REMINISCENCES OF LENIN

V. I. Lenin, January 1918

Reminiscences

of LENIN

by N. K. Krupskaya

International Publishers   New York

Translated by Bernard Isaacs

© by Lawrence & Wishart, 1960

First U.S. Edition by International Publishers, Co. Inc., 1970

Library of Congress Catalog Card Number: 67-27253

Printed in the United States of America

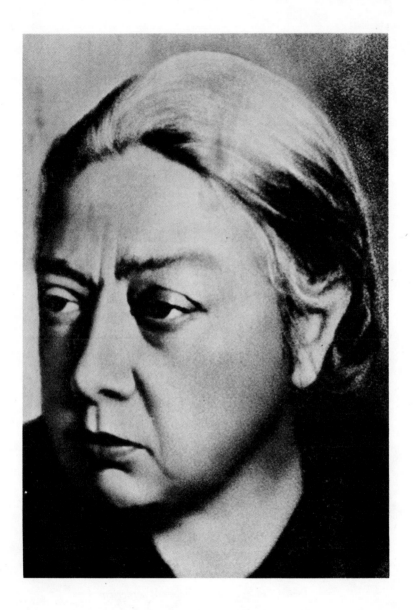

Nadezhda K. Krupskaya

Lenin in 1891

CONTENTS

3

INTRODUCTION

The reminiscences printed in this volume cover the period 1894 to 1917* from the time I first met Vladimir Ilyich up to the October Revolution. I have often been told that my reminiscences are rather sketchy. Everyone, of course, is eager to learn all he can about Ilyich, and besides, the epoch itself was one of tremendous historical importance. It saw the development of a mass movement among the workers, the creation of a strong staunch party of the working class, steeled under the most difficult conditions of underground activity and the steady growth of working-class consciousness and organization. It was an epoch of desperate struggle, which ended in the victory of the proletarian socialist revolution.

Heaps of interesting articles and books could be written both about that epoch and about Ilyich. The purpose of these reminiscences is to give a picture of the conditions under which Vladimir Ilyich lived and worked.

I wrote only of those things which stood out most vividly in my memory. These reminiscences were written in two stages. Part I, covering the period 1894-1907, was written a few years after Lenin's death. It contains recollections relating to his work in St. Petersburg, to the time of his Siberian exile, the Munich and London periods of his first emigration, the period preceding the Second Congress

* The writer has in mind only Parts I and II of *Reminiscences of Lenin* published in a separate volume in 1933.—*Ed.*

5

of the Party, the Second Congress itself and the period immediately following it right up to 1905. Then come recollections of 1905 both in Russia and abroad, and finally of the period 1905-1907. I wrote them for the most part at Gorki, where I roamed about the large house and the overgrown paths of the park in which Ilyich had spent the last year of his life. The years 1894-1907 saw the upsurge of the young working-class movement, and one's thoughts were involuntarily drawn back to that period, when the foundations of our Party were laid. I wrote the first part almost entirely from memory. The second part was written a few years later.

One had to study very hard during those years, to reread Lenin sedulously, to learn to link up the past with the present, to learn how to live with Ilyich without Ilyich. And so the second part of the book differs from the first. The first has a more personal touch, the second deals more with Ilyich's interests and thoughts. I think both parts should preferably be read together. The first part is closely linked with the second, and the latter, if read alone, may strike the reader as being less "reminiscential" than it really is.

Part II of the reminiscences was written at a time when many other recollections and symposiums, as well as the second edition of Lenin's *Works*, had come off the press. This, to a certain extent, determined the character of the reminiscences of the second period of emigration. It enabled me to check up on myself. Moreover, the period they deal with (1908-1917) was far more complex than the first.

The first period (1893-1907) covered the early steps of the working-class movement, the efforts to build up a Party, the rising wave of the first revolution directed chiefly against tsarism, and the defeat of that revolution.

The second period—that of the second emigration—was far more involved. It was a summing up of the revolutionary struggle of the first period, a period of struggle against the reaction, a period of fierce struggle against opportunism of every kind and description, a struggle for the necessity of adapting our work to every kind of condition without any falling off in its revolutionary content. The period of second emigration was a period of impending world war, when opportunism in the working-class parties led to the collapse of the Second International, when entirely new problems faced the world proletariat, when new paths had to be laid, and the foundation of the Third International built up stone by stone, when the struggle for socialism had to be started under the most adverse conditions. In emigration, all these problems were sharply focussed and concrete.

Unless these problems are understood it is impossible for anyone to grasp how Lenin rose to be the leader of October, the leader of the world revolution. Leaders are formed in and grow out of the struggle, from which they draw their strength. No reminiscences of Lenin during the period of emigration are conceivable that do not link up every little detail of his life with the struggle that he waged at that time.

The nine years of his second emigration had not changed Ilyich a bit. He worked just as hard and as methodically, he took the same keen interest in every little detail, was able to put two and two together and had lost none of his ability to see the truth and face it, no matter how bitter it was. He hated oppression and exploitation as cordially as ever, was just as devoted to the cause of the proletariat, the cause of the working people, and took their interests just as closely to heart. His whole life was bound up with that cause. It came naturally to him, he could not live in any other way. He fought opportunism and all and every backdown as passionately and sharply as ever. He was still capable of breaking with his closest friends if he saw them acting as a drag on the movement; he would go up to yesterday's opponent in a simple comradely way, if it was essential to the cause, and say what he had to say frankly and bluntly as he had always done. He was

7

just as fond of nature, of the spring woods, the mountain paths and lakes, the noise of the big cities, the working-class crowd; he loved his comrades, movement, struggle, life in all its numerous facets. The same Ilyich, except that, watching him day by day, one would notice that he had become more reticent, still more kindly towards people, and that he would often lapse into meditation, roused from which his eyes would have a fleeting shadow of sadness in them.

Those years of emigration had been trying ones, and had taken their toll of Ilyich's strength. But they had moulded a fighter out of him, the kind of fighter the masses needed to lead them to victory.

N. Krupskaya

PART I

Krupskaya in 1895

ST. PETERSBURG

1893-1898

Vladimir Ilyich came to St. Petersburg in the autumn of 1893, but I did not get to know him until some time later. Comrades told me that a very erudite Marxist had arrived from the Volga. Afterwards I was given a pretty well-thumbed copy-book "On Markets" to read. The manuscript set forth the views of technologist Herman Krasin,* our St. Petersburg Marxist, on the one hand, and those of the newcomer from the Volga on the other. The copy-book was folded down the middle, and on one side H. B. Krasin had set forth his views in a scrawly hand with many crossings out and insertions, while on the other side the newcomer had written his own remarks and objections in a neat hand without any alterations.

The question of markets interested all of us young Marxists very much at the time.

A definite trend had begun to crystallize among the St. Petersburg Marxist study-circles at that time. The gist of it was this: the processes of social development appeared to the representatives of this trend as something mechanical and schematic. Such an interpretation of social development dismissed completely the role of the masses, the role of the proletariat. Marxism was stripped

---

* A student of the St. Petersburg Technological Institute, brother of the late L. B. Krasin.—*Ed.*

of its revolutionary dialectics, and only the bare "phases of development" remained. Today, of course, any Marxist would be able to refute that mechanistic conception, but at that time it was a cause of grave concern to our St. Petersburg Marxist circles. We were still poorly grounded theoretically and all that many of us knew of Marx was the first volume of *Capital*; as for *The Communist Manifesto*, we had never even set eyes on it. So it was more by instinct than anything else that we felt this mechanistic view to be the direct opposite of real Marxism.

The question of markets had a close bearing on the general question of the understanding of Marxism.

Exponents of the mechanistic view usually approached the question in a very abstract way.

Since then more than thirty years have passed. Unfortunately, the copy-book has not survived,* and I can only speak about the impression which it made on us.

The question of markets was treated with ultra-concreteness by our new Marxist friend. He linked it up with the interests of the masses, and in his whole approach one sensed just that live Marxism which takes phenomena in their concrete surroundings and in their development.

One wanted to make the closer acquaintance of this newcomer, to learn his views at first hand.

I did not meet Vladimir Ilyich until Shrovetide. It was decided to arrange a conference between certain St. Petersburg Marxists and the man from the Volga at the flat of engineer Klasson, a prominent St. Petersburg Marxist with whom I had attended the same study-circle two years before. The conference was disguised as a pancake party. Besides Vladimir Ilyich, there were Klasson, Y. P. Korobko, Serebrovsky, S. I. Radchenko and others. Potresov

---

* Lenin's work *Concerning the So-Called Question of Markets* was considered lost, but the copy-book of which N. Krupskaya writes was found in 1917. This work is now included in Vol. I of Lenin's *Works*, 4th Russian edition.—*Ed.*

and Struve were to have been there, too, but I don't think they turned up. I particularly remember one moment. The question came up as to what ways we should take. Somehow general agreement was lacking. Someone (I believe it was Shevlyagin) said that work on the Illiteracy Committee was of great importance. Vladimir Ilyich laughed, and his laughter sounded rather harsh (I never heard him laugh that way again).

"Well, if anyone wants to save the country by working in the Illiteracy Committee," he said, "let him go ahead."

It should be said that our generation had witnessed in its youth the fight between the *Narodovoltsi** and tsarism. We had seen how the liberals, at first "sympathetic" about everything, had been scared into sticking their tail between their legs after the suppression of the *Narodnaya Volya* Party, and had begun to preach the doing of "little things."

Lenin's sarcastic remark was quite understandable. He had come to discuss ways of fighting together, and had had to listen instead to an appeal for the distribution of the Illiteracy Committee's pamphlets.

Later, when we got to know each other better, Vladimir Ilyich told me one day how this liberal "society" had reacted to the arrest of his elder brother Alexander Ulyanov. All acquaintances had shunned the Ulyanov family, and even an old teacher, who until then had come almost

---

* The *Narodovoltsi* were members of the illegal *Narodnaya Volya* (People's Will) organization set up by the *Narodnik* revolutionaries in 1879. They fought the tsarist autocracy by means of terrorist tactics. After the assassination of Alexander II by the *Narodovoltsi* (March 1, 1881) the tsarist government suppressed the organization. In the eighties and nineties of the 19th century *Narodism* abandoned propaganda of the revolutionary struggle. It began to express the interests of the rich peasants (liberal *Narodnik* trend) and preach reconciliation with the tsarist government and the landowners. It was opposed to Marxism and resisted its spread in Russia. The first blow against *Narodism* was dealt by Plekhanov, and its utter defeat as a political doctrine was consummated by Lenin.—*Ed.*

every evening to play chess, had left off calling. Simbirsk had no railway at the time, and Vladimir Ilyich's mother had had to travel to Syzran by horse-drawn vehicle in order to catch the train to St. Petersburg, where her son was imprisoned. Vladimir Ilyich was sent to find a way companion for her, but no one wanted to be seen with the mother of an arrested man.

This general cowardice, Vladimir Ilyich told me, had shocked him profoundly at the time.

This youthful experience undoubtedly affected his attitude towards so-called liberal society. He learned the true worth of all liberal rant at an early age.

No agreement was reached at the "pancake party," of course. Vladimir Ilyich spoke little, and was more occupied in studying the company. People who called themselves Marxists felt uncomfortable under his steady gaze.

I remember, as we were returning home from the Okhta District along the banks of the Neva, I first heard the story of Vladimir Ilyich's brother, a member of the *Narodnaya Volya*, who took part in the attempt on the life of Alexander III in 1887 and died at the hands of the tsarist executioners before he had even come of age.

Vladimir Ilyich had been very fond of his brother. They had had many tastes in common, and both liked to be left alone for long periods of time to be able to concentrate. They usually lived together and at one time shared a separate wing of the house, and when any of the young crowd dropped in (they had numerous cousins, boys and girls), the brothers would greet them with their pet phrase: "Honour us with your absence." They were both hard workers and revolutionary-minded. The difference in their age, though, made itself felt in various ways. There were certain things that Alexander did not tell Vladimir.

This is what Vladimir Ilyich told me:

His brother was a naturalist. On his last summer vacation at home he was preparing a dissertation on the *Annelida*, and was busy all the time with his microscope. To get all the light he could he got up at daybreak and started work at once. "No, my brother won't make a revolutionary, I thought at the time," Vladimir Ilyich related. "A revolutionary can't give so much time to the study of worms." It was not long before he saw his mistake.

The fate of his brother undoubtedly influenced Vladimir Ilyich profoundly. Another important factor was that he had begun to think for himself on many questions and had decided in his own mind the necessity of revolutionary struggle.

Had this not been so, his brother's fate would probably have caused him deep sorrow only, or at most, aroused in him a resolve and striving to follow in his brother's footsteps. As it was, the fate of his brother gave his mind a keener edge, developed in him an extraordinary soberness of thought, an ability to face the truth without letting himself for a minute be carried away by a phrase or an illusion. It developed in him a scrupulously honest approach to all questions.

In the autumn of 1894 Vladimir Ilyich read his *The "Friends of the People"** to our circle. I remember how it had thrilled us all. The aims of the struggle were set forth in the pamphlet with admirable clarity. Hectographed copies of it circulated afterwards from hand to hand under the name of "The Yellow Copy-Books." They were unsigned. Fairly widely read, they undoubtedly had a strong influence on the Marxist youth at the time. When I was in Poltava in 1896, P. P. Rumyantsev, who was then an active Social-Democrat just released from prison, described *The "Friends of the People"* as the best, the most powerful and complete formulation of the standpoint of the revolutionary Social-Democracy.

In the winter of 1894-95 I got more closely acquainted with Vladimir Ilyich. He was lecturing to workers' study-

---

* The full title of this pamphlet is *What the "Friends of the People" Are and How They Fight the Social-Democrats.—Ed.*

circles in the Nevskaya Zastava District, where I had been working for over three years as a teacher in the Smolenskaya Sunday Evening School for Adults and was therefore pretty familiar with life on the Schlüsselburg Post Road.* Quite a number of the workers who attended Vladimir Ilyich's circles were pupils of my Sunday School, among them Babushkin, Borovkov, Gribakin, the Bodrovs (Arseny and Philip) and Zhukov. In those days the Sunday Evening School offered an excellent opportunity for studying everyday working-class life, labour conditions and the temper of the masses. The Smolenskaya School had six hundred pupils, not counting the evening technical classes and the Women's and Obukhov schools attached to it. The workers, I must say, had full trust in their "school-mistresses." The dour-looking watchman of the Gromov timber-yards, for instance, told his teacher with a beaming face that a son had been born to him; a consumptive mill worker wished his teacher a bonny fiancé for having taught him to read and write; another workman, a member of a religious sect, who had been seeking God all his life, wrote with satisfaction that not until last Holy Week had he learned from Rudakov (another pupil) that there wasn't any God at all, and this made him feel so good, because the worst thing in the world was being a slave of God—you just had to grin and bear it— whereas being a slave of man was much easier—at least you could fight back; then there was a tobacco-worker, who used to get dead-drunk every Sunday and was so saturated with the smell of tobacco that it made you dizzy to stand near him. He wrote in a scrawl (leaving out most of the vowels) that they had picked up a girl of three in the street; she was living in their artel, but they would

---

* A working-class suburb of St. Petersburg beyond the Nevskaya Zastava. It used to be called the Nevsky District (now Volodarsky). A post road ran through it along the Neva to Schlüsselburg, along which most of the factories and mills of this district are situated.—*N. K.*

have to give her up to the police, which was a shame. A one-legged soldier came saying that "Mikhail—the chap you taught last year—has gone and done himself in with overwork, and before he died he asked to be remembered to you and to wish you long life." A textile worker, who stood up fiercely for the tsar and the priests, gave warning "to beware of that dark chap over there—he's always hanging about Gorokhovaya Street."* An elderly workman argued that he just could not chuck up his church-warden's job "because it makes me sick to see the way the priests are fooling the people, and somebody's got to show them up." As for the church, he wasn't struck on it a bit, and he'd cottoned to that phases-of-development stuff perfectly well, and so on and so forth.

Workers who belonged to the organization went to the school to get to know people and single out those who could be drawn into the circles and the organization. As far as these workers were concerned the teachers were no longer just a featureless set of women. They were already able to distinguish the extent to which this or that teacher was politically well-grounded. If they recognized a school-teacher to be "one of us" they let her know it by some phrase or word. For instance, in discussing the handicraft industry a man would say: "A handicraft worker cannot compete with large-scale production," or else he would ask a poser, like "What is the difference between a St. Petersburg worker and an Arkhangelsk peasant?" And after that he would have a special look for that teacher and would greet her in a special way, as much as to say, "You're one of us, we know."

If anything was doing locally they immediately told the teacher about it, knowing that it would be passed on to the organization. It was a sort of tacit understanding.

As a matter of fact we could talk almost about anything at school, although there was hardly a class that did not

---

* The secret political police had their headquarters there.—*Ed.*

have a police spy in it. If only you avoided such dreadful words as "tsar," "strike," and so on, you could touch on fundamental issues. Officially, of course, we were forbidden to talk about anything whatever. One day the Recapitulation Group was shut down because an inspector, on a surprise visit, had discovered that decimals were being taught there whereas the syllabus only allowed for the four rules of arithmetic.

I lived in Staro-Nevsky Street at the time, in a building that had a through courtyard, and Vladimir Ilyich used to drop in on Sundays after his circle work, when we would start endless conversations. I was in love with my school work and could talk about it for hours if you did not stop me—talk about the school, the pupils, the Semyannikov, Thornton, Maxwell and other factories and mills in the neighbourhood. Vladimir Ilyich was interested in every little detail that could help him to piece together a picture of the life and conditions of the workers, to find some sort of avenue of approach to them in the matter of revolutionary propaganda. Most of the intellectuals those days did not know the workers well. An intellectual would come to one of the study-circles and read the workers a kind of lecture. A manuscript translation of Engels' *The Origin of the Family, Private Property and the State* circulated among the circles for a long time. Vladimir Ilyich read Marx's *Capital* to the workers and explained it to them. He devoted the second half of the lesson to questioning the workers about their work and conditions of labour, showing them the bearing which their life had on the whole structure of society, and telling them in what way the existing order could be changed. This linking of theory with practice was a feature of Vladimir Ilyich's work in the study-circles. Gradually other members of our circle adopted the same method.

When the hectographed Vilna pamphlet *On Agitation* appeared the following year, the soil had been fully prepared for agitation by leaflets. The thing was to make a start. The method of agitation based on the workers' everyday needs struck deep root in our Party work. I did not fully appreciate how efficacious this method was until years later, when, living in France as a political emigrant, I observed how, during the great strike of the postal workers in Paris, the French Socialist Party stood completely aloof from it. It was the business of the trade unions, they said. In their opinion the business of a party was only political struggle. They had no clear idea whatever about the necessity of combining the economic with the political struggle.

Many of the comrades who worked in St. Petersburg at the time, seeing the effect this leaflet agitation had, were so carried away by the work that they entirely forgot that this was one of the forms, but not the only form of work among the masses, and took the path of notorious "Economism."*

Vladimir Ilyich never forgot that there were other forms of work. In 1895 he wrote the pamphlet *An Explanation of the Law Concerning Fines Levied on the Workers in the Factories,* in which he set a brilliant example of how to approach the average worker of that time, and, proceeding from the workers' needs, to lead them step by step to the question of the necessity of political struggle. Many intellectuals thought the pamphlet dull and prolix, but the workers read it avidly, for it was something clear and familiar to them. (It was printed at the *Narodnaya Volya*

---

* *"Economism"*—an opportunist trend among the Russian Social-Democrats at the end of the 19th and beginning of the 20th centuries. Its political programme advocated economic struggle for the workers, and political struggle for the liberals. The leaders of the Economists were Prokopovich, Kuskova, Krichevsky, Martynov and others. The "Economists' " organs of the press were the newspaper *Rabochaya Mysl (Workers' Thought)* and the journal *Rabocheye Delo (Workers' Cause).* An important role in the ideological defeat of Economism was played by Lenin's book *What Is To Be Done?* published in March 1902.—*Ed.*

printing plant and distributed among the workers.) At that time Vladimir Ilyich had made a thorough study of factory legislation. He believed that explaining these laws to the workers made it much easier to show them the connection that existed between their position and the political regime. Evidences of this study are traceable in quite a number of articles and pamphlets which Ilyich wrote at that time for the workers, notably in the pamphlet *The New Factory Act*, and the articles "On Strikes," "On Industrial Courts" and others.

A result of this going about round the workers' circles was that the police kept a closer watch on us. Of all our group Vladimir Ilyich was the most experienced in secrecy methods of work. He knew the through yards, and was a master hand at giving sleuths the slip. He taught us how to use invisible ink and to write messages in books by a dotted code and secret ciphers, and invented all kinds of aliases. One felt that he had been well-schooled in *Narodnaya Volya* methods. Indeed, he had good reason to speak with the great respect he did of the old *Narodovolets* Mikhailov, nicknamed "Dvornik" (Janitor) on account of his first-rate secrecy technique. Meanwhile, police surveillance kept growing stricter, and Vladimir Ilyich insisted that a "successor" should be appointed, someone who was not being shadowed and who would take over all contacts. As I was the "cleanest" of them all in the eyes of the police, it was decided to appoint me "successor." On Easter Sunday five or six of us went to Tsarskoye Selo to "celebrate the holiday" with Silvin, a member of our group, who lived there as a coach. In the train going down we pretended not to know each other. We sat nearly all day discussing which contacts had to be kept going. Vladimir Ilyich taught us the use of cipher, and we coded almost half a book. Afterwards, I am sorry to say, I was unable to decipher this first attempt at collective coding. There was one consolation, though—by the time it had to be deciphered most of the "contacts" no longer existed.

Vladimir Ilyich carefully built up these "contacts" by searching everywhere for people who were likely, in one way or another, to be of use in revolutionary work. I remember a conference that was held on Vladimir Ilyich's initiative between representatives of our group (Vladimir Ilyich and Krzhizhanovsky, if I am not mistaken) and a group of women teachers of the Sunday School. Nearly all of them afterwards became Social-Democrats. Among them was Lydia Knipovich, an old member of the *Narodnaya Volya*, who afterwards joined the Social-Democrats. Old Party workers remember her. A woman of great revolutionary self-discipline, exacting both to herself and others, a splendid comrade, an excellent judge of people, who surrounded those she worked with with love and solicitude, Lydia was quick to appreciate the revolutionary in Vladimir Ilyich.

Lydia undertook to handle all contacts with the *Narodnaya Volya* printing plant. She made all the arrangements for printing, passed over the MSS, took delivery of the printed pamphlets, carried them round to her friends in baskets, and organized the distribution of the literature among the workers. When she was arrested—betrayed by a compositor at the plant—twelve baskets with illegal pamphlets were confiscated from various friends of hers. The *Narodovoltsi* printed mass editions of pamphlets for the workers at the time, such as *The Working Day*, *Lives and Interests*, Vladimir Ilyich's pamphlet *On Fines*, *King Hunger*, etc. Two of the *Narodovoltsi*—Shapovalov and Katanskaya—who worked at the Lakhtinsky print-shop, are now in the ranks of the Communist Party.* Lydia Knipovich is no longer among the living. She died in 1920, when the Crimea, where she had been living for the last few years, was under the Whites. On her death-bed her soul yearned towards the Communists and she died with the name of the Communist Party on her lips.

---

* These reminiscences were written in 1930.—*Ed.*

Among the other participants of the conference were, I believe, the school-teachers P. F. Kudeli and A. I. Meshcheryakova (both at present members of the Party). One of the Nevskaya Zastava teachers was Alexandra Kalmykova—an excellent lecturer (I remember her lecture for workers on the state budget). She kept a bookstore in Liteiny St. Vladimir Ilyich became closely acquainted with her at the time. Struve was one of her pupils, and Potresov, an old school-mate of Struve's, was a frequent visitor at her place. Later Alexandra Kalmykova financed the old *Iskra* right up to the time of the Second Congress. She did not join Struve when he went over to the liberals, but definitely associated herself with the *Iskra*-ist organization. Her sobriquet was Auntie. She was very friendly with Vladimir Ilyich. Now she is dead, after having been bedridden for two years in a nursing home at Detskoye Selo. The children of the local orphanages used to visit her occasionally, and she told them about Ilyich. She had written to me in the spring of 1924 saying that Vladimir Ilyich's 1917 articles containing ardent appeals which had had such a powerful effect on the masses, ought to be published as a separate book. Vladimir Ilyich had written her in 1922 a few warm lines of greeting, such as only he could write.

Alexandra Kalmykova was closely associated with the "Emancipation of Labour" group.* At one time (in 1899, I believe), when Vera Zasulich came to Russia, Kalmykova arranged her illegal sojourn in the country and saw her very often. Influenced by the rising tide of the workers' movement, by the articles and books of the "Emancipation of Labour" group, and by the Petersburg Social-Democrats, Potresov, and for a time Struve, went Left. After a number of preliminary meetings, soundings were taken for

* *"Emancipation of Labour" group*—the first Russian Marxist group organized in Geneva in 1883 by G. Plekhanov, which did a great deal to disseminate Marxism in Russia.—*Ed.*

22

joint work. It was decided to publish jointly a symposium *Materials Characterizing Our Economic Development.* Our group was represented on the editorial board by Vladimir Ilyich, Starkov, and Stepan Radchenko, theirs—by Struve, Potresov and Klasson. The fate of that publication is common knowledge. It was consigned to the flames by the tsarist censor. In the spring of 1895, before going abroad, Vladimir Ilyich kept going more and more often to Ozernoy Street, where Potresov then lived, to speed up the work.

Vladimir Ilyich spent the summer of 1895 abroad, living part of the time in Berlin, where he attended workers' meetings, and partly in Switzerland, where he first met Plekhanov, Axelrod and Zasulich. He came back full of impressions, and brought with him a double lined suitcase crammed with illegal literature.

The police started shadowing him the moment he arrived. They had an eye on him and his suitcase. I had a cousin working at the time at the Address Bureau. Two days after Vladimir Ilyich had arrived she told me that a detective had come when she was on night duty, and had gone through the files (which were arranged in alphabetical order), saying boastfully: "There, we've tracked an important state criminal—Ulyanov, his name is. His brother was hanged, and this one's come from abroad. He won't get away now." Knowing that I was acquainted with Vladimir Ilyich, my cousin lost no time reporting this to me. Naturally, I warned Vladimir Ilyich at once. Extreme caution was necessary. But the work could not wait. We got busy. A division of labour was organized, and the work was divided by districts. We started to draw up and circulate leaflets. I remember Vladimir Ilyich drawing up the first leaflet to the workers of the Semyannikov Works.* We had no printing facilities at the time. The leaflet was copied out in print hand and distributed by Babushkin. Two of the

---

* The leaflet to the workers of the Semyannikov Works dates to the close of 1894. A part of the leaflet has survived.—*Ed.*

four copies were picked up by the watchmen, the other two circulated from hand to hand. Leaflets were distributed in other districts as well. One was got out on Vasilyevsky Island for the women workers of the Laferme Tobacco Factory. A. A. Yakubova and Z. P. Nevzorova (Krzhizhanovskaya) resorted to the following method of distribution: they rolled the leaflets up so that they could conveniently be peeled off one by one, and arranged their aprons in a suitable manner. Then, as soon as the whistle blew, they walked swiftly towards the women workers, who came pouring out of the factory gates, and thrust the leaflets into the hands of the puzzled women almost at a run. The leaflet was a great success.

Our leaflets and pamphlets roused the workers. It was decided—seeing that we had an illegal print-shop to do it in—to publish also a popular journal *Rabocheye Delo* (*Workers' Cause*). Vladimir Ilyich prepared the material for it with great thoroughness. Every line of copy passed through his hands. I remember a meeting at my place when Zaporozhets waxed very enthusiastic about the material which he had succeeded in collecting at a boot factory in the Moskovskaya Zastava neighbourhood. "They fine you there for everything," he said. "If you set a heel on crooked you get fined right away." Vladimir Ilyich laughed. "Well, if you set a heel on crooked," he said, "then you're asking to be fined." He collected and checked all the material very carefully. I remember, for instance, how the material about the Thornton Mills was collected. I was to call out my pupil Krolikov, who worked at the mills as a sorter (he had been deported from St. Petersburg once), and collect all the information from him according to the plan outlined by Vladimir Ilyich. Krolikov arrived in a posh fur coat which he had borrowed from somebody, and brought a bookful of notes which he supplemented verbally. His information was very valuable. Vladimir Ilyich fairly pounced on it. Afterwards A. A. Yakubova and I, with shawls over our heads to make us look like mill workers, went to the Thornton hostel, where we visited both the single and married quarters. Conditions there were appalling. It was only from information gathered in this way that Vladimir Ilyich wrote his correspondence and leaflets. Look at his leaflet to the men and women employees of the Thornton Mills. What a thorough knowledge of the subject it shows. And what a schooling this was for all the comrades who worked at that time. That was when we really learnt "to give attention to detail." And how deeply those details have engraved themselves in our minds.

Our *Rabocheye Delo* did not see the light of day. A meeting was held in my rooms on December 8, at which a final reading of the copy for the press was held. Vaneyev took the duplicate for a last look through, while the other copy remained with me. I went to Vaneyev the next morning to pick up the corrected copy, but the servant told me that he had moved out the night before. We had previously arranged with Vladimir Ilyich that in case anything went wrong I was to make enquiries of his friend Chebotaryov, who was a colleague of mine on the staff of the Central Railway Administration where I was employed. Vladimir Ilyich went there every day to dine. Chebotaryov was not in his office. I went to his house. Vladimir Ilyich had not been to dinner. Obviously, he had been arrested. Later in the day we found out that a good many of our group had been arrested. The copy of *Rabocheye Delo* left on my hands I gave to Nina Gerd for safe-keeping. Nina was an old school friend of mine, the future wife of Struve. Not to have any more of us arrested it was decided for the time being not to print *Rabocheye Delo*.

This St. Petersburg period of Vladimir Ilyich's work was of great importance, although the work itself was not noteworthy and hardly noticeable. He had described it so himself. It did not show. It was a matter not of heroic deeds but of establishing close contact with the masses, getting closer to them, learning to be the vehicle of their finest aspirations, learning how to win their confidence and rally them behind us. But it was during this period of his St. Petersburg work that Vladimir Ilyich was moulded as a leader of the working masses.

When I first came to the school after these arrests, Babushkin called me aside under the stairs and handed me a leaflet concerning these arrests written by the workers. The leaflet was of a purely political character. Babushkin asked me to get it printed and to let them have copies for distribution. Till then neither of us had ever directly mentioned my being connected with the organization. I passed the leaflet on to our group. I remember that meeting—it was at S. I. Radchenko's flat. All that remained of our group had gathered there. Lyakhovsky read the leaflet and exclaimed: "We can't print this leaflet—why, it's on a purely political subject." But since the leaflet had undoubtedly been written by the workers on their own initiative, and since they insisted on its being printed, it was decided to print it.

It wasn't very long before we got in touch with Vladimir Ilyich. In those days people committed for trial were freely permitted to receive books. They were given only a perfunctory examination, during which the tiny dots in the middle of the letters and the slightly changed colour of the paper where milk had been used for ink, escaped notice. The technique of secret correspondence had made swift progress with us. Vladimir Ilyich's concern for his imprisoned comrades was characteristic of him. There was not a letter he sent out that did not contain some request concerning a fellow prisoner. So-and-so had no one coming to visit him—it was necessary to get him a "fiancée";* or so-and-so had to be told through visiting relatives to look for letters in

---

* To ensure contact with prisoners who had no friends or relatives on the spot the Social-Democratic organization found fictitious "fiancés" and "fiancées" who went to the meetings with prisoners on visitors' days.—*Ed*.

such-and-such a book in the prison library, on such-and-such a page; another needed warm boots, and so on. He corresponded with many of his imprisoned comrades, to whom his letters meant a great deal. His letters dealing with work had a cheering effect. The man who received them forgot that he was in prison, and got down to work himself. I remember the impression those letters made (I was arrested myself in August 1896). They came written in milk every Saturday, which was book-receiving day. A glance at the secret mark would tell you that the book contained a message. Hot water for tea would be handed round at six o'clock, and then the wardress would conduct the non-political criminals to church. By that time you had the letter cut up in strips, and your tea brewed, and the moment the wardress went away you would begin dipping the strips in the hot tea to develop the text. (We couldn't very well use a candle for this in prison, and so Vladimir Ilyich hit on the hot water idea.) These letters were wonderfully cheering and so absorbingly interesting to read! The centre of all our work outside, Vladimir Ilyich even in prison was the centre of contact with the outside world.

Moreover, he worked a great deal in prison. It was there that he prepared *The Development of Capitalism in Russia*. He ordered all the necessary material and statistical handbooks in his legal letters. "I am sorry they have let me out so soon," Vladimir Ilyich said jokingly when he was released for deportation. "I haven't quite finished the book, and it will be difficult to get books in Siberia." Besides *The Development of Capitalism in Russia*, Vladimir Ilyich wrote leaflets and illegal pamphlets, and a draft programme for the First Congress (which did not take place until 1898, although it was planned for an earlier date), and gave his views on questions under discussion in the organization. To avoid being caught in the act of writing with milk, he kneaded little inkpots out of bread, which he promptly popped into his mouth whenever he heard the peep hole being opened. "Today I have eaten six inkpots," he would add to his letter by way of humorous remark.

But for all his self-discipline and restraint, Vladimir Ilyich could not help succumbing to the prison dumps. In one of his letters he suggested the following plan. When they were taken out for exercise one of the windows in the corridor afforded a momentary glimpse c the street pavement in Shpalernaya. His idea was that I and Appolinaria Yakubova, at a definite time, should come and stand on that bit of pavement so that he could see us. Appolinaria was unable to go for some reason, and so I went alone and stood on the pavement for a long time several days running. Only the plan did not work, I don't remember exactly why.

While Vladimir Ilyich was in prison, our work outside kept expanding, and the workers' movement grew spontaneously. With the arrest of Martov, Lyakhovsky and others, our group was weakened still further. True, new comrades joined the group, but these people were not so well up in theory and experience. There was no time for them to learn, as the movement had to be taken care of and demanded a lot of energy. Agitation was the order of the day. We simply had no time to think of propaganda. Our leaflet agitation was a great success. The strike of the thirty thousand textile workers of St. Petersburg, which broke out in the summer of 1896 and was influenced by the Social-Democrats, had turned many heads.

I remember Silvin reading out the draft of a leaflet at a secret meeting in the woods at Pavlovsk (at the beginning of August, I think it was). There was a phrase in it that definitely limited the workers' movement to the sphere of economic struggle. After reading it out, Silvin stopped and said laughingly: "Well I never, what on earth made me say that!" The phrase was crossed out. In the summer of 1896 our Lakhtinsky printing plant was suppressed, and we were no longer able to print our pamphlets. Arrangements for putting out the journal had to be postponed indefinitely.

During the strike of 1896 our group was joined by Takhtarev's group, known as "The Monkeys," and by Chernyshev's group, known as "The Cocks."* But so long as the "Decembrists"** were in prison and kept in touch with the organization outside, the work ran its usual course. When Vladimir Ilyich was released,*** I was still in prison. Despite the dazed state of joy a man finds himself in on coming out of prison, Vladimir Ilyich nevertheless contrived to write me a short note on Party affairs. My mother told me that he had even put on weight in prison and was as cheerful as ever.

I was released soon after the Vetrova affair (a prisoner named Vetrova had burned herself alive in the Peter and Paul Fortress).**** The gendarmes released quite a number of women prisoners, including myself. I was to remain in St. Petersburg until my case was finished, and two detectives were employed to shadow me. I found the organization in a very sad state. Stepan Radchenko and his wife were all that remained of the active members of our group. He could not carry on with the work for reasons of secrecy, but he continued to act as centre and maintained contacts. He was in touch with Struve too. Struve shortly afterwards married N. A. Gerd, the Social-Democrat—he was himself a Social-Democrat of a sort at that time. He was quite incapable of doing any work in the organization,

---

* Another breakdown took place on August 12, 1896, when practically all the Old Men and many of "The Cocks" were arrested. I was arrested too.—*N.K.*

** So called humorously because they were arrested in December (1895).—*Ed.*

*** Vladimir Ilyich was released from prison on February 26, 1897.—*Ed.*

**** A fortress on the Neva in the centre of St. Petersburg facing the Winter Palace. Used under the tsars as a prison for political offenders.—*Ed.*

leave alone underground work, but it flattered him, no doubt, to be called on for advice. He even wrote a manifesto for the First Congress of the Social-Democratic Labour Party. In the winter of 1897-98 I went to see Struve fairly often on behalf of Vladimir Ilyich. Struve was then publishing the *Novoye Slovo* (*New Word*) magazine, and besides, his wife was an old friend of mine. I studied Struve at the time. He was a Social-Democrat then, but what surprised me was his bookishness and his almost complete lack of interest in "the living tree of life,"* an interest which Vladimir Ilyich had so much of. Struve got a translation job for me and undertook to edit it. He found the work irksome, though, and quickly tired. (Vladimir Ilyich would sit with me for hours over similar work. But then his style of work was quite different; with him even such a job as translation was a labour of love.) Struve read Fet for relaxation. Someone has written of Lenin that he was fond of reading Fet. That isn't true. Fet was an out-and-out advocate of serfdom, with nothing in him you could get your teeth into. If anyone was fond of Fet, it was Struve.

I also knew Tugan-Baranovsky. I went to school with his wife, Lydia Davydova (whose mother was the publisher of the magazine *Mir Bozhy* (*God's World*) and I used to call on them at one time. Lydia was a very good and clever woman, although weak-willed. She was cleverer than her husband. You always felt in talking to him that he was not one of us. I once went to him with a collecting list to support a strike (the Kostroma strike, I believe it was). He gave me something—I don't remember how many rubles—but I was obliged to listen to a little lecture on the subject of "I don't understand why strikes should be supported—a strike is an inadequate method of fighting the employers." I took the money and hurried away.

---

* Slightly modified quotation from Goethe (used by Mephistopheles in *Faust*): "All theory, dear friend, is grey, but the golden tree of actual life springs ever green."—*Ed.*

I wrote to Vladimir Ilyich in exile about everything I saw and heard. There was little I could write about the work of the organization, however. At the time of the First Congress it consisted only of four people: S. I. Radchenko, his wife Lyubov, Sammer, and I. Our delegate was Radchenko. On his return from the Congress, however, he hardly told us anything about it. He took out the already familiar "Manifesto" by Struve, which was hidden between the covers of a book, and burst out crying. Nearly all the Congress delegates had been arrested.

I was banished to the Ufa Gubernia for three years, but obtained a transfer to the village of Shushenskoye in the Minusinsk Uyezd, where Vladimir Ilyich lived, by describing myself as his fiancée.

IN EXILE

1898-1901

I went out to Minusinsk at my own expense, accompanied by my mother. We arrived in Krasnoyarsk on the first of May, 1898, whence we had to go up the Yenisei by boat. Navigation, however, had not started yet. In Krasnoyarsk I made the acquaintance of the *Narodopravets** Tyutchev and his wife, who, being experienced people in these matters, arranged a meeting for me with a party of Social-Democrat exiles who were passing through Krasnoyarsk. Among them were two comrades—Lengnik and Silvin, who had been charged with me in the same case. The sol-

---

* *Narodopravets*—a member of the *Narodnoye Pravo* Party, an illegal organization of the petty-bourgeois intellectuals which came into being in 1893. Its founders were Natanson, Tyutchev, Aptekman and others. The *Narodopravtsi* rejected the struggle for socialism, and made it their aim merely to "unite opposition forces for the struggle with the autocracy for the sake of political freedom." The organization was suppressed by the government in the spring of 1894.—*Ed.*

diers brought the exiles down to be photographed and sat a little way off, munching the bread and sausage with which we had treated them.

In Minusinsk I went to see Arkady Tyrkov—one of the First of Marchers,* banished permanently to Siberia— to give him regards from his sister, an old school friend of mine. I also went to see Felix Kohn, the Polish comrade, who had been sentenced to penal servitude in 1885 in connection with the "Proletariat"** case and had had a very hard time in prison and exile. He had for me the aura of an old intransigent, and I liked him tremendously.

It was dusk when we arrived in Shushenskoye, where Vladimir Ilyich lived. He was out hunting. We unloaded and were shown into the cottage. In the Minusinsk district of Siberia the peasants live in very clean log-built cottages. The floors are covered with bright home-woven carpet strips, and the walls are whitewashed and decorated with branches of the Siberian fir. Vladimir Ilyich's room, though small, was spotlessly clean. My mother and I were given the rest of the cottage. Our landlord's family and all the neighbours crowded in and looked us over and questioned us with great curiosity. At last Vladimir Ilyich returned from the hunt. He was surprised to see a light in his room. The landlord told him that Oscar Engberg (an exiled St. Petersburg worker) had come in drunk and thrown all his books about. Ilyich ran up the steps. Just then I came out on the porch and we met. We had a good long talk that night.

There were only two other exiles in Shushenskoye, both workers. One was a Social-Democrat Prominski, a Polish hat-maker from Lódź, with a wife and six children, the

---

* *First of Marchers—Narodovoltsi* sentenced for the assassination of Alexander II on March 1, 1881.—*Ed.*
** *Proletariat*—first revolutionary Polish workers' party, which existed from 1882 to 1886.—*Ed.*

Members of St. Petersburg group of League of Struggle for the Emancipation of Labour, February 1897. Standing, left to right: A. L. Malchenko, P. K. Zaporozhets, A. A. Vaney. Sitting, Left to right: V. V. Starkov, G. M. Krzhizhanovsky, Lenin, L. Martov (Y. O. Zederbaum)

House in Shushenskoye where Lenin lived during Siberian exile

other was a Putilov worker named Oscar Engberg, of Finnish nationality. Both were very good comrades. Prominski was a calm, steady man with a very firm character. He read and knew little, but his class instinct was strikingly developed. His attitude towards his wife, then still a religious woman, was one of tolerant amusement. He was very good at singing Polish revolutionary songs, such as *Ludu roboczy, poznaj swoje sily, Pierwszy maj** and others. The children joined in the chorus, and so did Vladimir Ilyich, who sang a lot in Siberia and obviously enjoyed it. Prominski also sang Russian revolutionary songs, which Vladimir Ilyich had taught him. Prominski planned to go back to Poland to work, and slaughtered a little army of hares to make fur coats for the children. He never got back to Poland, though. He just moved a bit nearer to Krasnoyarsk with his family and got a job there on the railway. The children grew up. He became a Communist, his wife turned Communist, too, and so did the children. One of them was killed in the war, another barely escaped with his life during the Civil War, and is now in Chita. Prominski did not leave for Poland until 1923, but he died on the way from typhus.

The other worker, Oscar, was a different type altogether. He was a young man, who had been deported for taking part in a strike and behaving violently in the course of it. He had read a lot of all-sorts, but had only the faintest of ideas about socialism. He came back from a trip to the volost once and said: "A new clerk has arrived—he and I have the same convictions." "Meaning?" said I. "We are both against revolution," he answered. Vladimir Ilyich and I were just flabbergasted. The next day I sat down with him to study *The Communist Manifesto* (I had to translate it from the German), and when that was mastered, we passed on to *Capital*. During one of our lessons Prominski came in, and sat puffing at his pipe. I asked

---

* *Working People* and *First of May.—Ed.*

Oscar a question in connection with what we had been reading, but he could not answer it. Prominski answered it for him with calm smiling ease. Oscar dropped his lessons for a whole week after that. He was a good fellow, though. There were no other political exiles in Shushenskoye. Vladimir Ilyich said he had tried to strike up an acquaintance with the school-teacher, but nothing had come of it. The teacher was drawn towards the local aristocracy, that is, the priest and a couple of shopkeepers. Their only pastime was playing cards and drinking. The teacher had no interest whatever in social problems. Prominski's eldest son Leopold, who was already socialist-minded, was always arguing with him.

Vladimir Ilyich had a peasant of his acquaintance whom he was very fond of. He was Zhuravlyov, a consumptive man of about thirty. This Zhuravlyov had formerly been the village clerk. Vladimir Ilyich called him a revolutionary by nature, a protestant. Zhuravlyov came out boldly against the rich and would not put up with the slightest injustice. He was always travelling somewhere, and shortly died from consumption.

Another acquaintance of Ilyich's was a poor peasant, with whom he often went out shooting. He was the simplest of fellows—Sosipatych, his name was. He thought a lot of Vladimir Ilyich, though, and used to give him all kinds of odd presents. Once it was a live crane, once some cedar cones.

Through Sosipatych and Zhuravlyov Vladimir Ilyich studied the Siberian village. He told me once of a talk he had had with a well-to-do peasant in whose house he had lived. The man's farm labourer had stolen some hides from him. The peasant overtook him at a brook and finished him off. Ilyich in this connection spoke about the insensate cruelty of the petty proprietor, and his ruthless exploitation of his farm-hands. Indeed, the Siberian farm labourers worked like cart horses, and never got enough sleep except on holidays.

Ilyich had yet another method of studying the village. On Sundays he gave free legal advice. His reputation as a lawyer rose high after he had helped a gold-mine worker, who had been given the sack, to win his suit against his employer. The news of this success spread quickly among the peasants, and men and women came to Ilyich with their troubles. He heard them out attentively, went deeply into the matter and then gave his advice. Once a peasant came twenty versts to ask how he could prosecute his brother-in-law for not having invited him to his wedding, at which everyone had had a good time. "Will your brother-in-law treat you to a drink if you go and see him now?" "Aye, that he will." Vladimir Ilyich wasted an hour, trying to persuade the fellow to make it up with his brother-in-law. Sometimes you couldn't make head or tail of what they were talking about, and so Vladimir Ilyich always asked them to bring him a copy of the various papers in the case. Once a bull belonging to a rich farmer gored a poor woman's cow. The volost court ordered the owner to pay the woman ten rubles. The woman refused to accept the decision and demanded a "copy" of all the evidence in the case. "What do you want, a copy of a white cow?" the assessor said, laughing at her. The enraged woman came running to Vladimir Ilyich. Sometimes it was enough for the wronged party to threaten to take his complaint to Vladimir Ilyich to make the offender give in.

Vladimir Ilyich made a good study of the Siberian village. Till then he had known the Volga villages. Once he told me: "My mother wanted me to go in for farming. I started, but then I saw it was no good. My relations with the peasants became abnormal."

Strictly speaking, Vladimir Ilyich had no right as an exile to handle legal affairs, but those were liberal times in Minusinsk. Practically, surveillance did not exist.

The assessor—a local well-to-do peasant—was more concerned with selling us his veal than in seeing that "his" exiles did not run away. Life was surprisingly cheap in

Shushenskoye. Vladimir Ilyich's monthly allowance of eight rubles procured him clean lodgings, and meals, and paid for laundry and mending—and even that was considered dear. True, the dinner and supper were simple enough meals. One week a sheep would be slaughtered, and Vladimir Ilyich would be fed with it day in day out until it was all gone. Then they would buy meat for a week, and the servant girl would chop it up for cutlets out in the yard in a trough used for preparing the cattle feed. These cutlets were fed to Vladimir Ilyich for a whole week. But there was milk and cream enough for both Vladimir Ilyich and his dog, a fine Gordon setter named Zhenka, whom he taught to retrieve, and point, and do all other kinds of canine tricks.

As the Ziryanovs—our landlord's family—often had drinking parties at which the men used to get drunk, and as home life there was in many ways inconvenient, we shortly moved to another place, renting half a cottage with a vegetable garden for four rubles a month. We set up on our own. In the summer it was impossible to get anyone to help about the house. Mother and I tackled the Russian stove between us. Sometimes I would knock over the dumpling soup with the oven-fork, and upset the dumplings all over the coals. But I got used to it in time. We had all kinds of stuff growing in the garden—cucumbers, carrots, beetroots, pumpkins and what not. I was very proud of my little vegetable garden. Vladimir Ilyich and I had also made an orchard in the yard, fetching hops from the woods for the purpose. In October we got a girl-help—a skinny lass of thirteen with bony elbows named Pasha, who quickly took things in hand. I taught her to read and write, and she decorated the walls with specimens of my mother's instructions: "Neva waste eny tee," and kept a diary in which she made notes such as: "Oscar Engberg and Prominski came. They sang 'stump' and so did I."

I remember how we celebrated the First of May.

Prominski called in the morning, looking very festive in a clean collar and tie, and himself shining like a new penny. His mood quickly infected us, and we all three went to Oscar Engberg, taking the dog Zhenka with us. Zhenka ran on ahead, yapping joyfully. We walked along the bank of the River Shusha. The ice had broken up and was drifting down the stream. Zhenka waded into the icy water and defied the shaggy Shushenskoye watchdogs to follow his example.

Oscar was excited at our coming. We all sat down in his room and began singing together:

It's come, the merry First of May!
And let no sorrow bar its way.
Let songs ring out, sing loud and gay,
We'll have a jolly strike today!
Police arrive with no delay,
To prove they're worth their dirty pay:
Put us behind the bars, would they.
Police be damned! Is all we say,
And meet our May Day bold and gay.
Hooray, Hooray
For merry May!

Having sung the song in Russian, we sang it in Polish, and decided to celebrate May Day out in the fields after dinner. That is what we did. There were six of us in the field—Prominski took his two little boys along with him. He was as radiant as ever. Stepping on to a dry mound in the field, Prominski pulled a red handkerchief out of his pocket, laid it out on the ground and stood on his head. The children squealed with delight. In the evening we all got together at our place and sang songs again. Prominski's wife came too. My mother and Pasha also joined in the chorus.

That night Ilyich and I could not fall asleep for thinking of the huge workers' demonstrations in which we would some time take part.

There was a childish element too. A Lettish settler, a felt-boot maker by trade, lived across the way. He had had fourteen children, but only one survived—Minka. The father was an inveterate drunkard. Minka, who was six, was grave of speech, with a wan little face and bright eyes. He came to see us every day. We would hardly be up when the door would bang, and a small figure appear in a big cap and his mother's warm jacket with a scarf wrapped round him, exclaiming gladly: "It's me!" He knew that my mother doted on him, and Vladimir Ilyich would always say something funny and play with him.

Minka's mother would come running in.

"Darling, have you seen a ruble lying about?" she said.

"Yes, I saw it on the table, so I put it in the box."

When we went away Minka fell ill with grief. He is dead now, and his father wrote asking to be given a bit of land across the Yenisei—"as I'd like to be able to have enough to eat in my old age."

Our household kept growing. Our latest acquisition was a kitten.

First thing in the morning Vladimir Ilyich and I would sit down to the Webb translation, which Struve had got for me. After dinner we spent a couple of hours together copying out *The Development of Capitalism*. Then there were all kinds of odd jobs to do. One day Potresov sent us Kautsky's book criticizing Bernstein, which we were allowed to keep no longer than a fortnight. We dropped everything else we were doing and translated it exactly on time. After work we went out for walks. Vladimir Ilyich was a passionate hunter. He got himself a pair of leather breeches, and prowled about all the swamps in the neighbourhood! They teemed with game, I must say. Arriving as I did in the spring, I had been rather surprised at it all. Prominski would come in—he was passionately fond of hunting too—and say with a huge smile: "The ducks have come over—I have seen them." And then Oscar would come in, talking ducks. They would talk about them for hours, and the next spring found me, too, capable of talking about ducks and who had seen them, and where and when. Nature in the spring burst into riotous life after the winter frosts. Her sway grew powerful. Sunset. Wild swans swam in the vast puddles which spring had formed in the fields. Or we would stand on the fringe of the woods, listening to the babble of a brook and the mating call of the wood-grouse. Vladimir Ilyich would ask me to hold Zhenka while he went into the woods. I would stand there holding the dog, who trembled with excitement, while I felt this tempestuous awakening of nature tingling in all my veins. Vladimir Ilyich was a passionate hunter, but apt to get too excited over it. In the autumn we went far out into the forest cuttings. Vladimir Ilyich would say: "You know, if I come across a hare I won't shoot it, because I didn't bring my bags. It will be awkward to carry." Yet as soon as a hare came bounding out he would let go at it.

Late in the autumn, when sludge was already drifting down the Yenisei, we went out to the islands after the hares. The hares were already turning white. They could not escape from the island, and ran about like goats. Our hunters would sometimes shoot a boat-load of them.

When we lived in Moscow, Vladimir Ilyich in his latter years would still go hunting sometimes, but with nothing like the old zest. Once a fox battue was organized, and Vladimir Ilyich was greatly interested in the enterprise. "A clever idea," he said, when he saw the strung flags. The beaters drove the fox straight towards him, but he seized his gun when it was too late. The fox stopped and looked at him, then slipped away into the woods. "Why didn't you shoot?" I asked him. "The fox was so beautiful," he said.

Late in the autumn, when the rivers had frozen over but no snow had yet fallen, we went far upstream. Every little fish and pebble could be seen distinctly under the ice. It was like an enchanted kingdom. In the winter, when the mercury freezes in the thermometers and the rivers freeze right through, the water flows over the ice, and quickly forms a frozen crust. You could skate a couple of miles on this sagging ice crust. Vladimir Ilyich was terribly fond of this sport.

In the evenings Vladimir Ilyich usually read books on philosophy—Hegel, Kant or the French materialists—and when he grew very tired, Pushkin, Lermontov or Nekrasov.

When Vladimir Ilyich first turned up in St. Petersburg I had known him only from hearsay. Stepan Radchenko told me that he only read serious books and had never read a novel in his life. It had surprised me at the time. Afterwards, when I got to know him better, this question had somehow never come up, and it was only in Siberia that I found out that the story was sheer invention. Vladimir Ilyich had not only read Turgenev, L. Tolstoi, Chernyshevsky's *What Is To Be Done?* but reread them many times and was generally fond of the classics which he knew intimately. Afterwards, when the Bolsheviks came to power, he set Gosizdat* the task of reprinting the classics in cheap editions. His photo albums contained pictures of Zola and Herzen and several photos of Chernyshevsky,** as well as photos of his relatives and old political convicts.

The mail came twice a week. Our correspondence was extensive. Anna Ilyinichna—Lenin's sister—wrote fully about everything from St. Petersburg. Nina Struve wrote me, by the way, that her baby boy was "already holding his head up, and every day we show him the portraits of Darwin and Marx, and say: 'Nod to Uncle Darwin, nod to Uncle Marx'—and he nods in such an amusing way." We

---

* The State Publishing House.—*Ed.*
** Vladimir Ilyich was particularly fond of Chernyshevsky. On one of Chernyshevsky's photographs he had written "Born such-and-such a date, died in 1889."—*N.K.*

received letters from distant places of exile—from Martov in Turukhansk, from Potresov in Orlov, Vyatka Gubernia. Most of the letters, however, were from comrades scattered throughout the neighbouring villages. The Krzhizhanovskys and Starkov wrote from Minusinsk (fifty versts from Shushenskoye); thirty versts away, in Yermakovskoye, lived Lepeshinsky, Vaneyev, Silvin and Panin—the latter a friend of Oscar's. Seventy versts away, at Tes, lived Lengnik, Shapoval and Baramzin, while Kurnatovsky lived at a sugar refinery. We corresponded on every possible topic—the Russian news, future plans, books, new trends and philosophy. We corresponded also on chess problems, especially with Lepeshinsky. Vladimir Ilyich played games by correspondence. He would set out the figures and ponder over the board. He got so enthusiastic about it that he once cried out in his sleep: "If he moves his knight here, I'll put my rook there!"

Both Vladimir Ilyich and his brother Alexander had been enthusiastic chess players ever since they were children. Their father had played chess too. "Father used to beat us at first," Vladimir Ilyich once told me, "but then my brother and I got hold of a chess manual and started beating him. Once I met my father coming out of our room —it was upstairs—with a lighted candle in one hand and the chess manual in the other. He made a study of it too."

Vladimir Ilyich gave up chess when he returned to Russia. "Chess is too absorbing, it interferes with your work." And as Vladimir Ilyich was incapable of doing anything by halves, and always gave himself up wholeheartedly to whatever he was doing, it was usually with reluctance that he sat down to a game of chess when relaxing or when he lived abroad as a political emigrant.

Vladimir Ilyich, from his early youth, had a knack of being able to cast aside whatever interfered with his work. "When I was a schoolboy I went in for skating, but it made me tired and sleepy, and interfered with my studies, so I gave it up," he said.

"At one time," he related on another occasion, "I was very keen on Latin." "Latin?" I said, surprised. "Yes, but it interfered with my other studies, so I gave it up." Only recently, while reading an article in *Lef** dealing with the style and sentence structure of Vladimir Ilyich's writings, which were said to resemble those of the Roman orators, did I understand Vladimir Ilyich's interest in the Latin writers.

We not only corresponded with other comrades in exile, but sometimes, though not often, met them.

Once we went to see Kurnatovsky. He was a good comrade and a highly educated Marxist, but life had dealt harshly with him. An unhappy childhood dominated by a cruel father, and then exile after exile, prison after prison. He had hardly ever done any work—after a month or two of freedom he would be snatched back again for long terms. He never had any real life. One little incident stands out in my memory. We were passing the sugar refinery at which he was employed. Two girls were going along, the youngest quite a little one. The elder one was carrying an empty pail, the younger one a pail with beetroots. "Aren't you ashamed, a big girl like you making the little one carry things," Kurnatovsky said to the bigger girl. She just looked at him with a puzzled air. We also went to Tes. We had received a letter from the Krzhizhanovskys, saying: "The *ispravnik* is wild with us Tesians over some protest or other, and we are not allowed to go anywhere. We have a mountain here of geological interest. Write and say that you want to explore it." Vladimir Ilyich did so just for fun, and asked the *ispravnik* for permission to go to Tes both for himself and his wife, who was to assist him. The *ispravnik* sent his permission by messenger. We hired a dog-cart for three rubles—the woman assuring us that the horse was a strong beast and not a big eater at all—and

---

* *Lef*—abbreviation for Left Art Front, a literary group that arose in Moscow in 1923. It published a magazine called *Lef* (1923-25).—*Ed.*

off we drove. The "not-a-big-eater," however, proved to be a jibber, but we got to Tes all the same. Vladimir Ilyich discussed Kant with Lengnik and the Kazan study-circles with Baramzin. Lengnik, who had a fine voice, sang to us. That trip, on the whole, is a very pleasant memory.

We went to Yermakovskoye once or twice. The first time —to adopt a resolution on the "Credo,"* (Vaneyev, seriously ill with consumption, was dying, and his bed was carried out into the big room where we had all assembled). The resolution was adopted unanimously. The second time we went there was to attend Vaneyev's funeral.

Two of the "Decembrists" were soon put out of action— Zaporozhets, who went mad in prison, and Vaneyev, who died from an illness contracted there. Both passed away just when the flame of the working-class movement had begun to burn high.

On New Year's eve we went to Minusinsk, where all the exiled Social-Democrats had gathered.

There were also exiled *Narodovoltsi* in Minusinsk— Kohn, Tyrkov and others—but they kept aloof. These old revolutionaries were sceptical of the Social-Democratic youth. They did not believe that they were real revolutionaries. In this connection an incident occurred in the Minusinsk Uyezd shortly before my arrival in Shushenskoye. There was an exiled Social-Democrat named Raichin living in Minusinsk. He was connected with the "Emancipation of Labour" group abroad. He decided to run away. Money was provided for his escape, but the date for it had not been fixed yet. Raichin was worked up to such a nerv-

---

* The *"Credo"*—name given to the manifesto issued in 1899 by a group of "Economists" (Prokopovich, Kuskova and others) which most strikingly expressed the opportunism of Russian "Economism." Lenin retorted to the "Credo" with a sharp denunciatory protest. This document, known as *The Protest of the Russian Social-Democrats,* was discussed and unanimously adopted at a conference of seventeen political exiles in Siberia, and subsequently published abroad by Plekhanov.—*Ed.*

ous state when he got the money, that he ran away without telling anyone. The old *Narodovoltsi* accused the Social-Democrats of having known of Raichin's intended flight and not warned them about it so that they could have cleaned up in case the police made a search. Feeling ran high. Vladimir Ilyich told me about it when I arrived. "There is nothing worse than these exile scandals," he said. "They get people terribly worked up. These Old Men have bad enough nerves as it is after what they've been through, and all the convict prisons they've been in. We mustn't let ourselves get mixed up in such scandals—we have all our work ahead of us, we mustn't waste ourselves on such affairs." Vladimir Ilyich was for breaking with the Old Men. I remember the meeting at which that break occurred. The decision to break off with them had been made earlier, and it was now merely a question of putting it through as painlessly as possible. We made the break because we had to, but we did it without malice, in fact with regret. We kept apart after that.

On the whole, our exile was not so bad. Those were years of serious study. The closer the end of our exile drew in sight, the more did Vladimir Ilyich think about the work facing us. The news from Russia was scanty. "Economism" was gaining ground there, and there was no Party to speak of. We had no printing plants in Russia, and an attempt to arrange printing through the Bund had failed. On the other hand, we could no longer confine ourselves to writing popular pamphlets without expressing our views on the fundamental questions of our work. Party work was completely disorganized and constant arrests made any continuity impossible. People had gone to such lengths as the "Credo" and the ideas of *Rabochaya Mysl*, which had printed a letter from a worker, boosted by the "Economists," who wrote that "We workers do not want any of your Marxes or Engelses."

L. Tolstoi wrote somewhere that during the first part of his journey a person usually thinks of what he has left behind, and during the second part—of what is awaiting him ahead. It was the same in exile. At the beginning it was chiefly a matter of summing up the past. Later we thought more about what lay ahead of us. Vladimir Ilyich gave ever closer thought to the question of what was to be done to extricate the Party from the plight it was in, what was to be done to direct the work into the proper channels and ensure for it a correct Social-Democratic leadership. Where were we to begin? During the last year of his exile, Vladimir Ilyich had conceived the organizational plan which he afterwards developed in *Iskra,* in the pamphlet *What Is to Be Done?* and in his *Letter to a Comrade.* The thing was to start with the organization of an all-Russian newspaper. It was to be established abroad and linked up as closely as possible with the activities and organizations in Russia, and the best possible shipping arrangements had to be made. Vladimir Ilyich hardly slept at all, and grew terribly thin. He sat up all night, working out his plan in fullest detail. He discussed it with Krzhizhanovsky and with me, he corresponded with Martov and Potresov about it, and made arrangements with them for going abroad. He grew more and more impatient as time went on, eager to throw himself into the work. Just then, as luck would have it, the police came down on us with a search warrant. They had found somewhere a postal receipt for a letter which Lyakhovsky had written to Vladimir Ilyich. The letter was about a tombstone for Fedoseyev, and this was a good enough excuse for the gendarmes to make a search. This was done in May 1899. They found the letter—quite an innocent one—and went through our correspondence without finding anything of interest. By old habit acquired in St. Petersburg, we kept our illegal correspondence apart from the rest. It was not much of a hiding place, though—the bottom shelf of the bookcase. Vladimir Ilyich pushed up a bench for the gendarmes to stand on, and they began their search from the top shelves, which were lined with various statistical

45

publications. They got so tired that they did not even look at the bottom shelf, and were satisfied with my statement that it only contained my books on pedagogics. The search passed off safely, but we were afraid they might make this a pretext for adding a few more years to our term of exile. An escape in those days was not the common occurrence it became later. In any case it would have complicated matters, because, before going abroad, a good deal of organizing work had to be done in Russia. Everything went well, however, and our term was not increased.

In February 1900, at the end of Vladimir Ilyich's term of exile, we set out for Russia. Pasha, who had grown into a beautiful girl in two years, wept rivers of tears at night. Minka busied himself, collecting and lugging home the paper, pencils, pictures and other odds and ends that we were leaving behind. Oscar came in and sat down on the edge of a chair, evidently deeply agitated. He brought me a present—a hand-made brooch in the form of a book with the inscription "Karl Marx" on it, in memory of the lessons on *Capital* which he had taken with me. The landlady and her neighbours kept looking in. Our dog could not make out what all the fuss was about, and kept opening all the doors with his nose to make sure that everything was in its proper place. Mother busied herself with the packing, coughing from the dust, and Vladimir Ilyich tied the books up with a business-like air.

We arrived in Minusinsk, where we were to pick up Starkov and Olga Silvina. The whole exile fraternity were gathered there, and the mood was the usual one that prevailed whenever one of their number returned to Russia. Each was thinking when and where he would go himself when his time came, how he would work. Vladimir Ilyich had already made joint-work arrangements with all those who were expecting shortly to return to Russia, and now arranged for carrying on a correspondence with those who remained. Everyone was thinking about Russia while talking trivialities.

Baramzin was feeding sandwiches to Zhenka, who was being left him as an inheritance, but the dog took no notice of him. He lay at Mother's feet and did not take his eyes off her, watching her every movement.

At last, fitted out in high felt boots, heel-length fur coats, etc., we started out. We travelled 300 versts down the Yenisei by sledge day and night, taking advantage of a full moon. Vladimir Ilyich wrapped us up carefully at every stage-house, looked round to see that we had not forgotten anything, and joked with Olga Silvina, who was feeling the cold. We raced along at top speed, and Vladimir Ilyich—he rode without a top fur coat, assuring us that he felt too hot in it—sat with his hands thrust into a muff borrowed from Mother, his thoughts flying ahead of him to Russia, where he would be able to work to his heart's content.

At Ufa we received a visit from the local comrades on the day of our arrival—A. D. Tsyurupa, Svidersky and Krokhmal. "We've been to six hotels," Krokhmal said, stuttering. "At last we've found you."

Vladimir Ilyich spent two days in Ufa, and after having talked with the locals, he entrusted me and Mother to the care of our comrades and moved on nearer to St. Petersburg. All I remember of those two days was our visit to Chetvergova, an old *Narodovolets*, whom Vladimir Ilyich had known in Kazan. She had a bookshop in Ufa. Vladimir Ilyich went to see her the very first day, and there was a peculiar gentleness in his voice and face when he spoke to her. When, later, I read what Vladimir Ilyich had written at the end of his *What Is To Be Done?* I recalled that visit. "Many of them" (meaning the young Social-Democrat leaders of the workers' movement), Vladimir Ilyich wrote in *What Is To Be Done;* "began their revolutionary thinking as adherents of *Narodnaya Volya*. Nearly all of them in their early youth enthusiastically worshipped the terrorist heroes. It required a struggle to abandon the captivating impressions of these heroic traditions, and it was accompanied by the break of personal relations with people who were determined to remain loyal to the *Narodnaya Volya* and for whom the young Social-Democrats had profound respect." (*Works*, Vol. 5, pp. 483-84.)* This passage is a piece of Vladimir Ilyich's own biography.

It was a pity we had to part just when the "real" work was starting, but it did not even enter our heads that Vladimir Ilyich could remain in Ufa when he had a chance to move nearer to St. Petersburg.

Vladimir Ilyich went to live in Pskov,** where Potresov and L. N. Radchenko with his children afterwards resided. Vladimir Ilyich once laughingly related how Radchenko's little girls, Zhenyurka and Lyuda, used to mimic him and Potresov. They would walk up and down the room together with their hands behind their backs, one saying "Bernstein" and the other answering "Kautsky."

There, in Pskov, Vladimir Ilyich assiduously wove the threads of the organization that were to closely tie up the future all-Russian newspaper abroad with activities at home. He had meetings with Babushkin and many other comrades.

Gradually I acclimatized myself to Ufa and got translation work and some lessons.

There had been one of those exile scandals in Ufa shortly before my arrival, as a result of which the Social-Democrats had split up into two camps. In one camp were Krokhmal, Tsyurupa and Svidersky, in the other—the Plaksin brothers, Saltykov and Kvyatkovsky. Chachina and Aptekman were neutral and maintained relations with both groups. The first group stood nearer to me, and I soon became associated with it. This group did some work of a kind, and was the more active of the local fraternity.

---

* References to V. I. Lenin's *Works* apply throughout to the 4th Russian edition unless otherwise indicated.—*Ed.*
** Lenin arrived in Pskov on March 10, 1900.—*Ed.*

They had connections with the railway workshops, where there was a circle of twelve Social-Democratic workers. The most active worker was Yakutov. He often came to see me to get books and have a talk. He spoke a lot about "popularizing" Marx, but when he did manage to get the book he could not read it. "I haven't the time," he complained to me. "You know how it is, with the peasants coming to me with their troubles. You've got to talk with them all, so's they won't think bad of themselves—and it leaves you no time." He said that his wife Natasha was a sympathizer, and that exile did not scare them. He'd get on anywhere, his hands would always feed him. He was well up in secrecy technique, and there was nothing he hated more than heroics, boasting, and claptrap. Everything had to be done quietly and efficiently.

Yakutov was president of the republic that was set up in Ufa in 1905. Later, during the years of reaction, he was hanged in Ufa prison. He died in the prison yard, while the whole prison sang—they sang in every cell—and swore never to forget his death and never to forgive it.

I also helped other workers in their studies. One was a young metal-worker employed at a small factory, who told me about the life of the local workers. He was a very high-strung, nervous man. I learned afterwards that he went over to the Socialist-Revolutionaries and became insane in prison.

One of my visitors was a consumptive bookbinder named Krylov, who painstakingly made double bindings to hide illegal manuscripts in, and made pasteboard out of manuscripts to be used in binding. He told me about the work of the local printers.

Subsequent correspondence sent to *Iskra* was based on these stories.

We carried on our work at the neighbouring factories as well as in Ufa itself. The doctor's assistant at the Ust-Katavsk works was a Social-Democrat. She conducted propaganda there among the workers and distributed illegal popular literature, which we needed ever so badly.

There were several Social-Democratic students at the various factories. Our Ufa organization had an illegal agent in Ekaterinburg—a worker named Mazanov, who had returned from Turukhansk, where he had been in exile together with Martov. The work made no headway with him, though.

Ufa was the gubernia centre, and the exiles of Sterlitamak, Birsk and other uyezd towns were always trying to obtain permission to go there. Besides, Ufa lay on the road between Siberia and Russia. Comrades returning from exile stopped over to make arrangements about work. Among these were Martov (he had not been able to get away from Turukhansk for some time), G. I. Okulova, and Panin. Lydia Knipovich (Uncle) came illegally from Astrakhan, and Rumyantsev and Portugalov came from Samara.

Martov went to live in Poltava. We were in touch with him and hoped to receive literature through him. The literature arrived, I think, a week after my departure, and Kvyatkovsky, who went to fetch it, got five years in Siberia for his pains—the box containing the literature had broken open on the way. As a matter of fact, he was not an active member of the organization, and had only undertaken to go for the parcel because it was addressed to the brewery, the daughter of whose proprietor he had been giving lessons to.

There were *Narodovoltsi* in Ufa too—Leonovich, and afterwards Borozdich.

Just before leaving the country, Vladimir Ilyich had a narrow escape. He arrived in St. Petersburg from Pskov together with Martov. They were shadowed and arrested. He had two thousand rubles in his waistcoat, which he had received from Auntie (A. M. Kalmykova), and a list of contacts written in invisible ink on the back of an ordinary invoice. Had it occurred to the gendarmes to hold that invoice before a fire, Vladimir Ilyich would never have established an all-Russian newspaper abroad. But he was in luck, and after ten days or so he was released.

After that he came to Ufa to say good-bye to me. He told me what he had succeeded in doing since we had last met and the people he had managed to see. Naturally, a number of meetings were held on the occasion of his arrival. I remember that when it transpired that Leonovich, who considered himself a *Narodovolets*, had not even heard about the "Emancipation of Labour" group, Vladimir Ilyich flared up: "Fancy a revolutionary not knowing that? How can he intelligently choose a party he is going to work with when he does not know, has not studied, what the 'Emancipation of Labour' group has written?"

Vladimir Ilyich stayed about a week, I believe, in Ufa.

He wrote to me from abroad, chiefly by ciphered messages in books, which he addressed to various Zemstvo men. Things were not moving as fast with the newspaper as Vladimir Ilyich desired. He had trouble in coming to an understanding with Plekhanov. His letters were short and cheerless, and ended with: "I shall tell you all about it when you come over." "I have written down for you a full account of the conflict with Plekhanov."

I could hardly wait for the end of my exile. On top of it all I had not received any letters from Vladimir Ilyich for a long time.

I had intended going to Astrakhan to see Uncle (Lydia Knipovich), but was in too great a hurry.

Mother and I went to see Maria Alexandrovna—Vladimir Ilyich's mother—in Moscow. She was alone there at the time, her daughters Maria being in prison, and Anna abroad.

I was very fond of Maria Alexandrovna. She was always so tactful and considerate. Vladimir Ilyich loved his mother very much. "She has tremendous will-power," he told me once. "If this had happened to my brother when Father was alive, I don't know what there would have been."

Vladimir Ilyich inherited his mother's strength of mind as well as her tact and kindness towards people.

When we lived abroad I tried to describe our life to her in my letters in as lively a way as I could to make her feel a bit nearer to her son. When Vladimir Ilyich was in Siberian exile in 1897 (I had not joined him yet) the papers published an obituary notice on a Maria Alexandrovna Ulyanova, who had died in Moscow. Engberg told me: "I came to see Vladimir Ilyich, and he was as white as a sheet. 'My mother is dead,' he says." But the obituary notice turned out to be that on another woman of the same name.

Maria Alexandrovna had suffered much, what with the execution of her eldest son, the death of her daughter Olga, and the repeated arrests of her other children.

When Vladimir Ilyich fell ill in 1895, she came immediately to nurse him, and cooked his food herself. His arrest found her at her old post again, sitting for hours in the gloomy waiting-room of the House of Preliminary Detention, coming to see him on visiting day and bringing him parcels. But for a slightly shaky head, she had not changed a bit.

I promised her to look after Vladimir Ilyich, but I could not keep my promise....

From Moscow I took my mother to St. Petersburg, where I fixed her up and went abroad. I had some amusing adventures on that trip. I went to Prague in the belief that Vladimir Ilyich was living there under the name of Modráček.

I sent him a telegram. At Prague no one met me. I waited as long as I could, then, greatly embarrassed, I hailed a top-hatted cabby, piled my baskets into his cab and rode off. We arrived in a working-class quarter, and stopped outside a great tenement house in a narrow turning. A multitude of featherbeds were being aired in the open windows of the building.

I flew up to the fourth floor. A fair-headed little Czech

woman answered the door. All I could say was: "Modráček, Herr Modráček." A workman came out. "I am Modráček," he says. Bewildered, I stammered, "No, it's my husband." At last Modráček saw daylight. "Ah, you must be
the wife of Herr Rittmeyer. He lives in Munich, but sent
books and letters to you in Ufa through me." Modráček
spent the whole day with me. I told him about the Russian movement, and he told me about the Austrian movement. His wife showed me her needlework and treated me
to a meal of Czech dumplings.

I arrived in Munich* in a fur coat when people there
were going about in dresses. Made wise by experience, I
left my luggage in the cloak-room and went in search of
Rittmeyer by tram. I found the house. Flat No. 1 turned
out to be a beer-house. I approached the fat little German
behind the bar and timidly asked for Herr Rittmeyer with
a feeling that something was wrong again. "That's me,"
said the publican. Absolutely crushed, I mumbled: "No,
it's my husband."

And there we stood, staring at each other like a couple
of idiots. At last Rittmeyer's wife came in, and glancing at
me, said: "Ah, it must be Herr Meyer's wife. He is expecting his wife from Siberia. I'll take you to him."

I followed Frau Rittmeyer through the backyard of the
big building to an untenanted-looking flat. The door
opened, and there at a table sat Vladimir Ilyich, Martov
and Anna Ilyinichna. Forgetting to thank my guide, I
began to give Vladimir Ilyich a piece of my mind. "Damn
it all, couldn't you write and tell me where you were?"

"But I did! I've been going to the station to meet you
three times a day. How did you get here?"

As we afterwards learned, the Zemstvo man to whom the
book with the address had been sent had kept the book to
read.

---

* N. Krupskaya arrived in Munich about the middle of April
1901.—*Ed.*

Many a Russian travelled afterwards in the same manner. Shlyapnikov first went to Genoa instead of Geneva. Babushkin very nearly landed in America instead of London.

MUNICH

1901-1902

Although Vladimir Ilyich, Martov and Potresov went
abroad with legal passports, they decided in Munich to
live under false passports, and keep away from the Russian colony in order not to compromise our associates arriving from Russia and the better to be able to send illegal
literature to Russia in suitcases, letters, and so on.

When I came to Munich Vladimir Ilyich was living un-
registered with this Rittmeyer under the name of Meyer.
Although Rittmeyer kept a beer-house, he was a Social-
Democrat and sheltered Vladimir Ilyich in his flat. Vladimir Ilyich had a poor room, and lived in bachelor style,
having his meals at a German woman's, who kept him on
a *Mehlspeise* diet. In the morning and the evening he
drank tea out of a tin cup, which he carefully washed himself and hung up on a nail by the sink.

He looked worried. Things were going slower than he
wanted. Besides Vladimir Ilyich, there lived in Munich at
the time Martov, Potresov and Vera Zasulich. Plekhanov
and Axelrod wanted the paper to be published somewhere
in Switzerland under their direct control. They—and at
first Zasulich too—did not attach great significance to
Iskra, and failed completely to appreciate the organizing
role which it could and eventually did play. They were
much more interested in *Zarya.**

"That *Iskra* of yours is silly," Vera Zasulich said at the
beginning. Spoken in jest, it nevertheless betrayed a cer-

---

* *Zarya (Dawn)*—a Marxist scientific and political journal published in Stuttgart in 1901-1902 by the *Iskra* editorial board.—*Ed.*

tain underestimation of the whole enterprise. Vladimir Ilyich thought *Iskra* ought to be kept apart from the political emigrant centre, and run on secret lines. This was vitally important as a means of facilitating contact with Russia, correspondence and the arrival of agents. The Old Men were inclined to construe this as unwillingness to have the paper transferred to Switzerland, unwillingness to accept their leadership, a desire to pursue an independent course of action, and so they were in no particular hurry to help. Vladimir Ilyich sensed this and was worried about it. He had a soft spot for the "Emancipation of Labour" group, a great affection for both Axelrod and Vera Zasulich, not to mention Plekhanov. "Wait till you see Zasulich," he told me the first evening I arrived in Munich. "She is true to the core." And he was right.

Vera Zasulich was the only one of the "Emancipation of Labour" group to identify herself closely with *Iskra*. She lived with us in Munich and London, and *Iskra* and its editorial board were all she had in the world. Their joys and sorrows were hers, and tidings from Russia were the air she breathed.

"*Iskra* is coming along, you know," she said as the influence of the paper grew and extended. Vera Zasulich often spoke about the long bleak years she had lived in emigration.

We never experienced the kind of life in emigration that the "Emancipation of Labour" group had known. We were constantly and closely in touch with Russia and always had people from there coming to see us. We were better informed than if we had lived in some provincial town in Russia itself. We had no life outside the interests of our Russian work. Things in Russia were on the upgrade, the working-class movement was rising. The "Emancipation of Labour" group had been cut off from Russia, living abroad during the worst period of reaction, when a student arriving from Russia had been an event. Travellers had been afraid to call on them. When Klasson and Korobko visited them at the beginning of the nineties, they were summoned to the police as soon as they returned and asked why they had gone to see Plekhanov. Police detection was well organized.

Of all the "Emancipation of Labour" group Vera Zasulich lived the loneliest life. Plekhanov and Axelrod both had families. Vera Zasulich often spoke about how lonely she felt. "I have no one," she would say, then hasten to cover up her feelings with a joke: "You love me, I know, but when I die the most you'll do will be to drink one cup of tea less perhaps."

Her yearning for a home and family was all the more poignant for her having been brought up herself in a strange home as a ward. How lovingly she dandled Dimka's baby boy (Dimka was P. G. Smidovich's sister). She even displayed unsuspected gifts for housewifery and did the shopping when it was her turn to cook dinner for the "commune" (Vera, Martov and Alexeyev ran a communal household in London). Few people would have suspected such domestic inclinations in her, however. She always lived in nihilist style—dressed carelessly and smoked without a stop; her room was shockingly untidy, and she never allowed anyone to do it. Her eating, too, was rather fantastic. I remember her stewing some meat on an oil-stove and snipping pieces off it with a scissors and putting them into her mouth.

"When I lived in England," she told me, "the English ladies tried to be sociable, and asked: 'How long do you stew your meat?' 'All depends,' I said. 'If you're hungry ten minutes will do, if not—three hours or so.' That stopped them."

When Vera had any writing to do, she would shut herself up in her room and subsist on strong black coffee.

She was terribly homesick. In 1899, I believe, she went to Russia illegally—not to do any work, but just like that, "to have a look at the muzhik and see what kind of nose he has." And when *Iskra* began to appear, she felt that this was a piece of real Russian work, and clung to it desperately. For her to leave *Iskra* would have meant cutting herself off from Russia again, sinking back into the slough of emigrant life abroad.

That is why, when the question of *Iskra* editorship was brought up at the Second Congress, she was filled with indignation. For her it was not a question of ambition, but a matter of life and death.

In 1905 she went to Russia and stayed there.

Vera Zasulich, for the first time in her life, opposed Plekhanov at the Second Congress. She had been associated with him by years of joint struggle, she saw what a tremendous role he played in having the revolutionary movement guided into the proper channel, and appreciated him as the founder of Russian Social-Democracy, appreciated his intellect, his brilliant talent. The slightest disagreement with Plekhanov distressed her terribly. Yet in this case she went against him.

Plekhanov's was a tragic fate. In the theoretical field his services to the workers' movement are almost inestimable. Long years of life as a political emigrant, however, told on him—they isolated him from Russian realities. The broad mass movement of the workers started after he had gone abroad. He saw the representatives of different parties, writers, students, even individual workers, but he had not seen the Russian working-class mass, had not worked with it, nor felt it. Sometimes, when letters came from Russia that lifted the veil over new forms of the movement and revealed new vistas, Vladimir Ilyich, Martov and even Vera Zasulich would read them over and over again. Vladimir Ilyich would then pace the room for a long time and not be able to fall asleep afterwards. I tried to show those letters to Plekhanov when we moved to Geneva and was surprised at the way he reacted. He seemed to be staggered, then looked incredulous, and never spoke about them again.

His attitude towards those letters from Russia became more sceptical than ever after the Second Congress.

I felt hurt at this at first, and then I thought I began to see the reason. He had been away from Russia for such a long time that he had lost that capacity, developed by experience, which enables one to gauge the value of each letter and read between the lines.

Workers from Russia often came to *Iskra*, and all of them, of course, wanted to see Plekhanov. Seeing him was much more difficult than seeing us or Martov, and even when a worker did get to see him, he would come away feeling baffled. Plekhanov's brilliant intellect, knowledge and wit would impress the worker, but all that the latter felt on leaving him would be the vast gulf between himself and that brilliant theoretician. The things that had lain uppermost in his mind, the things he had been so eager to talk to him about and ask his advice on, had remained unuttered.

And if a worker differed with Plekhanov and tried to express his own opinion, Plekhanov would get angry and say: "Your daddies and mummies were knee-high when I...."

I daresay he was not like that at the beginning of his emigration, but by the turn of the century he no longer had the live feel of Russia. He did not go to Russia in 1905.

Axelrod was much more of an organizer than either Plekhanov or Zasulich. He saw much more of the new arrivals, who spent most of their time with him, and had their meals at his lodgings. He questioned them closely about everything.

He carried on a correspondence with comrades in Russia and was well up in secrecy techniques. One can well imagine how a Russian revolutionary organizer must have felt, living for years in Switzerland as a political emigrant! Axelrod worked at only a quarter of his former capacity; he did not sleep for nights at a stretch, and writing was a tremendous strain on him—it took him months to finish an article he had started, and his handwriting was almost illegible owing to the nervous way he wrote.

His handwriting always upset Vladimir Ilyich. "It's terrible to think of one reaching such a state as Axelrod," he would often say. He often spoke about Axelrod's handwriting to Dr. Kramer, who attended Ilyich during his last illness. When Vladimir Ilyich first went abroad in 1895 he had discussed organizational questions mostly with Axelrod. He told me a lot about him when I arrived in Munich. He asked me what Axelrod was now doing by pointing to his name in the newspaper when he himself could no longer write or even speak a word.

Axelrod reacted rather painfully to the fact that *Iskra* was not being published in Switzerland and that the flow of communications with Russia did not pass through him. That accounts for his bitter attitude on the question of an editorial trio at the Second Congress. *Iskra* to be the organizing centre, while he was removed from the editorial board! And this at a time when the breath of Russia made itself felt more strongly than ever at the Second Congress.

When I arrived in Munich the only member of the "Emancipation of Labour" group living there was Vera Zasulich. She had a Bulgarian passport and lived under the name of Velika Dmitriyevna.

All the others had Bulgarian passports too. Until my arrival Vladimir Ilyich had been living without any passport at all. When I came we took a passport in the name of Dr. Yordanov, a Bulgarian, with his wife Marica, and rented a room we saw advertised in a working-class home. The secretary of *Iskra* before me had been Inna Smidovich-Leman. She, too, had a Bulgarian passport, and her Party sobriquet was Dimka. Vladimir Ilyich told me when I arrived that he had arranged for me to be the secretary of *Iskra* on my arrival. This, of course, meant that all intercourse with Russia would be closely controlled by Vladimir Ilyich. Martov and Potresov had had nothing against this at the time, and the "Emancipation of Labour" group had put up no candidate of their own, as they had not attached any particular importance to *Iskra* at the time. Vladimir Ilyich told me he had felt very awkward about doing this, but had thought it necessary in the interests of the cause. I had my hands full at once. Things were organized in this way: letters from Russia were addressed to German comrades in various towns in Germany, and they readdressed them to Dr. Leman, who forwarded them on to us.

Shortly before this there had been quite a scare. Our comrades in Russia had succeeded at last in setting up a printing plant in Kishinev. The manager Akim (brother of Lieber—Leon Goldman) sent to Leman's address by post a cushion with copies of pamphlets published in Russia sewn up in it. Leman refused delivery of the parcel, thinking it a mistake, but when our people got to know about it and raised an alarm, he took the cushion from the post office and said that he would henceforth accept delivery of everything that was addressed to him, even if it was a trainload.

We had no transport facilities yet for smuggling *Iskra* into Russia. It was sent in mainly in double-bottom suitcases through various travellers, who delivered them at secret addresses in Russia.

One such secret rendezvous was the Lepeshinskys' in Pskov. Another was in Kiev and some other town. The comrades in Russia took the literature out of the suitcases and handed it over to the organization. Shipments had only just begun to be arranged through the Letts Rolau and Skubik.

All this took up a lot of our time. A good deal of time was also wasted on all kinds of negotiations, which led to nothing.

I remember wasting a week negotiating with a fellow who planned to get in touch with smugglers by travelling along the frontier with a camera, which he wanted us to buy for him.

We corresponded with *Iskra* agents in Berlin, Paris, Switzerland and Belgium. They tried to help as best they could by raising money and finding willing travellers, connections, addresses, and so on.

An organization called the League of Russian Revolutionary Social-Democrats Abroad was formed out of the sympathizing groups in October 1901.

Connections with Russia grew apace. One of the most active correspondents of *Iskra* was the St. Petersburg worker Babushkin. Vladimir Ilyich had seen him before leaving Russia and made arrangements with him to send in correspondence. He sent in a mass of reports from Orekhovo-Zuyevo, Vladimir, Gus-Khrustalny, Ivanovo-Voznesensk, Kokhma and Kineshma. He made a regular round of these towns and strengthened contacts with them. Letters also came from St. Petersburg, Moscow, the Urals and the South. We corresponded with the Northern Union.* Noskov, a representative of the Union, arrived from Ivanovo-Voznesensk. A more Russian type it is difficult to imagine. Fair-skinned and blue-eyed, with a slight stoop, he spoke with a broad country accent, and had arrived abroad with a small bundle to make all the necessary arrangements. His uncle, the owner of a small mill in Ivanovo-Voznesensk, had given him the money for the trip in order to get rid of his troublesome nephew, who was for ever being run in and having his room searched by the police. Boris Nikolayevich Noskov (Babushkin's alias, his real name and patronymic being Vladimir Alexandrovich) was an experienced

---

* The Northern Union of Russian Workers, or Northern Union, as it was called, was an association of members of the Social-Democratic organizations of the Vladimir, Kostroma and Yaroslavl (later Tver) gubernias. Founded in 1900. Membership included Varentsova, Noskov, Lyubimov and Karpov. The Union was dispersed by the tsarist police in the summer of 1902.—*Ed.*

practical worker. I had met him in Ufa where he had stopped over on his way to Ekaterinburg. He came abroad for contacts. Making contacts was his profession. I remember him sitting on the stove in our Munich kitchen, telling us with shining eyes about the work of the Northern Union. He was terribly enthusiastic, and Vladimir Ilyich's questions only added fuel to the flames. Boris kept a note-book while he lived abroad, in which he meticulously wrote down all contacts: where this or that one lived, what he did, and how he could be useful. He left us that note-book afterwards. His work as an organizer had a poetic sort of quality. He over-idealized his work and people, however, and lacked the ability to face up to reality. After the Second Congress he became a conciliator, and later disappeared from the political scene. He died during the years of reaction.

Other people came to Munich too. Struve had been there before my arrival. Things were already heading for a break with him. He was passing over from the Social-Democratic to the liberal camp. On the occasion of his last visit there had been a serious clash. Vera Zasulich had nicknamed him "the book-fed calf." Both Vladimir Ilyich and Plekhanov had given him up, but Vera Zasulich still thought there was hope for him. We jokingly called her and Potresov the *"Struve-freundliche Partei."*

Struve visited Munich again when I was there. Vladimir Ilyich refused to see him. I went to see Struve at Vera's rooms. The interview was a very painful one. Struve felt terribly hurt. There was a Dostoyevsky sort of touch about it all. He spoke about his being regarded as a renegade and other things in a similar strain, and acted the self-tormentor. I do not remember everything he said, but I do remember the heavy feeling with which I came away from that meeting. Plainly, he was a stranger, a man hostile to our Party. Vladimir Ilyich had been right. Afterwards Struve's wife, Nina Alexandrovna, sent us her regards and a box of sweets through somebody—I don't remember who now. She was powerless, and I doubt whether she realized where her husband was heading. He knew, though.

After my arrival we lived in rooms at a German working-class home. They were a family of six, and all lived in the kitchen and a tiny room, but everything was spotlessly clean. The children, too, were tidy and polite. I decided to put Vladimir Ilyich on home-cooked food and tackled the pots and pans. I did the cooking in the landlady's kitchen, but prepared everything in our own room. I tried to make as little noise as possible, because Vladimir Ilyich had then begun to write *What Is To Be Done?* When writing, he would usually pace swiftly up and down the room, whispering what he was going to write. I had already adapted myself to his mode of working, and when he was writing I never spoke to him or asked him any questions. Afterwards, when we went out for a walk, he would tell me what he had written and what he was thinking about. This became as much a necessity to him as whispering his article over to himself before putting it down in writing. We went for long rambles on the outskirts of Munich, choosing the loneliest spots where there were fewer people about.

A month later we moved into a flat of our own in Schwabing, a suburb of Munich, in one of the numerous newly erected buildings, and got ourselves some furniture (we sold it all for twelve marks when we left). We now settled down to real home life.

After lunch—which was at twelve—Martov and others came to attend the so-called editorial meeting. Martov spoke without a stop, jumping from one subject to another. He read a lot and was always chock-full of news. He knew everything and everybody. "Martov is a typical journalist," Vladimir Ilyich often said about him. "He is remarkably talented, quick at grasping things, terribly impressionable and easy-going." Martov was an indispensable man for *Iskra*. Those five-to-six-hour talks every day were very tiring for Vladimir Ilyich. He used to feel quite ill after them and was unfit for work. He asked me once to go and see Martov and tell him not to come to us. We arranged that I would call on him myself, and tell him what letters we had received and arrange everything with him. But nothing came of it. Two days later we were back again where we were. Martov could not live without these talks. From us he would go to a café with Vera Zasulich, Dimka and Blumenfeld* and sit there talking for hours.

Afterwards Dan arrived with his wife and children, and Martov spent most of his time with them.

We went to Zurich in October to amalgamate with *Rabocheye Delo*. Nothing came of it, though. Akimov, Krichevsky and others talked themselves silly. Martov worked himself up to such a pitch in his attack on the *Rabocheye Delo* adherents that he even tore his tie off. I had never seen him like that before. Plekhanov scintillated. A resolution was drawn up to the effect that amalgamation was impossible. Dan read it out at the conference in a wooden voice. "Papal nuncio," his opponents shouted at him.

This split was a painless one. Martov and Lenin had not collaborated with *Rabocheye Delo*, and strictly speaking no break had occurred since there had never been any cooperation. On the other hand, Plekhanov was in high feather. The opponent he had been grappling with for so long was at last worsted. Plekhanov was cheerful and chatty.

We lived in the same hotel, and had our meals together, and everything seemed to be going well. Only occasional-

---

* Blumenfeld set up *Iskra*, first in Leipzig, then in Munich at the printing shops of the German Social-Democrats. He was a splendid compositor and a good comrade, enthusiastic over his job. He was very fond of Vera Zasulich, and always took good care of her. He did not get on with Plekhanov.—*N.K.*

ly did a very slight difference in the approach to certain questions make itself felt.

One conversation sticks in my memory. We were sitting in a café, and in the room next to ours there was a gymnasium where fencing was in progress. Workers armed with shields and cardboard swords were engaged there in a sham battle. Plekhanov laughed, saying: "That's how we shall fight under the new order." Going home—I walked with Axelrod—he developed the theme touched on by Plekhanov. "Under the new order everything will be a deadly bore," he said. "There will be no struggle."

I was still painfully shy then and said nothing, but I remember being surprised at such an argument.

After we returned from Zurich Vladimir Ilyich sat down to finish his *What Is To Be Done?* Later the Mensheviks vehemently attacked that pamphlet, but at that time it gripped everybody, especially those who were more closely associated with Russian work. The pamphlet was an ardent appeal for organization. It outlined a broad plan of organization in which everyone would find a place for himself, become a cog in the revolutionary machine, a cog, which, no matter how small, was vital to the working of the machine. The pamphlet urged the necessity of intensive and tireless efforts to build the foundation that had to be built if the Party was to exist in deeds and not in words under the conditions then prevailing in Russia. A Social-Democrat should not be afraid of long, hard work. He must work and work unremittingly, and be ever ready *"for everything,* from upholding the honour, the prestige and continuity of the Party in periods of acute revolutionary 'depression,' to preparing for, fixing the time for and carrying out the *nation-wide armed insurrection,"* Vladimir Ilyich wrote in *What Is To Be Done?* (*Works,* Vol. 5, p. 481.)

Twenty-seven years have passed since that pamphlet was written, and what years! The conditions of work for the Party have changed completely and entirely new tasks confront the workers' movement, yet the revolutionary passion of this pamphlet is irresistible even today, and it should be studied by everyone who wants to be a Leninist in deeds and not in words.

Whereas The *"Friends of the People"* was of tremendous significance in defining the path which the revolutionary movement had to take, *What Is To Be Done?* can be said to have defined a plan for extensive revolutionary activities. It pointed out a definite task.

It was clear that a Party congress was still premature, that the conditions capable of preventing it from coming to nothing as the First Congress had done were lacking, and that long preparatory work was necessary. The attempt by the Bund,* therefore, to convene a congress in Belostok was not taken seriously by anybody. Dan went there from *Iskra*, taking with him a suitcase whose false lining was crammed with copies of *What Is To Be Done?* The Belostok Congress turned into a conference.

Vladimir Ilyich was particularly interested in the attitude of the workers to that pamphlet. He wrote to I. I. Radchenko on July 16, 1902: "I was ever so glad to read your report about the talk with the workers. We receive such letters much too rarely. They are really tremendously cheering. Be sure and convey this to your workers with our request that they should write to us themselves, *not just for the press,* but to exchange ideas, so that we do not lose touch with one another and for mutual understanding. Personally I am particularly interested to know what the workers think of *What Is To Be Done?* So far I have received no comments from the workers." *(Works,* Vol. 36, p. 86.)

---

* *Bund*—Jewish Workers' League in Lithuania, Poland and Russia, organized in 1897. Mainly an organization of Jewish artisans in the western provinces of Russia. The Bund was a vehicle of nationalism and separatism in the working-class movement of Russia and held Menshevik views.—*Ed.*

Iskra was going strong. Its influence was increasing. The Party programme was being prepared for the congress. Plekhanov and Axelrod came to Munich to discuss it. Plekhanov attacked parts of the draft programme which Lenin had drawn up. Vera Zasulich did not agree with Lenin on all points, but neither did she agree entirely with Plekhanov. Axelrod also agreed with Lenin on some points. The meeting was a painful one. Vera Zasulich wanted to argue with Plekhanov, but he looked so forbidding, staring at her with his arms folded on his chest, that she was thrown off her balance. The discussion had reached the voting stage. Before the voting took place, Axelrod, who agreed with Lenin on this point, said he had a headache and wanted to go for a walk.

Vladimir Ilyich was terribly upset. To work like that was impossible. The discussion was so unbusiness-like.

Organizing the work on a business-like footing without introducing any personal element into it, and thus ensuring that caprice or personal relations associated with the past would not influence decisions, had now become an obvious need.

All differences with Plekhanov distressed Vladimir Ilyich greatly. He fretted and did not sleep at night. Plekhanov on the other hand was sulky and resentful.

After reading through Vladimir Ilyich's article for the fourth number of *Zarya*, Plekhanov returned it to Vera Zasulich with marginal notes in which he gave full vent to his annoyance. When Vladimir Ilyich saw them he was greatly upset.

By this time it became known that *Iskra* could no longer be printed in Munich. The owner of the print-shop did not want to run the risk. We had to move. But where? Plekhanov and Axelrod were for Switzerland, the rest— after that whiff of the atmosphere that had prevailed during the discussion of the programme—voted for London.

We looked back on this Munich period afterwards as a bright memory. Our later years of life in emigration were a much more distressing experience. During the Munich days the rift in the personal relations between Vladimir Ilyich, Martov, Potresov and Zasulich had not been so deep. All energies had been concentrated upon a single object—the building up of an all-Russian newspaper. There had been an intensive rallying of forces around *Iskra*. All had had the feel of the organization's growth, a sense that the path for creating the Party had been rightly chosen. That explains the genuine spirit of jollification with which we had enjoyed the carnivals, the universal good humour that had prevailed during our trip to Zurich, and so on.

Local life held no great attraction for us. We observed it merely as bystanders. We went to meetings sometimes, but on the whole they were of little interest. I remember the May Day celebrations. For the first time that year the German Social-Democrats had been permitted to organize a procession, on condition that the celebrations were held outside the town and no crowds collected within the town.

Fairly large columns of German Social-Democrats with their wives and children, their pockets stuffed with horse-radishes, marched swiftly through the town in silence to drink beer in a suburban beer garden. There were no flags, no placards. That *Maifeier* bore very little resemblance to a demonstration of working-class triumph throughout the world.

We did not follow the procession to the suburban beer garden, but dropped behind and roamed the streets of Munich as was our habit, in order to let the feeling of disappointment that had crept into our hearts wear off. We wanted to take part in a real militant demonstration, and not a procession sanctioned by the police.

As we were working in strict secrecy, we never met any of the German comrades except Parvus, who lived near us in Schwabing with his wife and little son. Rosa Luxemburg came to see him once, and Vladimir Ilyich went there to meet her. Parvus was then an extreme Left-winger. He contributed to *Iskra* and was interested in Russian affairs.

We travelled to London via Liége. Nikolai Meshcheryakov was living in Liége at the time with his wife—both old Sunday School friends of mine. I had known him as a *Narodovolets*, but he had been the first to initiate me into illegal work, the first to teach me secrecy technique and help me to become a Social-Democrat by keeping me well supplied with the foreign publications of the "Emancipation of Labour" group.

Now he was a Social-Democrat. He had been living in Belgium for a long time and was familiar with the local movement. We decided to call on him en route.

There was tremendous excitement in Liége at that time. A few days previously the troops had fired on the strikers. The ferment in the working-class districts could be read in the faces of the workers and the people, who stood about in knots. We went to see the People's House. It was very inconveniently situated, and any crowd standing in front of the building could easily be cooped up and trapped. The workers were flocking to it. To avoid a crowd gathering there, the Party leaders had arranged meetings in all the working-class districts. This gave rise to a vague mistrust of the Belgian Social-Democratic leaders. It was very much like a division of labour, some shooting at the crowd, others seeking an excuse to pacify it. . . .

LIFE IN LONDON

1902-1903

We arrived in London in April 1902.

The immensity of London staggered us. Although the weather was filthy the day we arrived, Vladimir Ilyich brightened up at once and began to look round at this citadel of capitalism with curiosity, Plekhanov and the editorial conflicts for the moment forgotten.

At the station we were met by Nikolai Alexeyev—a political emigrant living in London, who had mastered the English language. He acted as our guide at the beginning, as we found ourselves rather helpless. We thought we knew English, having in fact translated a thick book in Siberia from English into Russian (the Webbs' book). I had studied English in prison from a self-instructor but had never heard a word of spoken English. When we started translating the Webbs in Sushenskoye Vladimir Ilyich had been horrified at my pronunciation. "My sister had an English teacher, but she never sounded like that," he said. I did not argue, and started learning over again. When we arrived in London we found we could not understand a thing, nor could anybody understand us. It got us into comical situations at first. It amused Vladimir Ilyich, but at the same time put him on his mettle. He tackled English in earnest. We started going to all kinds of meetings, getting as close as we could to the speaker and carefully watching his mouth. We went fairly often to Hyde Park at the beginning. Speakers there harangue the strolling crowds on all kinds of subjects. One man—an atheist—tried to prove to a group of curious listeners that there was no God. We particularly liked one such speaker—he had an Irish accent, which we were better able to understand. Next to him a Salvation Army officer was shouting out hysterical appeals to Almighty God, while a little way off a salesman was holding forth about the drudgery of shop assistants in the big stores. Listening to English speech helped us a lot. Afterwards Vladimir Ilyich found two Englishmen through an advertisement, who wished to take Russian lessons in exchange for English, and began studying assiduously with them. He got to know the language fairly well.

Vladimir Ilyich studied London too. He did not go to the museums—I mean the ordinary museums, not the British Museum, where he spent half his time, attracted not by the museum itself, but by the world's richest library and the facilities it offered for study. After ten minutes in the museum proper, Vladimir Ilyich got very tired, and we would usually make a very quick exit from the rooms hung about with medieval armour and the endless halls filled with Egyptian and other ancient vessels. I remember only one museum Vladimir Ilyich could not tear himself away from—the Museum of the 1848 Revolution in Paris, housed in one little room—in the Rue des Cordeliers, I believe—where he examined every little thing, every drawing.

Ilyich studied living London. He liked taking long rides through the town on top of the bus. He liked the busy traffic of that vast commercial city, the quiet squares with their elegant houses wreathed in greenery, where only smart broughams drew up. There were other places too—mean little streets tenanted by London's work people, with clothes lines stretched across the road and anaemic children playing on the doorsteps. To these places we used to go on foot. Observing these startling contrasts between wealth and poverty, Ilyich would mutter in English through clenched teeth: "Two nations!"

But even from the top of the bus one could observe many characteristic scenes. Ill-clad lumpen-proletarians with pasty faces hung around the pubs, and often one would see among them a drunken woman with a bruised eye wearing a trailing velvet dress from which a sleeve had been ripped off. Once, from the top of a bus, we saw a huge "bobby" in his typical helmet and chin strap hustling before him with an iron hand a puny little urchin, who had evidently been caught stealing, while a crowd followed behind them whooping and whistling. Some of the people on the bus jumped up and began hooting at the little thief too. "Well, well!" Vladimir Ilyich would mutter sadly. Once or twice we took a ride on top of the bus to some working-class district on pay-day evening. An endless row of stalls, each lit up by a flare, stretched along the pavement of a wide road; the pavements were packed with a noisy crowd of working men and women, who were buying all kinds of things and satisfying their hunger right there on the spot. Vladimir Ilyich always felt drawn to the working-class crowd. Wherever there was a crowd he was sure to be there—whether it was an outing in the country, where the tired workers, glad to escape from the city, lay about for hours on the grass, or a public house, or a reading room. There are many reading rooms in London—just a single room opening straight on to the street, where there is not even a seat, but just a reading desk with newspaper files. The reader takes a file and when he is finished with it, hangs it back in its place. Ilyich, in years to come, wanted to have such reading rooms organized everywhere in our own country. He visited eating houses and churches. In English churches the service is usually followed by a short lecture and a debate. Ilyich was particularly fond of those debates, because ordinary workers took part in them. He scanned the newspapers for notices of working-class meetings in some out-of-the-way district, where there were only rank-and-file workers from the bench—as we say now—without any pomp and leaders. These meetings were usually devoted to the discussion of some question or project, such as a garden-city scheme. Ilyich would listen attentively, and afterwards say joyfully: "They are just bursting with socialism! If a speaker starts talking rot a worker gets up right away and takes the bull by the horns, shows up the very essence of capitalism." It was the rank-and-file British worker who had preserved his class instinct in face of everything, that Ilyich always relied upon. Visitors to Britain usually saw only the labour aristocracy, corrupted by the bourgeoisie and itself bourgeoisified. Naturally, Ilyich studied that upper stratum, too, and the concrete forms which this bourgeois influence took, without for a moment forgetting the significance of that fact. But he also tried to discover the motive forces of the future revolution in England.

There was hardly a meeting anywhere we did not go to. Once we wandered into a socialist church. There are such churches in England. The socialist in charge was droning through the Bible, and then delivered a sermon to the effect that the exodus of the Jews from Egypt symbolized the exodus of the workers from the kingdom of capitalism into the kingdom of socialism. Everyone stood up and sang from a socialist hymn-book: "Lead us, O Lord, from the Kingdom of Capitalism into the Kingdom of Socialism." We went to that church again afterwards—it was the Seven Sisters Church—to hear a talk for young people. A young man spoke about municipal socialism and tried to prove that no revolution was needed, while the socialist who had officiated as clergyman during our first visit declared that he had been a member of the party for twelve years and for twelve years he had been fighting opportunism—and that was what municipal socialism was —opportunism pure and simple.

We know little about English socialists in their home surroundings. The English are a reserved people. They regarded the Bohemianism of the Russian emigrants with naive wonder. I remember an English socialist we once met at the Takhtarevs' asking me: "Do you mean to say you've been in prison? If my wife were put in prison I don't know what I'd do! I just can't imagine it!" How strong these petty-bourgeois prejudices were we had an opportunity of observing in the case of our landlady's family—a working-class family—and the Englishmen we exchanged lessons with. This was where we were able to study to our heart's content all the abysmal philistinism of petty-bourgeois English life. One of the Englishmen who came to us for his lessons was the manager of a large bookstore. He contended that socialism was a theory that set the most correct value on things. "I am a convinced socialist," he said. "At one time I even started to make socialist speeches. Then my employer sent for me and said he had no need for socialists, and if I wanted to keep my job I would have to hold my tongue. Well, I thought, socialism is inevitable, whether I speak for it or not, and I have a wife and children to look after. I no longer tell anyone that I'm a socialist, but you I can tell."

This Mr. Raymond, who has been nearly all over Europe, lived in Australia and other places, and spent most of his life in London, had not seen half of what Vladimir Ilyich had managed to see in London during his one year's stay there. One day Ilyich dragged him off to a meeting in Whitechapel. Like most Englishmen, Mr. Raymond had never been in that part of London, inhabited mostly by Russian Jews who lived a life of their own there unlike that of the rest of the city. He was astonished at what he saw.

We were in the habit of going for rambles in the suburbs too. More often than not we went to Primrose Hill. It was the cheapest trip—the fare only costing sixpence. The hill commanded a view of almost the whole of London—a vast smoke-wreathed wilderness of houses. From here we took long walks into the parks and country lanes. Another reason we liked going to Primrose Hill was because it was near the cemetery where Karl Marx was buried. We used to go there.

In London we met a member of our St. Petersburg group, Apollinaria Yakubova. Back in St. Petersburg she had been a very active worker. Everyone had thought highly of her and liked her, and she and I were bound still closer together by the fact that we had worked together in the Sunday School in the Nevskaya Zastava District and had a common friend in the person of Lydia Knipovich. After escaping from Siberian exile Apollinaria had married Takhtarev, former editor of *Rabochaya Mysl*. They were now living in London, but took no part in our activities. Apollinaria was delighted when we arrived. The Takhtarevs took us under their wing, and helped to fix us up in cheap and fairly comfortable lodgings. We saw Takhtarev very often, but as the subject of *Rabochaya Mysl* was generally avoided, our relations had a strained quality. Once or twice there was an explosion, and we had it out. In January 1903, I believe, the Takhtarevs officially declared their sympathy with the *Iskra* trend.

My mother was due to arrive soon, and we decided to set up on our own by renting two rooms and having our meals at home. We found that all those "ox-tails," skates fried in fat, and indigestible cakes were not made for Russian stomachs. Besides, we were living at the organization's expense, and that meant we had to economize every penny. Living at home would be cheaper.

As far as secrecy was concerned conditions could not have been better. No identity papers were needed in London at that time, and one could go under any name. We took the name of Richter. Another advantage was that all foreigners look alike to English people, and our landlady took us for Germans all the time we were there.

Shortly Martov and Vera Zasulich arrived and set up a communal household with Alexeyev in a continental-style apartment house not far away from us. Vladimir Ilyich made immediate arrangements to work at the British Museum.

He usually went there first thing in the morning, while Martov and I—Martov came early in the morning too—would go through the mail together. In this way Vladimir Ilyich was relieved of much of the tiresome routine.

The conflict with Plekhanov was over more or less. Vladimir Ilyich took a month off to go to Brittany to see his mother and sister Anna, and spend a few weeks with them by the seaside. He loved the sea with its incessant movement and vast spaces, and could relax properly there.

In London we immediately started getting visitors. Inna Smidovich (Dimka) came too—she soon after left for Russia. Another visitor was her brother Pyotr, who at the initiative of Vladimir Ilyich, had been christened

Matryona. He had just come out of prison after serving a long term, and become an ardent *Iskra*-ist. He considered himself an expert at erasing passports, the secret of which, he claimed, was "the use of sweat." He would turn all the tables in the commune upside down to serve as presses for sponging out the passports. The technique was extremely primitive, as was the whole of our secrecy technique at the time. Re-reading today the correspondence that we carried on with Russia makes one marvel at the naïveté of our secrecy methods. All those letters about handkerchiefs (meaning passports), brewing beer and warm fur (illegal literature), all those code-names for towns beginning with the same letter as the town itself (Osip for Odessa, Terenty for Tver, Peter for Poltava, Pasha for Pskov, and so on), all that substituting of women's names for men's and vice versa—the whole thing was so thin, so transparent. It had not struck us as naive at the time, and to a certain extent it had succeeded in throwing the police off the track. There had not been so many *agents provocateurs* at the beginning as there were later. All our people were trustworthy and well known to each other. *Iskra* agents were working in Russia, who took delivery of all literature from abroad—*Iskra* and *Zarya* and pamphlets. They saw to it that the *Iskra* literature was reprinted at the illegal printing plants and distributed to the various locals. They arranged for correspondence to be delivered to *Iskra*, saw to it that it was kept informed of all the illegal work being conducted in Russia, and collected money for the newspaper.

In Samara (at Sonya's) there were the Rodents—the Krzhizhanovskys (Clair—Gleb Krzhizhanovsky and Snail —his wife Zinaida). Lenin's sister Maria—Bear Cub, also lived there. A kind of centre was quickly formed in Samara. The Krzhizhanovskys had a knack of gathering people around them. Lengnik (Kurz) moved to the South, lived for a time in Poltava (at Petya's), then in Kiev. In Astrakhan there was Lydia Knipovich (Uncle). In Pskov

Lepeshinsky (Bast Shoe) and Lyubov Radchenko (Pasha).
Stepan Radchenko was utterly worn out and had given up
illegal work, but then his brother Ivan (alias Arkady, alias
Kasyan) worked unflaggingly for *Iskra*. He was a travelling agent. Another travelling agent who delivered
Iskra all over Russia was Silvin (Vagabond). In Moscow
there was Bauman (alias Victor, Tree, Rook), working in close contact with Ivan Babushkin (alias Bogdan). Other agents were Yelena Stasova (alias Thick and
Absolute), who was closely associated with the St. Petersburg organization, and Glafira Okulova, who, after the
arrest of Bauman, had moved to Moscow where she lived
(at the Old Woman's) under the name of Baby Hare. With
all these people *Iskra* carried on a lively correspondence.
Vladimir Ilyich looked through every letter. We knew
exactly what the various *Iskra* agents were doing and
discussed all their work with them. When they lost touch
with one another we put them in touch again, informed
them of arrests, and so on.

Iskra had a printing press working for it in Baku. The
work was carried on in strictest secrecy. The Yenukidze
brothers worked there, and Krasin (Horse) was the manager. The plant was called Nina. Afterwards an attempt
was made to run a printing press in Novgorod—Akulina,
we called it, but it was soon suppressed. The former secret
plant at Kishinev run by Akim (Leon Goldman) had fall-
en through by this time.

Shipments were made via Vilna (through Grunya).

The St. Petersburg comrades tried to arrange transportation through Stockholm. We had heaps of correspondence over this avenue, which operated under the name of
Beer. We shipped literature to Stockholm by the hundred-
weight and received confirmation that the Beer had been
delivered. We were sure that it was being received in St.
Petersburg and went on sending more literature to Stockholm. It was not until 1905, when we were returning to
Russia via Sweden, that we learnt the beer was still in

the brewery, in other words in Stockholm's People's House, where a whole cellar was stacked with literature. The "Smaller Casks" were shipped through Vardo. Only one parcel, I believe, was received, and then some hitch occurred. Matryona was sent to live in Marseilles. She was to arrange shipment through cooks working on boats going to Batum. There delivery of the literature was organized by the Baku comrades (the Horses). Most of the literature, though, was thrown into the sea (it was wrapped up in tarpaulin and dropped overboard at a prearranged spot, where our comrades fished it out). Mikhail Kalinin, a member of our organization, who was then working at a factory in St. Petersburg, gave a sailor an address in Toulon through Stasova (Thick). Literature was also shipped via Alexandria (Egypt), and transportation was arranged through Persia. Afterwards it was arranged through Kamenets-Podolsk and Lvov. All these shipments ate up a mass of money and energy, not to mention the tremendous risks involved, and yet not more than a tenth of all we sent probably ever reached destination. We also used double-bottomed trunks and bookbindings to smuggle literature through. It was snapped up immediately.

What Is To Be Done? was a great success. It supplied the answers to a number of vital and pressing questions. Everyone keenly felt the need for an underground organization working according to plan.

A conference was opened in Belostok in June 1902 by the Bund (Boris). All the delegates with the exception of the St. Petersburg delegate, were arrested. As a result, Bauman and Silvin were arrested too. The conference decided to set up an organizing committee for convening a Party congress. Delays occurred, however. Representation by the local organizations was required, but these were still of an extremely unorganized and heterogeneous nature. For instance, in St. Petersburg the organization was split up into a workers' committee (Manya), and an intellectuals' committee (Vanya). The workers' committee was chiefly to carry on the economic struggle, while the intellectuals' committee was to handle matters of high policy. This high policy, by the way, was of a very insignificant kind, and was more like liberal policy than revolutionary. This structure was a result of "Economism." Defeated in principle, it still held a secure footing locally. The *Iskra* group estimated this structure at its true worth. Vladimir Ilyich played an important part in the struggle for a proper structure of the organizations. His *Letter to Yerema*, better known as *Letter to a Comrade* (of which more anon) played an exceptionally important role in organizing the Party. It helped to strengthen the worker element in the Party and ensure the workers' active cooperation in deciding all urgent questions of policy. It broke down the wall which the *Rabocheye Delo* adherents had raised between the workman and the intellectual. The winter of 1902-03 saw a desperate struggle of tendencies within the organizations. The *Iskra*-ists steadily won ground, but sometimes they were "thrown out."

Vladimir Ilyich directed the struggle of the *Iskra*-ists, and warned them against a too vulgar interpretation of centralism. He combatted the tendency to regard every instance of live independent activity as "amateurish." This work of Vladimir Ilyich's, which so profoundly influenced the qualitative structure of the committees, is little known to the present generation, yet it was this that stamped the character of our Party and laid the foundation of its present organization.

The "Economists" of the *Rabocheye Delo* trend were strongly opposed to this struggle, as a result of which they had lost their influence, and resented "taking orders" from abroad.

Comrade Krasnukha arrived from St. Petersburg on August 6 to discuss organizational questions. His password was "Have you read No 47 of the *Citizen*?" Citizen became his Party sobriquet afterwards. Vladimir Ilyich had long talks with him about the St. Petersburg organization and its structure. Others who took part in these talks were P. A. Krasikov (alias Musician, Hairpin, Ignat and Pankrat) and Boris Noskov. From London Citizen went to Geneva to talk with Plekhanov and get properly "*Iskra*-fied." A week or two later we received a letter from Yerema giving his views about how the work ought to be organized locally. It was not clear from this letter whether Yerema was a single propagandist or a group of propagandists. But that was unimportant. Vladimir Ilyich began to think out a reply. The reply expanded into a pamplet *Letter to a Comrade on Our Organizational Tasks*. It was first hectographed and distributed, and later, in June 1903, printed illegally by the Siberian Committee.

Babushkin, who had escaped from prison in Ekaterinoslav, arrived at the beginning of September 1902. He and Gorovits had been helped to escape and cross the frontier by *gymnasium* schoolboys, who had dyed his hair. It turned crimson after a while, and attracted general attention. When he came to us he had crimson hair. In Germany he fell into the hands of commission agents and very nearly got himself shipped off to America. We fixed him up in the commune, where he lived throughout his stay in London. Babushkin had developed politically beyond recognition. He was now an experienced revolutionary with a mind of his own, a man familiar with all kinds of working-class organizations, who, being himself a worker, had nothing to learn in the matter of approaching the workers. When he first came to the Sunday School several years before he had been quite an inexperienced young man. I remember the following episode. At first he was in Lydia Knipovich's group. They were having a Russian lesson, and quoting grammatical examples. Babushkin wrote on the board: "There will soon be a strike in our factory." Lydia called him aside after the lesson and told him off: "If you want to be a revolutionary you must not try to show off that you are one. You must be able to control yourself." Babushkin had reddened, but afterwards regarded Lydia as his best friend, and often consulted her, speaking to her in a tone he used with no one else.

At that time Plekhanov arrived in London. A meeting was arranged with Babushkin. Russian affairs were discussed. Babushkin had opinions of his own and stood up for them very firmly, so much so that Plekhanov was impressed and began to study him more closely. About his future work in Russia, though, he spoke to no one but Vladimir Ilyich, with whom he was particularly intimate. I remember another small but rather characteristic incident. A couple of days after Babushkin's arrival we were astonished, on coming into the communal room, to find how tidy it was. All the litter had been cleared away, newspapers were spread on the tables, and the floor had been swept. We learnt that Babushkin had tidied up. "The Russian intellectual is so untidy—he needs a servant to tidy up for him, he can't do it himself," said Babushkin.

He soon went back to Russia. We did not see him any more. He was seized in Siberia in 1906 with a consignment of arms and was shot with other comrades over an open grave.

A group of *Iskra* comrades, who had escaped from prison in Kiev, arrived in London while Babushkin was still there. They were Bauman, Krokhmal, Blumenfeld (the latter had been caught on the frontier with a trunk of literature and addresses and taken to Kiev prison), Vallach (alias Litvinov, Daddy) and Tarsis (alias Friday).

We knew that a group of prisoners had been preparing to break jail in Kiev. Deutsch, an expert on breaking jail, who had just arrived, declared that it was impossible (he had first-hand knowledge of conditions in the Kiev prison). Nevertheless the prisoners succeeded in making their escape. Ropes, grappling irons and passports were smuggled into the prison. During the walk in the prison yard the guard and warder were gagged and bound, and the prisoners climbed over the wall. The last one in the queue—Silvin, who was holding the warder—failed to make good his escape.

Several hectic days followed.

In the middle of August we received a letter from the editors of *Yuzhny Rabochy**, a popular illegal organ of the workers, reporting arrests in the South and saying that they wished to establish close contact with the *Iskra* and *Zarya* organization. They also declared their solidarity with our views. This, of course, was a great step towards uniting our forces. In their next letter, however, the *Yuzhny Rabochy* group expressed disapproval with the sharp tone of *Iskra*'s polemics with the liberals. Then they went on to speak about the literary group of *Yuzhny Rabochy* continuing to preserve its independence, and so on. Obviously, they were keeping something back.

The Samara comrades ascertained by means of negotiations that *Yuzhny Rabochy*'s stand was characterized by: 1) underestimation of the peasant movement; 2) dissatisfaction at the sharp tone of the polemics with the liberals and 3) a desire to remain an independent group and publish their own popular organ.

At the beginning of October, Trotsky, who had escaped from Siberia, arrived in London. He considered himself then an *Iskra*-ist. Vladimir Ilyich studied him, and asked him many questions about his impressions of Russian work. Trotsky was being called back to Russia, but Vladimir Ilyich thought he ought to stay abroad to learn things and help in the work of *Iskra*. Trotsky went to live in Paris.

A new arrival was Ekaterina Alexandrova (Jacques), who had come from exile in Olekma. She had been a prom-

---

* *Yuzhny Rabochy (Southern Worker)*—a Social-Democratic group which published a newspaper under the same name. The paper existed from January 1900 to April 1903 and was distributed chiefly among the Social-Democratic organizations in the South of Russia. The group existed up till the Second Congress of the R.S.D.L.P.—*Ed.*

inent *Narodovolets,* and this had left its mark upon her. She was unlike our enthusiastic gushing girls, such as Dimka, and was highly self-possessed. She was an *Iskra*-ist now, and what she said carried weight.

Vladimir Ilyich held the old revolutionaries of the *Narodnaya Volya* in great respect.

When Alexandrova arrived, his attitude towards her was not uninfluenced by the fact that she was a former *Narodovolets,* who had now joined the *Iskra* group. As for me, I looked up to her. Before definitely becoming a Social-Democrat I had gone to the Alexandrovs (Olminskys) to ask to be given a study-circle of workers. I remember being greatly impressed by the simple furniture, the stacks of statistical manuals piled up everywhere, the figure of Mikhail Stepanovich sitting at the far end of the room, and the fervent speeches of Ekaterina, his wife, who urged me to join the *Narodnaya Volya.* I told Vladimir Ilyich this before her arrival. She became one of our current enthusiasms. Vladimir Ilyich was always being enthusiastic over somebody or other. On detecting in a person some valuable trait, he would fairly pounce on him. Ekaterina Alexandrova left London for Paris. She did not prove to be a very staunch *Iskra*-ist. The web of opposition against Lenin's "grasping" tactics at the Second Party Congress was spun not without her assistance. Later she was on the conciliatory Central Committee, and afterwards quitted the political arena.

Of the other comrades from Russia who visited London I remember Boris Goldman (Adele) and Dolivo-Dobrovolsky (Depth).

I had known Boris Goldman back in St. Petersburg, where he had been a technical worker of the organization engaged in printing leaflets for the League of Struggle. A great waverer, he was at that time an *Iskra*-ist. Dolivo was an amazingly quiet man. He used to sit as quiet as a mouse. Shortly after returning to St. Petersburg he went mad, and then, when half cured, shot himself. The underground in those days was a hard life, and not everyone could stand it.

Intensive preparations for the congress went forward all the winter. An Organizing Committee for preparing the congress was set up in December 1902, consisting of members of *Yuzhny Rabochy*, the Northern Union, of Krasnukha, I. I. Radchenko, Krasikov, Lengnik and Krzhizhanovsky; the Bund did not join it until afterwards.

The word "organizing" was very much to the point. Without the O.C. it would not have been possible to call the congress. The complicated task of organizationally and ideologically coordinating bodies which were either newly formed or still in the process of formation, and arranging for their representation on a congress to be held abroad, had to be carried out under the extremely difficult conditions of police regime. Actually the entire work of communicating with the O.C. devolved on Vladimir Ilyich. Potresov was ill—London's fogs did not agree with his lungs, and he was taking medical treatment somewhere. Martov found London and its secluded life trying, and had gone to Paris and stayed there. Deutsch, an old member of the "Emancipation of Labour" group, who had escaped from exile, was to have lived in London too. The group had had great hopes for him as an organizer. "Wait till Zhenka (Deutsch's alias) comes," Vera Zasulich said, "he will organize contacts with Russia splendidly." Plekhanov and Axelrod relied on him, too, hoping that he would represent them on *Iskra* and keep an eye on things. When Deutsch arrived, however, we found that being cut off for so many years from Russia had left its mark upon him. He was quite unfit to handle contacts with Russia and was unfamiliar with the new conditions. His hunger for companionship led him to join the League of Russian Revolutionary Social-Democrats Abroad.* He

---

* *The League of Russian Revolutionary Social-Democrats Abroad* was founded in 1901 after the failure of the attempt to unite with

established wide contacts with the Russian colonies abroad, and shortly also left for Paris.

Vera Zasulich resided permanently in London. She listened eagerly to stories about work in Russia but was herself incapable of handling contacts with Russia. Vladimir Ilyich bore the brunt of all this work. Correspondence with Russia frayed his nerves badly. Those weeks and months of waiting for answers to his letters, constantly expecting the whole thing to fall through, that constant state of uncertainty and suspense, were anything but congenial to Vladimir Ilyich's character. His letters to Russia were full of requests to write punctually. "We beg you again most earnestly and insistently to write us more often and more fully. Answer us without fail immediately you receive our letter, or at least drop us a line that you have received it." His letters were full of requests to act promptly. He did not sleep at night after receiving a letter from Russia saying that "Sonya is silent as the dead," or that "Zarin did not join the committee in time," or that "we have no contact with the Old Woman." I shall never forget those sleepless nights. It was Vladimir Ilyich's passionate desire to create a united solid party, merging into one all the detached groups whose attitude to the party was based on personal sympathies or antipathies. He dreamt of a party in which there would be no artificial barriers, national ones included. Hence the struggle with the Bund. The majority of the Bund at that time adopted the standpoint of *Rabocheye Delo*. Vladimir Ilyich had no doubts that if the Bund joined the Party and kept its autonomy only in purely national matters it would inevitably have to come into line with the Party. But the Bund wanted complete independence on all ques-

---

Rabocheye Delo (see above). It united all the revolutionary elements of the Russian Social-Democracy abroad, and included the "Emancipation of Labour" group, and the editorial staffs of the journal *Zarya* and *Iskra.—Ed.*

tions. Its leaders talked about a political party of their own, unconnected with the R.S.D.L.P., and agreed to affiliate only on a federal basis. Such tactics were disastrous to the Jewish proletariat. The latter could never win by itself. Only by joining with the proletariat of all Russia could it become a force. The Bundists failed to understand that. And so *Iskra* waged a fierce struggle with the Bund. It was a fight for unity, for solidarity of the working-class movement. The whole editorial board was in it, but the Bundists knew that the most ardent champion in the struggle for unity was Vladimir Ilyich.

The "Emancipation of Labour" group once more raised the question of moving to Geneva, and this time Vladimir Ilyich had been the only one to vote against it. We began making preparations for the journey. Vladimir Ilyich's nerves were in such a bad state that he developed a nervous disease caused by inflammation of the nerve endings of the back and chest.

As soon as I saw the redness I looked up a medical handbook. I made it out to be ring-worm. Takhtarev, who had been a medical student in his fourth or fifth year, confirmed my conjecture, and I painted Vladimir Ilyich with iodine, which caused him excruciating pain. It had not occurred to us to send for an English doctor, as that would have cost a guinea. Workers in England are usually their own doctors, since medical assistance is very expensive. During the journey to Geneva Vladimir Ilyich was in great pain, and on arriving there he took to bed and lay there for a fortnight.

A job which did not get on Vladimir Ilyich's nerves in London, but rather gave him satisfaction, was the writing of the pamphlet *To the Rural Poor*. The peasant uprisings of 1902 suggested to him the necessity of a pamphlet for the peasants. He explained in it what the workers' Party was out for and why the peasant poor should go with the workers. It was the first pamphlet in which Vladimir Ilyich addressed himself to the peasantry.

GENEVA

1903

We moved to Geneva in April 1903, and took up residence in the working-class suburb of Séchéron, where we rented a small house all to ourselves. There was a big kitchen with a stone floor downstairs, and three tiny rooms upstairs. The kitchen served as our living room. We made up for the scarcity of furniture by using the packing cases that had held our books and crockery. Ignat (Krasikov) dubbed our kitchen "smugglers' den." The place was terribly crowded. When we wanted to have a private talk with anyone we had to go to the park nearby or to the shore of the lake.

The delegates began to arrive. The Dementyevs came. Kostya (Dementyev's wife) amazed Lenin by her familiarity with the shipment business. "She's a real shipper!" he kept repeating. "That's real business, not idle talk." Another arrival was Lyubov Radchenko, with whom we were on intimate terms. We talked for hours. Then came the Rostov delegates—Gusev and Lokerman, then Zemlyachka, Shotman (Berg), Uncle, Youth (Dmitry Ilyich). Somebody turned up every day. We discussed questions concerning the programme and the Bund with the delegates, and listened to their stories. Martov was always at our place, and he never tired of talking with the delegates.

The delegates had to be told about the stand of the *Yuzhny Rabochy* group, who, under the guise of a popular newspaper, wanted to reserve the right to a separate existence. We had to explain that a popular newspaper could not become a mass medium under conditions of illegality, could not count on a mass circulation.

Differences of opinion arose on the editorial board of *Iskra.* The situation grew intolerable. The editors were generally divided into two trios: Plekhanov, Axelrod and Zasulich in one, Lenin, Martov and Potresov in the other.

Vladimir Ilyich again proposed what he had already proposed in March—that a seventh member be co-opted. Provisionally, until the congress, Krasikov was co-opted. The question of an editorial trio began to occupy Ilyich's thoughts more and more. It was a sore subject, but nothing had been said to the delegates about it. The fact that the *Iskra* editorial board as then constituted was no longer able to handle the job was too painful a thing to talk about.

The delegates complained about the O.C. members. One was accused of being too brusque and careless, another of being too passive. There were signs of discontent about *Iskra* wanting to boss the show, but the general impression was that there were no differences, and that after the congress everything would go swimmingly.

All the delegates had arrived except Clair (Krzhizhanovsky) and Kurz (Lengnik).

THE SECOND CONGRESS

July-August 1903

It was originally intended to hold the congress in Brussels, and in fact the first sittings were held there. Koltsov, an old Plekhanovite, lived in Brussels at the time, and he undertook to see to all the arrangements. As it turned out, however, it was not so easy to arrange the congress there. All the delegates were to have reported to Koltsov, but after four or five Russians had called on him his landlady told him that she would not stand any more of this coming and going, and if one more person called he would have to move out at once. Koltsov's wife after that stood on the street corner all day long, intercepting the delegates and directing them to the socialist hotel Coq d'Or as I believe it was called.

The delegates overran the whole hotel, and Gusev, after a drop of brandy, sang operatic arias in the evening in such a powerful voice that crowds collected at the windows outside. (Vladimir Ilyich liked Gusev's singing, especially the song *We Were Wedded Out of Church.*)

We overdid the secrecy precautions, though. The Belgian Party thought it would be safer to hold the congress in a vast flour warehouse. Our intrusion there only succeeded in astonishing the rats and the policemen. The word went round that Russian revolutionaries had got together to plot in secret.

The congress was attended by forty-three delegates with a deciding vote and fourteen with a deliberative vote. In comparison with present-day congresses, where the numerous delegates represent hundreds of thousands of Party members, this congress would seem a small one, but at that time we thought it big. The First Congress held in 1898 was attended by only nine persons. Everyone felt that considerable progress had been made in those five years. Most important of all, the organizations these delegates came from were no longer semi-mythical, they definitely existed and were already in touch with the working-class movement, which was beginning to spread ever wider.

How Vladimir Ilyich had dreamt of such a congress! He always, as long as he lived, attached tremendous importance to Party congresses. He held the Party congress to be the highest authority, where all things personal had to be cast aside, where nothing was to be concealed, and everything was to be open and above board. He always took great pains in preparing for Party congresses, and was particularly careful in thinking out his speeches.

Plekhanov looked forward to the congress just as eagerly as Vladimir Ilyich. He opened it. The big window of the flour warehouse near the improvised platform was covered with some red cloth. Everyone was excited. Plekhanov's speech, uttered with genuine deep feeling, sounded very solemn. And no wonder! The long years of emigrant life seemed to be a thing of the past. He was opening the Congress of the Russian Social-Democratic Labour Party.

Strictly speaking, the Second Congress was an inaugural congress. Fundamental questions of theory were raised there, and the foundations of Party ideology were laid. At the First Congress only the Party's designation and a manifesto on its formation had been adopted. Up to the time of the Second Congress the Party had had no programme. The editorial board of *Iskra* had drafted such a programme, and it had been under discussion for a long time. Every word, every sentence had been motivated, and weighed, and hotly debated. Correspondence on the programme had been carried on for months between the Munich and Swiss sections of the editorial board. Many practical workers regarded these disputes to be of a purely abstract nature, and did not think it mattered whether a "more-or-less" proviso was left standing in the programme or not.

Vladimir Ilyich and I were once reminded of a simile used by Lev Tolstoi. He was going along and saw from afar a man squatting and waving his arms about in a ridiculous way; a madman, he thought, but when he drew nearer, he saw it to be a man sharpening a knife on the kerb. The same thing happens in theoretical disputes. From the outside it seems a sheer waste of time, but when you go into the matter more deeply you see that it is a momentous issue. It was like that with the programme.

When the delegates began to arrive in Geneva the chief question discussed with them in greatest detail was that of the programme. That question went through at the congress more smoothly than any other.

Another question of tremendous importance discussed at the Second Congress was that of the Bund. It had been resolved at the First Congress that the Bund constituted a section of the Party, albeit an autonomous one. During the five years that had elapsed since the First Congress the Party, practically speaking, had not existed as a united whole, and the Bund had led a separate existence. Now the Bund wanted to make good this separateness and to establish merely federative relations with the R.S.D.L.P. The motive behind this was that the Bund, reflecting as it did the mood of the artisans of the small Jewish towns, was much more interested in the economic than in the political struggle, and therefore sympathized much more with the "Economists" than with the *Iskra*-ists. The issue at stake was whether the country was to have a strong united workers' Party, rallying solidly around it the workers of all nationalities living on Russian territory, or whether it was to have several workers' parties constituted separately according to nationality. It was a question of achieving international solidarity within the country. The *Iskra* editorial board stood for international consolidation of the working class. The Bund stood for national separatism and merely friendly contractual relations between the national workers' parties of Russia.

The question of the Bund had also been discussed in detail with the delegates as they arrived, and was likewise decided on *Iskra* lines by an overwhelming majority.

The vast importance of the fundamental issues dealt with and decided at the Second Congress was later overshadowed for many by the split. During the debates on these questions Vladimir Ilyich felt more than usually close to Plekhanov. The latter's speech to the effect that the thesis "the good of the revolution is the highest law" should be considered the basic democratic principle, and that even the idea of universal franchise should be regarded from the point of view of this principle, made a profound impression on Vladimir Ilyich. He recollected it fourteen years later, when the Bolsheviks were faced with the question of dismissing the Constituent Assembly.

Another speech of Plekhanov's that fell in with Vladimir Ilyich's ideas was that in which he spoke about the importance of popular education as being the "guarantee of the rights of the proletariat."

Plekhanov felt close to Lenin, too, at the congress.

Replying to Akimov, an ardent supporter of the *Rabocheye Delo* group, who was all out to create dissension between Plekhanov and Lenin, Plekhanov said humorously: "Napoleon had a craze for making his marshals divorce their wives. Some marshals submitted, although they loved their wives. Comrade Akimov reminds me of Napoleon in that respect—he wants to divorce me and Lenin at all costs. But I shall show more character than Napoleon's marshals—I shall not divorce Lenin and I hope he does not intend to divorce me." Vladimir Ilyich laughed and shook his head.

During the discussion of the first item on the agenda (the constitution of the congress) an unexpected incident occurred over the question of inviting a representative of the *Borba* (Struggle) group (Ryazanov, Nevzorov, Gurevich). The O.C. wanted to come forward with its own opinion. It was not a question of the *Borba* group at all; the O.C. was trying to impose a special discipline on its members in face of the congress. The O.C. wanted to act as a group, which had previously decided among themselves how they were going to vote, and to speak at the congress as a group. Thus the supreme authority for a member of the congress would be the group and not the congress itself. Vladimir Ilyich was fairly boiling with indignation. He was not the only one to support Pavlovich (Krasikov), when the latter protested against these tactics; he was backed by Martov, too, and others. Although the O.C. was dismissed by the congress, the incident was significant and augured all kinds of complications. The incident, however, was temporarily pushed into the background by such momentous issues as the Bund's place within the Party and the Party's programme. On the question of the Bund, the *Iskra* editorial board, the O.C. and the local delegates were of one mind. Yegorov (Levin),

representative of *Yuzhny Rabochy* and member of the O.C.
also came out emphatically against the Bund. Plekhanov
complimented him during the recess, saying that his
speech ought to be "spread wide through all the com
munes." The Bund was utterly defeated. The thesis that
national peculiarities must not interfere with the unity of
Party work and the monolithic unity of the Social-Democratic movement was securely established.

Meanwhile we were compelled to move to London. The
Brussels police made things difficult for the delegates,
and when they deported Zemlyachka and someone else,
we all got moving. In London the Takhtarevs did all they
could to make congress arrangements. The London police
raised no obstacles.

The discussion of the Bund question was continued.
Then, while the question of the programme was in its
committee stage, we passed to the fourth item of the
agenda—the question of approving the central organ.
Iskra was unanimously recognized as such, the *Rabocheye
Delo* group alone being against. *Iskra* was hailed with
enthusiasm. Even Popov (Rozanov), the representative of
the O.C., said: "Here, at this congress, we see a united
Party, created largely through the activity of *Iskra*." That
was the tenth sitting. There were thirty-seven sittings in
all. Clouds steadily began to gather. Three persons had
to be elected to the Central Committee. No nucleus of a
C.C. was yet available. One unquestionable candidature
was Glebov (Noskov), who had proved himself to be an
energetic organizer. Another would have been that of
Clair (Krzhizhanovsky), had he been at the congress. But
he was not. The voting for him and Kurz had to be done
by proxy, which was extremely awkward. On the other
hand, there were far too many "generals" at the congress
who were candidates for the Central Committee. These
were Jacques (Stein—Alexandrova), Fomin (Krokhmal),
Stern (Kostya—Rosa Galberstadt), Popov (Rozanov) and
Yegorov (Levin). All these were candidates for two seats

on the C.C. trio. We all knew one another not only as Party workers, but in intimate personal life. It was all a tangle of personal sympathies and antipathies. The atmosphere grew tenser as the time for voting approached. Although the accusations of the Bund and *Rabocheye Delo* about the foreign Centre wanting to control and dictate, etc., had met with a solid rebuff at the outset, they had done their work by influencing the Centre and the waverers, although they may not have been aware of it. Of whose "control" were people afraid? Not of Martov's Zasulich's, Starover's and Axelrod's, of course. They were afraid of Lenin's and Plekhanov's control. But they knew that the questions of personnel and Russian work would be decided by Lenin, and not by Plekhanov, who took no part in the practical work.

The congress had endorsed the *Iskra* line, but the *Iskra* editorial board had still to be elected.

Vladimir Ilyich moved that the editorial board of *Iskra* should consist of three members. He had told Martov and Potresov about this proposal beforehand. Speaking with the delegates on their arrival, Martov had supported the idea of three editors as being the most expedient. He realized then that the three-man proposal was aimed chiefly against Plekhanov. When Vladimir Ilyich handed Plekhanov his draft proposal for an editorial board of three, Plekhanov had read it and put it in his pocket without saying a word. He understood what it was about, and agreed to it. Once there was a Party, practical work was necessary.

Martov mixed more with the members of the Organizing Committee than anyone else on *Iskra*. It did not take long to persuade him that the three-man idea was directed against him, and that if he joined it he would be betraying Zasulich, Potresov and Axelrod. Axelrod and Zasulich were greatly upset.

In such an atmosphere, the dispute over the first paragraph of the Rules assumed an extremely acrimonious character. Lenin and Martov disagreed both politically and organizationally on the question of Paragraph 1 of the Party Rules. They had often disagreed before, but such differences had then been confined to narrow limits and had soon been sunk. Now they had come out at the congress, and everyone who had had a grudge against *Iskra*, against Plekhanov and Lenin, went out of his way to fan it up into a disagreement on a fundamental issue. Lenin was attacked for his article *Where to Begin?* and his pamphlet *What Is To Be Done?* and accused of being ambitious, and so on. In his booklet *One Step Forward, Two Steps Back* he wrote:

"I cannot help recalling in this connection a conversation I happened to have at the congress with one of the 'Centre' delegates. 'How oppressive the atmosphere is at our congress!' he had complained. 'This bitter fighting, this agitation one against the other, this biting controversy, this uncomradely attitude...' 'What a splendid thing our congress is!' I replied. 'A free and open struggle. Opinions have been stated. The shades have been brought out. The groups have taken shape. Hands have been raised. A decision has been taken. A stage has been passed. Forward! That's the stuff for me! That's life! That's not like the endless, tedious word-chopping of intellectuals which terminates not because the question has been settled, but because they are too tired to talk any more....' The comrade of the 'Centre' had looked at me with a puzzled expression and shrugged his shoulders. We were speaking in different tongues." (*Works*, Vol. 7, p. 320, *Note*.)

Here, in this quotation we have the whole of Ilyich.

His nerves had been keyed up from the very beginning of the congress. The Belgian woman worker with whom we lodged in Brussels was very upset at Vladimir Ilyich not eating the lovely radishes and Dutch cheese which she served up for breakfast every morning. He was too worried to be able to eat anything. In London he worried so much that he stopped sleeping altogether.

Vehement though he was in the debates, Vladimir Ilyich was absolutely impartial as chairman and never treated an opponent unfairly. Not so Plekhanov. When he was in the chair he liked to flash his wit and tease his opponent.

Although there were no differences among the overwhelming majority of the delegates on the question of the Bund's place in the Party, on the question of the programme, and the acceptance of the *Iskra* line as their banner, a definite rift made itself felt half-way through the congress, which deepened towards the end. Strictly speaking, no serious differences standing in the way of joint work or making such work impossible had yet come to light at the congress. They existed in a latent form, however, potentially, so to speak. Yet the congress was clearly divided. Many were inclined to blame Plekhanov's tactlessness, Lenin's "vehemence" and "ambition," Pavlovich's pinpricks, and the unfair treatment of Zasulich and Axelrod—and they sided with those who had a grievance. They missed the substance through looking at personalities. Trotsky was one of them. He became a fierce opponent of Lenin. And the substance was this—that the comrades grouped around Lenin were far more seriously committed to principles, which they wanted to see applied at all cost and pervading all the practical work. The other group had more of the man-in-the-street mentality, were given to compromise and concessions in principle, and had more regard for persons.

The struggle during the elections was very sharp. One or two scenes before the voting started are still fresh in my memory. Axelrod accused Bauman (Sorokin) of an alleged lack of moral sense, and brought up some gossip about an incident supposed to have taken place in Siberian exile. Bauman said nothing, but there were tears in his eyes.

Another scene. Deutsch was angrily telling off Glebov (Noskov), who looked up with flashing eyes and said with annoyance: "I'd keep my mouth shut if I were you, old boy!"

The congress ended. Glebov, Clair and Kurz were elected to the Central Committee, twenty out of the forty-four votes being abstentions. Plekhanov, Lenin and Martov were elected to the Central Organ. Martov refused to work on the editorial board. The split was obvious.

AFTER THE SECOND CONGRESS

1903-1904

Trying days set in for us when we got back to Geneva after the congress. First of all, Russian emigrants came pouring in from other Russian emigrant colonies abroad. League members came, asking: "What happened at the congress? What was the trouble about? Over what was the split?"

Plekhanov was fed up with these questions and one day he related: "X arrived. Kept asking me questions and repeating: 'I am like Buridan's ass.' I asked him: 'What has Buridan got to do with it?'"

People began to arrive from Russia too. Among them was Yerema from St. Petersburg, in whose name Vladimir Ilyich had addressed his letter to the St. Petersburg organization the year before. He promptly sided with the Mensheviks, and called on us. He put on an air of deep tragedy when he came in and turned to Vladimir Ilyich, exclaiming: "I am Yerema!" Then he began to talk about the Mensheviks being right. I remember another man, a member of the Kiev Committee, who was anxious to know what changes in technique had led to the split at the congress. I just stared at him—baffled by such a primitive understanding of the correlation between "basis" and "superstructure." I never thought it could exist.

People who had been assisting the cause with money or by offering their apartments for secret rendezvous and so forth, withdrew this help under the influence of Menshevik agitation. I remember an old acquaintance of mine coming with her mother to Geneva, where she had a sister. When we were children we had played together at such thrilling games of travellers and savages living up in the trees that I was overjoyed to hear she had come. She was a not-so-young girl now and quite a stranger. The subject of the assistance that their family had always rendered the Social-Democrats was mentioned. "We cannot give you our apartment now for secret rendezvous," she said. "We highly disapprove of this split between the Bolsheviks and the Mensheviks. These personal squabbles are very bad for the cause." Ilyich and I had some strong things to say about these "sympathizers" who belonged to no organization and imagined that their accommodation and paltry donations could influence the course of events in our proletarian Party!

Vladimir Ilyich wrote at once to Clair and Kurz in Russia, telling them what had happened. Beyond expressing their astonishment, they were unable to give any helpful advice, and seriously suggested recalling Martov to Russia and hiding him away in some remote corner to write popular pamphlets. It was decided to bring Kurz over from Russia.

After the congress Vladimir Ilyich did not object when Glebov suggested co-opting the old editorial board—better to rough it the old way than to have a split. But the Mensheviks refused. In Geneva Vladimir Ilyich tried to make it up with Martov, and wrote to Potresov, reassuring him that they had nothing to quarrel about. He also wrote to Kalmykova (Auntie) about the split, and told her how matters stood. He could not believe that there was no way out. Obstructing the decisions of the congress, staking the work in Russia and the efficacy of the newly formed Party struck him as sheer madness, something unbelievable. At times he saw clearly that a rupture was unavoidable. He started a letter to Clair once, saying that the latter simply could not imagine the present situation, that one had to realize that the old relations had radically changed, that the old friendship with Martov was at an end; old friendships were to be forgotten, and the fight was starting. Vladimir Ilyich did not finish that letter or post it. It was very hard for him to have to break with Martov. Their work together in St. Petersburg and on the old *Iskra* had drawn them close together. Extremely sensitive, Martov in those days had been very quick at grasping Ilyich's thoughts and developing them in a talented manner. Afterwards Vladimir Ilyich had fiercely fought the Mensheviks, but whenever Martov's line showed a tendency to right itself, his old attitude towards him revived. Such was the case, for example, in Paris in 1910, when Vladimir Ilyich and Martov worked together on the editorial board of *Sotsial-Demokrat* (*Social-Democrat*). Coming home from the office, Vladimir Ilyich often used to tell me in a pleased tone that Martov was taking a correct line and even coming out against Dan. Afterwards, in Russia, Vladimir Ilyich was very pleased with Martov's stand during the July days,* not because it was any good to the Bolsheviks, but because Martov bore himself as behooves a revolutionary.

Vladimir Ilyich was already seriously ill when he said to me once sadly: "They say Martov is dying too."

Most of the congress delegates (Bolsheviks) went back to Russia to work. Some of the Mensheviks remained, though, and were even joined by Dan. Their supporters abroad grew in number.

---

* *July days*—refers to the spontaneous demonstration of the St. Petersburg workers and soldiers on July 3-4 (16-17 New Style), 1917 against the bourgeois Provisional Government. The demonstration passed under the slogan of "All Power to the Soviets." Fire was opened on the demonstrators on July 4 (17) by order of the Provisional Government. Mass repressions were started against the Bolsheviks and the soldiers who had taken part in the demonstrations. The Bolshevik Party went underground and began preparing for an armed uprising.—*Ed.*

The Bolsheviks who remained in Geneva met periodically. Plekhanov took a very firm stand at these meetings. He cracked jokes and cheered people up.

At last Central Committee member Kurz, alias Vasilyev (Lengnik) arrived. The squabbles which he found raging in Geneva had a very depressing effect upon him. He was kept pretty busy settling disputes, sending people to Russia, and so forth.

The Mensheviks made a hit with people abroad and decided to challenge the Bolsheviks by calling a congress of the League of Russian Social-Democrats Abroad at which the League's delegate to the Second Congress—Lenin— was to report back. The management board of the League at the time consisted of Deutsch, Litvinov and myself. Deutsch pressed for the congress, but Litvinov and I were against it. We knew only too well that under the prevailing conditions the congress would degenerate into a downright brawl. Deutsch thereupon reminded himself that two other members of the management board were Vecheslov, who lived in Berlin, and Leiteisen, who lived in Paris. Although they had lately taken no part in the board's activities, they had not officially resigned from it. They were called upon to vote, and plumped for the congress.

Just before the League congress, Vladimir Ilyich, letting his thoughts wander, ran into a tramcar while out cycling and very nearly had his eye knocked out. He came to the congress pale and bandaged. The Mensheviks attacked him with bitter hatred. I remember one shocking scene when Dan, Krokhmal and others with furious faces leapt to their feet and banged the tops of their desks.

The Mensheviks were numerically stronger than the Bolsheviks at the League congress. Besides, the Mensheviks had more "generals" on their side. They adopted League Rules which turned the League into a Menshevik stronghold, gave them publishing facilities, and made the League independent of the Central Committee. Kurz

(Vasilyev) on behalf of the C.C. then demanded that the Rules should be modified, and as the League resisted this, he declared it dissolved.

The uproar raised by the Mensheviks was too much for Plekhanov's nerves. He declared: "I can't shoot at my own side."

At the meeting of the Bolsheviks Plekhanov said we ought to compromise. "There are moments," he said, "when even the autocracy is obliged to make concessions." "That's when we say it vacillates," Liza Knuniants threw in. Plekhanov glared at her.

In order, as he said, to preserve peace in the Party Plekhanov decided to co-opt the old *Iskra* editorial board. Vladimir Ilyich resigned from the board, saying that he would no longer collaborate and did not insist even on his resignation being reported. Plekhanov could try and make peace if he wanted; he, Lenin, would not stand in the way of peace within the Party. Not long before this he had written to Kalmykova, saying: "Quitting the job is a dead end." In resigning from the editorial board, that was what he was letting himself in for, and he realized it. The opposition further demanded that their representatives should be co-opted on the C.C., that two seats should be given them on the Council, and that the decisions of the League congress should be recognized as valid. The Central Committee agreed to co-opt two members of the opposition, to give them one seat on the Council, and to gradually reorganize the League. But peace there was none. Plekhanov's concession had encouraged the opposition. Plekhanov insisted on the second representative of the C.C. Rou (alias Horse, whose real name was Galperin) standing down from the Council in favour of a Menshevik. Vladimir Ilyich hesitated long before agreeing to this new concession. I remember the three of us— Vladimir Ilyich, Rou and I—standing on the shore of Geneva Lake, which was in a turbulent mood that evening. Rou urged Vladimir Ilyich to agree to his resignation. At last Vladimir Ilyich gave in, and went to Plekhanov to tell him that Rou would stand down.

Martov put out a pamphlet *State of Siege*, full of the wildest accusations. Trotsky also wrote a pamphlet entitled *Report of the Siberian Delegation*, in which events were depicted quite in the Martov strain, Plekhanov being represented as a pawn in the hands of Lenin, and so forth.

Vladimir Ilyich sat down to write his reply to Martov —his pamphlet *One Step Forward, Two Steps Back*, in which he gave a detailed analysis of what took place at the congress.

Meanwhile, a struggle was going on in Russia too. The Bolshevik delegates reported back on the congress. The programme and most of the resolutions adopted at the congress were hailed with great satisfaction by the local organizations. All the more puzzling to them was the position of the Mensheviks. Resolutions were passed demanding submission to the congress decisions. One of the most energetic of our delegates at the time was Uncle (Lydia Knipovich), who, being an old revolutionary, could simply not understand how the congress decisions could be flouted in such a way. She and other comrades wrote encouraging letters from Russia. The local committees sided with the Bolsheviks one after another.

Clair arrived. He had no idea what a barrier had arisen between the Bolsheviks and the Mensheviks and thought it was still possible to reconcile them. He went to see Plekhanov only to convince himself that a reconciliation was absolutely impossible. He went back in a depressed mood. Vladimir Ilyich was gloomier than ever.

Early in 1904 Celia Zelikson, Baron (Essen), a representative of the St. Petersburg organization, and the worker Makar, arrived in Geneva. All were Bolshevik supporters. Vladimir Ilyich saw them often. They talked about the work in Russia and the quarrel with the Mensheviks. Baron, who was quite a young man at the time, was enthusiastic about the St. Petersburg work. "Our organization is being run on collective lines now," he said. "We have separate bodies working—a propagandists' group, an agitators' group, and an organizers' group." Vladimir Ilyich heard him out, then asked: "How many people have you in the propagandists' group?" Baron was a bit put out, and answered: "I'm the only one so far." "Not many," observed Ilyich. "And how many have you in the agitators' group?" Baron reddened to the roots of his hair and said: "I'm the only one so far." Ilyich held his sides with laughter. Baron laughed too. Ilyich always had the knack, by means of one or two probing questions, of putting his finger on the weakest spot, and sifting the real facts from the husk of fine schemes and spectacular reports.

Afterwards Olminsky (M. S. Alexandrov), who joined the Bolsheviks, and Beast,* who had escaped from remote exile, arrived.

After her escape from exile Beast was full of cheerful energy, which communicated itself to all around her. Not a shadow of doubt or indecision weighed on her mind. She made fun of everyone who had the blues and moped over the split. All these emigrant squabbles did not seem to affect her. At that time we had started holding weekly "at homes" in Séchéron to bring the Bolsheviks closer together. We never got down to any "real" talk at these gatherings, but at least they helped to dispel the gloom cast upon us by all these squabbles with the Mensheviks. It was excellent fun to hear Beast strike up a rollicking song about "Vanka," and bald-headed Yegor, a worker, join in the chorus. Yegor had gone to have a heart-to-heart talk with Plekhanov, and had even put on a starched collar for the occasion. But he had come away disappointed and saddened. "Cheer up, Yegor. We'll win the day. Come on, let's get on with 'Vanka'!" Beast said. Ilyich would

---

* The alias of M. M. Essen.—*Ed.*

cheer up too—this boisterous gaiety dispelled gloomy thoughts.

Bogdanov appeared upon the scene. Vladimir Ilyich was not very familiar with his philosophical works at the time, and did not know him at all personally. Plainly, though, he was a man of calibre as far as the Party was concerned. He was on a temporary visit, and had extensive connections in Russia. The period of distressing squabbles was coming to an end.

Hardest of all was it for Vladimir Ilyich to break with Plekhanov.

In the spring Ilyich made the acquaintance of the old *Narodopravets* revolutionary Natanson and his wife. Natanson was a splendid organizer of the old type. He knew lots of people, was very good at sizing up a man, and could tell what he was capable of and what job he was best suited for. What struck Vladimir Ilyich about him was the fact that he was perfectly familiar with the personnel of both his own and our Social-Democratic organizations, which he knew better than many of our own Central Committee members. Natanson had lived in Baku, and knew Krasin, Postolovsky and others. Vladimir Ilyich thought that Natanson could be persuaded into becoming a Social-Democrat. He was very close to the Social-Democratic standpoint. We heard afterwards that that old revolutionary had sobbed when, for the first time in his life, he had seen an imposing demonstration in Baku. On one point Vladimir Ilyich and he could not see eye to eye: Natanson disagreed with the Social-Democrats' approach to the peasantry. The wooing of Natanson lasted a fortnight. Natanson was on familiar and even intimate terms with Plekhanov. Vladimir Ilyich fell into conversation with him about our Party affairs and the split with the Mensheviks. Natanson offered to talk things over with Plekhanov. He came away from Plekhanov in a state of perplexity. We would have to compromise, he said.

The romance with Natanson was broken off. Vladimir

Ilyich was annoyed with himself for having discussed Social-Democratic affairs with a man of another party, who had acted as a sort of go-between. He was annoyed with Natanson as well as with himself.

Meanwhile, in Russia, the Central Committee was pursuing a double-faced conciliatory policy, while the local committees backed the Bolsheviks. It was necessary to convene a new congress based on Russia.

In protest against the July declaration of the Central Committee,* which prevented him from defending his point of view and communicating with Russia, Vladimir Ilyich resigned from the C.C., and the Bolshevik group, numbering twenty-two, passed a resolution calling for a Third Congress.

Vladimir Ilyich and I took our rucks'acks and went out hiking in the mountains for a month. Beast joined us, but soon gave it up, saying: "You people like to go to places where there isn't even a living cat, but I must have human society." Indeed, we always chose the loneliest trails that led into the wilds, away from any people. We tramped about for a month, not knowing today where we would be tomorrow. After a weary day we would throw ourselves on our beds dead-tired and fall asleep instantaneously.

---

* This was the name given to the resolution adopted by the conciliatory section of the C.C., which was already pursuing a Menshevik policy, and by the Mensheviks in Lenin's absence. The resolution had twenty-six clauses, but only ten of them were published in No. 72 of *Iskra* of August 25, 1904. In the editorial reply to Lenin, who had protested against the Party being kept in ignorance of the decisions of its leading organ, Plekhanov had argued that the local committees need not know all the details about the leaders' differences. "To try to make the proletariat a judge in the innumerable disputes arising between the circles would mean inclining to the worst of all forms of pseudo-democratism." (*Iskra*, No. 53, November 25, 1903.)

One of the clauses of this resolution ran: "The C.C. is emphatically opposed to convening a special congress *at the present time*, and to any agitation in favour of such a congress."—*N.K.*

We had very little money, and lived mostly on cold food such as eggs and cheese, washed down with wine or water from a spring; we rarely had a proper dinner. At one little inn patronized by Social-Democrats a worker gave us a good tip. "Don't dine with the tourists, but with the coachmen, chauffeurs and labourers—it's twice as cheap and more filling." We took his advice. The civil servants and shopkeepers who ape the bourgeoisie would sooner stop going out altogether than sit down at the same table with a servant. This middle-class snobbery is very widespread in Europe. They talk a lot about democracy there, but to sit down at the same table with the servants —not at home, but in a smart hotel—is more than any snob trying to make his way in the world can stomach. It gave Vladimir Ilyich special pleasure, therefore, to sit down in the common room to have his meal. He ate there with a keener relish and was full of praise for the cheap but satisfying food. After that we would sling on our rucksacks and continue on our way. The rucksacks were pretty heavy. Vladimir Ilyich had a fat French dictionary in his, while I had in mine a no less heavy French book which I had just received for translation. Neither the dictionary nor the book, however, had once been opened during our trip. It was not at dictionaries we looked, but at the snow-capped everlasting mountains, at blue lakes and turbulent waterfalls.

A month of this restored Vladimir Ilyich's nerves to normal. It was as if he had bathed in a mountain stream and washed off all the cobwebs of sordid intrigue. We spent August with Bogdanov, Olminsky and Pervukhin in a remote village by the shore of Lac de Bré. The plan of work was arranged with Bogdanov, who proposed enlisting the cooperation of Lunacharsky, Stepanov and Bazarov. Plans were made to publish our own organ abroad and develop agitation for a congress in Russia.

Ilyich became his cheerful old self again. His return from a visit to the Bogdanovs in the evening was always announced by a furious barking from the chained dog outside, whom he teased in passing.

We went back to Geneva in the autumn and moved from the suburbs nearer to the centre. Vladimir Ilyich joined the Société de lecture, where there was a vast library and excellent facilities for work. They received lots of newspapers and magazines there in French, German and English. It was a very convenient place to study in. The members of the society—for the most part old professors—seldom visited the library, and Ilyich had the room to himself there, where he could write, pace up and down, think over his articles, and take down any book he wanted from the shelves. He could rest assured that no Russian comrade would come there and start telling him about the Mensheviks having said this and that or played a dirty trick in such-and-such a place. He could think there without having his thoughts diverted. And there was plenty to think about.

Russia has started the Japanese War, which glaringly revealed all the rottenness of the tsarist monarchy. Not only the Bolsheviks, but the Mensheviks and even the liberals, too, were defeatists in this war. A storm of popular protest was rising. The working-class movement entered a new phase. News of mass public meetings held in defiance of the police, and of direct clashes between the workers and the police, reached us ever more often.

In face of the growing mass revolutionary movement petty factional squabbles did not worry us as much as they recently had. These squabbles, though, sometimes assumed ugly forms. The Bolshevik Vasilyev, for instance, arrived from the Caucasus and wanted to make a report on the situation in Russia. At the opening of the meeting, however, the Mensheviks demanded the election of a presiding committee, although it was just an ordinary report which any Party member could come and hear, and not an organizational meeting. The Mensheviks tried to turn every report or lecture into a kind of electoral fight, hoping in this way to stop the mouth of the Bolsheviks "by democratic means." Things very nearly came to a hand to hand scuffle, a fight, over the insurance fund. During the uproar Bogdanov's wife Natalia had her mantle torn, and someone got knocked down. But now it did not affect us half as much as it used to.

All our thoughts were now in Russia. One felt a tremendous responsibility in face of the workers' movement that was growing out there—in St. Petersburg, Moscow, Odessa and other places.

All parties—liberals and Socialist-Revolutionaries—began to show themselves in their true colours. The Mensheviks, too, showed their real face. It became clear now what divided the Bolsheviks and the Mensheviks.

Vladimir Ilyich had implicit faith in the proletariat's class instinct, its creative powers, and historic mission. This faith had not come suddenly to Vladimir Ilyich, but had been hammered out during the years when he had studied and pondered Marx's theory of the class struggle, when he had studied Russian realities, and learnt, in fighting the ideas of the old revolutionaries, to offset the heroism of the solitary fighter by the strength and heroism of the class struggle. It was not just blind faith in an unknown force, but a deep-rooted belief in the strength of the proletariat and its tremendous role in the cause of working-class emancipation, a belief founded on a profound knowledge and thorough study of the facts of life. His work among the St. Petersburg proletariat had helped to identify this faith in the power of the working class with real live people.

At the end of December the Bolshevik newspaper *Vperyod* (*Forward*) began to appear. The editorial board, in addition to Ilyich, had Olminsky and Orlovsky* on it. Shortly afterwards Lunacharsky arrived to lend a hand.

---

* V. Vorovsky.—*Ed.*

His impassioned articles and speeches were consonant with the Bolsheviks' mood at the time.

The revolutionary movement in Russia was growing, and with it grew our correspondence with Russia. It soon reached a volume of three hundred letters a month, which was an enormous figure for those days. And what rich material it provided Ilyich with! He knew how to read workers' letters. I remember one from quarry workers in Odessa. It was a collective letter written in several uncultivated hands without subjects and predicates, stops and commas, but full of inexhaustible energy, a readiness to fight to the victorious end. That letter was colourful in every word, naive, but unshakable in its conviction. I do not remember what it was about but I remember how it looked—the paper and the watery ink. Ilyich read that letter over and over again, and paced up and down deep in thought. Not for nothing had the quarry workers of Odessa taken such pains when writing to Ilyich: they had written to the right man, one who could best understand them.

A few days after this letter, we received one from Tanya, a young Odessa propagandist, who gave a faithful and detailed report of a meeting of Odessa artisans. Ilyich read that letter, too, and sat down at once to answer Tanya. "Thank you for your letter. Write more often. We are tremendously interested in letters describing ordinary *workaday* activities. We get so few of them, worse luck."

Almost in every letter Ilyich asked the comrades in Russia to give us more contacts. "The strength of a revolutionary organization is in the number of its contacts," he wrote to Gusev, and asked him to put the Bolshevik centre abroad in touch with the youth. "Some of us have a kind of idiotic, philistine, Oblomov-like fear of the youth," he wrote. (*Works,* Vol. 34, p. 254.) Ilyich wrote to Alexei Preobrazhensky, an old Samara friend, who was then living in the country, asking him to put him in touch with the peasants. He asked the St. Petersburg comrades to forward original workers' letters to the Centre abroad and not just extracts or résumés. These letters told Ilyich more clearly than anything else that the revolution was drawing near, was rising. Nineteen 'Five was on the threshold.

THE YEAR 1905

LIFE IN EMIGRATION

In his pamphlet *The Zemstvo Campaign and "Iskra's" Plan*, written as far back as November 1904, and in his subsequent articles written in December in Nos. 1-3 of *Vperyod,* Ilyich had said that the hour of the masses' real open fight for freedom was approaching. He had clearly felt the gathering of the revolutionary storm. But it was one thing to feel it coming and another to learn that the revolution had already started. Therefore, when the news of January 9* reached Geneva, news telling of the concrete form in which the revolution had started, everything around us seemed to change, as if everything that had existed until then had suddenly receded into the distant past. The news of the events of January 9 reached Geneva the next morning. Vladimir Ilyich and I were going to the library when we met the Lunacharskys, who were on their way to us. I remember the figure of Anna Lunacharskaya, who waved her muff at us, too excited to speak. Instinct drew us, together with all the other Bolsheviks who had heard the news, to the emigrants' restaurant kept

---

* On January 9, 1905, a peaceful procession of St. Petersburg workers headed by a priest named Gapon, marched to the Winter Palace to present a petition to the Tsar. By order of the Tsar the procession was fired upon. Over a thousand people were killed and more than five thousand wounded that day. In protest against this wholesale massacre of unarmed workers, mass political strikes and demonstrations under the slogan "Down with autocracy" started all over Russia. The events of January 9 precipitated the Revolution of 1905-1907.—*Ed.*

by the Lepeshinskys. We sought each other's company. But hardly a word was spoken—we were all so excited. We sang the revolutionary funeral march *You Have Fallen in the Struggle...* with grim set faces. The realization came over everyone in a wave that the revolution had begun, that the shackles of faith in the tsar had been torn apart, and the hour was near when "tyranny shall fall, and the people shall rise up, great, powerful and free...."

We lived at one with all the Russian political emigrants in Geneva—from one number of the *Tribune** to the next. All Ilyich's thoughts were centred in Russia.

Presently Gapon arrived in Geneva. He was taken up first by the Socialist-Revolutionaries, who tried to make out that Gapon was their man, and that the whole labour movement in St. Petersburg was their handiwork, too. They boosted Gapon and made a terrible fuss of him. Gapon was in the limelight at that time and the London *Times* paid him fabulous sums for every line he wrote.

Some time after Gapon's arrival in Geneva a Socialist-Revolutionary lady called one evening and told Vladimir Ilyich that Gapon wished to meet him. A rendezvous was arranged on "neutral" ground in a café. That evening Vladimir Ilyich paced up and down his room without lighting the lamp.

Gapon was a living part of the growing revolution in Russia, a man closely bound up with the working-class masses who implicitly believed in him. Ilyich was excited at the prospect of meeting that man.

One comrade was recently shocked to learn that Vladimir Ilyich had had to do with Gapon.

Of course, one could simply have dismissed Gapon by deciding beforehand that nothing good could ever be expected of a priest. That is what Plekhanov did. He gave Gapon a very cool reception. But Lenin's strength lay in

---

* The newspaper *La Tribune de Genève* published in Geneva in French.—*Ed.*

the fact that to him the revolution was a living thing, like a face that one could study in all its varied features, because he knew and understood what the masses wanted. And a knowledge of the masses can only be obtained by contact with them. Ilyich was curious to know what influence Gapon could have had upon the masses.

Vladimir Ilyich related his impressions of Gapon after returning from the meeting. Gapon was still red-hot from the breath of the revolution. Speaking about the St. Petersburg workers, he stormed against the Tsar and his myrmidons. Naive though his indignation was in many ways, it was none the less honest. It was in keeping with the mood of the working-class masses. "He has a lot to learn, though," Vladimir Ilyich said. "I told him: 'Don't you listen to flattery, my dear man. If you don't study, that is where you'll be'—and I pointed under the table."

On February 8 Vladimir Ilyich wrote in No. 7 of *Vperyod*: "Let us hope that G. Gapon, who has had such acute personal experience of the change-over from views of a politically unconscious people to revolutionary views, will succeed in achieving that clarity of revolutionary outlook which is essential in a political leader." (*Works*, Vol. 8, p. 143.)

Gapon never achieved that clarity. He was the son of a rich Ukrainian peasant, and never lost touch with his family and his village. He knew the peasants' needs, and his speech was simple and familiar to the uneducated working masses. Very likely it was this origin of his, these links with the countryside, that accounted for his success; but it would be difficult to imagine anyone more thoroughly imbued with the priest psychology than Gapon was. He had never had any contact with revolutionary circles before, and was by nature not a revolutionary, but a sly priest, who was ready to accept any compromises. Once he related: "At one time I started having doubts, and my faith was shaken. I got quite ill and went to the Crimea. There was an old man there who was said to live a holy life. I went to see him so's to strengthen my faith. I came to the old man. People were gathered by a stream, and the old man was conducting a service. There was a little dent in that stream where St. George's steed was supposed to have stepped. That's nonsense, of course. The point is, I said to myself, this old man has profound faith. I went up to him after the service to get his blessing, and he slips out of his vestment and says: 'We've opened a candle-shop here and are doing a good trade!' There's faith for you! I got home more dead than alive. I had a friend then, the artist Vereshchagin. He says: 'Why don't you chuck up this priest business!' I thought—well, at home my parents are looked up to, my father is the village elder, everyone respects him, and then everyone will point and say—your son's unfrocked. No, I didn't do it."

That was Gapon all over.

He was no good at studying. He spent a lot of time learning target shooting and horseback riding, but when it came to books it did not work. True, on Ilyich's advice, he started to read Plekhanov's works, but did so as a matter of duty. He was unable to study from books. He was unable to learn from life either. The priest mentality blinded him. On his return to Russia he backslid into the mire of *agent provocateur* activities.

From the very first days of the revolution Ilyich had seen the whole thing in clear perspective. He realized that the movement would now grow like an avalanche, that the revolutionary people would not stop half-way, and that the workers would throw themselves into the fight against the autocracy. Whether they would win or lose, the outcome of that fight would show. In order to win they would have to be well armed.

Ilyich always had a remarkable flair for deeply sensing the moods of the working class at a given moment.

Taking their cue from the liberal bourgeoisie, who had not got moving yet, the Mensheviks talked about "untying" the revolution, whereas Ilyich knew that the workers were already determined to fight to the bitter end. And he was with them. He knew that there could be no stopping half-way, that this would so demoralize the working class, so weaken the impetus of their struggle and do such tremendous damage to the cause, that it was not to be thought of under any circumstances. History showed that in the Revolution of 1905 the working class was defeated but not vanquished. Its will to fight was not broken. This is what some people failed to understand, people who had attacked Lenin for his "downright views" and who had had nothing better to say after the defeat than that "they should not have taken to arms." If one was to remain true to one's class, it was impossible not to take to arms, it was impossible for the vanguard to leave its fighting class in the lurch.

And Ilyich was constantly calling upon the working-class vanguard—the Party—to fight, to organize, to work for the arming of the masses. He wrote of this in *Vperyod*, and in his letters to Russia.

"January 9, 1905 revealed all the gigantic reserves of revolutionary proletarian energy, and at the same time the utter inadequacy of the Social-Democratic organization," Vladimir Ilyich wrote at the beginning of February in his article *Should We Organize the Revolution?* (*Works*, Vol. 8, p. 144), every line of which is a clarion call to pass from words to deeds.

Ilyich had not only reread and very carefully studied and thought over all that Marx and Engels had written about revolution and insurrection, but had read many books dealing with the art of warfare, made a thorough study of the technique and organization of armed insurrection. He had given more thought to this than people know, and his talk about fighting squads in partisan war, about the squads of "five and ten," was not just the idle talk of a layman, but a well-thought-out plan.

The librarian at the Société de lecture was a witness of how a Russian revolutionary in cheap trousers with the bottoms turned up against the mud in Swiss style (he had forgotten to turn them down) would come early every morning, take the book on barricade fighting or the technique of attack left over from the day before, sit down with it at his customary place by the window, pat the sparse hair on his bald head with an habitual gesture, and become deeply absorbed in reading. Sometimes he would get up to take down a big dictionary to look up some unfamiliar term, then pace up and down a bit, and resume his seat at the desk, where he would start writing swiftly in a small hand on quarter sheets of paper with an air of deep absorption.

The Bolsheviks sought all possible means of sending weapons to Russia, but all this was a mere drop in the ocean. A Fighting Committee was set up in Russia (in St. Petersburg), but it worked too slow. Ilyich wrote to St. Petersburg:

"In an affair of this kind the last thing we need are schemes, and discussions and talk about the functions of the Fighting Committee and its rights. What we need is furious energy, and still more energy. I am horrified, absolutely horrified, to see people talking bombs *for over six months* and not a single bomb made yet. And those who do the talking are most learned people.... Go to the youth, gentlemen! That is the only saving remedy. Otherwise, take my word, you will be late (I can see this plainly), and will find yourselves with 'scientific' transactions, plans, drawings, schemes and excellent recipes, but without an organization, without anything to do.... For God's sake, never mind all the formalities and schemes, send all those 'functions, rights and privileges' to the devil." (*Works*, Vol. 9, pp. 315, 316.)

The Bolsheviks, in fact, did a great deal in the way of preparing the armed uprising. They often displayed wonderful heroism, and risked their lives every minute. Preparation of the armed uprising—such was the slogan of the Bolsheviks. Gapon, too, spoke about an armed uprising.

Shortly after his arrival he submitted a proposal for a militant agreement between the revolutionary parties. An appraisal of Gapon's proposal and a full examination of the whole question of militant agreements were given by Vladimir Ilyich in No. 7 of *Vperyod* for February 8, 1905.

Gapon undertook to supply arms to the St. Petersburg workers. All kinds of donations had been put at his disposal, and he used the money to buy weapons in England. All arrangements had been made at last. A ship was found—the *John Grafton*—whose skipper agreed to take a cargo of arms and discharge it on one of the islands near the Russian frontier. Gapon had no idea how illegal shipments were made, and thought it much simpler than it really was. He received an illegal passport from us and secret addresses and left for St. Petersburg to organize the business. To Vladimir Ilyich this whole enterprise was a passing from words to deeds. The workers had to receive arms at all costs. Nothing came of the enterprise, however. The *Grafton* ran aground, and in any case, approach to the island proved to be impossible. Gapon was unable to do anything in St. Petersburg either. He had to hide in the working-class slums and live under an assumed name. It was terribly difficult to contact people, and the addresses of the Socialist-Revolutionaries with whom arrangements had to be made for taking delivery of the consignments proved to be mythical. The Bolsheviks had been the only ones to send their people out to the island. All this had a stunning effect on Gapon. It was one thing to address crowded meetings without running any risks, and quite another thing to live underground, half-starving and not daring to show one's face anywhere. It needed people of quite a different revolutionary mould to organize illegal shipments of arms, people who were prepared to make any sacrifice in utter obscurity.

Another slogan advanced by Ilyich was that of support to the peasants' struggle for land. It would enable the working class to lean on the peasantry in their **struggle**.

Vladimir Ilyich always gave a great deal of attention to the peasant question. During the discussion of the Party programme at the Second Congress Vladimir Ilyich had put forward and strongly advocated the slogan of restoring to the peasants the *otrezki** of which they had been deprived during the Reform of 1861.

He believed that in order to win over the peasantry a concrete demand that would meet the peasantry's most urgent need had to be put forward. The peasantry had to be rallied around a concrete slogan as had been done in the case of the workers, when the Social-Democrats had launched their agitation among them with a campaign for tea service, for reducing working hours, and paying wages punctually.

The events of 1905 induced Ilyich to re-examine this question. His talks with Gapon (a peasant by origin, who had not lost touch with the village), with Matyushenko, a sailor off the *Potemkin*, and with a number of workers who had arrived from Russia and had first-hand knowledge of what was going on in the countryside, showed Ilyich that the *otrezki* slogan was no longer adequate, that a wider slogan than that was needed—one calling for the confiscation of the landowners' estates, and all the crown and church lands. Not for nothing had Vladimir Ilyich once delved into statistical reference books and fully established the economic connection between town and country, between big and small industry, between the working class and the peasantry. He saw that the time had come when this economic connection would serve the proletariat as a lever of powerful political influence upon the peasantry. He held the proletariat to be the only consistently revolutionary class.

---

* Russian word meaning lands "cut off" (seized) by the landowners during the Reform of 1861 in Russia at the time of the emancipation of the serfs. The landowners "cut off" from the peasants the best lands, such as meadows, pastures, etc.—*Ed.*

I remember an amusing incident, when Gapon once asked Vladimir Ilyich to listen to an appeal which he had written. He began to read it out with great fervour. The appeal was full of abusive terms against the Tsar. "We want no tsar," it ran, "let there be one master over the land—God, with all of you his tenants!" (At that time the peasant movement still had as its main objective a reduction in land rents.) Vladimir Ilyich burst out laughing. Naive though the figure of speech was, it revealed most strikingly the very traits that made Gapon stand so close to the masses: himself a peasant, he had stirred up in the workers, who were still half connected with the village, their age-old hunger for the land.

Gapon was put out by Vladimir Ilyich's laughter. "If it isn't right, tell me and I'll alter it," he said. Vladimir Ilyich became grave at once. "I'm afraid that wouldn't be of any use," he said. "My whole train of thought is different. Write it in your own way, in your own style."

I remember another scene. It was after the Third Congress, after the mutiny on the *Potemkin*. The crew had been interned in Rumania and were having a very hard time. Gapon had received a lot of money for his memoirs and by way of donations for the cause of the revolution, and he spent days on end running about buying clothes for the men of the *Potemkin*. The sailor Matyushenko, one of the most prominent participants in the mutiny, arrived in Geneva. He made friends with Gapon right away and the two of them were inseparable.

A young fellow came from Moscow about the same time (I forget his name now), a red-cheeked young salesman in a bookshop, who had recently joined the Social-Democrats. He had come on a Party errand from Moscow. He told us how and why he had become a Social-Democrat, and then began to enlarge on the subject of why he thought the programme of the Social-Democratic Party to be correct, expounding it point by point with the fervour of the convert. Vladimir Ilyich found it boring and went out to the library, leaving me to give the young man tea and get what I could out of him. The young man continued expounding the programme. Just then Gapon and Matyushenko arrived. I was about to offer them some tea, too, when the young man got to the clause dealing with the *otrezki*. On hearing this and the young man's argument that the peasants should not go beyond fighting for the recovery of the *otrezki*, Matyushenko flared up and shouted: "All the land to the people!"

I do not know how far things would have gone if Ilyich had not returned just then. He immediately grasped what the argument was about, but instead of going into the matter, he bore Gapon and Matyushenko off to his room. I got rid of the young man as quickly as I could.

A sweeping revolutionary movement was rising among the peasantry. At the December Conference in Tammerfors Ilyich had moved that the clause concerning the *otrezki* should be struck out of the programme altogether. A clause was inserted instead calling for support to the revolutionary measures of the peasantry, including confiscation of landowners', government, church, monastic and crown lands.

The German Social-Democrat Kautsky, who was then a very influential figure, took a different view of the case. He wrote in *Neue Zeit** at the time that the urban revolutionary movement in Russia should remain neutral on the question of the relations between the peasantry and the landowners.

Kautsky is now one of the most outstanding betrayers of the workers' cause, but at that time he was considered to be a revolutionary Social-Democrat. When Bernstein, another German Social-Democrat, raised the banner

---

* *Neue Zeit*—the theoretical organ of the German Social-Democrats, published from 1883 to 1923. Its editor-in-chief from the day it was founded up to 1917 was Kautsky. The journal ceased its existence in 1923.—*Ed.*

against Marxism at the end of the nineties by trying to prove that Marx's teaching needed revising, that much of it was out of date, and that the aim (socialism) was nothing, and the movement everything, Kautsky then came out against him in defence of Marx's teachings. As a result, Kautsky in those days enjoyed the reputation of being one of the most revolutionary and consistent of Marx's disciples. Kautsky's assertion, however, did not shake Ilyich's conviction that the Russian revolution could win only if it had the backing of the peasantry.

Kautsky's statement induced Ilyich to check up whether Kautsky was correctly presenting the case for Marx and Engels. He began to study Marx's views on the agrarian movement in America in 1848, and Engels' views on Henry George in 1885.* April already saw the publication of Vladimir Ilyich's article "Marx on the American 'Redistribution.'"

He ends this article with the words: "There is hardly another country in the world where the peasantry is experiencing such suffering, such oppression and degradation as in Russia. The more dismal this oppression of the peasantry has been, the more powerful will now be its awakening, the more invincible its revolutionary onslaught. It is the business of the class-conscious revolutionary proletariat to support this onslaught with all its might, so that it may leave no stone standing of this old, accursed, feudal and autocratic slavish Russia, so that it may create a new generation of bold and free people, a new republican country in which our proletarian struggle for socialism will have room to expand." (*Works*, Vol. 8, p. 300.)

The Bolshevik centre in Geneva stood on the corner of the famous Rue de Carouge—a street inhabited by Russian

---

* *Henry George* (1839-1897)—American economist, author of *Progress and Poverty*, who saw in the nationalization of the land and its renting out to those who worked it a panacea for all social ills.—*Ed.*

political emigrants—and the Arve embankment. The *Vperyod* editorial and dispatch offices, the Lepeshinskys' Bolshevik restaurant, and the apartments of the Bonch-Bruyeviches, the Lyadovs (Mandelstams) and the Ilyins were in the same building. Regular visitors at Bonch-Bruyeviches' were Orlovsky, Olminsky and others. Bogdanov, who returned from Russia, had made arrangements for Lunacharsky to come to Geneva to join the editorial staff of *Vperyod*. Lunacharsky proved to be a brilliant speaker, and did much towards strengthening the Bolshevik positions. Vladimir Ilyich became very friendly with him from then on and enjoyed his company. He was rather partial to him during his differences with the *Vperyod*-ists. As a matter of fact, Lunacharsky was always more than usually gay and witty in his presence. I remember an occasion—it was in 1919 or 1920, I believe—when Lunacharsky, who had returned from a visit to the front, described his impressions to Vladimir Ilyich, and the latter's eyes shone as he listened to him.

Lunacharsky, Vorovsky, Olminsky—the *Vperyod* had fine reinforcements there. Vladimir Bonch-Bruyevich, who was the business manager, went about beaming, full of grandiose schemes, for ever busy with the printing plant.

The Bolsheviks gathered almost every evening at the Café Landolt, and sat there for hours over a glass of beer, discussing events in Russia and making plans.

Many comrades had left for Russia, and many more were preparing to leave.

There was an agitation in Russia for a Third Congress. Many changes had taken place there since the Second Congress, and the new questions that had come up in the course of the daily struggle made a congress absolutely essential. Most of the committees were in favour of a congress. A Bureau of Majority Committees* was formed. The

Central Committee had co-opted a host of new members, including Mensheviks. It was in the main a conciliatory body, and hindered the convocation of the Third Congress in every way it could. After the raid on the Central Committee at the Moscow flat of Leonid Andreyev, the author, the unarrested members of the C.C. consented to the convocation of the congress.

The congress was held in London. The Bolsheviks had an obvious majority there, and so the Mensheviks kept away. Their delegates gathered at a conference of their own in Geneva.

The C.C. delegates from Russia were Sommer (alias Mark—Lyubimov) and Winter (Krasin). Mark was very gloomy, but Krasin looked just as if nothing had happened. The delegates furiously attacked the C.C. for its conciliatory stand. Mark sat as black as a thundercloud and said nothing. Krasin was silent, too, chin in hand, looking entirely unperturbed, as though all those vitriolic speeches did not concern him in the least. When his turn came, he made his report in a calm voice without even mentioning the attacks. Everyone understood that he had had a conciliatory bias, but that that had now passed, and from now on he had taken his stand with the Bolsheviks in whose ranks he would march to the end.

Party members now know the big and responsible job which Krasin did during the Revolution of 1905, when he had helped to arm the fighting ranks, directed the train-

---

will of the Party, the majority of which stood on the "majority" platform, i.e., the platform of the Bolsheviks, it was decided at the "Conference of Twenty-Two," held in Geneva in August 1904, to set up a Bolshevik organ to campaign for the convocation of the Third Party Congress. The candidates nominated at this conference (Gusev, Bogdanov, Zemlyachka, Litvinov and Lyadov) were afterwards endorsed at three illegal conferences held in Russia—the Northern, Southern and Caucasian. Thus a Bureau of Majority Committees was formed. In addition to agitating for the convocation of the congress the B.M.C. actually directed the practical work of the Bolshevik organizations in Russia.—*N.K.*

ing of the fighting squads, and so forth. All this had been done in secret, without any fuss, but the amount of energy that had gone into its doing was tremendous. Vladimir Ilyich knew more about this work than anybody else, and since then had always had a very high opinion of Krasin.

Four men came from the Caucasus—Mikha Tskhakaya, Alyosha Japaridze, Leman and Kamenev. There were only three mandates. Vladimir Ilyich wanted to know whose they were and how it was that four delegates had come on three mandates. Who had received the majority of votes? Mikha protested: "Whoever heard of anyone voting in the Caucasus! We settle all our business in a comradely way. Four of us have been sent, and the number of mandates doesn't matter." Mikha was the oldest member at the congress, and it was he who opened it. The Polesye Committee was represented by Lyova Vladimirov. We had often written to him in Russia about the split and never received any reply. In response to our letters describing the tricks the Martovists were up to we had received letters telling us what leaflets had been distributed and how many, and what strikes and demonstrations there had been in Polesye. At the congress he showed himself a staunch Bolshevik.

Other delegates from Russia included Bogdanov, Postolovsky (Vadim), P. P. Rumyantsev, Rykov, Sammer, Zemlyachka, Litvinov, Skrypnik, Bur (A. E. Essen), Shklovsky and Kramolnikov.

Everything at the congress pointed to the fact that the workers' movement in Russia was in full swing. Resolutions were passed on various questions, such as the armed uprising, a provisional revolutionary government, the attitude towards the government's tactics on the eve of the uprising, the question of open action by the R.S.D.L.P., the attitude towards the peasant movement, the attitude towards the liberals and the Social-Democratic organizations of the non-Russian nationalities, propaganda and agitation, the breakaway Party group, and so on.

The report on the agrarian question was made by Vladimir Ilyich, and on his motion the clause on *otrezki* was referred to the commentaries, while first-place prominence was given to the question of confiscating the lands of the landowners, the church and the crown.

Two other issues characteristic of the Third Congress were the question of two centres and the question of the relations between the workers and the intellectuals.

The predominating element at the Second Congress had been the literary intellectuals and practical Party workers, who had done a good deal for the Party one way or another but who had very weak ties with the organizations in Russia, which were then only just beginning to take shape.

The Third Congress was of quite a different character. The organizations in Russia definitely existed already in the shape of illegal local committees, which were obliged to work under extremely difficult conditions of secrecy. As a result, these committees everywhere practically had no workers among their membership, although they had a great influence on the workers' movement. The committees' leaflets and instructions reflected the mood of the working-class masses, who felt that they now had a leadership. The committees therefore were very popular with them, and for most of the workers their activities were cloaked in a veil of mystery. The workers often got together on their own apart from the intellectuals to discuss the fundamental issues of the movement. The Third Congress received a statement by fifty Odessa workers setting forth the main points of difference between the Mensheviks and the Bolsheviks, and mentioning that not a single intellectual had been present at the meeting where this question was discussed.

The "committeeman" was usually a rather self-assured person. He saw what a tremendous influence the work of the committee had on the masses, and as a rule he recognized no inner-Party democracy. "Inner-Party democracy only leads to trouble with the police. We are connected with the movement as it is," the "committeemen" would say. Inwardly they rather despised the Party workers abroad, who, in their opinion, had nothing better to do than squabble among themselves—"they ought to be made to work under Russian conditions." The "committeemen" objected to the overruling influence of the Centre abroad. At the same time they did not want innovations. They were neither desirous nor capable of adjusting themselves to the quickly changing conditions.

The "committeemen" had done a tremendous job during the period of 1904-1905, but many of them found it extremely difficult to adjust themselves to the conditions of increasing legal facilities and methods of open struggle.

There were no workers at the Third Congress—at least, none of any mark. The Babushkin who attended the congress was not the worker of that name, who was in Siberia at the time, but was the alias used by Shklovsky, as far as I remember. There was no scarcity of "committeemen" though. Unless this make-up of the congress is borne in mind a great deal of what the congress records contain will not be properly understood.

The question of "bringing to heel the Centre abroad" was raised by prominent Party workers besides the "committeemen." The opposition to this Centre was headed by Bogdanov.

A lot was said that were better left unsaid, but Vladimir Ilyich did not take it much to heart. He considered that the significance of the emigrants' Centre was diminishing hourly with the developing revolution. He knew that his own days abroad were "numbered," and his principal concern was that the Central Committee (in Russia) should promptly inform the Central Organ as to what was going on (the Central Organ was henceforth to be called *Proletary* and to be published abroad for the time being). He also urged that regular meetings should be arranged between the sections of the Central Committee in Russia and abroad.

The question of drawing workers into the committees was a sharper issue. Vladimir Ilyich warmly supported the idea. Bogdanov, the emigrants' Centre members and the writers were also in favour of it. The "committeemen" were against it. Both Vladimir Ilyich and the "committeemen" argued heatedly. The "committeemen" insisted that no resolution should be passed on this question—one could not very well carry a resolution to the effect that workers were not to be drawn into the committees!

Speaking in the debates, Vladimir Ilyich said:

"I think we ought to take a wider view of the matter. Drawing workers into the committees is not only a pedagogical but a political task. The workers have a class instinct, and given a little political experience they fairly quickly become staunch Social-Democrats. I would be strongly in favour of having eight workers on our committees to every two intellectuals. Since the advice given in literature—that workers were to be drawn into the committees wherever possible—proved to be insufficient, then it would be expedient for such advice to be given in the name of the congress. If you have a clear and definite directive of the congress you will have a radical means for combatting demagogy: that is the clear will of the congress." (*Works*, Vol. 8, p. 376.)

Vladimir Ilyich had repeatedly urged the necessity of drawing as many workers as possible into the committees. He had written about it as far back as 1903 in his *Letter to a Comrade*. And now, defending the same view at the congress, he became terribly excited and heckled his opponents. When Mikhailov (Postolovsky) said: "In practice, then, very little is required of intellectuals, and far too much of workers," Vladimir Ilyich cried out: "Quite right!" This was greeted by the "committeemen" with a chorussed "It's wrong!"

When Rumyantsev said: "The St. Petersburg Committee has only one worker on it, despite the fact that it has been working for fifteen years," Vladimir Ilyich shouted, "Shame!"

Afterwards, at the close of the debates, Ilyich said: "I could not sit calmly listening to people saying there were no workers fit to be members of the committees. It's just dodging the issue; obviously, this is an unhealthy symptom. The workers must be drawn into the committees." The only reason why Ilyich was not greatly upset at his point of view receiving such a severe rebuff at the congress was because he realized that the approaching revolution was bound to radically cure the Party of this incapacity to give the committees a more pronounced worker make-up.

Another important question before the congress was that of propaganda and agitation.

I remember a girl coming from Odessa who complained that "The workers are demanding the impossible of the local committee—they want us to give them propaganda. How can we? We can only give them agitation!"

The girl's statement made quite an impression on Ilyich. It served, as it were, as an introduction to the debate on propaganda. The old forms of propaganda—as could be gathered from the speeches of Zemlyachka, Mikha Tskhakaya and Desnitsky—were dead, and propaganda had turned into agitation. With the colossal growth of the working-class movement verbal propaganda and even agitation as a whole could not meet the needs of the movement. What was wanted was popular literature, a popular newspaper, literature for the peasants and for the non-Russian nationalities.

Life raised a hundred and one new questions which could not be decided within the limits of the old illegal organizations. They could only be dealt with by setting up a daily newspaper in Russia and wide facilities for legal publishing. Freedom of the press, however, had still to be won. It was decided to publish an illegal newspaper in Russia and form a group of writers there whose duty it would be to take care of the publication of a popular paper. It was clear nevertheless that all these measures were mere palliatives.

A good deal was said at the congress about the rising revolutionary struggle. Resolutions were adopted concerning the events in Poland and the Caucasus. "The movement is steadily spreading," said the delegate from the Urals. "It's high time we left off regarding the Urals as a backward sleepy region that was incapable of moving. The political strike in Lysva, the numerous strikes at the factories, and a variety of signs indicative of a revolutionary mood, which even goes to the extent of agrarian and factory terror in the form of all kinds of small spontaneous demonstrations—all these go to show that the Urals is on the verge of a big revolutionary movement. It is highly probable that this movement in the Urals will take the form of an armed uprising. The Urals was the first place where the workers used bombs and even brought out guns (at the Votkinsk Works). Comrades, don't forget the Urals!"

It goes without saying, Vladimir Ilyich had long talks with the Urals delegate.

On the whole the Third Congress correctly laid down the line of struggle. The same questions were decided by the Mensheviks quite differently. The fundamental differences between the resolutions of the Third Congress and those of the Menshevik Conference were dealt with by Vladimir Ilyich in his pamphlet *Two Tactics of Social-Democracy in the Democratic Revolution.*

We returned to Geneva. I had been elected to the committee for editing the congress minutes together with Kamsky and Orlovsky. Kamsky went away, and Orlovsky was very busy. Verification of the congress minutes was organized in Geneva, where quite a number of delegates had come after the congress. There were no stenographers in those days nor special secretaries, and the minutes were taken down in turn by two members of the congress, and afterwards handed to me. Not all the delegates were good secretaries. It goes without saying, there was no time to report the minutes at the congress. We went over them together with the delegates in Geneva at the Lepeshinskys' restaurant. Naturally, every delegate found that his thoughts had not been recorded correctly and wished to make insertions in the text. This was not allowed, however. Amendments could only be made if the other delegates agreed that they were warranted. It was very hard work, and not without the usual element of friction. Skrypnik (Shchensky) wanted to take the minutes home with him, and when I pointed out that in that case they would have to be given to everybody else and that there would be nothing left of them, he got angry and wrote a print-hand protest to the Central Committee.

When this work was finished in the rough Orlovsky, too, spent a good deal more time, editing the minutes.

In July we received the first minutes of the meetings of the new Central Committee. They reported that the Mensheviks in Russia disagreed with *Iskra*, and would also conduct a boycott,* and that although the C.C. had discussed the question of support to the peasant movement

---

* This alludes to the attitude of the Social-Democrats towards the commission headed by Senator Shidlovsky and appointed by the government after the events of January 9, 1905 "to enquire immediately into the causes of the discontent among the workers in the city of St. Petersburg and its suburbs and take steps to remove them." The Mensheviks were for cooperating with this commission. The Bolsheviks on the other hand considered it necessary to take part in the election of voters, and by electing class-conscious workers as voters, to present demands to the commission which it would refuse to meet, thus exposing in the eyes of the broad masses of workers the deceit and hypocrisy of the tsarist government's policy. These demands included the holding of the meetings of the commission in public, freedom of assembly and the press, the release of those who had been arrested, and so forth. The campaign was conducted with great success by the St. Petersburg Committee of our Party. The Shidlovsky Commission was a complete failure.—*Ed.*

it had not done anything yet as it wanted to consult the agronomists.

The letter struck us as being vexatiously laconic. The next letter about the work of the C.C. was more meagre still. Ilyich fretted very much. After that whiff of Russian air at the congress, it was more painful than ever to feel oneself cut off from the work in Russia.

In a letter written in the middle of August Ilyich urged the C.C. to "stop being dumb" and not confine themselves to discussing questions among themselves. "The C.C. has some kind of internal defect," he wrote to the C.C. members in Russia.

In subsequent letters he took them severely to task for not carrying out the decision to keep the C.O. regularly informed.

In his September letter addressed to August, Ilyich wrote: "To wait for complete solidarity in the C.C. or among its agents is sheer utopia. This is not a coterie but a Party, my dear fellow!"

In a letter to Gusev dated October 13, 1905, he pointed out the necessity of conducting a trade-union struggle simultaneously with preparations for an armed uprising. This struggle, however, had to be waged in a Bolshevik spirit and the Mensheviks would have to be challenged here too.

The harbingers of freedom of the press began to loom on the Geneva horizon. Publishers appeared who vied with each other in offering to legally publish pamphlets issued illegally abroad. The Odessa Burevestnik, the Malikh and other publishing houses all offered their services.

The C.C. asked us to abstain from signing any contracts as they were planning to set up publishing machinery of their own.

The question of Ilyich going to Finland for a meeting with the C.C. cropped up in the beginning of October, but the development of events caused a change of plan. Vladimir Ilyich intended to go to Russia. I was to remain in

Geneva a fortnight longer to wind things up. I helped Ilyich to sort out his papers and correspondence, and laid them out in envelopes. Ilyich made a note of the contents on each envelope. All this was packed up in a suitcase and handed over, I believe, to Karpinsky for safekeeping. This suitcase was preserved and forwarded to the Lenin Institute after Ilyich's death. It contained a mass of documents and letters which throw a vivid light on the history of the Party.

In September Ilyich wrote to the C.C.:

"As regards Plekhanov, I am giving you the local rumours for your information. He is obviously incensed against us for exposing him before the International Bureau. He swears like a trooper in No. 2 of the *Diary of a Social-Democrat.* Some rumours say he is planning a paper of his own, others that he is returning to *Iskra.* The inference is—growing mistrust of him on our part." (Lenin, *Miscellany,* V, p. 507.)

And on October 8 Ilyich continued: "I ask you earnestly—please drop the idea of Plekhanov and appoint your own delegate from the majority....* It would be good to appoint Orlovsky." (*Works,* Vol. 34, p. 302.)

But when, just as Ilyich was about to leave, news came that there was a possibility of setting up a daily paper in Russia, he wrote a warm letter to Plekhanov urging him to collaborate. "The revolution will itself sweep away our tactical differences with amazing rapidity...." "....All this will create *new ground,* upon which it will be easier to forget the past and work together for a real live cause." (*Works,* Vol. 34, p. 316.) Ilyich ended up by asking Plekhanov to meet him. I do not remember whether that meeting took place or not. Probably it did not, otherwise I would hardly have forgotten such an episode.

Plekhanov did not go to Russia in 1905.

---

* This refers to the sending of a delegate to the International Socialist Bureau of the Second International.—*Ed.*

Ilyich made detailed arrangements for his return to Russia in his letter of October 26. "Upon my word, our revolution in Russia is a jolly good thing!" he wrote. In reply to a question about the timing of the uprising, he says: "*I would put off the uprising till the spring. But we shan't be asked anyway.*"

BACK IN ST. PETERSBURG

A man was to meet Vladimir Ilyich in Stockholm and provide him with documents under another name so that he could enter the country and take up residence in St. Petersburg. Days passed and the man did not turn up. Vladimir Ilyich had to sit doing nothing while revolutionary events in Russia were assuming a more and more sweeping character. After a fortnight's wait in Stockholm, he arrived in Russia at the beginning of November. Ten days later I followed him out, after having settled all affairs in Geneva. A detective got on the boat with me at Stockholm and never let me out of his sight in the train all the way from Hangö to Helsingfors. In Finland the revolution was already in full swing. I wanted to send a wire to St. Petersburg, but the smiling cheerful Finnish girl told me she could not accept any telegrams because there was a strike of the post and telegraph workers. Conversation in the railway coaches was loud and excited. I got into conversation with a Finnish Activist,* who, for some reason, was speaking in German. He was describing the successes of the revolution. "We have arrested all the sleuths and put them in prison," he said. My glance fell

_____

* *Activists*—the Finnish Party of Active Resistance—a radical-bourgeois party of Finland whose object was to restore Finland's autonomy and even complete secession from Russia by means of "active resistance." In their methods of struggle the Activists were closely related to the Socialist-Revolutionaries with whom they even had a formal agreement. The Activists quitted the stage after the Revolution of 1905, and sided with the Whites in 1917.—*Ed.*

on the one who was travelling with me. "Yes, but others may come in their place," I said with a laugh, looking meaningly at my detective. The Finn grasped the situation. "Oh, you just say the word if you notice anybody," he cried. "We'll have him arrested at once." At the next wayside station my spy got up and went out, although the train only stopped there for a minute. And that was the last I saw of him.

I had been living abroad for close on four years and was just dying to be back in St. Petersburg. The city was seething, I knew, but the quietness of the Finland Station, where I got off the train, was so completely at variance with what I had imagined St. Petersburg and the revolution to be like, that I suddenly thought I had made a mistake and got off at Pargolovo instead of St. Petersburg. Puzzled, I asked a cabby standing there, "What stop is this?" The man was so surprised that he actually stepped back. Then, with arms akimbo he looked me over ironically, and said: "This isn't a stop, it's the city of Saint Petersburg."

Outside the station I was met by Pyotr Rumyantsev. He told me that Vladimir Ilyich was staying with them in the neighbourhood of Peski, and we drove down there together. I had first met Rumyantsev at Shelgunov's funeral (in 1891.—*Ed.*). He had then been a youngster with a curly mop, and had walked in front of the demonstration, singing. I met him again in Poltava in 1896 where he was at the centre of the Social-Democrats. He had just come out of prison, and was pale and nervous. An intelligent man, he had enjoyed great influence and seemed a good comrade.

In 1900 I saw him in Ufa, where he had arrived from Samara, and he had had a sort of disillusioned languid look about him.

He appeared on the scene again in 1905, this time as a literary man with a social position and a paunch, something of the *bon vivant*, but a clever and effective speaker.

He had conducted the campaign for boycotting the Shid-lovsky Commission splendidly, and had acquitted himself like a staunch Bolshevik. Shortly after the Third Congress he was co-opted to the Central Committee.

He had a pleasant well-furnished flat, and Vladimir Ilyich stayed there for the time being without registering.

Vladimir Ilyich always felt very uncomfortable living in strange homes. He could not work so well either. When I arrived he became urgent about taking lodgings together, and we moved into furnished apartments in Nevsky Pros-pekt without registering. I remember getting into con-versation there with the servant girls, who told me lots of things about what was happening in St. Petersburg with a mass of intimate and revealing details. Of course, I retold it all to Vladimir Ilyich at once. He complimented me on my ability to find things out, and from then on I became his sedulous reporter. Usually, when we lived in Russia, I could move about much more freely than he could, and speak with a much larger number of people. Two or three questions by Ilyich were enough to tell me exactly what he wanted to know, and I would keep my eyes open. I have still retained that habit of mentally for-mulating my every impression for Ilyich.

The very next day I managed to make a fairly rich haul in this respect. I went room hunting, and while looking over an empty flat in Troitskaya Street, I fell into conversation with the janitor. He told me quite a lot about the country-side and the landowner, and about how the land had to be taken away from the gentry and given to the peasants.

Meanwhile we had decided to take up legal residence. Maria Ilyinichna fixed us up with some friends in Gre-chesky Prospekt. The moment we registered our house was surrounded by a swarm of police spies. Our host was so scared that he did not sleep all night and walked about with a revolver in his pocket, determined to meet the po-lice arms in hand. "Drat the man, he'll only get us into trouble," said Ilyich. We took separate rooms and lived illegally. I was given a passport in the name of Prasko-via Onegina and lived with that document all the time. Vladimir Ilyich changed his passport several times.

When Vladimir Ilyich arrived in Russia the legal daily newspaper *Novaya Zhizn* (*New Life*) was already appearing. Its publisher was Maria Andreyeva (Gorky's wife), the editor was the poet Minsky, and contributors were Gorky, Leonid Andreyev, Chirikov, Balmont, Teffi and others. The Bolshevik collaborators on the paper were Bogdanov, Rumyantsev, Rozhkov, Goldenberg, Orlovsky, Lunacharsky, Bazarov, Kamenev and others. The secretary of *Novaya Zhizn* and of all subsequent Bolshevik newspapers at that period was Dmitry Leshchenko, who also acted as news editor, Duma reporter, copyman, etc.

Vladimir Ilyich's first article appeared on November 10. It began with the words: "The conditions of activity of our Party are undergoing a radical change. Freedom of assembly, of association and of the press has been seized." (*Works*, Vol. 10, p. 12.) And Ilyich hastened to make the most of these changed conditions by promptly dashing off with a bold stroke the main outlines of the "new course." The secret machinery of the Party was to be preserved. At the same time it was absolutely essential to set up more and more legal and semi-legal Party and affiliated organizations. More and more cadres of workers had to be enlisted in the Party. The working class was spontaneously and instinctively Social-Democratic, but ten odd years of Social-Democratic work had done quite a lot to turn this spontaneity into consciousness. "At the Third Congress of the Party," Vladimir Ilyich wrote in a footnote to this article, "I expressed the wish that the Party committees be formed in the proportion of about eight workers to two intellectuals. How obsolete this wish appears at the present time!

"Now we must wish for the new Party organizations to have one Social-Democratic intellectual to several hundred Social-Democratic workers." (*Ibid.*, p. 19.)

Addressing himself to the "committeemen" who feared that the Party would be swamped by the mass, Vladimir Ilyich wrote: "Do not invent bogies, comrades!" *(Ibid., p. 15.)* The Social-Democratic intellectuals now had to "go to the people." "The initiative of the workers themselves will now display itself on a scale that we, the undergrounders and circle-ists of yesterday, did not even dare dream of." *(Ibid., p. 18.)*

"Our task now is not so much to invent norms for the organizations on a new basis as to develop the most far-reaching and boldest work." *(Ibid., p. 19.)*

"In order to put the organization on a new basis, another Party congress must be called." *(Ibid., p. 12.)*

Such was the gist of Ilyich's first "legal" article. The methods of the study-circle stage, which were still in evidence everywhere, had to be combatted.

Naturally, one of the first things I did on my arrival was to go to the Nevskaya Zastava to visit the old Smolenskaya Sunday Evening School. No "geography" and natural history were being taught there now. Propagandist work was being conducted in the classrooms, which were packed with working men and women. The Party propagandists were reading lectures. I remember one of them, a young propagandist, who was dealing with a theme of Engels' *Socialism: Utopian and Scientific.* The workers sat without stirring, trying their hardest to grasp what the lecturer was telling them. No one asked any questions. Downstairs, our Party girls were arranging a club for the workers, setting out glasses which they had brought from town.

When I told Ilyich my impressions of what I had seen he became thoughtfully silent. It was not this he wanted to see, but the activity of the workers themselves. Not that such activity did not exist. It did, but it was not in evidence at Party meetings. The channels through which Party work and the workers' activity flowed somehow did not seem to meet. The workers had grown tremendously in stature during those years. I felt it more than ever when I met my former Sunday School "pupils." Once I was hailed in the street by a baker. He turned out to be a former pupil of mine—"Socialist Bakin," who had been deported to his home village ten years before as a result of a naive argument with the manager of the Maxwell Mills, to whom he had tried to prove that in changing over from two mule-jennies to three he would be increasing the "intensity of labour." He was now a fully conscious Social-Democrat, and we had a long talk about the growing revolution and the organization of the working-class masses. He told me all about the bakers' strike.

That first article of Ilyich's, in which he wrote openly about the Party congress and the Party's secret organization, turned *Novaya Zhizn* into a legal Party organ. It goes without saying that the presence on the paper of such men as Minsky, Balmont and their like was no longer conceivable. A dissociation took place and the newspaper passed completely into the hands of the Bolsheviks. It became a Party paper organizationally, too, and began to work under the control and guidance of the Party.

Ilyich's next article in *Novaya Zhizn* dealt with a fundamental issue of the Russian revolution—the relations between the proletariat and the peasantry. The Mensheviks were not the only ones to misinterpret these relations; even among the Bolsheviks certain comrades still had an "*otrezki* deviation." Instead of being a starting-point for agitation, this question of *otrezki* became for them an end in itself. They continued to uphold it even when the facts of reality had made it possible and necessary to conduct agitation and struggle on quite a different basis.

Ilyich's article "The Proletariat and the Peasantry" was a guiding article which supplied a clear Party slogan: The proletariat of Russia together with the peasantry is fighting for the land and freedom, together with the international proletariat and the agricultural workers it is fighting for socialism.

The Bolshevik representatives also began to defend this standpoint in the Soviet of Workers' Deputies. This Soviet came into being as a militant organ of the fighting proletariat on October 13, when Vladimir Ilyich was still abroad. I do not remember Ilyich's speech at the Soviet of Workers' Deputies.* I remember a meeting at the Free Economic Society,** where a large number of Party people had gathered to hear Vladimir Ilyich speak. Ilyich read a lecture on the agrarian question. It was there that he first met Alexinsky. Almost everything connected with that meeting has faded from my memory. I have a dim recollection of a grey door and Vladimir Ilyich making for the exit through the crowd. Other comrades will probably recollect it more clearly. All I remember is that the meeting was held in November and that Vladimir Nevsky was there.

Vladimir Ilyich was quick to note the fact in his November articles that the Soviets of Workers' Deputies were militant organizations of the people in revolt. He expounded the idea that a provisional revolutionary government could only be forged in the crucible of revolutionary struggle on the one hand, and that the Social-Democratic Party, on the other, should strive its hardest to win influence in the Soviets of Workers' Deputies.

---

* Lenin spoke at the seventeenth session of the Soviet on November 26 (13) in connection with the lockout by which the capitalists retaliated to the introduction of the eight-hour day in factories and mills on the part of the workers. Lenin's motion was carried next day at the meeting of the Soviet's Executive Committee. (*Works*, Vol. 10, p. 32.)—*Ed.*

** *Free Economic Society*—a scientific association founded in 1765 for the purpose, as stated in its charter, of "promulgating useful information for agriculture and industry within the country." The society's membership consisted of scientists from among the liberal nobility and the bourgeoisie; it carried out poll investigations and expeditions for studying various industries and districts in the country. It published periodically *The Transactions of the Free Economic Society*. N. Krupskaya has in mind Lenin's lecture delivered on the premises of the society.—*Ed.*

For reasons of secrecy Vladimir Ilyich and I lived apart. All day long he worked on the editorial board, which met not only at the *Novaya Zhizn* offices, but in a secret apartment or at the flat of Dmitry Leshchenko in Glazovskaya Street. It was not very convenient for me to go there for reasons of secrecy. More often than not we met at the *Novaya Zhizn* offices. Vladimir Ilyich was always busy there, however. It was not until he received a very good passport and moved to a place on the corner of Basseinaya and Nadezhdinskaya that I was able to visit him at home. I had to go in through the back entrance and speak in an undertone, but nevertheless we could have a good long talk about everything.

Vladimir Ilyich took a trip to Moscow from this flat. I went to see him as soon as he returned. I was struck by the number of spies lurking round every corner. "Why have they started shadowing you like this?" I asked Vladimir Ilyich. He had not been out of the house since his arrival and was unaware of it. I began to unpack his suitcase and suddenly came upon a pair of large blue spectacles. "What's this?" I asked. It appeared that the comrades in Moscow had rigged him out in those spectacles as a disguise, supplied him with a yellow Finnish box and put him on a non-stop train at the last minute. The sleuths were after him at once, evidently taking him for an expropriator. We had to get out as quickly as possible. We left the house arm-in-arm as if nothing had happened and walked in the opposite direction to the one we needed. We changed cabs three times, slipped through courtyards that had double entrances and arrived at Rumyantsev's after having shaken off our shadowers. We spent the night, I believe, with the Witmers, old friends of mine. We went there in a cab and drove past the house where Vladimir Ilyich had been living. The sleuths were still hanging about. Vladimir Ilyich did not return to those rooms. A fortnight or so later we sent a girl to fetch his things away and settle up with the landlady.

At that time I was a secretary of the Central Committee, and I got into full harness straightaway. The other secretary was Mikhail Sergeyevich (M. Y. Weinstein). My assistant was Vera Menzhinskaya. This constituted our secretariat. Mikhail Sergeyevich was engaged most of the time on the fighting organization, and was always busy carrying out the instructions of Nikitich (L. B. Krasin). I was in charge of the secret meeting places, contact with the local committees and individuals. It is difficult today to imagine what makeshift methods of work the secretariat of the C.C. employed in those days. We never attended the meetings of the C.C., no one was "in charge" of us, no minutes were taken, and ciphered addresses were kept in matchboxes, book covers and similar places. We had to rely on our memories. Crowds of people besieged us, and we gave them every possible attention, supplied them with whatever they needed—literature, passports, instructions and advice. It is inconceivable now how we ever managed to cope with such a rush of work, and how we had the complete and uncontrolled run of the whole business. Usually, on meeting Ilyich, I gave him a full account of everything The most interesting comrades on the most interesting business we referred direct to the C.C. members.

The pitched battle with the government was drawing near. Ilyich wrote openly in *Novaya Zhizn* that the army could not and should not be neutral; he wrote about the nation-wide arming of the people. On November 26 Khrustalev-Nosar* was arrested. His place was taken by Trotsky. On December 2 the Soviet of Workers' Deputies issued a manifesto urging nonpayment of government dues. On December 3 eight newspapers including *Novaya Zhizn*

---

* Khrustalev-Nosar—former chairman of the St. Petersburg Soviet of Workers' Deputies in 1905. A Menshevik member of the Social-Democratic Party. After the October Revolution he went over to the camp of the counter-revolution.—*Ed.*

were closed down for having printed this manifesto. When I went to the editorial office that day to keep a "secret appointment," loaded up with all kinds of illegal literature, I was intercepted outside by a newsman. *"Novoye Vremya!"** he shouted, muttering to me in an "aside" to be careful—"the police are on the premises." Vladimir Ilyich remarked in this connection, "The people are with us."

The Tammerfors Conference was held in the middle of December. What a pity the minutes of this conference have been lost! The enthusiasm that reigned there! The revolution was in full swing, and the enthusiasm was tremendous. Every comrade was ready for the fight. In the intervals we learned to shoot. One evening we attended a Finnish mass torchlight meeting, and the solemnity of it fully harmonized with the temper of the delegates. I doubt whether anyone who was at that conference could ever forget it. Lozovsky, Baransky, Yaroslavsky and many others were there. I remember these comrades because of the keen interest which their "local reports" aroused.

The Tammerfors Conference, which was attended only by Bolsheviks, passed a resolution calling for the immediate preparation and organization of an armed uprising.

The uprising in Moscow was developing apace, and so the conference had to be cut short. If I am not mistaken, we returned on the very eve the Semyonovsky Regiment was despatched to Moscow. One incident, at any rate, is fresh in my memory. Not far from the Trinity Church a soldier of the Semyonovsky Regiment was walking along with a sullen look. By his side walked a young worker, who, with his cap in his hand, was arguing warmly with the soldier and pleading with him. Their faces were so expressive that one could guess unerringly what the worker was pleading about—that the soldiers should not come

---

* *Novoye Vremya*—a reactionary newspaper.—*Ed.*

out against the workers. It was equally clear that the Semyonovsky soldier did not agree.

The Central Committee called upon the proletariat of St. Petersburg to support the uprising of the Moscow workers, but no concerted action was achieved. A comparatively raw district like the Moskovsky responded to the appeal, but an advanced district like the Nevsky did not. I remember how furious Stanislaw Wolski was—he had been agitating in that very district. He lost heart at once, and all but doubted whether the proletariat was as revolutionary as he had thought it to be. He failed to take into account that the St. Petersburg workers were worn out by previous strikes, and most important of all, they realized how badly organized and poorly armed they were for a decisive struggle with tsarism. And that it would be a struggle to the death, they had the example of Moscow to tell them.

ST. PETERSBURG AND FINLAND

1905-1907

The December uprising was crushed, and the government took harsh reprisals against the rebels.

In his article of January 4, 1906, ("The Workers' Party and Its Tasks in the Present Situation") Vladimir Ilyich evaluated the situation in the following words:

"Civil war is raging. The political strike, as such, is beginning to exhaust itself, is becoming a thing of the past, an obsolete form of the movement. In St. Petersburg, for instance, the wearied and exhausted workers were not able to carry out the December strike. On the other hand, the movement as a whole, though hard pressed by the reaction, has undoubtedly risen to a much higher plane....

"Dubasov's guns have revolutionized new masses of the people on an unprecedented scale.... What now? Let us look realities squarely in the face. We are now confronted with the new task of assimilating and studying the experience of the latest forms of struggle, with the task of training and organizing forces in *the most important centres of the movement.*" (My italics.—*N. K.) (Works.,* Vol. 10, pp. 75-76.)

Vladimir Ilyich felt the Moscow defeat very keenly. It was clear that the workers had been poorly armed, and that the organization was weak. Even the link between St. Petersburg and Moscow was poor. I remember the way Ilyich listened to his sister Anna Ilyinichna when she gave him an account of her meeting with a working woman from Moscow at the railway station. The woman had bitterly reproached the St. Petersburg comrades: "Thank you, Petersburgers, for your support. You sent us the Semyonovsky Regiment."

And as though in answer to this reproach Ilyich wrote:

"It would be greatly to the advantage of the government to suppress isolated actions of the proletarians as it has been doing. The government would like to challenge the workers of St. Petersburg to go into battle at once under circumstances that would be most unfavourable for them. But the workers will not allow themselves to be provoked and will be able to continue their path of independent preparation for the next all-Russian action." (*Ibid.,* p. 76.)

Ilyich believed the peasantry would rise, too, in the spring of 1906, and that this would affect the troops. He wrote:

"We must present the colossal tasks of a new action in a more definite and practical way, prepare ourselves for it in a more sustained, systematic and persistent fashion, and in doing so, *husband as far as possible the strength of the proletariat which has become exhausted by the strike struggle.*" (My italics.—*N.K.) (Ibid.,* p. 77).

"Let the party of the workers clearly realize its tasks. Down with constitutional illusions! *We must gather the new forces which are siding with the proletariat.* (My italics.—*N.K.) We must 'gather the experience' of the two great months (November and December) of the revolution. We must adapt ourselves again to the restored autocracy, and be able wherever necessary to go underground once more." (*Ibid.*)

And underground we went. We spun the network of the secret organization anew. Comrades arrived from all over Russia, and we made arrangements with them about the work and the line that had to be taken. People came first to the secret meeting places where they were received by Vera Menzhinskaya and myself or by Mikhail Sergeyevich. For the more intimate and important people I arranged interviews with Ilyich, while for those who came on military business Mikhail Sergeyevich arranged interviews with Nikitich (Krasin). The rendezvous were held at different places: at Dora Dvoires' dental surgery (somewhere in Nevsky), at the dentist Lavrentyeva's, (in Nikolayevskaya Street), at the *Vperyod* bookstore* and at the flats of various sympathizers.

I remember two incidents. One day Vera Menzhinskaya and I arranged to receive visitors at the *Vperyod* bookstore, where a special room had been set aside for the purpose. One local Party man came with a bundle of proclamations, while another sat waiting his turn. All of a sudden a police officer opened the door, stuck his head in, said, "Aha!" and locked us all in. What could we do? We couldn't very well climb out through the window, so we just sat there staring dumbly at one another. We decided meantime to burn the proclamations and other illegal stuff —that is what we did—and agreed among ourselves to say that we had come there to collect popular literature for the villages. The police officer sneered when we told him that, but he did not arrest us. He took our names and addresses. Naturally, we gave him false names and addresses.

---

* The *Vperyod* bookstore and publishing house belonged to the C.C. of the Party.—*Ed.*

On another occasion I nearly got into a mess. I went to a first secret meeting place at Lavrentyeva's, but instead of House No. 32 I was told No. 33. I was surprised to see that the name-card on the door had been pulled off. Funny sort of secrecy technique this, I thought. The door was opened by a soldier, obviously an officer's servant. I walked straight down the passage without saying a word, loaded up with ciphered addresses and literature. The servant dashed after me, deathly pale and trembling. I stopped and said: "Isn't the dentist in? I've got the toothache." The batman stuttered: "The Colonel is not at home." "The Colonel?" I said. "Yes, Colonel Riman." It appears I had blundered into the flat of Riman, Colonel of the very Semyonovsky Regiment which had crushed the Moscow uprising and taken punitive measures on the Moscow-Kazan Railway.

Obviously he feared an attempt on his life, and that accounted for the card being torn off the door. And here had I burst into his flat and rushed down the passage without announcing myself.

"I've come to the wrong place then, I want the dentist," I said, and beat a hasty retreat.

Sleeping at people's places tired Ilyich out, and besides, he found it very irksome. Being a shy man, he felt embarrassed by the attentions of the kind hosts. He liked to work in a library or at home, and here he had to accommodate himself every time to new surroundings.

I used to meet him at the Vienna Restaurant, but as it was not very convenient to talk there in public, we would sit there awhile, or, meeting at an agreed spot in the street, we would then take a cab to the hotel opposite the Nikolayevsky Station, where we would engage a private room and order dinner. Once we met Juzef (Dzerzhinsky) in the street. We stopped the cab and invited him to join us. He sat down next to the driver. Ilyich kept worrying whether he was comfortable, but he laughed and said that he had been brought up in the village and could ride on the driving-seat of a sledge.

Ilyich got fed up at last with this kind of life, and we took rooms together in Panteleimonovskaya (in a big building opposite the church of that name). Our landlady was a reactionary of the Black-Hundred type.

Of Ilyich's speeches at that period, I remember one on the peasant question at a meeting of propagandists from various districts held at Knipovich's flat. Nikolai from the Nevskaya Zastava district asked him some question. I did not like the stereotyped form in which the question was put nor the way in which Nikolai had spoken. After the meeting I asked Uncle, the local organizer in that district, what kind of a worker Nikolai was. She said he was an intelligent young man closely connected with the village, but complained that he was incapable of doing systematic mass work and wasted his gifts working only with a small group. In 1906 Nikolai was nevertheless an active worker. He turned *provocateur* during the period of reaction, but he could not stand it, and committed suicide. Nikolai belonged to a group of comrades who tried to penetrate among all sections of the poor population. I remember his going to a doss-house to carry on agitation. Krylenko, who was a cheeky young fellow at the time, gate-crashed at some meeting of a religious sect and nearly got a good hiding. Sergei Voitinsky was another one who was continually getting into all kinds of scrapes.

Ilyich had the sleuths after him. He had been to a meeting (at the lawyer Cherekul-Kush's, I believe), where he had made a report. He was so closely shadowed that he decided not to return home. I sat by the window all through the night, and concluded that he had been arrested. Ilyich barely managed to elude the sleuths, and with the aid of Bask (then a prominent member of Spilka*), he escaped

---

* *Spilka*—Ukrainian Social-Democratic organization, formed at the end of 1904, affiliated to the R.S.D.L.P. as an autonomous regional

to Finland, where he lived up to the time of the Stockholm Congress.

There, in April, he wrote the pamphlet *The Victory of the Cadets and the Tasks of the Workers' Party* and drafted the resolutions for the Unity Congress. They were discussed in St. Petersburg, Ilyich arriving there for the purpose. The discussion was held at the Witmer's in one of the classrooms (their house was used as a school).

It was the first time the Bolsheviks and Mensheviks had met together in congress since the Second Party Congress. Although the Mensheviks had shown themselves in their true colours during the last few months, Ilyich still hoped that the new wave of the revolution, of whose rise he had no doubt, would sweep them along with it and reconcile them to the Bolshevik line.

I was a bit late at the congress. I travelled there with Tuchapsky, whom I had known before (we had worked together in preparing the First Congress), and with Klavdia Sverdlova. Sverdlov himself had intended coming to the congress, too. He was a very big influence in the Urals. The workers there flatly refused to let him go. I had a mandate from Kazan, but was short of a few votes. The credentials committee therefore gave me only a deliberative vote. A few minutes with the credentials committee was enough to plunge one right away into the atmosphere of the congress—it was decidedly factional.

The Bolsheviks stood solid, united by the conviction that the revolution, despite its temporary setback, was on the upgrade.

I remember how busy Uncle was kept. She knew Swedish well and therefore was given the job of seeing the delegates fixed up. I remember Ivan Skvortsov and Vladimir Bazarov, and the way the latter's eyes used to gleam when he was in a fighting mood. I remember Vladimir Ilyich saying in this connection that Bazarov had a strong political streak in him and enjoyed a good fight. I remember a ramble we took in the country with Rykov, Stroyev and Alexinsky, when we talked about the temper of the workers. Voroshilov (Volodya Antimekov) and K. Samoilova (Natasha Bolshevikova) were at the congress too. Their two sobriquets alone, so full of youthful audacity,* were characteristic of the temper of the Bolshevik delegates at the Unity Congress. The Bolshevik delegates came away from it more strongly welded together than ever.

April 27 saw the opening of the First State Duma. There was a demonstration of the unemployed, among whom Voitinsky was working. May Day was marked with great enthusiasm. At the end of April the newspaper *Volna* (*Wave*) started publication in place of *Novaya Zhizn,* and a small Bolshevik magazine *Vestnik Zhizni (Herald of Life)* began to appear. The movement was building up again.

On our return from the Stockholm Congress we took rooms in Zabalkansky Street, I with a passport in the name of Praskovia Onegina, Ilyich in the name of Chkheidze. The building had a through courtyard, and we would have been fairly comfortable there but for one of the tenants, a military man, who knocked his wife about unmercifully and dragged her up and down the passage by her hair, and the too amiable landlady, who was very inquisitive about Ilyich's kin, and assured him that she had known him when he was a kid of four, only he had then been on the dark side....

Ilyich wrote a report about the Unity Congress to the St. Petersburg workers in which he high-lighted all the differences on vital issues. "Freedom of discussion, unity

---

* *Antimekov*—derived from the word "anti-Menshevik."—*Ed.*

of action is what we must strive for," Ilyich wrote in his report. "All Social-Democrats agree among themselves in supporting the revolutionary action of the peasantry and criticizing petty-bourgeois utopias...." "In the elections (to the Duma.—*N.K.*) complete unity of action is *imperative*. The congress has decided that we should *all* vote wherever there are any elections. No criticism for taking part in the elections is to be made during the elections. The *action* of the proletariat must be united." (*Works*, Vol. 10, pp. 348, 349.)

The report was published in *Vperyod* in May.

On May 9 Vladimir Ilyich, for the first time in Russia, addressed a huge mass meeting at Panina's People's House under the name of Karpov. The hall was packed with workers from all districts. The police were noticeably absent. The two police officers who had hung around at the beginning quickly disappeared. "You'd think someone had sprinkled insect-powder on 'em," some wag remarked. After Ogorodnikov, a Constitutional Democrat (Cadet), had spoken, the chairman called upon Karpov. I was standing among the crowd. Ilyich was terribly agitated. He stood silent for about a minute, very pale. All the blood had flowed to his heart. You could sense at once that the speaker's agitation was communicating itself to the audience. Then all of a sudden a burst of hand-clapping swept through the hall—the Party comrades had recognized Ilyich. I remember the puzzled excited face of a worker standing next to me. "Who is it? Who is it?" he asked. No one answered him. A hush descended upon the hall. A wave of extraordinary enthusiasm swept the audience after Ilyich's speech. At that moment everyone was thinking of the coming fight to the finish.

Red shirts were torn up to make banners, and the crowd dispersed to their respective districts with revolutionary songs.

It was a May night, one of those exhilarating St. Petersburg white nights. The police we had expected to be waiting outside were not there. After the meeting Vladimir Ilyich went to sleep at Dmitry Leshchenko's place.

Ilyich did not have another chance of addressing any big public meeting during that revolution.

On May 24 *Volna* was suppressed. On May 26 it resumed publication under the name of *Vperyod*, which existed until June 14.

It was not until June 22 that we succeeded in starting publication of a new Bolshevik newspaper *Ekho (Echo)* which existed up till July 7. The State Duma was dissolved on July 8.

At the end of June Rosa Luxemburg arrived in St. Petersburg. She had just been released from Warsaw prison. Vladimir Ilyich and our leading Bolsheviks met her. Old Papa Rode, a houseowner, whose daughter had been a fellow-teacher of mine in the Nevskaya Zastava and had afterwards been in prison with me, placed an apartment at our disposal for the meeting. The old man was anxious to help us in every way he could. The apartment he gave us for the meeting was a big empty place, and for the sake of greater secrecy, he had all the windows whitewashed, thus attracting the attention of all the janitors. At that conference we discussed the situation and the tactics that were to be employed. From St. Petersburg Rosa went to Finland, and thence abroad.

In May, when the movement was gathering momentum, Ilyich gave a good deal of attention to the Duma, which had begun to reflect the moods of the peasantry. During that period he wrote the following articles: "The Workers' Group in the State Duma," "The Peasant of 'Trudovik' Group and the R.S.D.L.P.," "The Land Question in the Duma," "Neither Land Nor Liberty," "The Government, the Duma and the People," "The Cadets Prevent the Duma from Appealing to the People," "The Hapless, the Octobrists and the Cadets," "Bad Advice," "The Cadets, the Trudoviks, and the Workers' Party." All these articles had in view a single object—the alliance of the working class with the peasantry, the necessity to rouse the peasants to the struggle for land and liberty, the necessity to prevent the Cadets from striking a bargain with the government.

Ilyich often made reports on this question during that period.

He addressed a delegates' meeting of the Vyborg District of St. Petersburg at the Engineers' Union in Zagorodny Prospekt. We had to wait a long time, as one hall was occupied by the unemployed, and the other by the longshoremen (their organizer was Sergei Malyshev). They had made a last attempt to come to an agreement with the employers and had failed again. We had to wait until they had gone.

I also remember Ilyich speaking to a group of schoolteachers. Socialist-Revolutionary moods then prevailed among the teachers, and the Bolsheviks had been debarred from the Teachers' Congress. A talk with a group of a few score teachers was arranged in one of the schools. Among those present I particularly remember the face of one of the school mistresses, a hunchbacked little woman. She was the Socialist-Revolutionary Kondratyeva. Ryazanov made a report on the trade unions at this meeting. Vladimir Ilyich spoke on the agrarian question. He was opposed by Bunakov, the S.-R., who accused him of contradicting himself and quoted Ilyin against him (Ilyin was Vladimir Ilyich's pen-name at the time). Vladimir Ilyich listened attentively, jotting down notes, then made short work of this S.-R. demagogy.

When the land question loomed large, and there openly appeared what Ilyich called "a league of the officials and liberals against the muzhiks," the vacillating Trudovik group sided with the workers. Seeing that the Duma could not be relied upon to back it, the government fought with the gloves off. Peaceful demonstrations were beaten up, buildings used for public meetings were set on fire, and *pogroms* started against the Jews. A government statement on the agrarian question in which violent attacks were made on the State Duma was issued on June 20.

Finally, on July 8, the Duma was dissolved, the Social-Democratic newspapers were shut down, and all kinds of repressions and arrests started. A revolt broke out in Kronstadt and Sveaborg. Our people took a very active part in it. Innokenty (Dubrovinsky) barely managed to get away from Kronstadt; he slipped through the fingers of the police there by pretending to be dead drunk. After a while our military organization was arrested. It had had an *agent provocateur* planted in its midst. This happened just at the time of the Sveaborg revolt. We waited despairingly that day for telegrams reporting the progress of the revolt.

We were sitting in the Menzhinskys' flat. The Menzhinsky sisters, Vera and Lyudmila, lived in a very convenient apartment, all on their own. Comrades often came to visit them. Frequent visitors were Rozhkov, Juzef and Goldenberg. On that occasion, too, several comrades had gathered there, among them Ilyich. He sent Vera to Schlichter with a message telling him to go to Sveaborg at once. Someone remembered that there was a comrade named Harrik working as proof-reader on the Cadet paper *Rech* (*Speech*). I cailed on him to find out whether there were any telegrams. He was not in the office, but I got the telegrams from another proof-reader. He advised me to make arrangements with Harrik, who lived nearby in Gusev Street. He even wrote the address for me on the galley-proofs on which the telegrams were printed. I went to Gusev Street. Two women were walking about arm-in-arm in front of the house. They stopped me. "If you are going to flat number so-and-so, you'd better not. The police are there—it's a trap. They're seizing everybody who goes in." I hastened to warn our people. As we afterwards found out, our whole military organization, including Vyacheslav Menzhinsky, had been arrested there. The insurrection was suppressed. The reaction began to put the screw on. The Bolsheviks resumed publication of the illegal *Proletary,* and went underground. The Mensheviks beat a retreat and began to write in the bourgeois press, putting forward the demagogic slogan of a non-party workers' congress, which, under the existing conditions, was tantamount to liquidating the Party. The Bolsheviks demanded the convocation of an emergency congress.

Ilyich was obliged to go into "semi-exile" in Finland. He put up with the Leiteisens in Kuokkala, not far from the railway station. The large rambling country house Vaasa had long been a refuge for revolutionaries. It had been formerly occupied by S.-R.'s, who had made bombs there, and afterwards the Bolshevik Leiteisen (Lindov) and his family lived there. Ilyich had a room to himself in a remote part of the house, where he wrote his articles and pamphlets, and received members of the Central Committee and the St. Petersburg Committee, and Party workers from the provinces. Ilyich practically directed all the activities of the Bolsheviks from Kuokkala. After a while I joined him there. I took a train to St. Petersburg every morning and returned late in the evening. The Leiteisens eventually went away, and we occupied the whole ground floor—my mother came to stay with us, and Maria Ilyinichna lived with us for a time. The top floor was occupied by the Bogdanovs, and then in 1907 by Dubrovinsky (Innokenty). In those days the Russian police judiciously kept away from Finland, and we enjoyed considerable freedom there. The door of the house was never locked, and every night a jug of milk and a loaf of bread were left in the dining room, where a bed was made on the sofa so that in the event of anyone coming down by the night train he could have a bite and go to sleep without disturbing anyone. In the morning we would often find comrades in the dining room who had come down during the night.

A special messenger came to Ilyich every day with copy, newspapers and letters. Ilyich would look through this mail, then sit down straightaway to write an article and send it back by the same man. Dmitry Leshchenko visited Vaasa nearly every day. In the evenings I would bring the latest news and messages from St. Petersburg.

Naturally, Ilyich yearned to be back in St. Petersburg, and although the closest possible contact was kept with him, a lonesome mood would come upon him sometimes, and we would all try our best to take him out of himself. And so it happened that all the inmates of Vaasa started playing *doorak**.

Bogdanov played a slow wary game, Ilyich played with careful zest, and Leiteisen with gusto. Sometimes a man calling on business from some Party local would be considerably taken aback to find the Central Committee members engaged in a lively game of *doorak*. But that was just an interlude.

Spending the whole day in St. Petersburg as I did, I saw very little of Ilyich. I came home late to find him always fretting, and so instead of asking him any questions I told him about all that I had seen and heard that day.

That winter Vera Menzhinskaya and I made our permanent rendezvous in the canteen of the Technological Institute. It was a very convenient place, as a great number of people passed through it in the course of the day. Sometimes as many as ten of us a day would meet there. We attracted no attention. On one occasion, though, Kamo came to a meeting there in full Caucasian kit, carrying a ball-shaped object in a serviette. Everyone in the canteen stopped eating and began to stare at the striking visitor. "He has brought a bomb," most of them probably thought. But it was not a bomb, it was a water-melon. Kamo had brought the water-melon and some candied nuts as a treat for Ilyich and me. "My Aunt sent them," he explained in his bashful way. A daredevil fighter of indom-

---

* *Doorak*—an amusing Russian card game.—*Tr.*

itable will and courage, Kamo was a man of the highest character, a rather naive and affectionate comrade. He was passionately devoted to Ilyich, Krasin and Bogdanov. He used to visit us at Kuokkala, where he made friends with my mother, and used to tell her all about his aunt and sisters. Kamo travelled frequently between Finland and St. Petersburg, and always took arms back with him. Mother used to help him strap the revolvers on his back with affectionate care.

The illegal paper *Proletary* began to appear in Vyborg in the autumn.* Ilyich devoted a great deal of time to it. Contact was maintained through Schlichter. The illegal newspaper was delivered in St. Petersburg and distributed there among the districts. Delivery arrangements were handled by Irina (Lydia Gobi). Although delivery and distribution went smoothly (literature went through the legal Bolshevik print-shop Delo), the addresses had to be obtained to which the literature was to be forwarded. Vera Menzhinskaya and I needed someone to help us. Komissarov, a district man, proposed his wife Katya as assistant. She came—a modest-looking woman with bobbed hair. An odd feeling came over me when first I saw her—a kind of sharp mistrust. I could not account for it, and soon it passed. Katya proved to be a very efficient assistant. She did everything quickly, accurately and with careful secrecy. She showed no curiosity, asked no questions. Once, though, when I asked her where she was going to spend the summer, she winced and gave me an ugly look. Katya and her husband turned out to be *agent provocateurs*. Katya received a consignment of arms in St. Petersburg and took it down to the Urals. The police came along as soon as she arrived and confiscated the arms which she had brought, and arrested everyone. We did not find that out until a long time afterwards. Her husband, Komissarov, became manager for Simonov, the proprietor of House No.

* The first number of *Proletary* appeared on August 21, 1906.—*Ed.*

9 in Zagorodny Prospekt. Simonov used to help the Social-Democrats. Vladimir Ilyich lived there at one time, then a Bolshevik club was organized there, and later Alexinsky lived there. Some time later, during the reaction, Komissarov fixed up illegal comrades there and supplied them with passports, and afterwards those comrades very quickly "happened" to get themselves arrested at the frontier. One of the comrades who fell into this trap was Innokenty, he had returned from abroad to work in Russia. It is difficult, of course, to say exactly when Komissarov and his wife turned *provocateurs*. At any rate, there were a good many things that the police did not know. They did not know Vladimir Ilyich's whereabouts, for one thing. In 1905 and throughout 1906 the police force was still pretty disorganized. The Second State Duma was to be convoked on February 20, 1907.

Fourteen delegates at the November Conference including those from Poland and Lithuania headed by Vladimir Ilyich had been in favour of the elections to the Duma, but against any bloc with the Cadets (as advocated by the Mensheviks). It was under this slogan that the Bolsheviks had worked for the Duma elections. The Cadets were defeated at the polls. The number of Cadet deputies returned to the Second Duma was only half of what they had had in the First. The elections were very late. A new revolutionary wave seemed to be rising. Ilyich wrote at the beginning of 1907: "How poor our recent 'theoretical' disputes have suddenly become in the light of the brilliant beam of the revolution that has now burst forth!"

The Second Duma deputies came to Kuokkala fairly often to have a talk with Ilyich. The work of the Bolshevik deputies was directed by Alexander Bogdanov. He lived in Kuokkala at the same country house as we did, and consulted Ilyich on everything.

I remember returning to Kuokkala late one evening from St. Petersburg and meeting Pavel Axelrod in the train. He said that the Bolshevik deputies, Alexinsky in particular, were not doing at all badly in the Duma. He began talking about a workers' congress. The Mensheviks were agitating strongly for a workers' congress in the hope that such a congress on a broad basis would help to fight the growing influence of the Bolsheviks. The latter pressed for a speedy convocation of the Party congress. It was finally fixed for April. There was a very big attendance. The delegates went there in a body. They came to the secret rendezvous one after another to show their credentials. The Bolshevik representatives there were Mikhail Sergeyevich (Weinstein) and myself, while the Menshevik representatives were Krokhmal and M. M. Shik (Khinchuk's wife). The police had us shadowed. Marat (Schanzer) and several other delegates were arrested at the Finland Station. We had to take extra measures of precaution. Ilyich and Bogdanov had already left for the congress. I was in no hurry to get back to Kuokkala. I did not arrive home until Sunday evening, and who should I find there but seventeen delegates, sitting cold and hungry and forlorn! The domestic help, who lived with us, was a Finnish Social-Democrat, and she had taken all day off on Sundays to go to the People's House where they held theatricals, and so on. It took me quite a time to feed that crowd. I did not attend the congress myself. There was no one I could turn over my secretarial duties to, and the times were difficult. The police grew more and more meddlesome, and people were afraid to let Bolsheviks have their rooms for sleeping in and holding secret rendezvous. I sometimes met our people in the *Vestnik Zhizni* office. Pyotr Rumyantsev, the editor of the magazine, was ashamed to tell me himself not to arrange any more meetings at the office, so he set his caretaker on to me. This caretaker was a worker with whom I had often talked about our Party affairs. I was vexed that Rumyantsev had not told me himself.

Ilyich was the last to return from the congress. He looked odd, with his moustache clipped short, his beard shaved off, and a big straw hat on his head.* On June 3 the Second Duma was dismissed. The Bolshevik group came down to Kuokkala in a body late in the evening, and sat up all night, discussing the situation. Ilyich had come back from the congress utterly worn out. He was overwrought and did not eat anything. I packed his things and sent him off to Styrsudd, where Uncle's family lived, while I remained to hastily wind things up. By the time I arrived in Styrsudd Ilyich had come to himself a bit. They told me there that he had kept falling asleep the first few days. He would sit down under a fir-tree and in a minute he would doze off. The children called him "sleepy-head." We had a wonderful time in Styrsudd—the forest, the sea, nature at its wildest, with only another large summer house next door belonging to engineer Zyabitsky, where Leshchenko and his wife and Alexinsky lived. Ilyich avoided conversations with Alexinsky—he wanted a rest. The latter felt hurt. Sometimes we got together at Leshchenko's to listen to music. Xenia Ivanovna—a relative of the Knipovichs'—was a professional singer with a lovely voice, and Ilyich used to enjoy her singing. Ilyich and I spent most of the day by the sea or cycling. Our machines were old ones and needed repairing all the time, which we did, sometimes with the help of Leshchenko, sometimes without it. We used old galoshes for patches, and I'm afraid we did more repairing than riding. But when we did go cycling it was wonderful. Uncle plied Ilyich with nourishing omelettes and deer ham. Ilyich steadily picked up and became fit again.

From Styrsudd we went to a conference at Terijoki. Ilyich had carefully considered the situation during his leisure hours, and spoke at the conference against the boycott-

---

* Immediately after the congress Ilyich reported back to a large gathering of workers who had arrived from St. Petersburg to hear him. He spoke at the hotel of a Finn named Kakko in Terijoki (the hotel was later destroyed by fire).—*Ed.*

ing of the Third Duma. War started on yet another front, a war against the boycottists, who refused to reckon with the grim realities and made themselves drunk with high-sounding phrases. Ilyich warmly defended his position in the little country house. Krasin rode up on a bicycle, and, standing by the window, listened attentively to Ilyich. Instead of going in, he walked away deep in thought. Indeed, there was food enough for thought.

Then came the Stuttgart Congress.* Ilyich was very pleased with it. He was pleased with the resolutions on the trade unions and on the attitude towards war.

AGAIN ABROAD

End of 1907

In Finland Ilyich was obliged to move still farther inland. The Bogdanovs, Innokenty (Dubrovinsky) and I stayed on at the Vaasa house in Kuokkala. There had already been police raids at Terijoki, and we were expecting them at Kuokkala. Natalia Bogdanova and I started cleaning up. We went through all the files, picking out everything of value and giving it to Finnish comrades to hide, while the rest we burned. We applied ourselves to the task with such zeal that we were surprised one day to find that the snow all round Vaasa was strewn with ashes. If the gendarmes had put in an appearance, though, they would still have found enough for their purpose. Stacks of papers had accumulated in the house. Special precautions had to be taken. One morning our landlady came running in to say that the gendarmes had turned up at Kuokkala. She took away as much illegal stuff as she could carry to hide in her own house. We sent Alexander Bogdanov and Innokenty for a walk in the woods, and

---

* The Stuttgart Congress of the Second International was held between August 18 and 24, 1907.—*Ed.*

sat waiting for the police to come with a search warrant. On that occasion, however, no search was made. They were looking for the fighting-squad comrades.

The comrades had sent Ilyich to the hinterland. He lived at Åggelby, a little station near Helsingfors, with two Finnish sisters. He felt an utter stranger in that spotlessly clean cold room, cosy in its Finnish way with lace curtains and everything standing in its proper place, and with the incessant sound of laughter, a piano and loud chatter in Finnish coming from the next room. Ilyich spent all day writing his paper on the agrarian question, during which he carefully weighed the experience of the recent revolution. He walked up and down the room for hours on tiptoes, so as not to disturb the landladies. I went to see him there once.

The police were looking for Ilyich all over Finland. He had to leave the country. Plainly, the reaction was going to last for years. We would have to move back to Switzerland. We had little heart for it, but there was no other way. Besides, it was necessary to arrange for the publication of *Proletary* abroad, since this was no longer possible in Finland. Ilyich was to leave for Stockholm at the first opportunity and wait for me there. I had to fix up my sick old mother in St. Petersburg, settle a number of other affairs and arrange future contacts before following Ilyich out.

While I was running about in St. Petersburg, Ilyich very nearly lost his life on his way to Stockholm. He was being so closely shadowed that to go the usual way, that is, by embarking at Åbo, would have meant being arrested for certain.* There had already been cases of our people being arrested when boarding the steamer. A Finnish comrade advised boarding the steamer at one of the nearby islands. This was safe as far as avoiding arrest was con-

---

* Steamers plied between Finland and Sweden in the winter with the help of ice-breakers.—*Ed.*

cerned, but it involved a three-mile walk across the ice to the island, and although it was December the ice was not very strong in some places. No guides were available, as no one cared to risk his life. At last two tipsy peasants in a pot-valiant mood undertook to escort Ilyich. Crossing the ice at night, all three nearly drowned when the ice in one place suddenly started to give way under them. They barely managed to jump for safety.

I learned afterwards from Borgo, a Finnish comrade (he was eventually shot by the White Guards), with whose help I crossed to Stockholm, how dangerous had been the path Ilyich had chosen and what a narrow escape he had had. Ilyich afterwards told me that when the ice began to give way, his first thought had been: "Ah, what a stupid way to die."

An exodus of Russians started again—Bolsheviks, Mensheviks, S.-R.'s left the country. On the boat going out I met Dan, Lydia Zederbaum, and a couple of S.-R.'s.

After a few days in Stockholm, Ilyich and I proceeded to Geneva via Berlin. Searches and arrests had been made among the Russians in Berlin on the eve of our arrival. We were met by Avramov, a member of the Berlin group, who therefore advised us not to go to the homes of any of our comrades. He led us about from café to café all day long. We spent the evening with Rosa Luxemburg. The Stuttgart Congress, at which Vladimir Ilyich and Rosa Luxemburg had been at one on the question of war, had brought them very close together. At that congress, as far back as 1907, they had said that the struggle against war should aim not only at peace but at the replacement of capitalism by socialism. The crisis created by war should be utilized for the speedy overthrow of the bourgeoisie. "The Stuttgart Congress," Ilyich wrote, "sharply set off the opportunist and the revolutionary wings of international Social-Democracy on a number of momentous issues and gave its decision on these issues in a spirit of revolutionary Marxism." (*Works*, Vol. 13, p. 65.) At the Stuttgart

Congress Rosa Luxemburg and Ilyich were at one. Their talk together that evening was therefore more than usually friendly.

We returned to our hotel in the evening feeling ill. Both of us had a white froth on our lips and felt extremely weak. As it transpired afterwards, we had got fish-poisoning somewhere during our round of the restaurants. A doctor had to be sent for during the night. Vladimir Ilyich was registered as a Finnish chef and I as an American citizen, and so the hotel attendant fetched an American doctor. He examined Ilyich and said it was very serious, then he examined me and said, "You will pull through all right!" He prescribed a heap of medicines, and, smelling a rat, charged us a terrific fee for the visit. We lay in bed for a couple of days, then dragged ourselves off, half-ill, to Geneva, where we arrived on January 7, 1908. Ilyich afterwards wrote to Gorky that we had "caught a cold" during the journey.

Geneva looked bleak. There was not a speck of snow about, and a cold cutting wind was blowing—the bise. Post cards with a view of the freezing water near the railings of the Geneva Lake embankment were being sold. The town looked dead and empty. Among the comrades living there at the time were Mikha Tskhakaya, V. Karpinsky and Olga Ravich. Mikha Tskhakaya lived in a small room and got out of bed with difficulty when we arrived. The conversation flagged. The Karpinskys were then living in the Russian library (formerly Kuklin's) where Karpinsky was manager. He had a very bad headache when we arrived and kept wincing all the time. All the shutters were closed, since the light hurt him. As we were going back from the Karpinskys through the desolate streets of Geneva, which had turned so unfriendly, Ilyich let fall: "I have a feeling as if I've come here to be buried."

We were beginning our second period of emigration, a much harder one than the first.

PART II

Lenin in 1910, Paris

SECOND EMIGRATION

The second emigration may be divided into three periods.

The first period (1908-1911) covers the years of rampant reaction in Russia. The tsarist government took savage reprisals against the revolutionaries. The prisons were full to overflowing, the prisoners were subject to brutal treatment, and death sentences followed one after another. The illegal organizations were driven deep underground, and even so they found it hard to escape detection. During the revolution the composition of the Party membership had undergone a change; new members joined the Party, who had no experience of the pre-revolutionary underground or of secrecy methods of work. On the other hand, the tsarist government did not stint any money for the organization of spying and stool-pigeoning. The system of spying was extremely well planned and ramified, and its network covered the central organs of the Party. The government's intelligence service was splendidly organized.

Simultaneously, a regular campaign of persecution was conducted against all legal societies, trade unions and the press. The government was all out to deprive the masses of the rights which they had won during the revolution. But there could be no return to the past; the revolution had left its mark on the masses, and the initiative of the workers found vent again and again through every possible crevice.

Those were years of the greatest confusion of ideas among the Social-Democrats. Attempts were made to revise the very foundations of Marxism, and philosophic trends arose which tried to shake the materialistic concepts on which the whole of Marxism is based. Those were dark days. Attempts were made to find a way out by inventing a new refined religion and giving it a philosophical basis. This new school of philosophy, which opened its doors to all kinds of "God-seekers" and "God-builders,"* was headed by Bogdanov and supported by Lunacharsky, Bazarov and others. Marx arrived at Marxism by way of philosophy, by way of the struggle against idealism. Plekhanov in his time had devoted considerable attention to building up evidence in support of the materialist philosophy. Lenin had made a very intensive study of their works and devoted a good deal of time to philosophy while in exile. He was fully alive to the implications of this attempt at revising the philosophic tenets of Marxism and its significance during the years of reaction, and opposed Bogdanov and his school very strongly.

Bogdanov was not only an opponent on the philosophic front. He rallied around him the Otzovists and Ultimatumists as well. The Otzovists said that the State Duma had become so reactionary that the Social-Democratic members of it should be recalled. The Ultimatumists held that an ultimatum should be presented to the Duma, and the Social-Democratic deputies should make speeches there which would have them thrown out. Strictly speak-

---

* *"God-seekers"* and *"God-builders"*—reactionary religious philosophical trends which arose in Russia after the defeat of the Revolution of 1905-1907 among the unstable elements of Social-Democracy (Bogdanov, Bazarov, Lunacharsky and others). They tried to set up a new "socialist" religion, to combine socialism with belief in God. The reactionary essence of these trends was exposed by Lenin in his book *Materialism and Empirio-Criticism.—Ed.*

ing, there was no difference between the Otzovists and the Ultimatumists. Among the Ultimatumists were Alexinsky and Marat. The Otzovists and Ultimatumists were opposed also to the Bolsheviks participating in the trade unions and the legal societies. A Bolshevik, they declared, should be hard and unyielding. Lenin considered this view fallacious. It would mean giving up all practical work, standing aside from the masses instead of organizing them on real-life issues. Prior to the Revolution of 1905 the Bolsheviks showed themselves capable of making good use of every legal possibility, of forging ahead and rallying the masses behind them under the most adverse conditions. Step by step, beginning with the campaign for tea service and ventilation, they had led the masses up to the national armed insurrection. The ability to adjust oneself to the most adverse conditions and at the same time to stand out and maintain one's high-principled positions—such were the traditions of Leninism. The Otzovists cut loose from these Bolshevik traditions. The fight against Otzovism was the fight for the tried and tested Bolshevik, Leninist tactics.

Finally, those years (1908-1911) were years of intense struggle for the Party, for its illegal organization.

Naturally, the first to show signs of pessimistic moods during the period of reaction were the Menshevik practical workers, who had always tended to swim with the stream and narrow down revolutionary slogans, and were closely linked with the liberal bourgeoisie. These pessimistic moods were strikingly manifested in a striving on the part of broad sections of the Mensheviks to dissolve the Party. These liquidators, as they were called, maintained that an illegal party only led to police raids and arrests, and narrowed the scope of the labour movement. As a matter of fact, liquidation of the illegal Party would have meant abandoning the independent policy of the proletariat, lowering the revolutionary spirit of the proletarian struggle, weakening the organization and unity of action of the proletariat. The liquidation of the Party meant rejecting the teaching of Marx and all its tenets.

Of course, Mensheviks like Plekhanov, who had done so much for the propagation of Marxism and the struggle against opportunism, could not but realize the reactionary character of these liquidationist moods; and when the preaching for the Party's liquidation developed into an agitation for the liquidation of the basic principles of Marxism itself, he dissociated himself from them completely and formed a group of his own, a group of Party-Mensheviks.

The ensuing struggle for the Party tended to shed light on a number of organizational issues and to give the rank and file of the Party a better and clearer understanding of the role of the Party and the duties of its members.

The struggle for a materialist philosophy, for contact with the masses, for Leninist tactics, the struggle for the Party, was waged under conditions of political emigration.

During the years of reaction the number of political emigrants from Russia increased tremendously. People fled abroad to escape the savage persecutions of the tsarist regime, people with frayed and shattered nerves, without prospects for the future, without a penny to their name, and without any help from Russia. All this tended to give to the political struggle an extremely painful twist. We had more than enough of squabbling and bickering.

Looking back over all those years, it is now transparently clear what the struggle was all about. Now that experience has so clearly demonstrated the correctness of Lenin's line, that struggle seems to be of little interest to many people. Without that struggle, though, the Party would not have been able to develop its activities as quickly as it did during the rising tide, and its progress towards victory would have been handicapped. The struggle took place at a time when the above-mentioned trends were just taking shape, and was waged between people who had only recently been fighting side by side, and many thought that the trouble was due to Lenin's quarrelsome disposition, his brusqueness and bad temper. Actually, it was a struggle for the Party's very existence, for its consistent line and correct tactics. Another reason for the sharp tone which the controversy assumed was the complicated nature of the issues, and Ilyich frequently presented them as sharply as he did because otherwise the essence of the question would have remained obscure.

The years 1908 to 1911 were not merely years of living abroad—they were years of intense struggle on a most important front—the ideological front.

The second period of the second emigration, the years 1911 to 1914, witnessed the rising tide of the movement in Russia. The growing strike movement, the Lena events,* which roused the whole working class to action, the development of the labour press, the elections to the Duma and the activity of the Social-Democratic deputies—all this called into being new forms of Party work, gave that work quite a new scope, made the Party membership far more proletarian, and brought the Party closer to the masses.

Contacts with Russia began to strengthen swiftly, and the influence on the work in Russia steadily increased. The Prague Conference held in January 1912 expelled the Liquidators from the Party and laid down the foundations of the illegal Party organization. Plekhanov did not join the Bolsheviks.

In 1912 we moved to Cracow. The struggle for the Party and for its consolidation was no longer waged be-

---

* *The Lena events*—the shooting of the workers during the suppression of the strike at the Lena gold-fields in the Siberian taiga in April 1912, during which 270 people were killed and 250 wounded. The workers of Russia protested against these atrocities by mass political strikes and demonstrations.—*Ed.*

tween small groups abroad. The Cracow period was one in which Lenin's tactics had been put to the test in Russia and proved their value in practice. The questions of practical work absorbed Lenin completely. But while the working-class movement was developing widely in Russia, the murmurings of an approaching storm could already be heard on the international front. The war clouds were gathering. Ilyich now began to give his attention to the new relationships that would have to be established between the different nationalities when the war that was then brewing would be converted into a civil war. While living in Cracow Ilyich was able to come into closer contact with the Polish Social-Democrats and to learn their point of view on the national question. He persistently combatted their mistakes and gave more definite and clearer point to his own formulations. During the Cracow period the Bolsheviks adopted a number of resolutions on the national question, which were of very great significance.

The third period of the second emigration (1914-1917) covers the war period, when the whole character of our life abroad underwent another sharp change. This was the period when international issues assumed decisive importance, and when our own Russian affairs could be dealt with only from the point of view of the international movement.

Inevitably, they were to be based on much wider ground now, on international ground. Everything a man could do while living in a neutral country was done in the way of propaganda for the struggle against the imperialist war and for converting this war into civil war, and for laying the foundations for a new International. This work absorbed all Lenin's energies during the early years of the war (the end of 1914 and throughout 1915).

Simultaneously, the events around him suggested to Lenin some new ideas. They impelled him to a deeper study of the questions of imperialism, of the nature of the war, of the new forms of state power that would take shape the day after the proletariat achieved victory, of the application of the dialectic method to the policy and tactics of the working class. We moved from Berne to Zurich, where there were better facilities for work. Ilyich started writing, and spent all day in the libraries until the news of the February Revolution came, and we started to make preparations for returning to Russia.

YEARS OF REACTION

GENEVA

1908

On the evening of our arrival in Geneva Ilyich wrote a letter to Alexinsky—the Bolshevik deputy in the Second Duma, who had been sentenced to penal servitude together with the other Bolshevik deputies, had emigrated abroad and was now living in Austria—in reply to his letter received in Berlin. A few days later he answered Maxim Gorky, who had been pressing Ilyich to visit him on Capri.

It was impossible to go to Capri, as work had to be started on *Proletary*, the illegal Central Organ of the Party. This had to be done as quickly as possible in order to provide a regular leadership through the Central Organ in those difficult days of reaction. Ilyich could not go, but he could dream of it when writing back to Gorky: "It would be wonderful to take a run over to Capri!" and continued: "I think it would be best to come over when you are not too busy with your work, so that we can loaf about and chat." (*Works,* Vol. 34, p. 323.) Ilyich had experienced and thought over so much in the last few years that he looked forward eagerly to a heart-to-heart talk with Gorky. He was obliged, however, to postpone his visit.

It had not been decided yet whether *Proletary* was to be published in Geneva or some other place. We had written about it to Adler, the Austrian Social-Democrat, and to Juzef (Dzerzhinsky), who lived in Austria too. Austria was closer to the Russian frontier, it would be more convenient in some ways to print the paper there, and easier to arrange transport facilities. Ilyich, however, had little hope of our being able to organize publication anywhere but in Geneva, and so he was taking steps to launch the paper there. We learned, to our surprise, that the type-setting machine we had used in the old days was still available. This cut down expenses and simplified matters.

Vladimirov, the old compositor, who had set the type for the Bolshevik paper *Vperyod* in Geneva before the 1905 Revolution, turned up. The general business management was entrusted to D. M. Kotlyarenko.

By February, all the comrades sent from Russia to organize *Proletary*—Lenin, Bogdanov and Innokenty (Dubrovinsky)—had assembled in Geneva.

Vladimir Ilyich wrote to Maxim Gorky on February 2: "We have everything ready and are announcing publication in a day or two. We have put you down as a contributor. Drop me a line whether you can give us anything for the first few issues (something in the style of *Notes on the Petty Bourgeois* from *Novaya Zhizn* or fragments from the story you are now writing, etc.)." (*Ibid.*, p. 328.) Ilyich had written about bourgeois culture and the petty bourgeois, which he deeply hated and despised, as far back as 1894 in his book *What the "Friends of the People" Are and How They Fight the Social-Democrats.* Gorky's notes on philistinism therefore greatly appealed to him.

Ilyich wrote to Lunacharsky, who was staying with Gorky at Capri: "Drop me a line whether you are fixed up all right and whether you are fit for work again." (*Lenin Miscellany*, I, p. 152.)

The editorial board (Lenin, Bogdanov and Innokenty)

wrote a letter to Trotsky in Vienna, asking him to contribute to the paper. Trotsky refused. He did not want to cooperate with the Bolsheviks, but he did not say so openly. He excused himself on the grounds that he was too busy.

Arrangements had to be made for shipping the paper to Russia. We started tracing old contacts. Our consignments used to be shipped by sea via Marseilles and other ports. Ilyich thought that shipment could now be arranged by way of Capri, where Gorky lived. He wrote to Maria Andreyeva, Gorky's wife, to arrange for the literature to be forwarded on to Odessa through the ships' employees and workers. He got in touch with Alexinsky for shipment via Vienna, but had little hope of success in that quarter. Alexinsky was quite unfitted for that kind of work. We invited over our "shipping expert" Pyatnitsky, now a worker on the Comintern, who had done a good job in the past in smuggling literature across the German frontier. But it took Pyatnitsky (who was in Russia) nearly eight months to throw the police off the scent, evade arrest and cross the frontier. On arriving abroad he tried to organize shipments through Lvov, but nothing came of it. He arrived in Geneva in the autumn of 1908. We arranged that he was to take up his residence again in Leipzig, where he had lived before, and pick up old contacts and organize shipments across the German border as he had done in the past.

Alexinsky decided to move to Geneva. It was intended to enlist his wife Tatyana to help me with our Russian mail. But these were only plans. As for letters, we expected them more than we received them. Shortly after our arrival in Geneva an incident occurred with the changing of money.

In July 1907 an expropriation raid had been made in Erivan Square in Tiflis. At the height of the revolution, when the fight against the autocracy was waged on an extended front, the Bolsheviks considered it permissible to seize tsarist funds by making raids of expropriation. The money obtained in the Tiflis raid was handed over to the Bolsheviks for revolutionary purposes. But the money could not be used. It was all in 500-ruble notes, which had to be changed. This could not be done in Russia, as the banks always had lists of the note numbers in such cases. Now when the reaction was rampant, it was necessary to arrange escapes from prison, where the tsarist government was brutally treating the revolutionaries; to keep the movement alive it was necessary to organize illegal printing plants, etc. The money was badly needed. And so a group of comrades made an attempt to change the 500-ruble notes simultaneously in various towns abroad, just a few days after our arrival. Zhitomirsky, an *agent provocateur*, knew about this and took part in organizing the exchange. No one knew at the time that he was a spy, and he enjoyed full confidence, although he had already betrayed Comrade Kamo, who was arrested in Berlin with a suitcase containing dynamite. Kamo was kept in a German prison for a long time and then handed over to the Russian authorities. Zhitomirsky had warned the police about the attempt to change the ruble notes, and those involved in it were arrested. A member of the Zurich group, a Lett, was arrested in Stockholm, and Olga Ravich, a member of the Geneva group, who had recently returned from Russia, was arrested in Munich with Bogdassarian and Khojamirian. In Geneva N. A. Semashko was arrested after a post card addressed to one of the arrested men was delivered to his house.

The Swiss burgher was frightened to death by this incident. The "Russian expropriators" were the talk of the town. The thing was discussed with horror around the table of the boarding-house where Ilyich and I used to go to dine. Mikha Tskhakaya, our Caucasian comrade, chairman of the Third Party Congress in 1905, lived in Geneva at the time, and when he first came to see us his foreign appearance gave our landlady such a fright that she slammed the door in his face with a shriek of terror, taking him for a real expropriator.

Ultra-opportunist moods prevailed in the Swiss Party at the time, and in connection with the arrest of Semashko, the Swiss Social-Democrats declared that theirs was the most democratic country in the world, that justice reigned supreme there, and that therefore they could not tolerate crimes against property in their territory.

The Russian Government demanded the extradition of the arrested persons. The Swedish Social-Democrats were prepared to intervene, but demanded only that the Zurich group, to which one of the arrested comrades belonged, should confirm that the lad who had been arrested in Stockholm was a Social-Democrat and had been living all the time in Zurich. The Zurich group, in which the Mensheviks predominated, refused to do it. The Mensheviks hastened also to dissociate themselves from Semashko in the local Berne press, in which they tried to make out that Semashko was not a Social-Democrat and had not represented the Geneva group at the Stuttgart Congress.

The Mensheviks had condemned the Moscow uprising of 1905; they were against anything that was likely to scare away the liberal bourgeoisie. The fact that the bourgeois intelligentsia had swung away from the revolution at the moment of its defeat was accounted for by them as being due not to its class character but to the fact that the Bolsheviks had frightened it by their methods of struggle. The Bolsheviks' contention that expropriation from the expropriators during the height of the revolutionary struggle was a legitimate method of raising funds for revolutionary purposes, was strongly condemned by them. The Bolsheviks, they said, had frightened away the liberal bourgeoisie. The fight against the Bolsheviks played into the hands of the Mensheviks, and in this fight all means were fair.

In a letter dated February 26, 1908, to Plekhanov, P. B. Axelrod set forth his plan of making use of this incident to discredit the Bolsheviks in the eyes of the foreigners. He suggested that a report should be drawn up, translated into German and French, and forwarded to the German Party headquarters (Vorstand), to Kautsky, Adler, the International Socialist Bureau, to London and so forth.

This letter of Axelrod's, published many years later (in 1926), is striking proof of how widely the paths of the Bolsheviks and Mensheviks had diverged already at that time.

In connection with the arrest of N. A. Semashko, Vladimir Ilyich, in his capacity of R.S.D.L.P. representative, sent an official statement to the International Socialist Bureau. He also wrote to Gorky, saying that if he knew Semashko personally from Nizhny days he ought to come out in his defence in the Swiss press. Semashko was soon released.

It was difficult for us, after the revolution, to get used to life in emigration again. Vladimir Ilyich spent all his days in the library, and in the evenings we did not know what to do with ourselves. We had no desire to sit in the cold cheerless room we had rented and longed to be among people. Every evening we went to the cinema or the theatre, although we seldom stayed to the end, and usually left in the middle of a show to wander about the streets, most often around the lake.

At last, in February, the first Geneva issue of *Proletary* (No. 21) came out. Vladimir Ilyich's first article in it was characteristic. He wrote:

"We knew how to work during the long years preceding the revolution. Not for nothing do they say we are as firm as a rock. The Social-Democrats have formed a proletarian party which will not lose heart at the failure of the first armed onslaught, will not lose its head, and will not be carried away by adventures. That party is marching towards socialism, without binding itself or its future with the issue of any particular period of bourgeois revolutions. Precisely for that reason it is also free from the weak sides of bourgeois revolutions. And that proletarian party is marching to victory." (*Works*, Vol. 13, p. 409.)

These words of Vladimir Ilyich's expressed thoughts that dominated the whole of his life at the time. At the moment of defeat he was thinking of the proletariat's sweeping victories. He talked about this during our evening walks along the shore of Lake Geneva.

Adoratsky, who was deported from Russia in 1906 and went back at the beginning of 1908, was still in Geneva when we arrived. He recalls the talks he had with Ilyich concerning the character of the next revolution and that this revolution was bound to place the power in the hands of the proletariat. Adoratsky's reminiscences fully dovetail with the spirit of the article mentioned above and with everything else that Ilyich said at the time. That the defeat of the proletariat was merely a temporary setback Ilyich never for a moment doubted.

Adoratsky also recalls that Vladimir Ilyich made him "write a full account of the events of 1905 and the October days, with special reference to the lessons to be drawn from such questions as the arming of the workers, the organization of fighting squads, the organization of the uprising and the seizure of power."

Vladimir Ilyich held that the experience of the revolution should be studied very carefully, as this experience would come in useful. He got hold of every participant in the recent struggle and had long talks with him. He considered that it was the task of the Russian working class "to safeguard the traditions of the revolutionary struggle, which the intelligentsia and the petty bourgeoisie were hastening to renounce; to develop and strengthen these traditions, inculcate them into the minds of the broad masses of the people, and sustain them for the next inevitable upswing of the democratic movement." (*Works*, Vol. 15, p. 37.)

"The workers themselves," he wrote, "are pursuing this line spontaneously. They lived through the great struggle of October and December too passionately; they saw only too clearly that their conditions could change *only* as a result of this direct revolutionary struggle. They say now, or at least they feel like that mill worker, who in a letter to his trade-union paper declared: 'The bosses have robbed us of our gains, the foremen are bullying us again the way they did before; *but you wait, we'll have another 1905.*'

"Wait, we'll have another 1905. That is how the workers look at it. To the workers that year of struggle was an example of *what to do.* To the intelligentsia and the renegade petty bourgeois it was a 'mad year,' an example of *what not to do.* To the proletariat, the study and critical assimilation of the experience of the revolution means learning to apply the methods of struggle *of that time more effectually,* learning to convert that October strike movement and December armed struggle into something broader, more concentrated and more class-conscious." (*Ibid.*, p. 38.)

Ilyich saw the years ahead as years of preparation for a new onslaught.

The "respite" in the revolutionary struggle had to be used for the purpose of deepening its content still more.

In the first place a line of struggle adapted to the conditions of reaction had to be worked out. It was necessary to plan the Party's switch over to underground activities while enabling it at the same time to make use of legal facilities and keep the Duma forum as a means of speaking to the broad masses of the workers and peasants. Ilyich noticed a tendency among many Bolsheviks, the so-called Otzovists, to simplify the problem; in their anxiety at all cost to preserve the forms of struggle that had proved expedient when the tide of the revolution was at its highest, they were actually quitting the struggle in face of the difficult conditions created by the reaction, withdrawing in face of the difficulties of adapting the work to the new conditions. Ilyich qualified Otzovism as Liquidationism from the Left. An avowed Otzovist was

Alexinsky. When he returned to Geneva relations between him and Ilyich quickly deteriorated. Ilyich had to deal with him on quite a number of questions, and the man's self-opinionated narrow-mindedness repelled him more than ever. The fact that the Duma, even under the reaction, could be used as a medium of contact with the broad masses of the workers and peasants, did not interest Alexinsky in the least. All the same he could not use this rostrum any more since the Second Duma had been dissolved. The self-centred piggishness of the man stood out in glaring relief against the Geneva background, and yet he was still considered a Bolshevik at the time. I remember the following incident. I was walking down the Rue Carouge one day (the "Caruzhka," as we called it, had long been a Russian emigrant centre), when I saw two Bundists standing in the middle of the pavement with a bewildered air. Together with Alexinsky, they constituted a committee elected for editing the minutes of the London Congress (these minutes first came out in Geneva in 1908). After an argument about some formulation, Alexinsky had begun to shout, then had snatched up all the papers from the table and run away. I looked round and saw his short figure turning the corner in the distance. He was striding along swiftly with his head proudly raised and a batch of huge files under his arms. It was not even funny.

It was not a matter of Alexinsky alone, though. Obviously, the former unity among the Bolshevik group was lacking and a split threatened, a split with Bogdanov in the first place.

A volume entitled *Studies in the Philosophy of Marxism* appeared in Russia containing essays by Bogdanov, Lunacharsky, Bazarov, Suvorov, Berman, Yushkevich and Gelfand. These *Studies* were an attempt to revise the materialist philosophy, the Marxist materialist conception of the development of humanity, the conception of the class struggle.

The new philosophy was a loophole for a hodgepodge of mysticism. Decadent moods among the intelligentsia during the years of reaction were favourable to the spread of revisionism. Obviously the line had to be drawn.

Ilyich had always been interested in questions of philosophy. He had studied it closely in exile, was familiar with everything that Marx, Engels and Plekhanov had written in that field. He had studied Hegel, Feuerbach and Kant. While still in exile in Siberia he had had heated discussions with comrades who inclined towards Kant, he followed all that was written on the subject in the *Neue Zeit*, and was on the whole fairly well-grounded in philosophy.

The story of his differences with Bogdanov was told by Ilyich in his letter of February 25 to Gorky. Ilyich had read Bogdanov's book *Fundamentals of the Historical Conception of Nature* in Siberian exile, but Bogdanov's position at the time had been a stage in his transition to his later philosophic views. In 1903, when Ilyich was working with Piekhanov, the latter had often criticized Bogdanov for his philosophic opinions. Bogdanov's book *Empiriomonism* appeared in 1904, and Ilyich told Bogdanov outright that he considered Plekhanov's view right and not his, Bogdanov's.

"In the summer and autumn of 1904 Bogdanov and I came to terms as Bolsheviks," Ilyich wrote to Gorky, "and concluded that tacit bloc tacitly ruling out philosophy as neutral ground, which existed throughout the revolution and enabled us to jointly carry out the tactics of revolutionary Social-Democracy (=Bolshevism), tactics, which, I am profoundly convinced, were the only correct ones to adopt.

"There was little time for philosophy at the height of the revolution. Bogdanov wrote another thing in prison at the beginning of 1906—Part III of his *Empiriomonism*, I believe. He presented me with a copy of it in the summer of 1906 and I sat down to make a careful study of it. After reading it I was furious. It became clearer to me than ever before that he was taking an absolutely wrong non-Marxist line. I wrote him then a 'declaration of love' —a little letter on philosophy running into three note-books. I explained to him there that I was, of course, just an *ordinary Marxist* in philosophy, and that it was his clear, popularly and splendidly written works that had definitely convinced me that he was essentially wrong and Plekhanov right. I showed those note-books to some friends (Lunacharsky among them) and was going to have them published under the title *Notes of an Ordinary Marxist on Philosophy*, but did not do so. I am sorry now that I did not publish them immediately.

"Now the *Studies in the Philosophy of Marxism* has appeared. I have read all the articles except Suvorov's (which I am reading now), and every article made me positively furious. I would rather be drawn and quartered than agree to cooperate with a publication or body which preaches this sort of thing.

"I was tempted to take up again the *Notes of an Ordinary Marxist on Philosophy* and I started to write them, but in the opinions I expressed to Bogdanov in the course of reading the *Studies* I was, of course, blunt and outspoken." (*Works*, Vol. 13, pp. 412-15).

That is how Vladimir Ilyich described the affair to Gorky.

At the time the first number of *Proletary* published abroad made its appearance (February 13, 1908), the relations between Ilyich and Bogdanov were strained to the utmost.

At the end of March Ilyich had been of the opinion that philosophical disputes could and should be detached from political groupings within the Bolshevik section. He believed that such disputes in the section would show better than anything else that Bogdanov's philosophy could not be put on the same level as Bolshevism.

It grew clearer every day, however, that the Bolshevik group would soon fall apart.

During that difficult time Ilyich became more friendly than ever with Innokenty (Dubrovinsky).

Up to 1905 we had known Innokenty only by hearsay. Uncle (Lydia Knipovich), who had met him in exile in Astrakhan, had spoken favourably of him. The Samara comrades (the Krzhizhanovskys) had praised him highly, too, but we had never met him. We had not corresponded with him either. Only once, after the Second Congress of the Party, when the squabble with the Mensheviks flared up, did we receive a letter from him in which he wrote about the importance of preserving Party unity. Afterwards he was a member of the conciliatory Central Committee and was arrested with the other C.C. members at Leonid Andreyev's flat.

In 1905 Ilyich saw Innokenty at work. He saw how utterly devoted Innokenty was to the revolutionary cause, how he undertook the most dangerous and difficult jobs—a fact that accounts for his having been unable to attend a single Party congress; he always got arrested just before the congress was held. Ilyich saw what a resolute fighter Innokenty was—he had taken part in the Moscow uprising, and had been in Kronstadt during the rising there. Innokenty was not a literary man. He spoke at meetings of workers, at the factories, and his speeches inspired the workers in their struggle. No one wrote those speeches down, of course. Ilyich thought a lot of Innokenty for his wholehearted devotion to the cause and was very glad when he arrived in Geneva. They had much in common to draw them together. Both attached tremendous importance to the Party and considered it necessary to wage a determined struggle against the Liquidators, who argued that the illegal Party should be dissolved because it only hindered the work. Both had a very high opinion of Plekhanov, and were glad that he had not sided with the Liquidators. Both held that Plekhanov was right in the philosophic field, that it was essential to dissociate definitely from Bogdanov on philosophic issues, and that the fight on the philosophic front had now assumed particular importance. Ilyich saw that there was no one so quick to understand him as Innokenty was. Innokenty used to have his meals with us, and after dinner they would sit for a long time discussing the plans of work and the situation that had arisen. In the evenings they would meet in the Café Landolt to continue their discussions. Ilyich was so "drunk with philosophy," as he called it, that he infected Innokenty with it. All this tended to draw them still closer together. Ilyich became strongly attached to Inok (Innokenty) at the time.

They were difficult times. In Russia the organizations were going to pieces. The police, with the aid of *agent provocateurs*, had arrested the leading Party workers. Big meetings and conferences became impossible. It was not so easy for people, who had only recently been in the eye of the public, to go underground. In the spring (April-May) Kamenev and Warski (a Polish Social-Democrat and intimate friend of Dzerzhinsky, Tyszka and Rosa Luxemburg) were arrested in the street. A few days later Zinoviev, and then N. A. Rozhkov (a Bolshevik, member of our C.C.) were arrested, too, in the street. The masses withdrew into themselves. They wanted to think things over, try to understand what had happened; agitation of a general kind had palled and no longer satisfied anyone. People readily joined the study-circles, but there was no one to take charge of them. These moods provided a favourable soil for Otzovism. Left without the leadership of the Party organization, acting on their own apart from and independently of the main mass struggle, the fighting squads degenerated, and Innokenty was obliged to handle many a difficult case which had arisen in consequence.

Gorky invited Ilyich to Capri (where Bogdanov, Bazarov and others were living at the time) in order to come to a general agreement, but Ilyich did not want to go—

he had a presentiment that no understanding was possible. In his letter of April 16 to Gorky he wrote:

"My going is useless and harmful. *I cannot* and will not have anything to do with people who have set out to preach a union of scientific socialism and religion. The days of copy-book controversy have passed. There is nothing to argue about, and it's silly to upset one's nerves for nothing." (*Works*, Vol. 34, p. 343.)

Yielding to Gorky's urgent requests, however, Ilyich did go to Capri in May, but he spent only a couple of days there. The visit, of course, brought no conciliation with Bogdanov's philosophical views. Ilyich afterwards related how he had told Bogdanov and Bazarov—"I'm afraid we'll have to separate for two or three years," and how Maria Fyodorovna, Gorky's wife, had laughingly called him to order.

Gorky's place was filled with a crowd of noisy bustling people playing chess or boating. Ilyich did not have very much to say about this trip. He spoke mostly about the beautiful scenery, the sea, and the local wine, but was reticent about the talk on painful subjects that had taken place there.

Ilyich took up the study of philosophy again.

This is how he describes the situation in a letter to Vorovsky which he wrote in the summer of 1908. Vorovsky was a comrade he had worked with on *Vperyod* and during the Revolution of 1905. He lived in Odessa at the time.

"My dear friend,

"Thanks for your letter. Both your 'suspicions' are wrong. I was not fretting, but the situation here is a difficult one. We are heading for a break with Bogdanov. The real reason is that he has taken offence at the sharp criticism of his papers (by no means on the editorial board) on philosophy. Bogdanov now is trying to find points of difference. He has dragged out the boycott theme again together with Alexinsky, who is kicking up the devil of a row, so much so that I have been obliged to break off all relations with him.

"They are building up a split on empiriomonistic-boycottist grounds. Things are quickly coming to a head. A fight at the next conference is unavoidable. A split is highly probable. I will leave the group as soon as the line of 'Left' and true 'boycottism' gains the upper hand. I asked you to come because I thought your speedy arrival would help to keep them quiet. We absolutely count on you attending the conference in August, New Style. You must arrange it in such a way that you can come out. We shall send money for the journey for all the Bolsheviks. Pass the slogan down to the local organizations that mandates should be given only to local and actual Party workers. We ask you earnestly to write for our paper. We can pay now for articles, and will pay regularly. Sincerely yours."

"Do you know a publisher who would undertake to publish what I am now writing on philosophy?" (*Ibid.,* p. 345.)

At that time the Bolsheviks were well provided with funds.

Twenty-three-year-old Nikolai Schmidt, a nephew of Morozov* and owner of a furniture factory in Moscow (Presnya District), went over to the workers in 1905 and became a Bolshevik. He provided money for *Novaya Zhizn* and for the purchase of weapons, and became a close friend of the workers. The police called his factory a "devil's nest." The factory played an important part during the Moscow uprising. Schmidt was arrested and brutally treated in prison. They took him to see what they had done to his factory, showed him the murdered workers, and finally killed him in prison. Before he died he

---

* The Morozovs were a family of millionaires who owned large textile mills in pre-revolutionary Russia.—*Ed.*

managed to let his friends outside know that he was bequeathing his property to the Bolsheviks.

His younger sister, Elizaveta Schmidt, decided to give her share of the inheritance to the Bolsheviks. As she was not yet of age, however, a fictitious marriage had to be arranged so that she could dispose of her money at her own discretion. She went through a form of marriage with Ignatyev, a member of the fighting squad who had managed to keep on a legal footing, and she could now dispose of her legacy, for which the consent of her husband was needed. Actually, Elizaveta was the wife of another Bolshevik, Victor Taratuta. The fictitious marriage enabled her to obtain the legacy immediately and hand the money over to the Bolsheviks. That explains why Ilyich wrote so confidently about *Proletary* now being able to pay for contributions and money being sent to the delegates for the journey.

Victor Taratuta came to Geneva in the summer, and gave a hand in business matters. He conducted the correspondence with other foreign centres in the capacity of secretary of the Foreign Bureau of the Central Committee.

Contacts with Russia were gradually restored and correspondence resumed, but I still had a lot of free time on my hands. It looked as if we would have to stay on abroad for a long time yet, and I decided to tackle French in real earnest so as to be able to take part in the work of the local Social-Democratic Party. I took a course in French arranged in the summer for foreign teachers of French at the Geneva University. I studied the methods of foreign teachers, and learned Swiss efficiency as well as the French language.

Tired out by work on his book on philosophy, Ilyich would take my French grammars and books dealing with the history of the language and the study of its idiom, and read them for hours, lying in bed, until his nerves, unstrung by philosophic disputes, relaxed again.

I also began to study the system of school training in

Geneva. I realized for the first time what a bourgeois school "for the people" was. I saw excellent buildings with lofty windows in which the children of workers were trained to be docile slaves. I saw the school-masters in one and the same classroom boxing the ears of workers' children and never touching the children of the rich. I saw how every child's mind was stifled of independent thought, how all learning was taught by cramming, and how at every step the worship of power and wealth was inculcated in the children. I never imagined that anything of the kind could exist in a democratic country. I shared my impressions with Ilyich, and he would hear me out attentively.

During our first emigration (up to 1905), when Ilyich observed life abroad, it was the labour movement that claimed his chief attention; he was interested most of all in workers' meetings, demonstrations, etc. Up to the time Ilyich left the country in 1901 we had had nothing of the kind in Russia. Now, after the Revolution of 1905, after having experienced the mighty upsurge of the workers' movement in Russia, after the struggle between the parties, the experience of the Duma, and especially after the appearance of the Soviets of Workers' Deputies, he still took an interest in the forms of the labour movement abroad, but was particularly interested in seeing what a bourgeois democratic republic was in real life, what role the masses of the workers played in it, how great their influence in it was, and how great the influence of other parties.

I particularly remember the tone of mingled astonishment and scorn in which Ilyich repeated the words of a Swiss M.P. who, in connection with the arrest of Semashko, had said that their republic had existed for hundreds of years and could not tolerate any encroachment on the rights of property.

"The struggle for a democratic republic" was a point in our programme at the time. Ilyich now visualized the bourgeois democratic republic more vividly than ever as something more subtle than tsarism, but nevertheless an instrument for enslaving the working masses. The whole political structure in a democratic republic tended to imbue all social life with the bourgeois spirit.

I think that if Ilyich had not lived through the Revolution of 1905 and his second period of emigration, he would not have been able to write his book *The State and Revolution*.

The controversy on philosophic questions called for the speedy publication of the book on philosophy which Ilyich had started.* He needed some material which he could not get in Geneva. Besides, the squabbling that was such a marked feature of life among the political emigrants, was a great hindrance to his work. Ilyich therefore decided to go to London to work in the British Museum and finish his book there.

In his absence, a lecture by Lunacharsky was announced in Geneva. Innokenty attended and took part in the debate. Ilyich had sent him the theses, to which Innokenty had made some amendments. He was very nervous before lecture day, and sat at our place all day long with books all round him, making notes. He spoke well, and declared in his own name and Lenin's that Bolshevism had nothing in common with the philosophical trend of Bogdanov (empiriomonism), that he and Lenin advocated dialectic materialism and sided with Plekhanov.

Although the paper was read by Lunacharsky, the principal advocate of empirio-criticism at the meeting was Bogdanov. He made a violent attack on Innokenty. He knew Innokenty well, knew that Innokenty stood for a straightforward open fight on the philosophical front, knew what a strong sense of revolutionary honour he possessed, and he went out of his way to wound that feeling. Referring to the lecturer, he said: "A knight rode forth

---

* *Materialism and Empirio-Criticism, Works,* Vol. 14.—*Ed.*

in a garland of roses, but he was stabbed in the back." Innokenty was not put out by this thrust, of course. He gave Ilyich, on his return from London, a full account of the lecture.

Ilyich was pleased with his trip to London, where he had succeeded in collecting the necessary material and working it up.

On August 24, shortly after Ilyich's return, a plenary meeting of the Central Committee was held. It was decided at the meeting to hasten the convocation of a Party conference. Innokenty went to Russia to organize the conference. By that time Liquidationism among the Mensheviks had gained considerable ground. The Liquidators were out to dissolve the Party and its illegal organization, which in their opinion only led to failures and arrests. They wanted to pursue a course of purely legal activities in the trade unions and various other societies. In view of the prevailing reaction this meant complete rejection of all revolutionary activity, rejection of leadership, the surrender of all positions. On the other hand, the Ultimatumists and Otzovists in the ranks of the Bolshevik group went to the other extreme: they were opposed to working not only in the Duma but also in cultural and educational organizations, clubs, schools, legal trade unions and workers' insurance societies. They withdrew completely from wide activity among the masses, and abandoned the leadership of them.

Innokenty and Ilyich often discussed the necessity of combining Party leadership (for which purpose the illegal Party machinery had to be retained at all costs) with broad work among the masses. Preparations for the Party conference were the order of the day. The elections of delegates to it would have to be utilized for launching an extensive campaign against Liquidationism from the Right and Left.

It was to carry out this plan that Innokenty went to Russia. He took up residence in St. Petersburg, where he organized the work of the C.C. Five, consisting of himself, Meshkovsky (Goldenberg), the Menshevik M. I. Broido, a representative of the Bund and a Lettish representative. He also organized a bureau of which Golubkov, afterwards a delegate of the C.C. Bureau to the Party conference, was a member. Innokenty himself did not attend the conference, which was held in December 1908—about a fortnight before the conference was to take place he was arrested at the Warsaw Railway Station just as he was about to leave the country, and was exiled to the Vologda Gubernia.

The police happened to be very well informed about Innokenty's mission in Russia. There is no doubt that this was the handiwork of Zhitomirsky. Another person drafted in to help with the work of the C.C. Bureau which Innokenty had organized was Lucy, the wife of Serov, deputy to the Second Duma. This Lucy soon turned out to be an *agent provocateur* too.

Ilyich finished his book on philosophy in September, after Innokenty had left for Russia. It was not published until much later—in May 1909.

We had settled down in Geneva for good.

My mother arrived and we set up house on our own in a small apartment. On the surface our life dropped into a smooth rut. Maria Ilyinichna arrived from Russia too; other comrades began to arrive. I remember Skrypnik arriving— he was studying cooperative problems at the time. I went with him as interpreter to the Swiss M.P. Sigg (a terrible opportunist); Skrypnik discussed the cooperative movement with him, but these talks yielded little results, for Sigg and Skrypnik approached the question from different angles. Skrypnik's approach was that of a revolutionary, whereas to Sigg the cooperative movement was nothing but well-organized "shopkeeping."

Zinoviev and Lilina arrived from Russia. A baby boy had been born to them, and they settled down to build a nest. Kamenev and his family arrived. After St. Petersburg, everyone found life dull and nostalgic in this quiet little backwood of Geneva. Everyone longed to move to some big centre. The Mensheviks and Socialist-Revolutionaries had already moved to Paris. Ilyich was in two minds. One advantage of Geneva was that life there was cheaper, and provided better facilities for studying. Then Lyadov and Zhitomirsky arrived from Paris and urged us to go there. Various arguments were used: 1. We would be able to take part in the French movement; 2. Paris was a big city, and we were less likely to be spied on there. The latter argument clinched the matter for Ilyich. Late in the autumn we began preparing to leave for Paris.

In Paris we spent the most trying years of our emigrant life abroad. Ilyich always looked back upon them with a heavy feeling. He would often remark later: "What the devil made us go to Paris!" It was not the devil who drove us there but the need to swing into the struggle for Marxism, the struggle for Leninism and the Party in that centre of the Russian political emigrants such as Paris was during those years of reaction.

PARIS

1909-1910

We left for Paris in the middle of December. A Party conference was to take place there on the 21st jointly with the Mensheviks. Vladimir Ilyich was utterly engrossed in this conference. The situation called for proper appraisal, and the Party line had to be straightened out to ensure that the Party remained a class party, the vanguard, capable even during the hardest times of keeping in close touch with the rank and file, the masses, of helping them to overcome all difficulties and organize themselves for fresh battles. A check had to be given to the Liquidators. Contacts with the organizations in Russia were poor, and the conference could not rely on any appreciable support from that quarter (the only delegates from Russia were two Muscovites—Baturin from the Urals, followed the next day by Third Duma member Poletayev from St. Petersburg). The Otzovists, rallied in a separate group, were worked up to a strong pitch of excitement. Prior to the conference the Mensheviks had convened a congress of their emigrant groups in Basle, at which a number of breakaway resolutions were adopted. The atmosphere was tense.

Ilyich might not have noticed the great stir and fuss we women made in fixing up our new domestic den for all the interest he took in it. We rented an apartment right on the edge of the town in the Rue Bonier, a street running off the Avenue d'Orléans not far from the Parc Montsouris. It was a large airy flat, which even had mirrors over the fireplaces—a fixture in all the new houses. There was my mother's room, Maria Ilyinichna's (she had arrived in Paris by this time), our own room and a living room. This rather luxurious apartment, however, did not fit in with our way of living and with the "furniture" which we had brought from Geneva. The scorn with which the *concierge* eyed our white deal tables, plain chairs and stools! Our living room contained just a couple of chairs and a small table. The place was anything but cosy.

I had my hands full right away with all kinds of domestic cares. Household affairs had been much simpler in Geneva. Here it was a great bother. To get the gas connected I had to go up to town three times before I received the necessary written order. The amount of red-tape in France is unbelievable. To get books from the lending library you must have a householder to stand surety for you, and our landlord, seeing our miserable furniture, hesitated to do so. The housekeeping, too, at the beginning was a terrible bother. I was not much of a housekeeper; Ilyich and Innokenty were of a different mind, but people who were accustomed to seeing a house run properly were extremely critical of my facile approach.

Life in Paris was a hectic affair. Russian political emigrants were flocking to Paris at that time from all over Europe. Ilyich seldom sat at home during that year. Our people used to sit about in the cafés till late at night. Taratuta was a great lover of café life. Gradually the others acquired the habit.

After heated debates at the December Party Conference, we managed nevertheless to chart out a common line. *Sotsial-Demokrat* was to become the organ of the Party as a whole. At the plenary meeting held after the conference a new editorial board was elected, consisting of Lenin, Zinoviev, Kamenev, Martov and Marchlewski. Nine issues of the paper were put out during the year. Martov was in a minority of one on the new editorial board, and he often forgot about his Menshevism. I remember Ilyich once remarking with satisfaction that it was good to work with Martov, as he was an exceedingly gifted journalist. But that was only until Dan arrived.

As to the position within the Bolshevik group, relations with the Otzovists became more strained than ever. The Otzovists became very assertive. By the end of February relations with them were broken off completely.

For about three years prior to this we had been working with Bogdanov and the Bogdanovites hand in hand, and not just working, but fighting side by side. Fighting for a common cause draws people together more than anything. Ilyich, on the other hand, was wonderful at being able to fire people with his ideas, infect them with his enthusiasm, while at the same time bringing out the best in them, taking from them what others had failed to take. Every comrade working with him seemed, as it were, to have a part of Ilyich in him, and that perhaps is why he was so close to them.

The conflict within the group was a nerve-wracking business. I remember Ilyich once coming home after having had words with the Otzovists. He looked awful, and even his tongue seemed to have turned grey. We decided that he was to go to Nice for a week to get away from the hurly-burly and take it easy in the sunshine. He did, and returned fit again.

Studying in Paris was very inconvenient. The Bibliothèque Nationale was a long way off. Vladimir Ilyich usually cycled there, but riding a bicycle in Paris was not what it was in the suburbs of Geneva. It was a great strain. Those cycle rides tired him out. The library closed at lunch time. There was a lot of red-tape in the arrangements for ordering books, and Ilyich swore at the library, and while he was at it, at Paris in general. I wrote to a French professor who had been giving French lessons at the summer courses in Geneva, asking him to recommend some other good libraries. I received an immediate reply, giving me the necessary information. Ilyich made the round of all the libraries mentioned but none of them was suitable. In the end his bicycle was stolen. He used to leave it on the stairs of a house next door to the Bibliothèque Nationale and pay the *concierge* ten centimes a day for it. When he came for the bicycle and found it gone, the *concierge* declared that she had not been hired to look after the bicycle but only to let Ilyich keep it on the stairs.

Riding a bicycle in Paris and the suburbs required great care. Once, on his way to Juvisy, Ilyich was nearly run over by a motor-car. He barely managed to jump clear, and the bicycle was wrecked.

Innokenty arrived after his escape from Solvychegodsk. Zhitomirsky very kindly offered him lodgings in his flat. Innokenty was very ill when he arrived. The chains he had worn going out to his place of exile had chafed his leg so badly that they had left deep wounds on it. Our doctors examined his leg and said a lot of alarming things about it. Ilyich went to consult Professor Dubouché, an excellent French surgeon, who had worked in Odessa during the Revolution of 1905. Ilyich went to see him together with Natasha Gopner, who had known him in Odessa. When Dubouché heard the awful things our doctor comrades had told Innokenty, he laughed, and said: "Your doctor comrades are good revolutionaries, but as doctors they are asses!" Ilyich laughed until he cried, and afterwards often repeated the story. Innokenty nevertheless had to take a long course of medical treatment for his leg.

Ilyich was very glad that Innokenty had arrived. Both were elated at the fact that Plekhanov had begun to dissociate himself from the Liquidators. Plekhanov had already announced his withdrawal from the editorial board of *Golos Sotsial-Demokrata* (*Voice of the Social-Democrat*), where the Liquidators had gained control in December 1908. Afterwards he withdrew his resignation, but his relations with the Liquidators kept growing more strained, and when the first volume of the Menshevik symposium *The Social Movement in Russia at the Beginning of the Twentieth Century* appeared in 1909 containing an article by Potresov denying the leading role of the proletariat in the bourgeois-democratic revolution, Plekhanov on May 26 definitely resigned from the editorial board of *Golos Sotsial-Demokrata*. Both Ilyich and Innokenty still hoped that cooperation with Plekhanov would be possible. The younger generation did not have the same feelings for Plekhanov that the older generation of Marxists had, since in the lives of the latter he had played a decisive role.

Ilyich and Innokenty took the struggle on the philosophic front very much to heart. To them philosophy was a weapon in the struggle, organically bound up with the question of evaluating all phenomena from the point of view of dialectic materialism, with the questions of the practical struggle in all directions. Ilyich wrote to Anna Ilyinichna in Russia, asking her to speed up the publication of his book. An enlarged meeting of the editorial board of *Proletary* was planned, at which it was intended to make a complete break with the Otzovists. "Things look sad over here," Vladimir Ilyich wrote to his sister Anna Ilyinichna on May 26. "There will probably be *Spaltung* (a split); I hope in about a month or six weeks to be able to give you exact information about it." (*Letters to Relatives*, Partizdat Publishing House, 1934, p. 344.)

May saw the appearance of Ilyich's book *Materialism and Empirio-Criticism*. In this book he crossed all the t's and dotted all the i's of the controversy. For Ilyich the questions of philosophy had a direct bearing on those of the struggle against religion. That is why he read a paper on the subject of "Religion and the Workers' Party" at the *Proletary* club in May, and wrote an article "Attitude of the Workers' Party towards Religion" for No. 45 of *Proletary* and another entitled "Classes and the Party in Their Attitude towards Religion and the Church" for No. 6 of *Sotsial-Demokrat*. These articles, especially the one in *Proletary*, have not lost their significance to this day. They lay heavy stress on the class character of religion, and show that in the hands of the bourgeoisie religion is a means of diverting the masses from the class struggle and for drugging their minds. The fight on this front could not be ignored or underestimated, but neither could it be oversimplified; the social roots of religion had to be shown up, and the question dealt with in all its complexity.

Ilyich realized the harmfulness of religion when still a boy of fifteen. He stopped wearing the cross and going to church. In those days this was not such a simple thing as it is now.

Most harmful of all, according to Lenin, was the subtle type of religion, shorn of too patent absurdities and external slavish forms. Such a religion, he believed, was liable to have a stronger influence on people. "God-building," the attempt to create a new religion, a new belief, was to him such a subtle religion.

In June the delegates began to arrive for the enlarged meeting of the *Proletary* editorial board. As a matter of fact this enlarged editorial board was the Bolshevik Centre, which at that time also included the *Vperyod-ists.**

Golubkov (Davydov) arrived from Moscow. He was a Party worker on the Central Committee Bureau in Russia, where he worked under the direction of Innokenty, and had attended the Paris Conference in 1908. Shulyatikov (Donat) and Shurkanov, a Duma deputy (who later turned out to be an *agent provocateur*), arrived as well. The latter did not come to attend the conference, though. Following the French custom, our comrades went to a café with them. Shurkanov attacked the beer, drinking mug after mug. Shulyatikov drank, too, although it was bad for him—he suffered from hereditary alcoholism. The beer brought on a sharp nervous fit, and on leaving the café he suddenly attacked Shurkanov with his walking stick. Innokenty and Golubkov could barely manage him. They brought him to our place. I sat with him while they went to look for a doctor and rent a room for him in the suburbs. They found a room in the Fontenay-aux-Roses, where Semashko and Vladimirsky lived.

I sat with the sick man in our bare living room for about two hours. He tossed about nervously and kept jumping up, seeing visions of his sister, who had been hanged. I tried to calm him, and divert his thoughts, and held his hand. As soon as I let it go he became restless again. I was greatly relieved when Innokenty and Golubkov at last came for him.

The conference of the enlarged editorial board was attended by members of the editorial board—Lenin, Zinoviev, Kamenev and Bogdanov, representatives of the Bolshevik locals Tomsky (St. Petersburg), Shulyatikov (Mos-

---

* *Vperyod*-ists—adherents of the anti-Party *Vperyod* group, consisting of Otzovists, Ultimatumists and God-builders. The group was organized in December 1909 on the initiative of Bogdanov and Alexinsky. It had its own organ of the press under the same name. The group had no support among the workers and actually fell to pieces in 1913. It's final break-up occurred in 1917 after the February Revolution.—*Ed:*

cow) and Nakoryakov (the Urals); members of the Central Committee Innokenty, Rykov, Goldenberg, Taratuta and Marat (Schanzer). Others present were Skrypnik (Shchur), Lyubimov (Sommer, Mark), Poletayev (a deputy of the Third Duma), and Golubkov (Davydov). The conference lasted from July 4 to 13.

Resolutions were adopted on the Otzovists and Ultimatumists, for Party unity, and against the holding of a special Bolshevik congress. The Capri school was a question apart. Bogdanov had seen clearly that the Bolshevik group was bound to break up, and had begun in good time to select and organize his own group. Bogdanov, Alexinsky, Gorky and Lunacharsky had organized a Social-Democratic propagandist high school for workers. Pupils for the school were drafted in Russia by a worker named Vilonov. Staunch reliable men were chosen. After the experiences of the revolution the workers keenly felt the need for theoretical training, and besides, the lull in the struggle now allowed time for that sort of thing. Although they went to Capri to study, it was clear to anyone with experience of Party work that the school at Capri would lay the foundations for a new group. And so the meeting of the enlarged editorial board of *Proletary* condemned the organization of a new group. Bogdanov declared that he would not accept the decisions of the conference, and was expelled from the Bolshevik group. Krasin supported him. The Bolshevik group was breaking up.

Maria Ilyinichna had fallen seriously ill in the spring, before the enlarged meeting of the editorial board. Ilyich was greatly upset. Luckily, a timely operation checked the disease. The operation was made by Dubouché. The convalescence, however, was rather slow. What she needed was to get out of town somewhere in the country.

The conference had told on Ilyich, and he, too, was in need of a holiday somewhere out in the country, away from all the petty strife and squabbles of emigrant life.

Ilyich **began** to scan the French papers for notices of

cheap boarding-houses. He found one such pension in the village of Bombon in the Department of Saône-et-Loire, where they charged only ten francs a day for four persons. We found it very comfortable and spent about a month there.

Ilyich did not work at Bombon, and we tried to avoid talking shop. We went out for walks and cycled almost every day to the Clamart woods fifteen kilometres away. We also observed French ways of life. Among the boarders in our pension were various clerks, a saleswoman from a big store with her husband and daughter, a valet to some count, and others of that class. This petty-bourgeois crowd, steeped in middle-class notions and prejudices, made a very interesting study. On the one hand, they were a downright practical crowd, who took good care that the food was up to standard and everything was made comfortable for them. On the other hand, they all aped the gentry, for whom they were anxious to be taken. Madame Lagourette (the saleswoman) was typical in this respect. She had obviously been through the mill, and liked to tell risqué stories of which she had a large fund, yet at the same time she dreamt of how she would lead her daughter Martha to her first communion, saying how touching it would be, etc., etc. Of course, too large a dose of this mediocrity was rather boring. It was a good thing that we were able to keep aloof from them and live our own way. On the whole, Ilyich had a good holiday at Bombon.

We changed our quarters in the autumn, moving to an apartment in a quiet side-street—Rue Marie Rose—in the same neighbourhood. We had two rooms and a kitchen, with windows overlooking a garden. We made our living room in the kitchen this time, and it was there that all heart-to-heart talks were held. In the autumn Ilyich was all set for work. He laid down a rigorous "regime" as he called it. He got up at eight, went to the Bibliothèque Nationale and came home at two. He did a lot of work at home. I tried my best to keep people away from him. We always had crowds at our place, a regular crush, especially now that with the reaction rampant in Russia and the adverse conditions of work prevailing there the number of Russian political emigrants kept growing swiftly. People arriving from Russia were full of enthusiastic accounts of what was going on there, and then somehow they gradually wilted. The petty worries of emigrant life, the daily cares and struggles to make a living got them down.

In the autumn the pupils of the Capri school invited Ilyich to come over and read them some lectures. Ilyich flatly refused. He explained to them the factional character of the school and invited them to Paris. A factional fight started within the Capri school. At the beginning of November five pupils (there were twelve in all) including Vilonov, the school's organizer, took their stand as definite Leninists and were expelled from the school. Nothing could better have illustrated how right Ilyich had been in pointing out the factional character of the school. The expelled pupils came to Paris. I remember our first meeting with Vilonov. He began to speak about his work in Ekaterinoslav. We had frequently received correspondence from a worker in Ekaterinoslav who had signed himself "Misha Zavodsky." His correspondence had been very interesting and dealt with the most pressing problems of Party and factory life. "Do you happen to know Misha Zavodsky?" I asked Vilonov. "Why, that's me," he answered. This immediately disposed Ilyich in his favour, and he and Misha had a good long chat that day. Later in the day Ilyich wrote to Gorky: "Dear Alexei Maximovich. I have been fully convinced all this time that you and Comrade Misha were the firmest supporters of the new faction, with whom it would be absurd for me to attempt to speak in a friendly way. Today I met Comrade Misha for the first time and had a heart-to-heart talk with him about Party affairs and about yourself, and I see how

Lenin playing chess with A. A. Bogdanov while visiting Maxim Gorky in Capri, Italy, 1908. Gorky is in center, rear

Anna I. Ulyanova-Yelizarova and Maria I. Ulyanova, Lenin's
sisters, 1912

badly mistaken I was. My word, the philosopher Hegel was right: life advances by way of contradictions, and living contradictions are much richer, more varied and pithy than the human mind is at first able to grasp. I regarded the school *only* as the centre of a new faction. This proved to be wrong—not in the sense that it is not the centre of a new faction (the school has been and still is such a centre), but in the sense that this is not complete, it is not the whole truth. Subjectively, certain persons were making such a centre of the school, and objectively that is what it was, but apart from this the school drafted real foremost workers from real working-class life."

And what passionate faith in the strength of the working class is implicit in the end of this letter, in which Ilyich writes about the working class being obliged to forge a party out of heterogeneous and mixed elements. "It will forge it in any case, it will forge a splendid revolutionary Social-Democracy in Russia, forge it sooner than it sometimes seems possible from the point of view of this thrice cursed state of political emigration, forge it sooner than we imagine, judging by certain outward symptoms and separate incidents. Men like Misha are a guarantee of this." (*Works*, Vol. 34, pp. 353, 354.)

Five other pupils of the Capri school arrived together with Misha. Vanya Kazanets (Pankratov) stood out among the others for his activity and forthright views. He was more strongly opposed to the Capri school than the rest. The others were Lyushvin (Pakhom), Kozyrev (Foma), Ustinov (Vasily) and Romanov (Alya Alexinsky). Ilyich read lectures to them with pleasure. They went back to Russia. Misha had tuberculosis, contracted in the convict labour gangs, where he was brutally treated. We fixed him up in Davos. He did not live long there, however. He died on May 1, 1910.

The rest of the Capri students arrived in Paris at the end of December when their studies were over, and Ilyich delivered lectures to them too. He spoke on current topics, on the Stolypin reform* with its "rich peasant" slant, on the leading role of the proletariat and on the Duma group. Kozyrev said that one of the Capri pupils, at the beginning, tried to accuse Ilyich of attaching more importance to the work of the Duma than to agitation among the troops. Ilyich smiled, and went on to talk about the importance of Duma work. Of course, the idea of work among the troops being slackened in the least degree was farthest from his thoughts, but what he did think was that it should be carried on in greater secrecy. This work, he said, should be done and not talked about. As it happened, a letter had recently been received from Toulon from a group of Social-Democrat sailors on the cruiser *Slava*, asking for literature and, more particularly, for someone to be sent to help carry on revolutionary work among the sailors. Ilyich had sent a comrade there who was experienced in secret work. The man had settled in Toulon. Ilyich did not mention a word about this to the students, of course.

Living with Russia for ever in his thoughts, Ilyich at the same time made a careful study of the French labour movement. The French Socialist Party at the time was out-and-out opportunistic. In the spring of 1909, for instance, there was a great strike of the postal employees. The whole city was stirred up over it, but the Party kept aloof. "This is the business of the trade unions and not ours," the leaders said. To us Russians such a division of labour, the withdrawal of the Party from all participation in the economic struggle was simply monstrous.

Ilyich closely followed the election campaign. All

---

* *The Stolypin reform*—an allusion to the agrarian laws issued by the tsarist Minister Stolypin in 1906-1907, under which the peasants were able to leave the village communities and set up in homesteads as owners of their own holdings. The reform was aimed at strengthening the rich peasants who would serve as a mainstay of the autocracy in the countryside.—*Ed.*

political issues were submerged in a morass of personal squabbles and mutual recriminations. As a matter of fact political issues were not discussed at all. Only a few of the meetings were interesting. I saw Jaurès at one of them. His sway over the crowd was tremendous, but I did not like his speech—every word seemed to be so carefully calculated. I liked Vaillant's speech much more. This old Communard was a special favourite with the workers. I remember the figure of a tall worker who had come straight from work with his shirt sleeves rolled up. He listened to Vaillant with rapt attention. "That's the stuff to give 'em, old man!" he exclaimed. Two youngsters, the sons of this worker, gazed at the speaker with the same ecstatic admiration. But not all the meetings had a Jaurès or a Vaillant to address them. The ordinary speakers played down to their audiences, saying one thing to a working-class audience, and another thing to an audience of intellectuals. Attending the French election meetings gave us a striking picture of what elections are in a "democratic republic." To an outside observer, it was simply astonishing. That is why Ilyich was so fond of the revolutionary music-hall singers who ridiculed the election campaign. I remember a song describing how a candidate went canvassing in a village; he drinks with the peasants, tells them a lot of twaddle, and the tipsy peasants vote for him, singing: *"T'as bien dit, mon gars!"* (What you say is true, lad!) Having got the peasants' votes, the candidate begins to draw his fifteen thousand francs salary as deputy, and betrays the interests of the peasants.

A Socialist member of the Chamber of Deputies by the name of Dumas visited us once and told us how he had toured the countryside canvassing for votes, and it made me think of that music-hall song I had heard. One of the most popular music-hall singers was Montegus, the son of a Communard and a great favourite of the *faubourgs* (the working-class districts). His songs were a mixture of petty bourgeois sentimentality and genuine revolutionism.

Ilyich liked to go to the suburban theatres and watch the working-class crowd. I remember once going to see a play with Ilyich describing the brutal treatment of army offenders in Morocco. It was interesting to watch the way the audience, mostly workers, responded to every incident. The show had not yet begun, when suddenly the whole theatre started shouting in one voice: "Hat! Hat!" A lady had come into the theatre in a high fashionable hat with feathers, and the audience was demanding that she take it off. She was obliged to submit. The show started. In the play a soldier is sent off to Morocco, while his mother and sister are left to live alone in poverty. The landlord is willing to let them live rent free if the soldier's sister becomes his mistress. "The swine! The canaille!" cries flew from all over the hall. I do not remember the details, but the play showed the brutal way in which soldiers were treated for refusing to obey their officers. It ended with a revolt and the singing of the *Internationale*. This play had been banned for performance in the centre of the city, but it was performed in the suburbs to cheering audiences. A demonstration about one hundred thousand strong was held in 1910 to protest against the adventure in Morocco. We went to see it. The demonstration was held with the permission of the police. It was headed by Socialist M.P.'s wearing red sashes. The workers were in an aggressive mood and shook their fists as they passed the houses of the wealthy residential districts. Shutters were hastily put up here and there, but the demonstration passed off very peacefully. It was not like a protest demonstration at all.

Ilyich got in touch with Paul Lafargue through Charles Rappoport. Lafargue, the son-in-law of Karl Marx, was a well-tried fighter, of whose opinion Ilyich thought very highly. Paul Lafargue, with his wife Laura—Marx's daughter—lived in Draveil, about 25 kilometres from Paris. They had already retired from active work. One day Ilyich and I cycled down to see them. They received us very kindly. Vladimir Ilyich began to talk to Lafargue about his book on philosophy, while Laura Lafargue took me for a walk in the park. I was quite excited—I was actually walking with the daughter of Karl Marx! I scrutinized her face eagerly, anxious to find traits of resemblance with Marx. In my confusion I babbled incoherently about women taking part in the revolutionary movement, about Russia. She answered me, but somehow the conversation flagged. When we got back Lafargue and Ilyich were discussing philosophy. "He will soon prove the sincerity of his philosophic convictions," Laura said, referring to her husband, and they looked at each other rather strangely. I did not understand the meaning of those words and that glance until I heard of the death of the Lafargues in 1911. They both died as atheists, having committed suicide together because old age had come and they had no strength left for the struggle.

A plenary meeting of the Central Committee was held in 1910. Resolutions in favour of Party unity and against calling a special Bolshevik congress had been adopted previously at the enlarged meeting of the editorial board of *Proletary*. Ilyich and the group of comrades who had rallied round him upheld the same line at the plenary meeting of the Central Committee. It was extremely important, during the period of reaction, to have a Party that boldly spoke the whole truth, albeit from underground. It was a time when the reaction was wrecking the Party, when the Party was being overwhelmed by opportunism, when it was important to keep the banner of the Party flying at all cost. In Russia the Liquidators had a strong legal opportunist centre of their own. The Party was needed in order to stand up against that centre.

The experience of the Capri school had shown how often the factionalism of the workers was relative and peculiar. The thing was to have a united Party centre, around which the Social-Democratic worker masses could rally. The struggle in 1910 was a struggle waged for the very existence of the Party, for exercising influence on the workers through the medium of the Party. Vladimir Ilyich never doubted that within the Party the Bolsheviks would be in the majority, that in the end the Party would follow the Bolshevik path, but it would have to be a Party and not a group. Ilyich took the same line in 1911, when a Party school was being organized near Paris to which *Vperyod*-ists and pro-Party-Mensheviks as well as Bolsheviks were admitted. The same line was pursued at the Prague Party Conference in 1912. Not a group, but a Party pursuing a Bolshevik line. Naturally, there was no room in such a Party for Liquidators, against whom forces were being rallied. Obviously, there could be no room in the Party for people who had made up their minds beforehand that they would not abide by the Party decisions. With some comrades, however, the struggle for the Party assumed the form of conciliation; they lost sight of the aim of unity and relapsed into a man-of-the-street striving to unite all and everyone, no matter what they stood for. Even Innokenty, who fully subscribed to Ilyich's opinion that the main thing was to unite with the pro-Party-Mensheviks, the Plekhanovites, was so keen to preserve the Party that he began himself to incline towards a conciliatory attitude. Ilyich set him right, however.

On the whole the resolutions were passed unanimously. It is absurd to believe that Ilyich was voted down by the conciliators and gave ground. The plenary meeting lasted three weeks. Ilyich believed that the utmost concession should be made on organizational issues without yielding an inch of ground on fundamental issues. The organ of the Bolshevik group—*Proletary*—was closed down. The remaining 500-ruble notes were burnt. The funds of the Bolshevik group were handed over to three trustees—Kautsky, Mehring and Clara Zetkin—to be issued by them only for general Party needs. In the event of a split, the money left over was to be refunded to the Bolsheviks. Kamenev was sent to Vienna where he was to represent the Bolsheviks on the Trotskyist *Pravda*. "Things have been very 'stormy' here recently, but the end of it was an attempt to make peace with the Mensheviks," Vladimir Ilyich wrote to his sister Anna Ilyinichna. "Yes, strange as it may seem, the organ of our group has been closed down and we are trying to make a stronger move towards unity."

Innokenty and Nogin went to Russia to organize a collegium of the Central Committee on the spot. Nogin was a conciliator who was out to unite all and everyone, and his speeches met with a rebuff on the part of the Bolsheviks. Innokenty took a different line, but Russia was not abroad, where every word was common property. His words were interpreted Nogin's way—the non-Bolsheviks saw to that all right. Lindov and V. P. Milyutin were co-opted on the Central Committee. Innokenty was soon arrested. Lindov supported Nogin's point of view and was not very active. Things were in a bad way with a Russian C.C. in 1910.

They were not much better abroad either. Mark (Lyubimov) and Lyova (Vladimirov) were "conciliators in general" and very often took for granted the stories that were retailed about the Bolsheviks being prone to squabbling and disloyalty. Mark, particularly, heard many of these stories, as he was a member of the united Bureau of the Central Committee Abroad,* at which all groups were represented.

---

* *The B.C.C.A.* was set up by the plenary meeting of the C.C. of the R.S.D.L.P. in August 1908 to represent the Party abroad and was under the auspices of the Russian Collegium of the C.C. Soon after the January Plenary Meeting of the C.C. in 1910 a Liquidator majority was formed in the B.C.C.A., which became a rallying point for anti-Party forces. The Liquidator tactics of the B.C.C.A. forced the Bolsheviks to recall their representative from it in May 1911. The B.C.C.A. went into voluntary liquidation in January 1912.—*Ed.*

The *Vperyod*-ists continued to organize. Alexinsky's group once broke into a meeting of the Bolshevik group, who had gathered in a café in Avenue d'Orléans. Alexinsky sat down at the table with an insolent air and demanded to be given the floor. When this was refused he gave a whistle, and the *Vperyod*-ists who had come with him attacked our comrades. Two members of our group, Abram Skovno and Isaac Krivoi, were about to hurl themselves into the fray, but Nikolai Sapozhkov (Kuznetsov), a man of tremendous physical strength, snatched Abram up under one arm and Isaac under the other, while the proprietor of the café, an experienced man in the matter of brawls, turned off the lights. The fight was thus nipped in the bud. But Ilyich roamed the streets of Paris almost all night after that, and when he came home he could not fall asleep.

"So there you are," Ilyich wrote in a letter to Gorky dated April 11, 1910, "the 'anecdotic' is the dominant note in unity at the present moment, it is pushed into the forefront, it evokes jeers, and giggles, etc.

"Living in the midst of this 'anecdotic' situation, amidst these squabbles and scandals, this hell and ugly scum is sickening. To watch it all is sickening too. But one must not be influenced by one's moods. Emigrant life now is a hundred times worse than it was before the revolution. Emigrant life and squabbling are inseparable.

"But the squabbling can be dismissed—nine-tenths of it takes place abroad; squabbling is a minor detail. The thing is that the Party, the Social-Democratic movement are developing and going forward in face of all the hellish difficulties of the present situation. The purging of the Social-Democratic Party of *its* dangerous 'deviations,' Liquidationism and Otzovism *is going ahead* unswervingly, and within the framework of unity it *has moved ahead far more* than before."

Further he writes: "I can imagine how hard it must be to watch this painful growth of the new Social-Democratic movement for those who have not seen or experienced the painful growth at the end of the eighties and the beginning of the nineties. At that time such Social-Democrats could be counted in dozens if not in units, whereas now there are hundreds and thousands of them. Hence the crisis and crises. And Social-Democracy *as a whole* is weathering these crises openly and honestly." (*Works*, Vol 34, pp. 369, 370.)

The squabbling roused in one a desire to get away from it all. Lozovsky, for example, gave himself up entirely to the French trade-union movement. We, too, felt drawn closer to the French movement. We thought this would be made easier by our living in the French Party colony. It was situated on the seashore near the village of Pornic in the famous Vendée. I first went there with my mother. But our life in the colony was not a success. The French there kept to themselves, each family holding aloof from the others, while the attitude to us Russians was not at all friendly, especially on the part of the manageress of the colony. I became rather friendly with a French teacher. There were hardly any workers there. Presently the Kostitsins and Savvushka—*Vperyod*-ists— arrived, and the first thing they did was to have a row with the manageress. We then all decided to move to Pornic and board together. Mother and I rented two small rooms in the house of the customs caretaker. Soon Ilyich arrived. He went sea bathing a lot, cycled a good deal—he loved the sea and the sea breezes—chatted gaily with the Kostitsins on everything under the sun, and enjoyed eating the crabs which our landlord caught for us. He took a great liking to him and his wife. The landlady, a stout loud-voiced laundress, told us about the war she waged with the Catholic priests. She had a boy who went to the secular school, and the youngster being an excellent scholar, a bright and clever boy, the priests kept urging her to send him to the monastery to be educated and promised to pay her an allowance. The laundress indignantly related how she had turned the Catholic priest out of the house. She had not brought a son into the world, she said, in order to make a contemptible Jesuit out of him. Ilyich praised the crabs all the more highly.

Ilyich arrived at Pornic on August 1, and the 26th found him already in Copenhagen where he had gone to attend the meeting of the International Socialist Bureau and the International Congress. Describing the work of the congress Ilyich wrote: "Differences with the revisionists are looming, but the revisionists are still a long way from coming out with any programme of their own. The fight with revisionism has been postponed, but the fight is inevitable." (*Works*, Vol. 16, p. 257.)

The Russian delegation at the congress was a fairly large one—twenty in all, of whom ten were from the Social-Democrats, seven from the Socialist-Revolutionaries and three from the trade unions. The Social-Democratic group was represented by all trends—Lenin, Zinoviev, Kamenev, Plekhanov, Warski, Martov and Martynov; Trotsky, Lunacharsky and Kollontai had deliberative votes. There were numerous guests at the congress. A conference was held during the congress in which Lenin, Plekhanov, Zinoviev, Kamenev and members of the Third Duma Poletayev and I. P. Pokrovsky took part. It was decided at this conference to publish abroad a popular newspaper *Rabochaya Gazeta* (*Workers' Newspaper*). Plekhanov played the diplomat, but nevertheless wrote an article for the first number of the paper, entitled "Our Position."

After the Copenhagen Congress Ilyich went to Stockholm to see his mother and sister Maria Ilyinichna. He was there ten days. This was the last time he was to see his mother. He had a premonition of it, and it was with sad eyes that he watched the departing steamer. When he returned to Russia seven years later—in 1917—she was already dead.

Ilyich related on his return to Paris that he had

managed to have a good talk with Lunacharsky. Ilyich always had a weak spot for Lunacharsky. He was charmed by the man's gifted nature. However, an article by Lunacharsky appeared soon afterwards in *Le Peuple** entitled "Tactical Trends in Our Party," in which all issues were dealt with from the Otzovist standpoint. Ilyich read it and said nothing, but he retorted with an article of his own. Others who attended the congress commented on it too. Trotsky anonymously wrote an article in *Vorwärts* in connection with the congress in which he attacked the Bolsheviks and praised his own Vienna *Pravda*. Congress delegates Plekhanov, Lenin and Warski protested against the publication of this article in *Vorwärts*. Plekhanov was hostile towards Trotsky as far back as 1903, when Trotsky first made his appearance abroad before the Second Congress. They had had an angry argument on the question of a popular newspaper then. At the Copenhagen Congress Plekhanov signed the protest against Trotsky's article without reservation. Trotsky retaliated with a campaign against *Rabochaya Gazeta*, which the Bolsheviks had started to publish, declaring it to be a narrow factional organ. He also addressed a meeting on the subject at the Vienna club. Kamenev, by way of protest, resigned from the editorial board of the Trotskyist *Pravda*, to which he had been sent to work after the January Plenary Meeting. Influenced by Trotsky, the Paris conciliators headed by Mark raised a campaign, too, against *Rabochaya Gazeta*, fearing factionalism. Ilyich simply could not stand this diffuse, unprincipled conciliationism, conciliationism with anyone and everyone, which was tantamount to surrendering one's positions at the height of the struggle.

No. 50 of *Neue Zeit* for 1910 carried an article by Trotsky entitled "Tendencies in the Development of

---

* *Le Peuple*—mouthpiece of the Belgian Social-Democratic Party, headed by Vandervelde.—*Ed.*

Russian Social-Democracy," and No. 51 an article by Martov "Prussian Discussion and Russian Experience." Lenin replied with an article "The Historical Meaning of the Internal Party Struggle in Russia," but the editors of *Neue Zeit*—Kautsky and Wurm, refused to publish it. Marchlewski (Karsky) replied to Trotsky and Martov after consulting Vladimir Ilyich by letter.

In 1911 Comrade Kamo arrived in Paris. He had been arrested in Berlin early in 1908 while carrying a valise with dynamite. He had been kept in a German prison for over a year and a half, where he had feigned madness. In October 1909 he was deported to Russia and kept in prison there for another sixteen months in the Metekh fortress in Tiflis. He was certified to be hopelessly insane and transferred to the Mikhailovsky mental hospital, whence he escaped, then came to France on board a ship as a stowaway, and arrived in Paris to have a talk with Ilyich. He was very distressed to hear that a rupture had occurred between Ilyich and Bogdanov and Krasin. He was greatly attached to all three. Besides, he was unable to grasp the situation that had developed during the years he had spent in prison. Ilyich told him how things stood.

Kamo asked me to buy him some almonds. He sat in our Paris kitchen eating almonds, as if in his native Georgia, and telling us about his arrest in Berlin, about the way he had simulated insanity, about the sparrow he had tamed in prison, etc. Listening to his stories, Ilyich felt extremely sorry for that brave, devoted, childishly naive man with the warm heart, who was so eager to perform deeds of valour, but who now did not know what to turn his hand to. His schemes were fantastic. Ilyich did not argue with him, but tried delicately to bring him back to earth with suggestions about organizing the transportation of literature and so forth. In the end it was decided that Kamo was to go to Belgium, have an operation on his eyes there (he was cross-eyed, and this always gave him away to the police spies), and then make his way south to Russia and the Caucasus. Ilyich examined Kamo's coat and said: "Haven't you got a warm coat? You'll be cold in this, walking about on deck." Ilyich himself always promenaded the deck incessantly when travelling by boat. Hearing that Kamo had no other coat, Ilyich got out the soft grey cloak which his mother had given him as a present in Stockholm and of which he was very fond, and gave it to Kamo. His talk with Ilyich, and the latter's kindness, somewhat soothed Kamo. Afterwards, during the period of Civil War, Kamo was back in his own element again, and displayed miracles of heroism. True, with the passing over to the New Economic Policy, he was off the rails again and kept talking about wanting to go and study, while all the time he dreamt of derring-do. He was killed during Ilyich's last illness. He was cycling downhill in Tiflis and ran into a motor-car.

Inessa Armand arrived in Paris from Brussels in 1910 and immediately became an active member of our Paris group. Together with Semashko and Britman (Kazakov) she was elected to the presidium of the group and started an extensive correspondence with the other groups abroad. She had a family of two little girls and a boy. She was a hot Bolshevik, and before long our whole Paris crowd had gathered round her.

Our Paris group, as a matter of fact, was steadily gaining strength. It was becoming ideologically welded too. The trouble was that many of us were hard up. The workers managed somehow to make a living, but the intellectuals were in dire straits. They could not always become workers. To live at the expense of the political emigrants' benefit fund and feed on credit at the emigrants' restaurant was humiliating in the extreme. I remember several sad cases. One comrade became a furniture polisher, but it was a long time before he learned the job, and he had to change his place of work. He lived in a working-class district, far away from where the other emigrants lived. He got so weak from lack of food that he could not get up from his bed, and he wrote a note, requesting money, and asking that it should not be brought directly to him but left with the *concierge*.

Nikolai Sapozhkov (Kuznetsov) had a hard time too. He and his wife got a job painting pottery, but they earned very little at it. It was painful to see the ravages of starvation gradually showing on the face of this once healthy giant of a man, who never, by the way, complained about his circumstances. There were many such cases. The saddest of all was that of Comrade Prigara, a participant of the Moscow uprising. He lived somewhere in a working-class suburb, and the comrades knew little about him. One day he came to us in a very excitable state and began talking a lot of nonsense without a stop—something about chariots full of corn sheaves with a beautiful girl standing in one of them. Clearly, the man had gone mad. It struck us at once as being the result of starvation. Mother began hastily to prepare something to eat for him. Ilyich, white with emotion, sat with him while I ran off to fetch a psychiatrist, an acquaintance of ours. The doctor came, had a talk with the patient, then said it was a serious case of insanity as a result of starvation. He was not so bad just now, but when it developed into a persecution mania the patient was likely to commit suicide. He would have to be watched. We did not know his address even. Britman went to see him home, but on the way Prigara gave him the slip. Our whole group searched for him, but could not find him. Later his body was found in the Seine with stones tied to his neck and feet. He had committed suicide after all.

Another year or two of life in this atmosphere of squabbling and emigrant tragedy would have meant heading for a breakdown. But the years of reaction were followed by years of upsurge.

The death of L. Tolstoi sparked off demonstrations in Russia. The first issue of *Zvezda* (*The Star*) was published. In Moscow the Bolshevik *Mysl* (*Thought*) began to appear. Ilyich picked up at once. His article "The Beginning of the Demonstrations," written on December 31, 1910, is full of an inexhaustible buoyancy and vigour. It ends with the appeal: "To work, comrades! Begin everywhere to build up your organizations, to set up and strengthen Social-Democratic Party workers' units, develop economic and political agitation. In the first Russian revolution the proletariat taught the masses to fight for liberty; in the second revolution it will lead them to victory!" (*Works*, Vol. 16, p. 328.)

THE YEARS OF NEW REVOLUTIONARY UPSURGE

1911-1914

PARIS

1911-1912

The end of 1910 was marked by a revolutionary upsurge. Between 1911 and 1914 every month, right up to the outbreak of the war in August 1914, saw symptoms of the rising working-class movement. This movement, however, was now developing under conditions different from those that prevailed before 1905. It now had the experience of the 1905 Revolution to go by. The proletariat was not what it had been. It had behind it an experience of strikes, of a number of armed uprisings, of a sweeping mass movement, and years of defeat. That was the crux of the matter. This made itself evident in all ways, and Ilyich, who threw himself into the living vortex with all his ardour, who was always able to decipher the meaning and significance of every phrase uttered by the worker, felt this growth of the proletariat in every fibre of his being. On the other hand, he knew that not only the proletariat but the whole situation was not what it had been. The intelligentsia had changed too. In 1905 the broad sections of the intelligentsia had supported the workers. Not so now. The nature of the struggle which the proletariat was going to wage was now clear. It was going to be a fierce grim struggle, in which the proletariat would overthrow everything that stood in its way. There was to be no more using the proletariat to fight for a meagre constitution, the way the liberal bourgeoisie wanted. The working class would not have it. It would lead now, and not be led. The conditions of the struggle were different too. The tsarist government had the experience of the 1905 Revolution behind it too. It now had the whole workers' organization enmeshed in its network of spies and *agent provocateurs*. They were not the old type of spies who used to hang around the street corners and whom it was possible to evade. There were now the Malinovskys, the Romanovs, the Brendinskys and the Chernomazovs, who held high Party posts. The business of spying and making arrests was no longer done haphazardly. It was carefully planned.

These conditions served as a regular breeding-ground for opportunists of the worst kind. The striving of the Liquidators to dissolve the Party—the vanguard of the working class—was supported by the wide sections of the intelligentsia. The Liquidators sprang up right and left like mushrooms. Every other Cadet tried to take a smack at the illegal Party. It was impossible not to fight them tooth and nail. The struggle was unequal though. The Liquidators had a strong legal centre in Russia and facilities for carrying on broad activities among the masses, whereas the Bolsheviks had to fight for every inch of ground under the most difficult conditions of illegal work which then prevailed.

The year 1911 started with a break-through of the censorship barriers on the one hand, and a vigorous struggle for strengthening the illegal Party organization on the other. The struggle started inside the united organization abroad, set up at the January Plenary Meeting in 1910, but soon broke banks and got out of control.

The publication of *Zvezda* in St. Petersburg and *Mysl* in Moscow delighted Ilyich. The smuggling into Russia of illegal newspapers published abroad was very badly organized, worse than in 1905. The police had *agent provocateurs* everywhere, both in Russia and abroad, and things were always going wrong because of them. That is why Ilyich was so pleased at the publication of legal newspapers and magazines in Russia to which the Bolsheviks could contribute.

The editorial board of *Zvezda* consisted of V. Bonch-Bruyevich (Bolshevik), N. Iordansky (a Plekhanovite at the time), and I. Pokrovsky (a deputy of the Duma who sympathized with the Bolsheviks). The newspaper was considered the mouthpiece of the Duma group. The first issue contained an article by Plekhanov. Vladimir Ilyich was not very pleased with the first issue—he thought it rather dull. But then he was delighted with the first issue of the Moscow *Mysl*.

"*All* ours, and it pleases me immensely," Ilyich wrote to Maxim Gorky about it. (*Works*, Vol. 34, p. 385.) He started writing a lot for *Zvezda* and *Mysl*. Publishing legal newspapers at that time was no easy matter. In February Skvortsov-Stepanov was arrested in Moscow, and Bonch-Bruyevich and Lydia Knipovich in St. Petersburg. The latter worked together with Poletayev and others. In April *Mysl* was closed down, and in June *Zvezda* ceased publication as the organ of the Duma group after putting out twenty-five issues. *Zvezda* did not resume publication until November (No. 26 came out on November 5). By that time it had become definitely Bolshevik. Another Bolshevik paper *Sovremennaya Zhizn* (*Contemporary Life*) began to appear in Baku.

In July talks were held with Savelyev about the publication of a legal journal called *Prosveshchenie* (*Enlighten-

ment) in St. Petersburg. Publication of this magazine was not started until the end of 1911.

Ilyich closely followed these publications and wrote for them.

As regards contact with the workers, an attempt was first made to repeat the Capri experiment with the students of the Bologna school, but nothing came of it.

The Otzovists had organized a school in Bologna, Italy, in November 1910, and the students had invited down various lecturers including Dan, Plekhanov and Lenin. Vladimir Ilyich refused the invitation and asked the pupils to come to Paris. Grown wise with the experience of the Capri school, however, the *Vperyod*-ists began to fence and demanded an official invitation from the Bureau of the Central Committee Abroad, in which the Mensheviks predominated at the time. And when they arrived in Paris together with the students, who were to counteract Lenin's influence, they demanded autonomy. In the long run, no studies were held, and the B.C.C.A. sent the students back to Russia.

In the spring of 1911 we succeeded at last in setting up a Party school of our own near Paris. It was open to workers and pro-Party-Mensheviks and *Vperyod*-ist workers (Otzovists), but the two latter elements were a small minority. The first to arrive at the school were St. Petersburg comrades—two metal-workers Belostotsky (Vladimir) and Georgi (I do not remember his surname), a *Vperyod*-ist and Vera Vasilyeva, a woman worker. They were an advanced intelligent group of people. The first evening they arrived Ilyich invited them to supper in a café, and I remember how earnestly he talked to them all the evening, asking them about St. Petersburg and their work, fishing eagerly for details and symptoms of the upswing of the workers' movement in Russia. Nikolai Semashko fixed them up for the time being in Fontenay-aux-Roses, a suburb of Paris not far from where he lived, and they spent their time reading up while waiting for the others to arrive. Then came two Muscovites, one a tanner named Prisyagin, the other a mill worker whose name I forget. The St. Petersburg comrades soon made friends with Prisyagin. He was no ordinary worker, and had edited the illegal paper of the leather workers *Posadchik*. He wrote well, but was terribly shy. He got so nervous when he spoke that his hands would tremble. Belostotsky chaffed him.

During the Civil War in Russia, Prisyagin was shot by Kolchak. He was then chairman of the Gubernia Trade-Union Council in Barnaul.

Belostotsky poked fun at the Moscow mill worker, too, but in anything but a kindly way. The man was intellectually undeveloped and self-opinionated. He wrote poetry and expressed himself in a high-flown style. I remember once visiting the students in their rooms, and this Muscovite met me, and called the students together, saying: "*Mister* Krupskaya has come." This "Mister Krupskaya" made him the butt of Belostotsky's merciless jests. They were constantly at loggerheads. The end of it was that the St. Petersburgers insisted on his removal from the school. "The fellow does not know a thing, and the nonsense he talks about prostitution!" they said. We tried to argue that the lad would learn better in time, but the St. Petersburgers insisted on his being sent back to Russia. We fixed him up temporarily with a job in Germany.

It was decided to organize the school in the village of Longjumeau, fifteen kilometres from Paris, a locality in which there were no Russians or summer residents. Longjumeau was a straggling French village stretching along the highroad along which carts with farmers' produce for *le ventre de Paris* rolled endlessly all through the night. There was a small tannery there, and all around lay fields and orchards. The arrangements were these: the students rented rooms in the village, while Inessa

Armand rented a house, in which a canteen for the students was organized. We and the Zinovievs moved to Longjumeau too. All the housekeeping was done by Katya Mazanova, the wife of a worker who had been in Siberian exile together with Martov (in Turukhansk) and later had worked illegally in the Urals. Katya was a good housekeeper and a good comrade. Things went swimmingly. Some of the students lodged in Inessa's house. These were Sergo (Orjonikidze), Semyon (Schwartz) and Zakhar (Breslav). Sergo had only recently arrived in Paris. Until then he had lived for a time in Persia, and I remember the long correspondence we had had with him in clarifying the line which Ilyich had taken in regard to the Plekhanovites, the Liquidators and the *Vperyod*-ists. We had always conducted a lively correspondence with the group of Caucasian Bolsheviks. For a long time we had received no reply to our letter concerning the struggle that was going on abroad, and one day the *concierge* came in and said: "There's a man downstairs who doesn't speak a word of French. I suppose he's come to see you." I went down and saw a Caucasian-looking man standing there and smiling. He was Sergo. From that time on he became one of our most intimate comrades. Semyon Schwartz we had known for a long time. He was a particular favourite of my mother's, in whose presence he had once related how, at the age of nineteen, he had first distributed leaflets in a factory by pretending to be drunk. He was a worker from Nikolayev. We had known Breslav too since 1905 in St. Petersburg, where he had worked in the Moskovsky District.

Inessa's house was thus occupied entirely by our own crowd. We lived at the other end of the village and took our meals in the common dining room, where it was pleasant to chat with the students, ask them about all kinds of things, and discuss current topics with them.

We took two rooms in a small two-storey brick house (all the houses in Longjumeau were brick-built) tenanted by a tannery worker, and were able to observe at first-hand the life of a small-factory employee. He went to work early in the morning and came home in the evening dog tired. The house did not have a bit of garden round it. Sometimes a table and chair would be carried outside, and he would sit there for hours, resting his tired head on his toil-worn arms. None of his work-mates ever dropped in. On Sundays he went to the church, which towered across the road. Music had him spellbound. Nuns with lovely operatic voices came to the church to sing. They sang Beethoven, etc., and it was no wonder that it captivated this tanner, whose life was so drab and hard. One could not help comparing him with Prisyagin, who was also a tanner by trade. Prisyagin's life was no easier, but he was an intelligent fighter for the cause, a general favourite among his comrades. The French tanner's wife put on her clogs every morning, took a broom, and went to work in the neighbouring *château* where she was employed as a charwoman. The house was left on the hands of her daughter, no more than a child, who was busy all day in the damp gloomy kitchen and looked after her younger brothers and sisters. No play-mates came to see her either, and her life, too, was just a round of drudgery on weekdays and visits to the church on Sundays. It never entered anyone's mind in the home of the tanner that it would be a good thing to change the existing social system. "Was it not God who created the rich and the poor—and everything was as it should be," the tanner argued.

The French nurse whom the Zinovievs employed for their three-year-old son held similar views, and when her charge tried to get into the *château* park adjoining the village, she told him: "This is not for us, it is for the masters." We were highly amused when the child repeated his nurse's phrase to us with an air of wisdom.

At last all the students were assembled: Andreyev, a Nikolayev worker, who while in exile (in Vologda, I believe) had taken a peculiar course of training (Ilyich jestingly called him the best pupil), Dogadov from Baku (Pavel) and Sema (Semkov); two came from Kiev— Andrei Malinovsky and Chugurin, the latter a Plekhanovite. Andrei Malinovsky afterwards turned out to be an *agent provocateur.* He was not distinguished in any way except that he had a fine voice. He was quite a young man and not very observant. He told me how he had eluded the police spies on his way to Paris, and although his story did not sound very plausible to me at the time, it did not arouse any suspicions in my mind. The other man, Chugurin, considered himself a Plekhanovite. He was a Sormovo worker, who had spent a long time in prison. He was very intelligent, but highly strung. Before long he became a Bolshevik. Another Plekhanovite was Savva (Zevin) who came from Ekaterinoslav. When renting rooms for the students we said that they were Russian country teachers. Savva contracted typhus during his stay in Longjumeau, and the French doctor who attended him afterwards remarked with a smile: "What odd teachers you have." What surprised the French most of all was the fact that our "teachers" went about barefooted (the heat that summer was terrific).

Six months later Zevin took part in the Prague Party Conference and fought for a long time in the ranks of the Bolsheviks until he was killed by the White Guards. He was one of the twenty-six Baku commissars.

Vasily (S. Iskryanistov) arrived from Ivanovo-Voznesensk. He studied well, but behaved rather strangely. He shunned everybody and locked himself up in his room. When he went back to Russia he flatly refused to deliver any messages. He was an able Party worker, and for some years occupied executive posts. He was refused employment at the factories because he was considered "unreliable," and he could not find a job anywhere. He, his wife, and their two children lived for a long time on the meagre earnings of his wife, who was a mill hand. As we learned afterwards, Iskryanistov was unable to keep it up and became an *agent provocateur*. He began to drink heavily. In Longjumeau he did not drink, but when he returned to Russia he committed suicide. He drove his wife and children out of the house one evening, heated up the stove, and shut the flue. In the morning he was found dead. He received a miserable pay for his "job"— about ten rubles. He was a *provocateur* for less than a year.

The Poles were represented by Oleg (Próchniak). Half way through the term Mantsev arrived.

The lessons were held with strict regularity. Vladimir Ilyich read lectures on political economy (thirty lectures), on the agrarian question (ten lectures) and on the theory and practice of socialism (five lectures). The seminars on political economy were conducted by Inessa. Zinoviev and Kamenev lectured on the history of the Party, and Semashko delivered a couple of lectures too. Other lecturers were Ryazanov, who lectured on the history of the West-European labour movement, Charles Rappoport, who lectured on the French movement, Steklov and Finn-Yenotayevsky, who lectured on public law and finance, Lunacharsky—on literature, and Stanislaw Wolski on newspaper printing.

The students studied hard and diligently. In the evenings they sometimes went out into the fields, where they would sing a lot of songs, or lie about under the haystacks, talking about this and that. Ilyich sometimes joined them.

Kamenev did not live in Longjumeau, and he only came there to deliver his lectures. He was writing his book *Two Parties* at the time. He discussed it with Ilyich. I remember them lying in the grass in a ravine outside the village, while Ilyich expounded his view to Kamenev. He wrote a preface to the book.

I often went to Paris, where I saw our comrades on business. This was necessary in order to keep them from coming to Longjumeau. All the students intended going back to Russia to work as soon as the course was over, and their stay in Paris had to be kept as secret as possible. Ilyich was very pleased with the work of the school. In our spare time we went out cycling together as usual, going up the hill and riding out fifteen kilometres to a place where there was an aerodrome. Being further inland, this was much less frequented than the aerodrome at Juvisy. We were often the only spectators, and Ilyich was able to watch the evolutions of the aeroplanes to his heart's content.

In the middle of August we moved back to Paris.

The unity of all the groups, achieved with such difficulty in January 1910, swiftly began to break up. As the practical problems of the work in Russia began to crop up it became ever more clear that cooperation was impossible. The exigencies of practical work tore away the mask of Party principle that some of the Mensheviks wore. The meaning of Trotsky's "loyalty"—under the mask of loyalty he had been trying to unite the Liquidators and *Vperyod*-ists—stood forth in its true colours. As soon as the necessity of better organization for work in Russia made itself felt the artificiality of this unity became at once apparent. Lenin, Zinoviev and Kamenev, already at the end of December 1910, had submitted a proposal to the B.C.C.A. urging that a plenary meeting of the Central Committee should be convened abroad. The reply to this proposal did not come until a month later. The Menshevik B.C.C.A. rejected it. Negotiations on the subject dragged on until the end of May 1911. It was clear that all talk with the B.C.C.A. was a waste of time. The Bolshevik representative on the Bureau, Semashko, resigned, and the Bolsheviks began to convene a conference of members of the Central Committee who were abroad at the time. There were nine such members in June 1911. The Bundist Ionov being ill, the others assembled on June 10, but the Menshevik Gorev and the Bundist

Liber walked out. The rest discussed the most pressing problems, debated the question of convening a Party conference, and decided to set up in Russia an Organizing Committee for convening the Party conference. In August several comrades left for Russia—Breslav (Zakhar) went to St. Petersburg and Moscow, Semyon Schwartz to the Urals and Ekaterinoslav, and Sergo Orjonikidze to the south. Rykov went to Russia too, but was arrested in the street as soon as he arrived. The newspapers reported that many addresses had been found on him. That was not true. A number of Bolsheviks had been arrested at the same time as Rykov, but afterwards we learned that in Leipzig, where Pyatnitsky was then working on the shipping of literature to Russia and where Rykov had called on his way to Russia, there lived a man named Brendinsky, our shipping agent, who turned out to be an *agent provocateur.* He coded the addresses for Rykov. Therefore, although the police found nothing on Rykov when they arrested him, all the addresses became unusable.

A conference was called in Baku. Its members escaped arrest by a mere accident, as one of its most prominent members—Stepan Shaumyan, and a number of other Baku Party workers had been arrested. The conference was transferred to Tiflis and held there. Representatives of five organizations were present. Schwartz, Sergo and others were there. Bolsheviks and Plekhanovites were represented. Chernomazov was there too—he proved later to be an *agent provocateur.* The Russian Organizing Committee, however, had done its work—a Party conference was convened in January 1912.

The Bolshevik group in Paris in 1911 was a fairly strong organization. Among its members were Semashko, Vladimirsky, Antonov (Britman), Kuznetsov (Sapozhkov), the Belenkys (Abram, and later his brother Grisha), Inessa Armand, Staël, Natasha Gopner, Kotlyarenko, Chernov (whose real name I do not remember), Lenin, Zinoviev, Kamenev, Lilina, Taratuta, Mark (Lyubimov) and

Lyova (Vladimirov). There were over forty people all told. On the whole this group had fairly large contacts with Russia and considerable revolutionary experience. The struggle with the Liquidators, Trotskyites and others had steeled it. The group had done a great deal towards helping the work in Russia and carried on a certain amount of work among the French workers and the Russian emigrant public at large. This public in Paris was fairly numerous. At one time Staël and I had tried to do some work among the mass of emigrant women, such as milliners, dressmakers, etc. We organized a number of meetings, but underestimation of this work was a hindrance. At every meeting someone was bound to kick up a row, and raise the question: "What's the idea of a women's meeting, anyway?" And so the thing petered out, although it might have done some good. Ilyich thought it a useful job.

At the end of September Vladimir Ilyich went to Zurich to attend a meeting of the International Socialist Bureau. Molkenburg's letter to the Central Committee of the German Social-Democratic Party was discussed. The letter urged that criticism of the colonial policy in connection with the Morocco incidents should not be stressed too hard owing to the forthcoming elections. Rosa Luxemburg had published that letter. Bebel resented it. Vladimir Ilyich defended Rosa. The opportunist policy of the German Social-Democrats was strikingly revealed already at this meeting.

On this trip Ilyich read a number of papers in Switzerland.

In October the Lafargues committed suicide. Their death was a great shock to Ilyich. We recalled our visit to them. Ilyich said: "If you can't do any more work for the Party you must be able to face the truth and die like the Lafargues." And he wanted to say over their graves that their work had not been in vain, that the cause which they had launched, the cause of Marx, with whom both Paul and Laura Lafargue had been so closely associated, was growing and spreading to distant Asia. At that time the tide of the mass revolutionary movement was rising in China. Vladimir Ilyich wrote the speech and Inessa translated it. I remember with what deep emotion he delivered it at the funeral on behalf of the Russian Social-Democratic Labour Party.

On the eve of the New Year the Bolsheviks called a conference of the Bolshevik groups abroad. The temper of the conference was a cheerful one, although life in foreign exile had frayed people's nerves pretty badly.

EARLY 1912

Preparations for the conference were energetically being made. Vladimir Ilyich got in touch with Nemec, the Czech representative on the International Socialist Bureau, on the question of arranging the conference in Prague. The advantage of holding it in Prague was that there was no Russian colony there, and, besides, Ilyich knew Prague, where he had lived during his first emigration at Modráček's.

Two incidents connected with the Prague Conference stand out in my memory (I was not present at the conference itself). One was the dispute between Savva (Zevin), the Ekaterinoslav delegate and former student of the Longjumeau school, and the Kiev delegate David (Schwartzman) and also, I believe, Sergo. I remember Savva's excited face. I forget exactly what the dispute was about, but Savva was a Plekhanovite. Plekhanov had not come to the conference. "The make-up of your conference," he had written in reply to the invitation, "is so uniform that it would be better, that is, more in the interests of Party unity, if I took no part in it." He worked Savva up accordingly, and the latter moved protest after protest at the conference in the Plekhanov spirit. Later, as we know, Savva became a Bolshevik. The other Plekhanovite, David, sided with the Bolsheviks. The talk, as far as I remember,

227

was about whether Savva should go to the conference or not. In Longjumeau Savva had always been a cheerful steady man, and this excitement of his surprised me.

Another incident. Vladimir Ilyich had already gone to Prague, when Philip (Goloshchokin) and Brendinsky arrived to go together to the Party conference. I had known Brendinsky only by name as a transport man. He lived in Dvinsk. His main duty was to forward the literature on to the organizations, chiefly to Moscow. Philip began to have his doubts about Brendinsky. He had a father and sister living in Dvinsk. Before going abroad Philip went to see his father. Brendinsky lived in rooms at the home of Philip's sister. The old man warned Philip not to trust Brendinsky, who, he said, was behaving strangely and lived above his means, throwing money about. A fortnight before the conference took place Brendinsky was arrested and released within a few days. While he was in custody, however, several people came to see him. These people were arrested. Who they were is unknown. Crossing the frontier together was another suspicious circumstance in Philip's mind. Philip came to our house together with Brendinsky and I was very glad to see them, but Philip squeezed my hand meaningly and looked at me in a way that told me he had something to say to me about Brendinsky. Afterwards, in the passage, he told me about his suspicions. We arranged that he would go away and we would see each other later. Meanwhile I was to have a talk with Brendinsky to sound him out, and we would decide what to do afterwards.

My talk with Brendinsky was a very odd one. We had been receiving information from Pyatnitsky that the literature was being safely transported and delivered in Moscow, but the Muscovites complained that they were not getting anything. I began asking Brendinsky to whom he was sending the literature, to what address. He looked embarrassed and said that he was not forwarding it to the organization as that was dangerous now. He was handing it to workers of his acquaintance. I asked their names. He gave them obviously at random, saying that he did not remember their addresses. The man was clearly lying. I began to question him about his round of the towns, and asked him about one town—Yaroslavl, I believe. He said he could not go there because he had been arrested there once. "On what charge?" I asked him. And he answered: "On a criminal charge." I was taken aback. His answers became more and more confused. I told him a story about the conference being held in Brittany and about Ilyich and Zinoviev having already left for that place. Afterwards I arranged with Philip that he and Grigory were to leave for Prague in the night and leave a note for Brendinsky saying that they had gone to Brittany. That is what they did. After that I called on Burtsev, who, at that time, had specialized in detecting *agent provocateurs*. "He's obviously an *agent provocateur*," I told him. Burtsev heard me out and said: "Send him to me." But there was no need to. A telegram was received from Pyatnitsky, whose suspicions had been aroused, too, saying that Brendinsky should be kept away from the conference. It was followed by a detailed letter. Brendinsky was thus prevented from attending the conference. He never returned to Russia. The tsarist government bought him a villa outside Paris for forty thousand francs.

I was very proud of the fact that I had been responsible for keeping an *agent provocateur* away from the conference. Little did I know that two other *provocateurs* were present at the Prague Conference—Roman Malinovsky and Romanov (Alya Alexinsky), a former Capri student.

The Prague Conference was the first conference with Party workers from Russia which we succeeded in calling after 1908 and at which we were able in a business-like manner to discuss questions relating to the work in Russia and frame a clear line for this work. Resolutions were adopted on the issues of the moment and the tasks of the Party, on the elections to the Fourth Duma, on the

Social-Democratic group in the Duma, on the character and organizational forms of Party work, on the tasks of the Social-Democrats in the anti-famine campaign, on the attitude towards the State Insurance for Workers' bill before the Duma, and on the petition campaign.*

The results of the Prague Conference were a clearly defined Party line on questions of work in Russia, and real leadership of *practical* work.

Therein lay its tremendous significance. A Central Committee was elected at the conference, of which Lenin, Zinoviev, Orjonikidze (Sergo), Schwartzman (David), Goloshchokin (Philip), Spandaryan** and Malinovsky were members. Candidates were nominated to replace arrested members, if any. Soon after the conference Stalin and

---

* *Petition campaign*—a propaganda hullabaloo raised by the Liquidators and Trotsky in support of a "petition" drawn up by the St. Petersburg Liquidators in December 1910. This petition calling for freedom of trade-union organization, assembly, and strikes was to have been presented to the Third Duma on behalf of the workers. The petition campaign had no success among the mass of the working class.—*Ed.*

** Suren Spandaryan was the delegate from Baku. When Ilyich was in Berlin after the conference, Suren, who was there too, introduced him to an old friend of the family—Voski-Jonisyan, who had rendered all kinds of services to the Party. It was planned to carry on a correspondence with Russia through her medium. Suren did not last long. At the end of April he was reported to have been arrested. Suren's father lived in Paris. Ilyich and I went to see him to learn the details of his son's arrest.

Suren's father was a sick destitute old man, who lived all alone. He did not even have any money to pay the rent, and his memory failed him. He would write a letter and forget to write the address. Ilyich was terribly sorry for the old man. The news from Baku was anything but cheering. Suren was having a very bad time in prison, and had no one to look after him. When we got home Ilyich immediately wrote a letter to Voski, asking her to do something for both the Spandaryans. "The old man's plight is a very sad one, a desperate one, I should say," he wrote. "We gave him a small loan, I decided nevertheless to write to you. Probably you have acquaintances and friends of Spandaryan in Baku and Paris. Do you know anyone in Baku who could be written to about Suren and asked to take care of him? If you have

Belostotsky (a student of the Longjumeau school) were co-opted to the C.C. A unity was achieved on the C.C. without which it would have been impossible to carry on the work at such a difficult time. Undoubtedly the conference was a big step forward in that it put a stop to the disintegration of the work in Russia. Although the acrimonious abuse of the Liquidators and Trotsky, and the diplomacy of Plekhanov and the Bundists called for a stern rebuff and exposure, these disputes did not loom large at the conference, where attention was focussed on the work in Russia. The fact that Malinovsky was a member of the C.C., the fact that the meeting with the representatives of the Third Duma, Poletayev and Shurkanov, held in Leipzig after the conference, had also become known to the police (Shurkanov turned out to be an *agent provocateur* too) — all this was no great harm. Undoubtedly, the *agent provocateurs* got Party workers into trouble and weakened the organization, but the police were powerless to stem the rising tide of the working-class movement. On the other hand the framing of a correct policy guided the movement into the right channel and stimulated the steady growth of new forces.

From Leipzig, where he had gone to confer with Poletayev and Shurkanov, Vladimir Ilyich went to Berlin to make arrangements with the "trustees" for refunding the money, which was now needed more than ever for the work. Meanwhile Shotman arrived in Paris to see us. He had been working lately in Finland. The Prague Conference had adopted a resolution strongly condemning the policy of tsarism and the Third Duma towards Finland, and emphasizing the common aims of the workers of Finland and Russia in the struggle against tsarism and the Russian counter-revolutionary bourgeoisie. Our organiza-

---

common acquaintances, it would be extremely important to take care of the father too.... I trust you will do what you can for both Spandaryans and drop me a line about it."—*N.K.*

tion was working illegally in Finland at the time. Work was being carried on among the sailors of the Baltic Fleet, and Shotman had come to report that all was set for the rebellion in Finland. The illegal organization working among the Russian troops was ready for action (they had planned to seize the Sveaborg and Kronstadt forts). Ilyich was still away. When he returned he questioned Shotman closely about the organization, the very existence of which was an interesting fact (Rahja, S. Vorobyov and Kokko were working in it), but he pointed out that such action at the present moment was inadvisable. It was doubtful whether the St. Petersburg workers would support the rebellion at this moment. Things never reached the rebellion stage, however. The organization was discovered, and presently wholesale arrests were made, fifty-two persons being committed for trial on a charge of conspiring to insurrection. The uprising was still a long way off, of course, but the Lena gold-fields shootings in the middle of April and the widespread protest strikes vividly revealed the extent to which the proletariat had developed in recent years, and showed that they had forgotten nothing, that the movement was rising to a higher stage, and that quite new conditions of work were being created.

Ilyich became another man. His nerves were steadier, he became more concentrated, and gave more thought to the tasks that now confronted the Russian working-class movement. His mood was perhaps best expressed in his article on Herzen, written in the beginning of May. There was so much of Ilyich in that article, so much of the Ilyich ardour that gripped one and swept one off one's feet.

"In commemorating Herzen we clearly see the three generations, the three classes that were active in the Russian revolution," he wrote. "At first—nobles and landlords, the Decembrists and Herzen. The circle of these revolutionaries was a narrow one. They were very far removed from the people. But their work was not in vain.

The Decembrists awakened Herzen. Herzen launched revolutionary agitation.

"This agitation was taken up, extended, strengthened, and tempered by the revolutionary commoners, beginning with Chernyshevsky and ending with the heroes of the *Narodnaya Volya*. The circle of fighters widened, their contacts with the people became closer. 'The young helmsmen of the impending storm,' Herzen said of them. But as yet it was not the storm itself.

"The storm is the movement of the masses themselves. The proletariat, the only class that is revolutionary to the end, rose at the head of the masses and for the first time aroused millions of peasants to open revolutionary struggle. The first onslaught in this storm took place in 1905. The next is beginning to develop before our very eyes." (*Works*, Vol. 18, pp. 14-15.)

Only a few months before this Vladimir Ilyich had said with a touch of sadness to Anna Ilyinichna, who had arrived in Paris: "I do not know whether I'll live to see the next rise of the tide," and now he felt the gathering storm, the movement of the masses themselves, with all his being.

When the first number of *Pravda* came out we were preparing to move to Cracow. In many ways Cracow was more convenient than Paris. It was more convenient in regard to the police. The French police cooperated closely with the Russian, whereas the Polish police were hostile to the Russian police, as they were to the Russian Government as a whole. In Cracow we could rest assured that our letters would not be tampered with and that new arrivals would not be spied on. Another advantage was the proximity of the Russian frontier. People could cross it very often. The mail to Russia was not held up. We made hasty preparations for departure. Vladimir Ilyich cheered up and became more than usually solicitous of the comrades who were remaining behind. Our flat was crowded with comers and goers.

I remember Kurnatovsky came too. We had known Kurnatovsky in Siberian exile in Shushenskoye. This was his third term of exile. He had graduated the Zurich University, was a chemical engineer by trade, and worked in a sugar refinery near Minusinsk. On returning to Russia he was arrested again in Tiflis. He spent two years in prison in the Metekh fortress, and was then deported to Yakutsk. On the way there he got mixed up in the "Romanov affair"* and was sentenced in 1904 to twelve years' penal servitude. He was amnestied in 1905, organized the "Chita Republic,"** was seized by Meller-Zakomelsky*** and handed over to General Rennenkampf. He was sentenced to death and taken by train to see the revolutionaries shot. Afterwards, his sentence was commuted to exile for life. Kurnatovsky succeeded in making his escape from Nerchinsk to Japan in 1906. He made his way to Australia, where he had a very tough time. He worked for a while as a lumber-jack, caught a cold, got an inflammation or something in his ear, and seriously impaired his health. He barely managed to make his way to Paris.

His hard life had taken it out of him. On his arrival in the autumn of 1910 Ilyich and I went to see him in the

* *Romanov affair*—an attack on the exiles in Yakutsk Region in 1904 made by order of the authorities because of their having protested against the tyranny and the brutal treatment of the political exiles. On February 18 they locked themselves up in the house of a Yakut by the name of Romanov (hence the name). During the shooting an exile named Matlakhov was killed and three others wounded, and two soldiers were killed. On March 7 the "Romanovites" surrendered. The participants of the protest were tried by the Yakutsk court. All the 55 defendants were sentenced to twelve years' penal servitude each.—*N.K.*
** *The Chita, or Trans-Baikal, Republic*—a period at the end of 1905 in which the power was seized in Chita by the workers of the railway workshops aided by soldiers who had returned from Manchuria after the Russo-Japanese War. A punitive force headed by General Rennenkampf arrived in Chita on January 21 and drowned the movement in its own blood.—*N.K.*
*** *General Meller-Zakomelsky* was notorious for his punitive expeditions to the Baltic region and Siberia in 1905-1906.—*N.K.*

hospital. He suffered from terrible headaches. Ekaterina Okulova visited him with her little daughter Irina, who used to write him notes in her childish scrawl, as he was half deaf. He recovered slightly, then fell in with the conciliators and began to talk their way. After that our friendship cooled off a bit. We were all highly strung. In the autumn of 1911 I dropped in to see him once—he lived in a small room on the Boulevard Montparnasse. I brought him some of our newspapers, told him about the school in Longjumeau, and had a good long talk with him. He agreed unreservedly with the line of the Central Committee. Ilyich was pleased, and began to visit him frequently. Kurnatovsky looked at us packing our things; and watching my mother's cheerful activity, he said: "Some people have got energy." In the autumn of 1912, when we were already in Cracow, Kurnatovsky died.

We gave our flat over to a Pole, a Cracow precentor, who took it furnished. He kept asking Ilyich all kinds of domestic questions: "What's the price of geese? How much is veal?" Ilyich was at a loss. "Geese? Veal?" He had had very little to do with the housekeeping, and I was not helpful either, because we had never eaten goose or veal during our stay in Paris. I could have told the precentor the price of horse-flesh and lettuce, but he was not interested in them.

Our people in Paris felt strongly drawn towards Russia at the time. Inessa, Safarov, and others were preparing to go there. As for us, we decided to move a little nearer to Russia for the time being.

CRACOW

1912-1914

Political-emigrant life in Cracow was unlike that in Paris or Switzerland. As a matter of fact, it was only half emigration. In Cracow the chief interest of our life, practically speaking, was the work in Russia. Contacts with Russia were quickly established. Newspapers arrived from St. Petersburg in two or three days. At that time *Pravda* was being published in Russia. "And in Russia there is a *revolutionary* upsurge, not just any kind of upsurge, but precisely a *revolutionary* one," Vladimir Ilyich wrote to Gorky. "We succeeded after all in setting up a daily *Pravda*—incidentally thanks to the very (January) conference which fools are barking at." (*Works*, Vol. 35, p. 26.) The closest possible contacts were established with *Pravda*. Ilyich wrote articles for *Pravda* almost every day, sent letters there, followed its work, and recruited contributors for it. He urged Gorky to write for it. Zinoviev and Lilina wrote regularly, too, and the latter collected interesting foreign material for it. Such regular collaboration would have been inconceivable from Paris or Switzerland. Correspondence with Russia was also quickly established. The Cracow comrades taught us how to arrange this with the utmost secrecy. The thing was not to have a foreign cancellation-stamp on the letters. Then the Russian police would not take so much notice of them. Peasant women coming to the market-place from Russia would take letters across and post them in Russia for a small fee.

There were about four thousand Polish emigrants from Russia living in Cracow.

On our arrival there we were met by Comrade Bagocki, a Polish political emigrant, who immediately took us under his wing and helped us with all our domestic affairs and secret work. He taught us how to use the *polupaski* (special passes issued to the local inhabitants to enable them to cross and recross the frontier). These *polupaski* cost very little, and the important thing was that they greatly facilitated the work of our illegal comrades who travelled back and forth with them. We sent many comrades across with these *polupaski*. Varvara Yakovleva was one of them. She had escaped from

Siberian exile, where she had contracted tuberculosis, and gone abroad to get medical treatment and see her brother in Germany. She went back through Cracow, as arrangements had to be made for corresponding and work. She got through safely. Only recently did I learn that when crossing the frontier she attracted the attention of the gendarmes by reason of the large suitcase which she carried. They wanted to know whether she was really travelling to the place she had booked her ticket to. The car attendant, however, warned her about it, and offered to buy her a ticket to Warsaw for a tip. She did so, and continued her journey without mishap. Once we sent Stalin across with a *polupaska*. The thing was to answer promptly in Polish *jestem*—"present"—when the name of the pass owner was called out at the frontier. I remember trying to teach our comrades this little trick. Soon we had this illegal crossing of the frontier properly organized. On the Russian side the secret rendezvous were arranged through Krylenko, who lived in Lublin at the time, not far from the frontier. We used the same means for smuggling illegal literature across. The police in Cracow gave us no trouble, and our mail was not tampered with. Generally speaking, they had no contacts with the Russian police. We had this brought home to us on one occasion. Shumkin, a Moscow worker, came to us once for literature, which he wanted to smuggle through in a special waistcoat made for the purpose. He was a great one for secrecy technique, and used to walk about the streets with his cap jammed down over his eyes. We went to a meeting and took him with us. He did not walk with us, though, and kept at some distance behind for safety sake. He looked so patently conspiratorial that he attracted the attention of the Cracow police. A police officer called on us the next day and asked us whether we knew this man and could vouch for him. We said we could. Shumkin nevertheless insisted on taking the literature, although we tried to dissuade him, and smuggled it through safely.

We had arrived in Cracow in the summer and Bagocki advised us to take rooms in the Zweiżyńce suburb. We rented rooms in the same house as the Zinovievs. It was a terribly muddy place, but the Vistula was quite near and offered enjoyable bathing, while about five kilometres away there was the Las Wolski, a vast beautiful forest which Ilyich and I often went to on our bicycles. In the autumn we moved to another part of the town, in a newly built quarter, together with Bagocki and the Zinovievs.

Ilyich liked Cracow very much. It reminded him of Russia. The new surroundings and the absence of emigrant squabbles tended to soothe his nerves. Ilyich closely observed the everyday life of the Cracow population, its workers and its poor. I liked Cracow, too. I had lived in Poland once when I was a child from the age of two to five, and I had still retained some memories of it. I liked the open wooden galleries in the courtyards; they reminded me of those on whose steps I used to play with the Polish and Jewish children; I liked the little gardens—ogródki, where they sold *kwaśne mleko z ziemniakami* (sour milk and potatoes). My mother, too, was reminded of her young days. As for Ilyich, he was glad to have escaped from Paris at last; he cracked merry jokes, and praised both the *kwaśne mleko* and the Polish *mocna starka* (strong liquor).

Lilina knew more Polish than any of us. I knew it poorly; I remembered a little from my childhood days and had studied it a bit in Siberia and Ufa, and now I was obliged to make immediate use of the language along domestic lines. The housekeeping there was much more difficult than in Paris. There was no gas, and we had to light a wood fire in the kitchen. I tried asking for meat without bones at the butcher's, the way they used to sell it in Paris. The butcher looked at me and said: "The Lord God has created cows with bones, so how can I sell you meat without bones?" We had to stock up on loaves for Monday, because on Mondays the bakers would be having their hangover and the bakeries would be closed. One had to learn how to haggle. There were Polish shops and Jewish shops. You could buy everything at the Jewish shops at half the price, but you had to haggle there, pretend to go away, then come back again, and so on. It was a shocking waste of time.

The Jews lived in a separate quarter of the town and dressed differently. In the waiting room at the out-patient hospital, the patients would seriously discuss whether a Jewish child was the same as a Polish child or not, whether it was cursed or not. And a little Jewish boy sat there listening to it all. The power of the Catholic clergy in Cracow was boundless. The priests rendered relief to the victims of fires, to old women and orphans, the convents found employment for domestic servants and defended their rights, and church services were the only recreation the downtrodden ignorant population enjoyed. Feudal customs still survived in Galicia, and the Catholic Church kept them alive. For example, a lady would come to the market to hire a servant. A dozen or so peasant women who had come to hire themselves as servants would stand round the lady kissing her hand. Tips were given everywhere. On receiving a tip, the carpenter or cabby would drop on his knees and bow down to the ground. But then hatred of their masters lived strongly in the masses. The nurse whom the Zinovievs had hired for their little boy went to church every morning, and was wan with fasting and praying. Nevertheless, when I fell into conversation with her once, she told me how bitterly she hated the masters; she had worked for an officer's wife once for three years; like all ladies of the gentry, she slept till eleven o'clock, took her coffee in bed, and made the servant dress her and pull on her stockings. This fanatically religious nurse said that if there was a revolution, she would be the first to go against the gentry with a pitchfork. The poverty and downtrodden state of the peasantry and the poor were apparent at every step, and were much worse even than they were with us in Russia.

In Cracow Vladimir Ilyich met Ganiecki, who had been a delegate of the Social-Democratic Party of Poland and Lithuania to the Second, and then the Stockholm and London congresses of our Party. He had been delegated by the Central Board.* Vladimir Ilyich learned the details about the split among the Polish Social-Democrats from Ganiecki and other Polish comrades. The Central Board had started a campaign against the Warsaw Committee, which was backed by the whole Warsaw organization. The Warsaw Committee had demanded of the Central Board a more principled policy and a definite attitude towards the internal Party affairs of the Russian Social-Democratic Labour Party. The Central Board had dissolved the Warsaw Committee and begun to spread rumours alleging that the latter was connected with the secret police. Vladimir Ilyich sided with the Warsaw Committee (the Rozłamowcy, as they were called). He wrote an article in their defence, and sent a protest to the International Socialist Bureau. The Warsaw Committee was closely connected with the masses of Warsaw and other working-class centres (Lódź, etc.). Vladimir Ilyich did not consider that they were fighting for some alien interests; their cause had a very close bearing on the general struggle within the Party, which was very acute at the moment. Vladimir Ilyich, therefore, could not remain a mere bystander. Russian affairs, nevertheless, claimed his chief attention.

Lenin's close comrades, Safarov and Inessa, went to St. Petersburg from Paris to make arrangements for the election campaign. They travelled with other people's passports. Inessa called on us in Cracow when we were still living in Zwieżyńce. She stayed with us for two days,

---

* The Central Committee of the Polish Social-Democratic Party. —*Ed.*

and we went into all the details with her and supplied her with all the addresses and connections. She and Ilyich discussed the whole plan of work. Inessa was to call on Krylenko on the way—he lived in Lublin, not far from the Galician border—in order to organize through him the crossing of the frontier by comrades bound for Cracow. Inessa and Safarov sent us fairly detailed reports of what was going on in St. Petersburg. They made contacts there and did a good deal towards acquainting the workers with the resolutions of the Prague Conference and the tasks which then confronted the Party. They set up their headquarters in the Narva District. The St. Petersburg Committee was re-established, and subsequently a Northern Regional Bureau was formed, members of which, in addition to Inessa and Safarov, were Shotman and his comrades Rahja and Pravdin. A sharp struggle was going on in St. Petersburg against the Liquidators. The activities of the Northern Regional Bureau prepared the ground for the election of Badayev, a Bolshevik railway worker, as deputy for St. Petersburg. The Liquidators were losing influence among the working-class masses of St. Petersburg; the workers saw that instead of fighting a revolutionary struggle, the Liquidators were taking the way of reform and actually pursuing a liberal-labour policy. An irreconcilable struggle had to be waged against the Liquidators. That is why Vladimir Ilyich was so upset when *Pravda* at first persistently kept striking out of his articles his polemics with the Liquidators. He wrote angry letters to *Pravda*. Only gradually did *Pravda* join in the struggle.

The election of deputies in the worker curia in St. Petersburg was fixed for Sunday, September 16. The police, too, were preparing for the elections. Inessa and Safarov were arrested on the 14th. But the police did not know yet that Stalin, who had escaped from exile, had arrived on the 12th. The elections in the worker curia passed off very successfully. Not a single candidate of the Right went through, and everywhere resolutions of a political character were passed.

Throughout October all attention was focussed on the elections. Traditionally and through ignorance, the working-class masses in a number of districts showed a lack of interest in the elections and did not attach any importance to them. Wide agitation was needed. Nevertheless, the workers everywhere elected Social-Democrats. The elections in all the worker curiae of the big industrial centres resulted in a victory for the Bolsheviks. Party workers were elected who enjoyed great prestige among the working class. Six Bolsheviks and seven Mensheviks were returned to the Duma, but the six Bolshevik deputies represented a million workers, whereas the seven Menshevik deputies represented less than a quarter of a million. What is more, the Bolshevik group at the very outset showed that they were better organized and welded. The opening of the Duma on October 18 was ushered in by workers' demonstrations and strikes. The Bolshevik deputies in the Duma had to work together with the Mensheviks, although internal Party relations between them had become very strained of late.

In January the Prague Conference took place. It played an important part in organizing the Bolshevik forces.

A so-called Party conference, sponsored by Trotsky, was convened in Vienna at the end of August 1912. The avowed object of this conference was to unite all Social-Democratic forces; the fact that the ways of the Liquidators and the Bolsheviks had sharply diverged and that the conduct of the Liquidators was profoundly antagonistic to the Party line was completely ignored. The *Vperyod*-ists were also invited to the conference. As was to be expected, the conference was markedly Liquidationist in character. The Bolsheviks grouped around the Central Committee took no part in it, and even the Menshevik Plekhanovites and Bolshevik conciliators grouped around Plekhanov's journal *Za Partiu* (*For the Party*) (published abroad), refused to attend it. The Poles did not take part in it either, and Alexinsky, who went to the conference on behalf of the *Vperyod* group, exposed the weakness of its composition. The great majority of the conference delegates were people who lived abroad; two Caucasians were delegated to it from the Caucasian Regional Bureau, and on the whole all the delegates were elected by very narrow bodies. The resolutions of the conference were the quintessence of Liquidationism. The slogan of a democratic republic was thrown out of the election platform entirely, and the slogan of "revision of the agrarian legislation of the Third Duma" was substituted for that of "confiscation of the landowners' estates."

Boris Goldman (Gorev), one of the principal speakers, said that the old Party no longer existed, and that the conference was to become an "inaugural" one. Even Alexinsky protested against this. This August unification, or August bloc as it was called, set itself in opposition to the Central Committee and tried to discredit the decisions of the Prague Conference. Under the guise of unity of all Social-Democratic forces, a union against the Bolsheviks was established.

Meanwhile the workers' movement in Russia was growing. This was proved by the elections.

Soon after the elections Muranov visited us. He had crossed the frontier illegally. Ilyich was shocked. "What a scandal there would have been if you had been caught," he told Muranov. "As a deputy of the Duma you enjoy immunity, and there would have been no harm if you had travelled legally. As it is there might have been a scandal." Muranov told us many interesting things about the elections in Kharkov, about his Party work, about how he distributed leaflets through his wife, how she went to the market with them, and so forth. Muranov was so well up in secrecy technique that parliamentary immunity meant nothing to him. Ilyich spoke to him about his future work in the Duma and urged him to go back as soon as possible. Subsequently, the Duma deputies travelled openly.

The first conference with the deputies took place at the end of December and the beginning of January.

The first to arrive was Malinovsky. He was very excited, and I did not like him very much at first. I did not like his eyes, his free and easy manner, which was so obviously put on. The impression wore off the very first time we talked business with him. Then Duma deputies Petrovsky and Badayev arrived. They told us about their first month of work in the Duma, and their work among the masses. I can see Badayev, standing in the doorway, waving his cap about and saying: "The masses have grown up these last few years, you know." Malinovsky gave one the impression of being a very intelligent and influential worker. Badayev and Petrovsky, although somewhat shy, were obviously real dependable proletarians. At this conference a plan of work was drawn up, and the nature of the speeches to be delivered in the Duma and of the work to be carried on among the masses was discussed with special stress on the importance of closely linking this up with the work of the Party, its illegal activity. Badayev was put in charge of *Pravda*. Medvedev, who had come with the Duma deputies, told us about his work in connection with the printing of leaflets. Ilyich was very pleased. "Malinovsky, Petrovsky and Badayev," he wrote to Gorky on January 1, 1913, "send you their warm regards and best wishes." And added: "Cracow headquarters have proved useful. Our moving to Cracow has proved a paying proposition (from the point of view of the cause)." (*Works*, Vol. 35, pp. 42-43.)

In the autumn, owing to the intervention of the Great Powers in Balkan affairs, the war clouds began to gather. The International Socialist Bureau organized protest meetings everywhere. One such meeting was held in Cracow. It was a peculiar one, though, being more like a hate meeting against Russia than one of protest against war.

The International Socialist Bureau held an emergency congress of the Socialist International in Basle on November 11 and 12. The Central Committee of the R.S.D.L.P. was represented at the Basle Congress by Kamenev.

Vladimir Ilyich's indignation was aroused by an article by Kautsky in *Neue Zeit*, an out-and-out opportunist article, arguing that it would be a mistake for the workers to organize armed uprisings or strikes against war. Vladimir Ilyich had written a good deal about the organizing role of strikes during the Revolution of 1905. After Kautsky's article he dealt with the subject more thoroughly still in a number of articles. He attached tremendous importance to strikes, as he did to all forms of direct action by the working class.

The question of war had been discussed at the Stuttgart Congress in 1907, five years before the Basle Congress, and had been decided in the spirit of revolutionary Marxism. Opportunism had made tremendous headway during the intervening five years. Kautsky's article was a striking illustration of this. The Basle Congress, however, unanimously adopted a manifesto against war, and a great anti-war demonstration was organized. The extent to which the Second International was corroded by opportunism was not revealed until 1914.

During the Cracow period—in the years immediately preceding the imperialist war—Vladimir Ilyich devoted a great deal of attention to the national question. Ever since his youth he had hated national oppression in every form. Marx's saying that there could be no greater misfortune for a nation than to subjugate another nation, was near and comprehensible to him.

With war impending, the nationalist temper of the bourgeoisie kept rising, and national hatred was fomented by it in every possible way. The impending war meant oppression of the weak nationalities and the suppression of their independence. But the war—Ilyich had no doubts about that—would inevitably grow into rebellion; the oppressed nationalities would fight for their independence. It was their right. The Internationl Socialist Congress held in London in 1896 had confirmed that right. Underestimation of the right of nations to self-determination in the face of imminent war at such a moment—the end of 1912 and beginning of 1913—roused Vladimir Ilyich's indignation. Instead of rising to the occasion and high-lighting this issue, the August bloc passed a resolution to the effect that cultural-national autonomy,* which had been a controversial issue as far back as 1903 at the Second Congress of the Party and had then been voted down, was allegedly compatible with the clause in the Party programme dealing with the right of nations to self-determination. This meant surrendering the position on the national question, and confining the whole struggle to a fight for culture only, as if it were not clear that culture and the whole political system were bound together by a thousand ties. Ilyich held this to be opportunism carried to extreme lengths. The main dispute on the question of the right of nations to self-determination was carried on with the Poles. They contended—the Rozłamowcy as well as Rosa Luxemburg —that the right of nations to self-determination did not imply the right to secession. Ilyich understood the reason for the Poles' attitude on the question of self-determination. The Polish masses hated tsarism—this could be observed daily in Cracow. One man related what his father had lived through during the Polish insurrection,

---

* The demand for cultural-national autonomy was put forward by the Bund in 1905 and formulated in the following way: all functions connected with questions of culture (public education, etc.) were to be withdrawn from the jurisdiction of the state and the organs of local and regional self-government and vested in the nation as represented by special institutions—local and central—elected by all its members on the basis of universal, equal, direct and secret ballot.—*N.K.*

when he had barely escaped the gallows; another recalled
how the tsarist authorities had desecrated the graves of
his near and dear ones by turning pigs into the cemetery,
etc., etc. Russian tsarism not only oppressed peoples, but
mocked and humiliated them.

With war on the horizon, there was a revival not only
of Black-Hundred nationalism and chauvinism on the part
of the bourgeoisie of the ruling states, but of the hopes of
emancipation of the oppressed nationalities. The Polish
Socialist Party was fired more and more by dreams of
Polish independence. The growing separatism of the
P.S.P.—a party that was petty-bourgeois to the core—
caused alarm among the Polish Social-Democrats. The
latter, therefore, were opposed to secession. Ilyich met
members of the P.S.P., had several talks with one of their
prominent workers Iodko, and heard Daszyński speak. He
was therefore able to appreciate the reasons for the Poles'
alarm. "But one cannot approach the question of the
right of nations to self-determination only from the point
of view of the Poles!" he said.

The controversy on the national question, which had
arisen as far back as the Second Congress of our Party,
flared up sharply on the eve of the war in 1913-1914 and
continued in 1916, during the height of the imperialist
war. Ilyich played a leading role in these disputes; he
went to the heart of the problem, and the controversy
was a useful one. It enabled our Party to find a correct
solution of the national question within the Soviet state,
to establish a Union of Soviet Socialist Republics in which
inequality of nations and restriction of their rights are
unknown. We see in our country the rapid cultural growth
of the nationalities which formerly lived under unbearable
conditions of oppression, we see the ties being drawn ever
closer and closer between the nationalities of the U.S.S.R.,
united on a common basis of socialist construction.

It would be a mistake, however, to think that the national question obscured from Ilyich during the Cracow period

such questions as the peasant question, to which he always attached great importance. During the Cracow period Ilyich wrote over forty articles on the peasant question. He wrote a complete paper for Duma deputy Shagov "The Question of the (General) Agrarian Policy of the Present Government" and a paper for G. I. Petrovsky "On the Question of the Estimates of the Ministry of Agriculture." He started a big work in Cracow based on a study of American sources—"New Data on the Laws of Development of Capitalism in Agriculture." America is famous for the precision and wealth of its statistics. In this work Ilyich set out to refute the view of Himmer (the name of the now notorious Sukhanov, involved in the sabotage case).

"Mr. Himmer," Vladimir Ilyich wrote, "is not a stranger, not a casual author of a casual magazine article, but one of the most prominent economists representing the most democratic, the extreme left, *bourgeois* trend in Russian and European social thought. It is precisely for this reason that Mr. Himmer's views may become—and among the non-proletarian strata of the population have already become to a certain extent—particularly widespread and influential. For these are not his personal views, his individual mistakes; they are the expression of *common* bourgeois views—only particularly democratized, particularly embellished with pseudo-socialist phraseology—which in the conditions of capitalist society are most readily accepted by official professors who follow the beaten track, and by those small farmers who are distinguished among the millions of their kind for their intelligence.

"The theory of the non-capitalist evolution of agriculture in capitalist society advocated by Mr. Himmer is in essence the theory of the vast majority of bourgeois professors, bourgeois democrats, and opportunists in the labour movement throughout the world...." (*Works*, Vol. 22, p. 6.)

Started in Cracow, this booklet on American agriculture was finished in 1915 but not published until 1917.

Eight years later, in 1923, when Ilyich was already ill, he scanned Sukhanov's notes about the revolution and dictated an article on them which was published in *Pravda* under the title of "Our Revolution." In this article he wrote: "And now there can be no doubt that in the main we have been victorious." (*Works*, Vol. 33, p. 439.) Sukhanov had not realized this. Ilyich went on to say: "I have lately been glancing through Sukhanov's *Notes on the Revolution*. What strikes one particularly is the pedantry of all our petty-bourgeois democrats, as of all the heroes of the Second International. Apart from the fact that they are all extraordinarily faint-hearted... what strikes one is their slavish imitation of the past.

"They all call themselves Marxists, but their conception of Marxism is impossibly pedantic. They have completely failed to understand what is decisive in Marxism, namely, its revolutionary dialectics.... Their whole conduct betrays them as cowardly reformists, who are afraid to take the smallest step away from the bourgeoisie, let alone break with it." (*Ibid.*, p. 436.)

Further on Ilyich speaks about the imperialist world war having created conditions "which enabled us to achieve precisely that union of a 'peasant war' with the working-class movement which no less a 'Marxist' than Marx himself had in 1856 suggested as a possible prospect for Prussia?" (*Ibid.*, p. 438.)

Eight more years have passed since then. Ilyich is no longer among the living. Sukhanov still does not see what conditions for the building up of socialism the October Revolution has created, and actively strives to prevent us from tearing up the last roots of capitalism; he does not see how the face of our country has changed. The collective farms and state farms are being consolidated, harvester combines are turning up the virgin soil, the old unploughed bound strips are becoming a thing of the past, labour is being organized on new lines, and the very face of agriculture has changed.

In his numerous articles written during the Cracow period, Ilyich covers a number of very important questions giving a striking picture of the state of peasant and landlord farming, describing the agrarian programme of the different parties, exposing the character of the government measures, and calling attention to a number of momentous problems, such as the settler movement, wage labour in agriculture, child labour, the sale and purchase of land, the concentration of peasant lands, etc. Ilyich had a first-hand knowledge of the countryside and the peasants' needs, and the workers and peasants always felt and saw this.

The rising tide of the revolutionary workers' movement at the end of 1912 and the role which *Pravda* played in that movement were obvious to all, including the *Vperyod*-ists.

Alexinsky on behalf of the Paris group of the *Vperyod*-ists made an offer of cooperation to the *Pravda* editorial board in November 1912. He wrote a number of articles for *Pravda*, and in No. 3 of the *Vperyod*-ists' symposium *Na Temi Dnya* (*Current Topics*), he even urged the necessity of calling off the fight within the Bolshevik ranks and of forming a bloc of all Bolsheviks for the purpose of combatting the Liquidators. The editorial board of *Pravda* included in its list of contributors not only the members of the Paris group to which Alexinsky belonged, but also Bogdanov. Ilyich got to know of this only through the press. It was characteristic of Ilyich that he was able to draw the line between disputes on fundamental issues and squabbling and personal grievances, was able to set the interests of the cause above all else. Plekhanov might heap abuse on his head, but if the cause required unity with him, Ilyich was not one to hold back. Alexinsky might fight his way into a meeting of the group and conduct himself disgracefully, but once he realized that it was necessary to work wholeheartedly in *Pravda*, to fight the Liquidators and stand up for the Party, Ilyich was well pleased. One could cite dozens of examples like this. Ilyich hit back hard when he was attacked, and defended his point of view, but when new problems had to be tackled and it was found possible to cooperate with his opponent, Ilyich was able to approach his opponent of yesterday as a comrade. He did not have to make any special effort to do this. Herein lay Ilyich's tremendous advantage. Very guarded though he always was on matters where principles were involved, he was a great optimist as far as people were concerned. Despite an occasional error of judgement, this optimism of his was, on the whole, very useful to the cause. But where there was no agreement on matters of principle, there was no reconciliation.

In a letter to Gorky Ilyich wrote: "I am wholeheartedly prepared to share your joy at the return of the *Vperyod*-ists *provided* that your supposition about 'Machism, God-building and all that stuff having gone for good,' as you say, is really true. If that is so, if the *Vperyod*-ists have realized this or will realize it now, then I heartily share your joy at their return. But I emphasize the '*if*,' for so far this has been more a wish than a fact.... I do not know whether Bogdanov, Bazarov, Wolski (the semi-anarchist), Lunacharsky and Alexinsky are *capable* of *learning* anything from the painful experiences of 1908-1911. Have they learned that *Marxism* is a much more serious and profound thing than they had believed, that you cannot scoff at it the way Alexinsky did, or slight it as a dead thing the way the others did? *If* they have, then a thousand greetings to them, and all the personal things (inevitably involved in acute struggles) will go by the board in a twinkling. And if they have not realized this, not learned anything, then don't blame me—friendship is one thing, duty is another. Any attempt to throw mud at

Marxism or confuse the policy of the workers' Party will make us fight to the death.

"I am *very* glad that a *way* has been found for a gradual return of the *Vperyod*-ists through *Pravda*, which did not hit them directly. I am very glad. But if this rapprochement is to be *durable*, we must go about it slowly and *cautiously*. That is what I wrote in *Pravda*. The friends who are anxious to bring about a reunion between us and the *Vperyod*-ists should direct their efforts towards this too. A careful *return* of the *Vperyod*-ists (tested by experience), *from* Machism, Otzovism and God-building, may do a devil of a lot of good. The slightest carelessness and 'a relapse to the disease of Machism, Otzovism, etc.,' may make the struggle flare up worse than ever.... I have not read Bogdanov's *Philosophy of Living Experience*; I suppose it is the same old Machism in a new garb...." (*Works*, Vol. 35, pp. 43-44.)

Reading those lines today brings up the whole path of struggle against the *Vperyod*-ists in that period of profound cleavage between 1908 and 1911. Now that that period was over, Ilyich was completely absorbed in Russian work, carried away by the rising tide of the movement. He could speak more calmly now about the *Vperyod*-ists, but he hardly believed, if he believed at all, that Alexinsky was capable of learning by experience or that Bogdanov would cease to be a Machist. Things turned out just as Ilyich had anticipated. Before long a sharp conflict broke out with Bogdanov, who, under cover of supplying a popular explanation of the word "ideology," attempted to smuggle his philosophy into *Pravda*. The end of it was that Bogdanov was crossed out of the list of *Pravda*'s contributors.

During the Cracow period Vladimir Ilyich's mind was already running on socialist construction. Of course, this can only be said conditionally, since the direction which the socialist revolution would take in Russia was not yet clear at the time. Nevertheless, without the Cracow experience of semi-emigration, when the leadership of the political struggle of the Duma group came to grips with all the concrete problems of economic and cultural activity, it would have been difficult, during the period immediately following the October Revolution, to tackle all the essential aspects of Soviet construction in their entirety. The Cracow period was a sort of preparatory class for socialist construction. Naturally, the problems were posed in bare outline, but they were so vital and real that they have lost none of their significance to this day.

Vladimir Ilyich devoted a good deal of attention at that time to questions of culture. At the end of December arrests and searches were made among the pupils of the Witmer *gymnasium* in St. Petersburg. This school, of course, was unlike the others of its type. The head mistress and her husband took an active part in the first Marxist circles formed in the nineties, and rendered various services to the Bolsheviks in 1905-1907. In the Witmer *gymnasium* no one was forbidden to go in for politics, organize circles, etc. It was this *gymnasium* that the police raided. The question of the students' arrests was raised in the Duma, and the Minister for Education, Kasso, gave an explanation. His explanation was rejected as unsatisfactory by a majority of votes.

In an article entitled "Growing Incongruity," written for Nos. 3 and 4 of *Prosveshchenie*, Vladimir Ilyich pointed out in Chapter X that the State Duma passed a vote of no confidence in Kasso, the Minister of Education, in connection with the arrests of the students of the Witmer *gymnasium*. This, he said, was not the only thing the people ought to know. "The people and democracy must know the *motives* for this vote of non-confidence in order to *understand* the reasons of things regarded as abnormal in politics, and to find a *way out* to the normal." (*Works,* Vol. 18, p. 537.) Ilyich goes on to examine the formulas of the various parties for proceeding to the next business. He examined the formula of the Social-Democrats, and writes:

"This formula can hardly be regarded as faultless either. One cannot help wishing it a more popular and comprehensive style of exposition, one cannot help regretting that it does not mention the legitimacy of engaging in politics, etc., etc.

"But our criticism of *all the formulas* is in no way directed against a particular style of editing; it is directed exclusively against the *basic political ideas* of the authors. A democrat should have said the main thing— that circles and talks are *natural and gratifying*. That is the point. Condemnation of political activity, albeit at an 'early age,' is hypocrisy and obscurantism. A democrat should have raised the question *from* that of a 'united cabinet' *to* that of the political regime. A democrat should have pointed out the 'indissoluble connection' first 'with the dominance of the secret police,' secondly, with the dominance of the class of large landowners of the feudal type in the economic life." (*Ibid.*, p. 541.) Thus did Vladimir Ilyich teach how to link up concrete questions of culture with important political issues.

Speaking of culture, Ilyich always emphasized the connection between culture and the general political and economic system. He severely criticized the slogan of cultural-national autonomy, and wrote: "So long as various nations live in a single state they are bound together by millions and billions of threads of an economic, legal and social nature. How can school education be torn away from these links? How can it be 'removed from the jurisdiction' of the state, to use the classic and emphatic absurdity of the Bund formula? If economics unite nations living in a single state, then any attempt to divide them once for all in the sphere of 'culture,' and especially on school questions, is ridiculous and reactionary. On the contrary, we should strive to *unite* the nations in school matters, in order that the school may prepare for what is carried out in life. At present we witness the inequality of nations and dissimilarity in their levels of development; under such conditions the division of school education by nationalities will *actually* make it inevitably *worse* for the more backward nations. In the southern, former slave states of America. Negro children attend separate schools to this day, while in the northern states white and Negro children go to the same schools." (*Works*, Vol. 19, pp. 455-56.) In February 1913 Vladimir Ilyich wrote a special article "Russians and Negroes," in which he tried to show how the ignorance and cultural backwardness of one nationality affects the culture of another, how the cultural backwardness of one class leaves its mark upon the culture of the entire country.

Vladimir Ilyich's remarks about proletarian policy in the field of school education are extremely interesting. Protesting against cultural-national autonomy and the removal of school education "from the jurisdiction" of the state, he wrote: "The interests of democracy, in general, and of the working class, in particular, demand the exact opposite. We must strive to *bring* the children of *all* nationalities *together* in the *same* school of a given locality. The workers of all nationalities must carry out *together* the proletarian policy in school education that was so well expressed by Samoilov, a deputy of the Vladimir workers, on behalf of the R.S.D.L.P. group in the State Duma." (*Works*, Vol. 19, p. 482.) Samoilov had demanded the separation of the church from the state and the school from the church; he had demanded the complete secularization of the schools. Vladimir Ilyich also said that facilities for the children of the national minorities to study their own culture would easily be arranged under a real democracy, when bureaucratism and "Peredonovism"* would be completely ousted from the schools.

---

* *Peredonov*—a *gymnasium* teacher, a character in Sologub's novel *Little Demon* typifying a vulgar sordid bureaucrat and petty tyrant, snob and sneaking cad.—*N.K.*

In the summer of 1913 Ilyich drafted a Duma speech for Badayev "In Reference to the Policy of the Ministry of Education." Badayev delivered it, but was prevented from finishing it by the Chairman of the Duma.

In this draft Ilyich cited statistical data showing the unbelievable cultural backwardness of the country and the paltry sums allocated for education. He showed that the policy of the tsarist government barred nine-tenths of the population from education. In this draft speech Ilyich wrote about "the government's mean, shameless and disgustingly tyrannical treatment of the teachers." He drew a comparison again with America. There were 11 per cent of illiterates in America, and as much as 44 per cent among the Negroes. "But the American Negroes are *more than twice* better off than the Russian peasants in respect of "popular education." (*Works*, Vol. 19, p. 115.) The Negroes in 1900 were more literate than the Russian peasants because half a century before that the American people had utterly defeated the American slaveowners. The Russian people, too, should have overthrown their government in order to make their country a literate, cultured country.

In a speech drafted for Shagov, Ilyich wrote that the only way for Russia to become a literate country was to give the landowners' estates over to the peasants. In an article "What Can Be Done for Education?" written at that period, Ilyich gave a detailed account of library organization in America and urged the necessity of doing the same job in Russia. In June he wrote his article "The Working Class and Neo-Malthusianism," in which he said: "We are fighting better than our fathers did. Our children will fight still better, and *they will win.*

"The working class is not finished, it is growing, maturing, becoming stronger, more united and enlightened, and hardened in the struggle. We are pessimists as regards serfdom, capitalism and small-scale production, but we are ardent optimists as far as the working-class movement and its aims are concerned. We are laying the foundations of the new edifice, and our children will complete it." (*Works*, Vol. 19, p. 206).

Ilyich was interested not only in questions of cultural development, but in a number of other questions of practical importance in socialist construction.

Characteristic of the Cracow period were articles such as "A Great Victory of Technics," in which Vladimir Ilyich compares the role of great inventions under capitalism and under socialism. Under capitalism, inventions go to enrich a handful of millionaires, tending to worsen the general conditions of the workers and increase unemployment. "Under socialism, the application of Ramsey's system would 'emancipate' the toil of millions of mining workers, etc., and would immediately make it possible to reduce the eight-hour working day *for all* workers from eight to, say, seven and even less hours. 'Electrification' of all the factories and railways would make the conditions of work more hygienic, would rid millions of workers of dust, smoke and dirt, and quicken the process of converting the filthy workshops into clean and airy laboratories fit for human beings. Electric lighting and heating in all houses would save millions of 'domestic drudges' from wasting three-quarters of their lives in smelly kitchens.

"Capitalist technics every day are steadily *outgrowing* the social conditions, which condemn the working people to hired drudgery." (*Ibid.*, p. 42.) Eighteen years ago Ilyich was thinking about "electrification," a seven-hour day, kitchen-factories and the emancipation of women.

Ilyich's article "A Young Industry" shows him eighteen years ago pondering the problems and significance of automobile developments under socialism. In his article "Metals in Agriculture," Ilyich described iron as "the iron foundation of a country's culture." "We are all fond of chattering about culture, about the development of productive forces, about raising the level of peasant farming, etc.," he wrote. "But the moment the question is brought up of removing the barrier that prevents millions of impoverished, downtrodden, hungry, barefooted, neglected peasants from being 'raised,' our millionaires' tongues stick in their throats.... Our industrial millionaires prefer to share their medieval privileges with the Purishkeviches and sigh about liberating the 'muterlend' from medieval backwardness...." (*Works,* Vol. 19, pp. 276, 277.)

Of especial interest, however, is Ilyich's article "The Ideas of Advanced Capital." In this article he examined the ideas of an American millionaire businessman by the name of Filene, who tried to impress upon the masses that the employers were bound to become their leaders, because they were learning ever better and better to understand the community of interests between themselves and the masses. Democracy was spreading, the strength of the masses was increasing, the cost of living was rising. Parliamentarism and the daily Press with its vast circulation were keeping the masses increasingly well informed. The ideas of advanced capital were designed to dupe the masses, make them believe that there was no antagonism of interests between labour and capital, for the sake of which they were prepared to go to a certain expense (by giving office employees and skilled workers a share in the profits). Having got to the bottom of these ideas of advanced capital, Ilyich exclaims: "My most esteemed Mr. Filene! Are you quite sure that the workers of the world are the simpletons you take them for?" (*Ibid.*, p. 246.)

Written eighteen years ago, these articles show what problems of construction Ilyich was interested in at the time, problems, which, at the time the Soviet power was established, already proved to be familiar ones; all that had to be done was to put in effect ideas that had already been worked out.

In the autumn of 1912 we made the acquaintance of Nikolai Bukharin. Besides Bagocki, whom we saw pretty often, we received visits at the beginning from Kazimierz

Czapiński, a Pole who worked on the Cracow newspaper *Naprzód* (*Forward*). This Czapiński told us a lot about the famous Cracow health resort Zakopane, about the lovely mountains there and the wonderful scenery, and incidentally mentioned that a Social-Democrat by the name of Orlov lived there, who made fine paintings of the Zakopane mountains. Shortly after this we moved into town from Zwieżyńce, and looking through the window one day we saw a young fellow coming up to the house with a huge canvas bag on his back. It turned out to be Orlov—otherwise Bukharin. He and Ilyich had a fairly long talk together. Bukharin lived in Vienna. We were in close touch with Vienna ever since. The Troyanovskys lived there too. When we asked Bukharin about his paintings he pulled a number of splendid reproductions of German painters out of his bag. We examined them with great interest. Some of the pictures were by Boecklin. Vladimir Ilyich was fond of paintings. I remember how surprised I was when Ilyich once brought home from Vorovsky's a heap of illustrated write-ups of various painters over which he spent hours in the evenings.

We had lots of visitors in Cracow. Comrades going to Russia used to call on their way to make arrangements about their work. Nikolai Yakovlev, the brother of Varvara Nikolayevna, stayed with us a fortnight once. He was on his way to Moscow to start the Bolshevik paper *Nash Put* (*Our Way*). He was a staunch and reliable Bolshevik. Ilyich had long talks with him. Yakovlev got the paper going, but it was soon suppressed and he was arrested. This was not surprising, since the man who had "helped" him start the newspaper was the Duma deputy from Moscow—Malinovsky. The latter told us a great deal about his tours of the Moscow Gubernia and the workers' meetings which he had conducted. I remember him telling us about a meeting at which a policeman had been present; the policeman had listened very attentively and had been very obliging. In relating this incident Malinovsky had laughed. He told us a good deal about himself. One story was about how he came to volunteer for the Russo-Japanese War. During the recruiting a demonstration passed by, he said, and he couldn't resist making a speech from the window. He was arrested for it, and afterwards the colonel of the police spoke to him and said he would leave him to rot in jail or pack him off to a military convict gang unless he volunteered to join up. He had no alternative, Malinovsky said. He also told us that his wife was religious and when she found out that he was an atheist, she all but committed suicide; she suffered from nervous fits ever since. His stories sounded queer. No doubt there was a particle of truth in them. In talking about his past experiences, he held certain things back, omitted important points, and gave things a wrong twist.

Later on I thought perhaps that recruiting story of his was true, and maybe that was the reason why, on returning from the front, he had had an ultimatum put to him—either to become an *agent provocateur* or to go to prison. His wife was really under great emotional stress, and had actually attempted suicide, but the reason may have been something else—perhaps she suspected her husband of being an *agent provocateur*. At any rate, Malinovsky's stories were a mixture of truth and lies, and it was this that made them sound so plausible. It never occurred to anyone at the time that he was a police spy.

Besides Malinovsky, the government took care to have a spy on *Pravda,* too. He was Chernomazov. He lived in Paris, and called on us in Cracow on his way to Russia, where he was going to work on *Pravda.* We took a dislike to him, so much so that I did not offer him to stay the night with us, and he was obliged to walk the streets of Cracow all night. Ilyich attached tremendous importance to *Pravda.* He sent articles there almost every day, carefully counted up what collections had been made for the paper and where, how many articles had been written for it and on what subjects, etc. He was very glad when the paper carried good articles and took the correct line. Once, at the end of 1913, Ilyich asked *Pravda* to send him its lists of subscribers, and my mother and I sat right through the evenings for over a fortnight cutting them up and sorting them out by towns and villages. Nine-tenths of the subscribers were workers. Sometimes you would come across a small town with a large number of subscribers, and on looking it up, you would find that it contained a big factory of which we had known nothing. This chart of *Pravda* distribution turned out to be an interesting one. It was never printed, however. Chernomazov must have thrown it into the wastepaper basket. Ilyich had liked it very much. Worse things than that happened, though. Sometimes—but not often—Ilyich's articles got lost. At other times they were held up and inserted only after some delay. Ilyich used to worry; he wrote angry letters to *Pravda*, but that did not help much.

Not only people going to Russia called on us at Cracow. We had visitors from Russia, too, who came to consult us on various matters. I remember Krylenko arriving shortly after Inessa Armand had visited him. He came to arrange closer contacts. I remember how glad Ilyich was to see him. In the summer of 1913 Gnevich and Dansky came to see us to make arrangements for publishing the journal *Voprosy Strakhovania* (*Insurance Questions*) under the auspices of the Priboy Publishing House. Ilyich attached great importance to the insurance funds campaign, which he believed would strengthen the Party's ties with the masses.

A conference of Central Committee members was held in Cracow in the middle of February 1913, to which our Duma deputies arrived. Stalin arrived too. Ilyich had met Stalin at the Tammerfors Conference and the Stockholm and London congresses. This time Ilyich had long talks with Stalin on the national question. He was glad to have met a man who was seriously interested in that question and well informed on it.

Previously Stalin had spent two months in Vienna, where he had studied the national question. He had become closely acquainted with our comrades there, notably Bukharin and the Troyanovskys. After the conference Ilyich wrote to Gorky about Stalin: "We have a wonderful Georgian here who is writing a long article for *Prosveshchenie*, for which he has collected *all* the Austrian and other materials on the subject." (*Works*, Vol. 35, p. 58.) Ilyich was worried about *Pravda*, and so was Stalin. They discussed ways of putting things right. Troyanovsky, if I am not mistaken, was invited to these talks. They talked about *Prosveshchenie*. Vladimir Ilyich set great hopes on the Troyanovskys. Elena Troyanovskaya (Rozmirovich) was preparing to go to Russia. A scheme for the publication by *Pravda* of a series of pamphlets was discussed. We had big plans.

Just before this we had received a parcel from home containing various fish products—salmon, caviar and cured fillet of sturgeon. I got Mother's cookery book out for the occasion and made a pancake party. Vladimir Ilyich was tickled by the whole affair—he loved to treat his comrades to good and satisfying fare.

On his return to Russia, Stalin was arrested in St. Petersburg on February 22.

Life in Cracow was rather monotonous when there were no visitors. "We are living here as if in Shushenskoye—from one mail to another," I wrote to Ilyich's mother. "Until eleven o'clock we manage somehow to pass the time, waiting for the first post, and after that we have another long wait of six dreary hours." Vladimir Ilyich found the Cracow libraries rather inconvenient to work in. He started going in for ice-skating, but spring soon came. At Easter we went for a walk in the Wolski forest. Springtime in Cracow is lovely and in the woods it was simply glorious. The bushes were a riot of yellow blossoms and the trees were budding. The heady scents of spring were in the air. We had a long walk back to town, and had to cross the whole city on foot to reach home, as the trams were not running on account of the Easter holidays. I felt quite done up. In the winter of 1913 I felt rather low; my heart became tricky, my hands trembled, and I suffered from general debility. Ilyich insisted on my going to see a doctor. The doctor said my case was serious—my nerves and heart were out of order as a result of goitre. He advised the mountains of Zakopane. I came home and related what the doctor had said. The charwoman—a cobbler's wife—waxed indignant. "Fancy saying you have nerves! It's the rich ladies who have nerves and throw crockery at your head!" I did not throw crockery about, but in the state I was in I was hardly fit for work.

We moved out to Poronino, seven kilometres from Zakopane, for the summer together with the Zinovievs and the Bagockis with their famous dog Zhulik. Zakopane was overcrowded and expensive; Poronino was simpler and cheaper. We rented a large summer house together. It stood on high ground, some 2,300 feet above sea-level, in the Tatra foothills. The air was wonderful, although there were frequent mists and drizzling rains. But the view of the mountains during clear spells was beautiful. We would climb to the plateau near our house and feast our eyes on the snow-capped summits of Tatra. Sometimes Ilyich would go to Zakopane with Bagocki, and take long walks in the mountains with the local comrades (Vigelev). Ilyich was terribly fond of hiking. The mountain air did not do me any good, and I steadily got worse. After consulting Bagocki (who was a neurologist), Ilyich insisted on my going to Berne to be operated on by Kocher. We went there in the middle of June, stopping over at Vienna, where we visited the Bukharins. Bukharin's wife Nadezhda was ill in bed, and he was obliged to look after the house and do the cooking. He put sugar into the soup instead of salt while engaged in an animated conversation with Ilyich about matters that Ilyich was interested in and about our comrades who lived in Vienna. We met several of them, and went for a ramble about the city. This large charming city was a very pleasant contrast to Cracow. In Berne we were taken charge of by the Shklovskys, who made quite a fuss of us. They rented a little house with a garden. Ilyich joked with the younger girls and teased Zhenyurka. I was in the hospital for about three weeks; Ilyich sat at my bedside half the day and spent the rest of the day in the libraries. He read a great deal. He even waded through a number of medical books on thyroid complaints and jotted down notes for himself. While I was in the hospital he visited Zurich, Geneva and Lausanne to read lectures on the national question. He also lectured on the same subject in Berne. After I came out of the hospital a conference of Party groups abroad took place in Berne, at which the state of affairs in the Party was discussed. I was to have spent another fortnight after the operation convalescing in the mountains of Beatenberg on Kocher's advice, but we got word from Poronino that a lot of urgent business was waiting to be attended to, and a telegram was received from Zinoviev, which induced us to go back.

We stopped at Munich on the way. Boris Knipovich, a nephew of Lydia Knipovich, lived there. I had known him since he was a child, when I used to tell him fairy-tales. Four-year-old blue-eyed little Boris used to climb up on my knees, put his arms round my neck, and demand, "Krupa, tell me the story about the little tin soldier." In 1905-1907 Boris was an active organizer of Social-Democratic study-circles in the *gymnasiums*. In the summer of 1907, after the London Congress, Ilyich had lived with the Knipoviches in the country in Finland, at Styrsudd. Boris was a *gymnasium* student at the time, but already took an interest in Marxism, and lent an eager ear to Ilyich, knowing in what high esteem his Aunt Lydia held Ilyich.

Boris was arrested in 1911 and later deported abroad, where he studied at the University of Munich. His first book *The Differentiation Among the Russian Peasantry* was published in 1912. He sent a copy of it to Ilyich. Ilyich's letter to Boris shows a keen interest in the young author "I read your book with great pleasure," he wrote, "and I was very glad to see that you were tackling something serious and important. A work of this kind should enable you to test, deepen and strengthen your Marxian convictions." Ilyich then went on to make several very tactful remarks and suggestions as to method.

Rereading this letter reminds me of Ilyich's attitude towards inexperienced writers. He always went to the heart of the matter, and considered in what way he could help to improve it. He did this very tactfully, however, so that the writer was hardly aware he was being corrected. Ilyich was really wonderful at helping people in their work. For instance, wanting to ask someone to write an article and not being sure whether that person would do it properly, he would first draw him out on the subject, unfold his own ideas, and get the person interested. After sounding him out, Ilyich would suggest: "What about your writing an article on the subject?" And the writer would not even have noticed how helpful this preliminary discussion with Ilyich had been to him, and he would use the latter's own turns of phrase and expressions without being aware of it.

We had planned to stay in Munich for a couple of days to see what changes had taken place there since we lived there in 1902, but as we were in a great hurry to get back we only stayed a few hours and caught the next train out. Boris and his wife had come to meet us, and we spent the time together in the Hof Bräu restaurant, which was famous for its beer. The initials "H.B." inscribed on the walls and the beer mugs read N. V. in Russian, and I laughingly deciphered them as *Narodnaya Volya*. We spent the whole evening with Boris in that *Narodnaya Volya* place. Ilyich praised the beer with the air of a connoisseur. He and Boris discussed class differentiation

among the peasantry, and we all talked about Uncle—
Lydia Knipovich—who was also seriously ill with the
same thyroid trouble as I had. Ilyich dashed a letter off
to her there and then, urging her to go abroad and be
operated on by Kocher. We arrived in Poronino at the
beginning of August—the 6th, if I am not mistaken—to
find it still drizzling there. Lev Kamenev gave us the
latest news about Russia.

A conference of members of the Central Committee had
been arranged for the 9th. *Pravda* had been suppressed
Rabochaya Pravda (*Workers' Truth*) started coming out,
but almost every number was confiscated. The strike wave
was mounting. Strikes had broken out in St. Petersburg,
Riga, Nikolayev and Baku.

Kamenev moved into the rooms above ours, and in the
evenings after dinner he and Ilyich sat on for a long time
in our big kitchen discussing the news from Russia.

Preparations were going forward for the Party conference which became known as the "Summer Conference."
It was held in Poronino between September 22 and October 1. All the Duma deputies arrived except Samoilov;
others attending were two Moscow electors—Novozhilov
and Balashov, Rozmirovich from Kiev, Sima Deryabina
from the Urals, Shotman from St. Petersburg and others.
Prosveshchenie was represented by Troyanovsky, and the
Poles by Ganiecki and Domski and two other Rozłamowcy (the influence of the Rozłamowcy at that time extended to the four largest industrial centres of Warsaw,
Lódź, Dabrowa and Kalisz).

Of the Duma deputies present I remember only Malinovsky. The conference discussed the affairs of *Rabochaya
Pravda*, of the Moscow newspaper, of *Prosveshchenie*,
the Priboy Publishing House, and the tactics to be pursued at the forthcoming cooperative and shop-assistants'
congresses and other current tasks.

Inessa Armand arrived at the conference when it was
half through. Arrested in September 1912, she had been

kept in prison under an assumed name in conditions that had seriously undermined her health (she developed symptoms of tuberculosis). She had lost none of the old energy, however, and threw herself into Party work with all her usual zest. All our people in Cracow were delighted to see her.

In all there were twenty-two persons present at the conference. It was decided to raise the question of convening a Party congress. The Fifth London Congress had been held six years ago, and since that time many changes had taken place. The growth of the working-class movement made a congress imperative. The questions before the conference were the strike movement, preparation for a general political strike, the tasks of agitation, the publication of a number of popular pamphlets, and the inadmissibility of watering down the slogans calling for a democratic republic, the confiscation of the land-owners' estates and the eight-hour day, in the course of agitation work. The questions of conducting activities in the legal societies and Social-Democratic work in the Duma were also discussed. Of special significance were the decisions on the need for securing equal rights for the Bolshevik and Menshevik groups in the Social-Democratic group of the Duma, on the inadmissibility of the Bolsheviks being voted down in the group by a majority of one on the part of the "Seven,"* who represented the views of only a negligible minority of the workers. Another im-

---

* The Social-Democratic group in the Fourth Duma consisted of thirteen members (not counting one representative of the Polish Socialist Party Jagiello, who had no vote), of whom six were Bolsheviks and seven Mensheviks. The Bolshevik group consisted exclusively of workers and represented the broad masses of the Russian proletariat, whereas the "Seven" represented mostly the interests of the petty bourgeoisie and the radical intelligentsia. The Mensheviks forced an advantage for themselves out of this one-man majority by putting through their own resolutions on all fundamental issues in the name of the whole group. The "Six" demanded equal rights in making decisions on all

portant resolution adopted was that on the national question which wholly reflected the views of Vladimir Ilyich. I remember the arguments on that question in our kitchen, the heat with which it was discussed.

Malinovsky worried more than ever. He got drunk night after night, became maudlin and complained that he was being treated with suspicion. I remember Balashov and Novozhilov, the Moscow electors, resenting his behaviour. They sensed a false note and play-acting in the way he carried on.

We stayed in Poronino for about another fortnight after the conference. We took long walks, went once to Czarny Staw, a mountain lake of remarkable beauty, and other places in the mountains.

That autumn all of us—our entire Cracow group—were drawn very close to Inessa. She was just brimming with vitality and exuberant good spirits. We had known her in Paris, but the colony there had been a large one, whereas in Cracow we lived together in a small close and friendly circle. Inessa rented a room in the same house where Kamenev lived. My mother was greatly attached to her. Inessa often came to have a chat with her, or sit and smoke. Things seemed cosier and more cheerful when Inessa was there.

We were completely absorbed by Party cares and affairs. Our home life was more like that of students, and we were very glad to have Inessa. During this visit of hers, she told me a great deal about her life and her children, and showed me their letters. There was a delightful warmth about her stories. Ilyich and I went for long walks with Inessa. Kamenev and Zinoviev called us the "gadding party." We used to go for long walks outside the town, to the meadows—called *błoń* in Polish. Inessa in

---

Duma questions. The Mensheviks refusing, the "Six" withdrew from the united S.-D. group and formed a Russian Social-Democratic group of their own.—*N.K.*

fact took the pseudonym of Blonina. She loved music, and persuaded us all to attend the Beethoven concerts. She was a good musician herself and played many Beethoven pieces very well. A particular favourite of Ilyich's was the *Sonate pathétique*, and he always asked her to play it. He loved music. Later, in Soviet times, he would go to Tsyurupa's to hear that sonata played by some famous musician. We talked a lot about literature—fiction. "What we are really starved for here is fiction," I wrote home to Ilyich's mother. "Vladimir knows Nadson and Nekrasov almost by heart, and has read *Anna Karenina*— the only odd volume we have—about a hundred times. We left our fiction library in Paris (an insignificant part of what we had in St. Petersburg), and here no Russian books are obtainable. We sometimes read with envy the advertisements of second-hand book-dealers offering twenty-eight volumes of Uspensky, or ten volumes of Pushkin, etc. As luck would have it, Vladimir has taken a sudden liking to belles-lettres. And he's such an out-and-out nationalist, too. You couldn't get him to go and see the Polish painters for love or money, yet he picked up an old catalogue of the Tretyakov Gallery at a friend's place and very often buries himself in it." (*Letters to Relatives*, pp. 396-97.)

It was originally planned that Inessa was to remain in Cracow and bring her children over from Russia. I had even gone with her to look for rooms. Life in Cracow, however, was very secluded, and reminded one a bit of Siberian exile. Inessa's energies, with which she was bubbling over at that time, found no outlet there. She decided to make the round of our groups abroad and deliver there a series of lectures before taking up her residence in Paris, where she was to organize the work of our Committee of Organizations Abroad. Before her departure we had long talks together about women's work. Inessa strongly urged that propaganda work be widely developed among the women workers and a special women workers' magazine be published in St. Petersburg. Ilyich wrote to his sister Anna about the necessity of such a magazine, which began to make its appearance shortly afterwards. Inessa eventually did a great deal towards developing work among working women, and devoted no little time and energy to the business.

In January 1914 Malinovsky arrived in Cracow, and together with Vladimir Ilyich, went to Paris, and thence to Brussels to attend the Fourth Congress of the Lettish Social-Democrats, which opened on January 13.

In Paris Malinovsky delivered what Ilyich described as a very able report on the work of the Duma group, while Ilyich delivered a lengthy address on the national question. He also spoke at a 9th of January commemoration meeting, and at a meeting of the Bolshevik group in Paris in connection with the attempt of the International Socialist Bureau to intervene in Russian affairs with the aim of reconciliation and in connection with Kautsky's speech at the December meeting of the International Bureau to the effect that the Social-Democratic Party in Russia was dead. This meddling in Russian affairs on the part of the International Socialist Bureau worried Ilyich, who was afraid that it would merely act as a drag on the growing influence of the Bolsheviks in Russia. Ilyich sent a report to Huysmans concerning the state of affairs in the Party. The Fourth Congress of the Lettish Social-Democrats resulted in a victory for the Bolsheviks. Among those who attended the congress were Bērziņš, Lācis and Hermans. Ilyich spoke at the congress and appealed to the Letts to line up with the Central Committee. In a letter to his mother Ilyich wrote that his trip to Paris had refreshed him.

"Paris is an uncomfortable place for anybody with modest means to live in, and very tiring," he wrote. "But for a short visit or a joy-ride there is no better or jollier city. It did me good." (*Letters to Relatives*, pp. 400-01.)

In the winter, shortly after Vladimir Ilyich had returned from Paris, it was decided to send Kamenev to Russia to run *Pravda* and direct the work of the Duma group. Both *Pravda* and the Duma group were in need of help. Kamenev's wife came for him with their little son.

Kamenev's little boy and Zinoviev's son, Styopa, gravely debated whether St. Petersburg was a city or Russia. Preparations were made for departure. We all went to the station to see them off. It was a cold wintry evening. Very little was said. Kamenev's boy alone kept up a steady chatter. Everyone was wrapped up in his own thoughts. Would Kamenev hold out long there, we wondered. When would we meet again? How long would it be before we went to Russia? Everyone was thinking about Russia, longing to be back there. I used to dream of Nevskaya Zastava in my sleep. We avoided the subject, although secretly it was on everyone's mind.

The first number of the popular magazine *Rabotnitsa* (*Woman Worker*) came out in St. Petersburg on March 8, 1914. It cost four kopeks. The St. Petersburg Committee issued leaflets on Women's Day. Inessa and Staël sent in articles for the magazine from Paris, and Lilina and I from Cracow. Seven numbers of this magazine were published. The eighth was to carry articles on the forthcoming Socialist Women's Congress in Vienna, but that issue never appeared—the war broke out.

We planned to hold the Party congress at the same time as the International Socialist Congress, which was to take place in Vienna in August. We hoped that some of the delegates would be able to come legally. As for the rest, we planned to organize the crossing of the border *en masse* under the guise of an excursion party. This plan was to be carried through by the Cracow printers.

In May we moved back to Poronino again.

Kisilev, Glebov-Avilov and Anya Nikiforova were specially assigned to conduct the campaign of preparation for the congress in St. Petersburg. They came to Poronino to make arrangements about it all with Vladimir Ilyich. On the day of their arrival we sat for a long time on the slope near our country house, listening to them talk about the work in Russia. They were all young people, full of energy, and Ilyich took a liking to them. Glebov-Avilov had been a pupil at the Bologna school, and was now a staunch Leninist. Ilyich advised the visitors to go for a walk in the mountains. As he was feeling indisposed, they went without him. On their return, they gave us a humorous account of the climbing they had done (they had climbed a very steep height), of how their knapsacks had been a nuisance, and they had carried them in turns, and how, when it was Anya's turn, all the passers-by had laughed at them and advised her to carry her gentlemen friends as well while she was at it.

The nature of the agitation for the congress was decided upon. Having received all the necessary instructions, Kiselev went to the Baltic provinces, and Glebov-Avilov and Anya Nikiforova went to the Ukraine.

Romanov, an ex-pupil of the Capri school, who had become an *agent provocateur*, arrived from Moscow too. I forget on what pretext he came, but it was in connection with the forthcoming congress. The secret police wanted all the information they could get about it.

Inessa had had her children over from Russia for the summer, and lived in Trieste by the seaside. She was preparing a report for the International Women's Congress, which was to be held in Vienna at the same time as the International Socialist Congress. She had work to do in other fields too. The International Socialist Bureau planned a conference in Brussels for the middle of June consisting of representatives of eleven organizations of the R.S.D.L.P. of all trends in order to organize an exchange of opinions there with the aim of establishing unity. It was obvious, however, that things would be carried further, that the Liquidators, the Trotskyists, the Bundists and others would take this opportunity to limit the activities of the Bolsheviks and bind them by a number of resolutions. The influence of the Bolsheviks in Russia was growing. As Badayev pointed out in his book *The Bolsheviks in the State Duma*, by the summer of 1914 the Bolsheviks had a majority on the executives of fourteen out of the eighteen trade unions that existed in St. Petersburg. The biggest trade unions, including the Metal-Workers' Union, which was the largest and most powerful in St. Petersburg, were on the side of the Bolsheviks. The same ratio existed among the workers' group of the insurance institutions. Of the Insurance Fund delegates elected in St. Petersburg and Moscow, thirty-seven were Bolsheviks and only seven Mensheviks, while in the case of the all-Russian insurance institutions forty-seven were Bolsheviks and ten Mensheviks.

Election of delegates to the International Socialist Congress in Vienna was organized on a broad scale. The majority of the workers' organizations elected Bolsheviks.

Preparations for the Party congress were making good headway too. Beginning with the spring this campaign steadily gained strength. "The task confronting us," Badayev writes, "during the period preceding the congress —namely, the consolidation and extension of the local Party units, was largely fulfilled thanks to the tremendous upsurge of the revolutionary movement in the country during the past few months. The workers' swing towards the Party increased; new cadres of revolutionary-minded workers joined the Party organizations, and the work of the leading bodies showed a steady improvement. In this connection, the forthcoming congress and the questions on its agenda were assured of a heightened interest on the part of the working-class masses of the Party." (A. Y. Badayev, *The Bolsheviks in the State Duma*, State Publishing House, 1932, pp. 293-94.)

Badayev received considerable sums of money collected for the organizing fund of the congress. He had already received a number of mandates, draft resolutions, instructions, etc. He gives a striking picture of how legal activities were linked with illegal. "The summertime," he writes, "favoured the organization of illegal meetings in the woods outside the city, where we were more or less safe from police raids. When it was necessary to call wider meetings, these were arranged under the guise of country excursions supposedly sponsored by some educational society. After riding out of St. Petersburg some twenty or thirty versts we would strike off into the woods 'for a walk,' and once there, we would post patrols to show people the way after the password had been given, and then hold our meeting. Police spies fairly swarmed around all the labour organizations, paying particular attention to the editorial offices of *Pravda* and our group premises, which were known to be the centres of Party work. But while the secret police increased their activity, our own secrecy technique steadily improved as well. Of course, comrades were still being arrested, but there were no big and disastrous breakdowns." (*Ibid.,* pp. 294-95.)

Thus, the line adopted by the Central Committee aimed at increasing legal publications, and giving the legal press a definite angle towards developing the work of the Duma group inside and outside of the Duma, towards framing all questions in a clear and definite manner and combining legal with illegal work, proved to be absolutely correct.

The attempt to override this policy through the International Socialist Bureau made Ilyich furious. He decided not to go to the Unity Conference in Brussels, but to send Inessa instead. She knew French well (it was her mother tongue), was able to keep a cool head, and had plenty of character. She could be depended upon not to surrender positions. Inessa lived in Trieste, and Ilyich sent her the report of the Central Committee which he had drafted, together with instructions how she was to act in particular circumstances. He thought out every detail. The delegation of the Central Committee, in addition to Inessa, consisted of M. F. Vladimirsky and N. F. Popov. Inessa read out the report of the C.C. in French. As was to be expected, things went beyond a mere exchange of opinions at the conference. Kautsky, on behalf of the Bureau, submitted a motion condemning the split and declaring that no serious differences existed. All voted for the resolution except the delegates of the Central Committee and the Letts. The latter refused to vote in spite of Huysmans' threat that he would report to the Vienna Congress that those who did not vote were taking upon themselves the responsibility for side-stepping the attempt to bring about unity.

At a private meeting in Brussels the Liquidators, Trotskyists, *Vperyod*-ists, Plekhanovists and the Caucasian regional organization formed a bloc against the Bolsheviks, and decided to take advantage of the situation to bring pressure to bear on the Bolsheviks.

Another very painful affair that completely absorbed Ilyich in the summer of 1914 besides this Brussels unity business was the Malinovsky affair.

When General Junkovsky, the newly appointed Deputy Minister of the Interior, discovered the role of *agent provocateur* that Malinovsky was playing, he reported it to Rodzyanko, the Chairman of the Duma, with a view to preventing a grave political scandal.

On May 8 Malinovsky handed Rodzyanko his resignation from the Duma and left the country. The local and central Party organizations condemned Malinovsky's action as being anarchistic and disruptive, and expelled him from the Party. As for the charge of being a police spy, this seemed to be so monstrous at the time, that the Central Committee appointed a special commission of enquiry under the chairmanship of Ganiecki, with Lenin and Zinoviev as members.

Rumours that Malinovsky was an *agent provocateur* had been creeping about for a long time. These rumours originated in Menshevik circles. Elena Rozmirovich had

strong suspicions of him in connection with her arrest—
she had been working for the Duma group, and the gendarmes who interrogated her were informed of details
which only an inside agent could have supplied them
with. Bukharin, too, had heard various reports about Malinovsky. Vladimir Ilyich thought it utterly incredible
that Malinovsky could be an *agent provocateur.* Only
once did a fleeting suspicion cross his mind. I remember
once in Poronino, as we were returning from the Zinovievs
and talking about these sinister rumours, Ilyich suddenly
stopped on the bridge we were crossing and said: "What
if they are true!" A look of dismay showed on his face.
"That's impossible," I answered. Reassured, Ilyich fell to
cursing the Mensheviks, who had no scruples as to the
means they used in fighting the Bolsheviks. He had no
further doubts on this score.

The commission of enquiry investigated all the rumours
about Malinovsky, received Burtsev's statement to the effect that he considered the charge improbable, considered the evidence of Bukharin and Rozmirovich, but could
not establish Malinovsky's guilt.

Malinovsky hung around in Poronino, feeling utterly
miserable and lonely. God knows what he must have lived
through during that time. Then he disappeared from Poronino. No one knew where he had gone to. The February
Revolution showed him up in his true colours.

He returned to Russia of his own free will after the
October Revolution and gave himself up to the Soviet authorities. He was sentenced to death by the Supreme Trib-
unal and shot.

Meanwhile, in Russia the struggle was becoming more
acute. The strike movement was building up, particularly
in Baku. The working class supported the Baku strikers.
The police opened fire on a crowd of 12,000 Putilov
workers gathered at a meeting in St. Petersburg.
Clashes with the police assumed a more violent character. The Duma deputies were becoming leaders of the

rising proletariat. Mass strikes became the order of the day.

A hundred and thirty thousand workers came out on strike in St. Petersburg on July 7. The strike grew in intensity rather than waned. Barricades were erected on the streets of red St. Petersburg.

But war broke out.

Germany declared war on Russia on August 1, on France on August 3, and on Belgium on August 4. On the same day Britain declared war on Germany. On August 6 Austria-Hungary declared war on Russia, and on August 11 France and Britain declared war on Austria-Hungary.

It was the beginning of the world war, which temporarily checked the rising revolutionary movement in Russia, turned the whole world upside down, precipitated a number of grave crises, gave new and much sharper emphasis to vital issues of the revolutionary struggle, accentuated the role of the proletariat as the leader of all the working people, roused new strata to the struggle, and made the victory of the proletariat a question of life or death for Russia.

THE YEARS OF THE WAR

CRACOW

1914

Although war had been in the air for a long time it came as a shock to all of us. We had to get out of Poronino, but had no idea where to go. Lilina was seriously ill at the time, and Zinoviev could not leave in any case. They lived in Zakopane at the time, and there were doctors there. We decided to stay on in Poronino for the time being. Ilyich wrote to Kobetsky in Copenhagen, asking to be kept informed, to establish contacts with Stockholm, etc. The local hill people were utterly depressed when mobilization started. No one had the faintest idea what the war was all about and against whom it was being fought. There was no enthusiasm whatever; men went like dumb animals to the slaughter. Our landlady, a peasant woman who owned the summer house, was numb with grief when her husband was called up. The Catholic priest tried to fan a patriotic spark from the pulpit. Rumours were rife, and the six-year-old boy of the poor family next door, who was always hanging around our house, told me confidentially that the Russians were putting poison in the wells—so the priest had said.

The local gendarme officer came to our house on August 7 with a witness—a local peasant armed with a rifle —to make a search. What exactly he was to search for, the officer did not know himself. He rummaged about in the book-case, found an unloaded pistol, took several notebooks with figures on the agrarian question, and asked a few irrelevant questions. The embarrassed witness sat on the edge of a chair, staring around with a puzzled air, while the officer poked fun at him. He pointed to a jar of paste and assured him it was a bomb. Then he told Vladimir Ilyich that they had received information against him, and that he really ought to arrest him, but as he would have to take him down to Nowy Targ (the nearest place where there were military authorities) the next morning in any case, Vladimir Ilyich might just as well come down himself tomorrow in time to catch the six o'clock morning train. One thing was clear—he was going to be arrested, and in war-time, especially during the early days of the war, it did not want much to have a man put out of the way. Vladimir Ilyich went to see Ganiecki, who lived in Poronino at the time, and told him what had happened. Ganiecki wired immediately to the Social-Democratic Deputy Marek, and Vladimir Ilyich wired to the Cracow police, who knew him as a political emigrant. The thought of Mother and me remaining alone in Poronino in a big house worried Ilyich, and he arranged with Tikho-mirnov for the latter to move into an upstairs room for the time being. Tikhomirnov had recently returned from exile in Olonets, and the *Pravda* editors had sent him to Poronino to take a holiday and rest his shattered nerves, and, incidentally, to help Ilyich to draw up reports in connection with the current campaigns for a workers' press, etc. based on data published in *Pravda*.

Ilyich and I sat up all night. We were very upset. I saw him off in the morning and returned to an empty room. The same day Ganiecki hired a farm cart which took him to Nowy Targ. He managed to see the district officer in charge—the Royal Imperial *starosta*—kicked up a row, told him that Ilyich was a member of the International Socialist Bureau, a man who was in the public eye and for whose life he, the officer, would have to answer. Then he saw the inspector who was handling the case, told him who Ilyich was, and got a permit for me to see Ilyich the next day. When Ganiecki got back from Nowy Targ we both drew up a letter to the Austrian Social-Democrat M.P. and member of the International Bureau Victor Adler. At Nowy Targ I was permitted to see Ilyich. I was left alone with him, but he spoke very little—the situation was still extremely confused. The Cracow police wired that there were no grounds for suspecting Ulyanov of espionage. A similar telegram was received from Marek in Zakopane, and a well-known Polish writer went to Nowy Targ to intercede on Ilyich's behalf. On learning of Ilyich's arrest, Zinoviev, who lived in Zakopane, cycled down in a pouring rain to see Doctor Dlusski, the old Polish *Narodovolets* who lived ten versts away. Dlusski immediately hired a phaeton and drove to Zakopane, where he began sending telegrams, writing letters, and seeing people. I was allowed to see Ilyich every day. I took the six o'clock train to Nowy Targ every morning—it was an hour's ride—then hung about the station, the post office and the market-place until eleven, then I would have an hour's meeting with Vladimir Ilyich. Ilyich told me about his prison mates. There were a lot of local peasants in jail—some for having allowed their passports to expire without renewal, some for not having paid their taxes, others for wrangling with the local authorities, etc. One of the prisoners was a Frenchman, another was a Polish government clerk who had used someone's travelling pass to get a cheap ride, a third was a Gypsy who carried on a shouted conversation with his wife across the prison wall, where she would take up her stand at set hours. Ilyich recalled his legal practice in Shushenskoye among the peasants, whom he had helped out of all kinds of predicaments, and he set up an improvised legal advice office in prison, wrote petitions, etc. His prison mates called Ilyich *byczy chlop* which means a "corker." The "corker" gradually got used to prison life in Nowy Targ, and was more composed and animated at our meetings. In this prison, at night, when the inmates were asleep, he lay pondering and planning what the Party had to do now, what steps had to be taken in order to convert the world war into a world struggle with the bourgeoisie on the part of the proletariat. I gave Ilyich all the news about the war I was able to obtain.

What I did not tell him was this. Returning from the station one day, I heard some peasant women coming out of the church talking in loud voices—apparently for my benefit—about what they would do to a spy if they got hold of one. If the authorities by any chance let a spy go, they would see to it themselves that he had his eyes put out, his tongue cut off, and so forth. Clearly, we could not remain in Poronino after Ilyich was released. I began packing up, sorting out what we needed to take with us and what we could leave behind. Our household went to pieces. We had a servant, whom we had hired for the summer because of Mother's illness. She had been telling the neighbours all kinds of stories about us and our connections with Russia, and I got rid of her as fast as I could by paying her fare to Cracow, where she had been eager to go, and her wages in advance. Our neighbour's girl helped us to heat the stove and do the shopping. My mother—she was already 72 years old—was feeling very poorly. She could see that something was wrong, but could not make out exactly what it was. Although I had told her that Vladimir Ilyich had been arrested, she would talk at times about his having been called up. She worried whenever I left the house—she had an idea that I would disappear the way Vladimir Ilyich had done. Our lodger Tikhomirnov smoked with a pensive air, while he helped with packing up the books. Once I had to get some kind of certificate from the peasant witness whom the gendarme officer had made fun of during the search of our rooms. I went to see him at the other end of the village, and we had a long talk together in his hut—the typical hut of a poor peasant—about what the war was all about, why people were fighting it, and who was interested in having it. We parted afterwards in a very friendly way.

At last, the pressure brought to bear by the Vienna M.P. Victor Adler and the Lvov M.P. Diamand, who both vouched for Vladimir Ilyich, had its effect. On August 19 Vladimir Ilyich was released from prison. I was at Nowy Targ as usual since early in the morning, and this time they even let me go into the prison to help take Ilyich's things. We hired a cart and went to Poronino. There we were obliged to stay for about a week until we received permission to move to Cracow. In Cracow we went to the landlady with whom Kamenev and Inessa had lodged. Most of the rooms were being used as a medical station, but she found a place for us. She had other things to worry about, though. The first battle had just been fought at Krasnik, in which two of her sons were engaged. They had signed up as volunteers, and she did not know what had become of them.

The next day we witnessed a harrowing scene from the window of the hotel to which we had moved. A train had arrived from Krasnik with the dead and wounded. Relatives of the men who had fought in the battle ran after the stretchers peering into the faces of the dead and dying, trying yet dreading to identify their kin. Those who were less seriously wounded walked slowly from the station with bandaged heads and arms. The people who had come to meet the train helped them to carry their things, offered them food and mugs of beer obtained from nearby restaurants. "So this is war!" one could not help thinking. And it was only the first battle.

In Cracow it did not take us long to get permission to go abroad to a neutral country—Switzerland. Certain matters had to be attended to first. A little while before that my mother had become a "capitalist." Her sister, a school-mistress, had died in Novocherkassk and left all her property to her—silver spoons, icons, articles of dress, and four thousand rubles saved up during thirty years of teaching. The money was deposited in a Cracow bank, and to get it from there we had to resort to a broker in Vienna, who got the money for us and took exactly half of it for his fee. We lived mainly on this money during the war, husbanding it so carefully that we still had some of it left on our return to Russia in 1917. And it was this money, a certificate for which was issued during a police search of our rooms in St. Petersburg during the July days of 1917, that served as evidence alleging Vladimir Ilyich to have received money from the German Government in payment for espionage.

We were a whole week travelling from Cracow to the Swiss frontier. Our train made long stops along the line to let military trains pass. We observed the chauvinistic agitation which the nuns and their active women associates carried on. At the railway stations they distributed sacred images, prayer books and so on to the soldiers. Dandyish military men sauntered about the stations. The coaches had mottoes pasted all over them telling men what to do with the French, the English and the Russians:

"Jedem Russ ein Schuss!" (A Shot for Every Russian.)
Several carloads of insect powder stood on one of the sidings, waiting to be shipped to the front.

We stopped for a day in Vienna to get the necessary papers, arrange our money affairs, and send a wire to Switzerland to get someone to go surety for us to enable us to enter the country. Greulich—a veteran member of the Swiss Social-Democratic Party—went surety for us. In Vienna Ryazanov took Vladimir Ilyich to see Victor Adler, who had helped to secure Ilyich's release. Adler related his conversation with the Minister. "Are you sure that Ulyanov is an enemy of the tsarist government?" the Minister had asked. "Oh, yes," Adler had answered. "He is a more implacable enemy than Your Excellency." From Vienna we travelled to the Swiss frontier fairly quickly.

BERNE

1914-1915

At last, on September 5, we entered Switzerland and proceeded to Berne.

We had not definitely decided yet where we were going to live—in Geneva or Berne. Ilyich felt drawn to the old familiar home—Geneva, where he had worked so well in the old days at the Société de lecture, where there had been a good Russian library. Our Berne comrades, however, assured us that Geneva had changed a good deal and was now crowded with emigrants from other cities and from France, and the place was a regular hurly-burly. We took a room in Berne for the time being without definitely deciding anything.

Ilyich immediately got in touch with Geneva to find out whether there were any people there who were going to Russia (they had to be made use of for establishing contacts with Russia), whether the Russian printing plant still existed, whether Russian leaflets could be printed there, and so on.

The day after our arrival from Galicia, all the Bolshe viks then living in Berne—Shklovsky, the Safarovs, Duma Deputy Samoilov, Goberman, and others—got together and arranged a conference in the woods, at which Ilyich expounded his views on current events. As a result a resolution was adopted characterizing the war as an imperialist predatory war and the conduct of the leaders of the Second International, who had voted for war credits, as a betrayal of the cause of the proletariat. The resolution stated that "from the point of view of the working class and the toiling masses of all the peoples of Russia the lesser evil would be the defeat of the tsarist monarchy and its armies, which are oppressing Poland, the Ukraine and various other peoples in Russia." (*Works*, Vol. 21, p. 3.) The resolution launched the slogan of propaganda for a socialist revolution, civil war, and an implacable struggle against chauvinism and patriotism to be waged in all countries without exception, and outlined a programme of action for Russia, namely, struggle against the monarchy, propaganda for the revolution, the fight for a republic, for the liberation of the nationalities oppressed by the "Great Russians," for the confiscation of the landowners' estates and for the eight-hour day.

The Berne resolution was in substance a challenge to the whole capitalist world. It was not written, of course, to be shelved. It was first of all sent to all the Bolshevik sections abroad. Then Samoilov took the theses with him for discussion with the Central Committee section in Russia and the Duma group. It was not known yet what stand they took Communication with Russia was broken off. We did not learn until later that the Russia section of the Central Committee and the Bolshevik section of the Duma group had struck the right note from the very start. For the advanced workers of our country, for our Party organization, the resolutions of international congresses on the war were not mere scraps of paper. They were a guide to action.

In the early days of the war, when mobilization had only just been declared, the Central Committee issued a leaflet with the appeal: "Down with war! War against war!" A number of factories in St. Petersburg went on strike on the day the reserves were mobilized, and an attempt was even made to organize a demonstration. But the war had called forth such a violent outburst of Black-Hundred patriotism and strengthened the military reaction to such an extent that nothing much could be done. Our Duma group took a firm stand against war and continued the line of struggle against the tsarist rule. This firmness impressed even the Mensheviks, and the Social-Democratic group as a whole adopted a resolution which was read from the Duma tribune. The resolution was very cautiously worded and left many things unsaid, but it was a resolution of protest nevertheless, and roused indignation among the rest of the Duma deputies. Feeling ran particularly high when the Social-Democratic group, still acting together, abstained from voting on war credits and walked out in a body as a demonstration of protest. The Bolshevik organization quickly went deep underground and began to issue leaflets containing directions how to utilize the war in the interests of developing and intensifying the revolutionary struggle. Anti-war propaganda was started in the provinces too. Local reports pointed to the fact that this propaganda had the support of the revolutionary-minded workers. We abroad learned about all this much later.

Fretting as they did in the dreary atmosphere of emigrant life abroad, from which they were so eager to escape, and having had no direct experience of the revolutionary upsurge which had taken place in Russia in recent months, our Bolshevik groups abroad lacked the firmness which our Duma deputies and the Bolshevik organizations in Russia had evinced. People were not clear on the question, and spoke mostly about which side was the attacking side.

In Paris, in the long run, the majority of the group expressed themselves against the war and volunteering, but some comrades—Sapozhkov (Kuznetsov), Kazakov (Britman, Sviagin), Misha Edisherov (Davydov), Moiseyev (Ilya, Zefir) and others—joined the French army as volunteers. The Menshevik, Bolshevik and Socialist-Revolutionary volunteers (about eighty men in all) adopted a declaration in the name of the "Russian Republicans," which was printed in the French press. Plekhanov made a farewell speech in honour of the volunteers before they left Paris.

The majority of our Paris group condemned volunteering. But in the other groups, too, there was no definite clarity on the question. Vladimir Ilyich realized how important it was at such a serious moment for every Bolshevik to have a clear understanding of the significance of events. A comradely exchange of opinions was necessary: it was inadvisable to fix all shades of opinion right away until the matter had been threshed out. That is why, in his answer to Karpinsky's letter framing the views of the Geneva section, Ilyich wrote: "Would not this 'criticism' and my 'anti-criticism' make a better subject for discussion?"

Ilyich knew that an understanding could more easily be reached in a comradely discussion than by correspondence. Of course, this was no time to keep such an issue long confined to comradely talks within a narrow circle of Bolsheviks.

Early in October we found out that Plekhanov, who had returned from Paris, had already addressed a meeting in Geneva and was going to read a paper in Lausanne.

Plekhanov's position worried Ilyich very much. He could not believe that Plekhanov had become a "defencist." "I just can't believe it," he said, adding thoughtfully, "it must be the effect of his military past." When a telegram was received from Lausanne on October 10, saying that the lecture was scheduled for the next day, the 11th, Ilyich got busy preparing his speech, and I took care to relieve him of all other business, and arranged with our people who was to go from Berne, etc. We had settled down in Berne for good. The Zinovievs were living there, too, by that time (they had arrived a fortnight after us), and so was Inessa.

I could not go to the lecture myself, and learned all about it afterwards from the others. After reading F. Ilyin's memoirs about that lecture in the *Transactions of the Lenin Institute*, and knowing what it had meant to Ilyich at the time, I can picture the whole thing quite vividly. Inessa gave me a full account of it afterwards too. Our people came to the lecture from all over. Zinoviev, Inessa and Shklovsky came from Berne, Rozmirovich, Krylenko, Bukharin and the Lausanne comrades came from Baugy, near Clarens.

Ilyich was afraid he would not be admitted to Plekhanov's lecture and say what he had to say—the Mensheviks might not let in so many Bolsheviks. I can imagine how reluctant he was to see people and carry on small talk with them, and I can understand the naive ruses he devised to shake them off. I can clearly see him amid the dinner-table bustle at the Movshovichs', so withdrawn, absorbed and agitated that he could not swallow a bite. One can understand the rather forced humour of the remark uttered in an undertone to those sitting next to him about Plekhanov's opening speech, in which the latter had declared that he had not been prepared to address such a large audience. "The slyboots," Ilyich muttered, and gave himself up entirely to hearing what Plekhanov had to say. The first part of the lecture in which Plekhanov attacked the Germans had his approval, and he applauded it. In the second part, however, Plekhanov set forth his "defence-of-the-country" views. There was no room for doubt any more. Ilyich asked for the floor—he was the only one to do so. He went up to the speaker's table with a pot of beer in his hand. He spoke calmly, and only the pallor of his face betrayed his agitation. He said in effect that the war was not an accidental occurrence, that the way for it had been paved by the whole nature of the development of bourgeois society. The International congresses at Stuttgart, Copenhagen and Basle had defined what the attitude of the Socialists should be towards the impending war. Only by combatting the chauvinist intoxication in their countries would the Social-Democrats be fulfilling their duty. The war, which had just begun, ought to be converted into a decisive fight against the ruling classes on the part of the proletariat.

Ilyich had only ten minutes. He could only deal with the bare essentials. Plekhanov retorted with his usual display of wit. The Mensheviks, who were an overwhelming majority, wildly applauded him. The impression was that Plekhanov had won the day.

Three days later, on October 14, in the same hall where Plekhanov had spoken—the Maison du Peuple—Ilyich was to deliver his own lecture. The hall was packed. The lecture was a great success. Ilyich was in a buoyant fighting mood. He elaborated his views on the war, which he branded as an imperialist war. He pointed out in his speech that a leaflet against the war had already been issued in Russia by the Central Committee and that similar leaflets had been issued by the Caucasian organization and other groups. He pointed out that the best socialist newspaper in Europe at the moment was *Golos* (*Voice*), in which Martov was writing. "The more often and seriously I have disagreed with Martov," he said, "the more definitely must I now say that this writer is doing just what a Social-Democrat should do. He is criticizing his government, denouncing the bourgeoisie of his own country, railing against its ministers."

In private conversation Ilyich often remarked what a good thing it would be if Martov came over to our side altogether. But he doubted whether Martov would stick to his present position for long. He knew how prone Martov was to yield to outside influences. "He writes like that while he is alone," Ilyich added. Ilyich's lecture was a tremendous success. He repeated the same lecture—"The Proletariat and the War"—in Geneva at a later date.

Ilyich returned from his lecture trip to find a letter of Shlyapnikov's from Stockholm informing him about the work in Russia, about Vandervelde's telegram to the Duma group and the replies of the Menshevik and Bolshevik deputies. When war was declared Émile Vandervelde, Belgian representative on the International Socialist Bureau, accepted a ministerial post in the Belgian Government. He had been in Russia shortly before the war and seen the struggle which the Russian workers were waging against the autocracy, but had failed to grasp its full import. Vandervelde had sent telegrams to both sections of the Social-Democratic group of the Duma. He called on the group to help the Russian Government conduct a determined war against Germany on the side of the Entente.

The Menshevik deputies, who, for the moment, had refused to vote for war credits, began to vacillate when they learned what position the majority of the Socialist parties had taken up. Their answer to Vandervelde, therefore, showed a complete change of front. They declared in it that they would not oppose the war. The Bolshevik group sent a reply emphatically rejecting any suggestion of supporting the war and discontinuing the struggle against the tsarist government. Much was left unsaid in this reply, but the main line was correct. It showed how important it was to maintain contact with Russia, and Ilyich strongly insisted that Shlyapnikov should remain in Stockholm and establish still closer contact with the Duma group and the Russians at large. This could best be arranged through Stockholm.

As soon as Ilyich arrived in Berne from Cracow, he wrote to Karpinsky, enquiring whether it was possible to have a leaflet printed in Geneva. The theses were adopted in Berne soon after our arrival, and a month later it was decided to recast and publish them in the form of a manifesto. Ilyich got in touch with Karpinsky again concerning its publication. He sent him letters by trusted messengers, avoiding the post and maintaining strict secrecy. It was not clear at the time what attitude the Swiss Government would adopt towards anti-militarist propaganda.

The day after receiving Shlyapnikov's first letter, Vladimir Ilyich wrote to Karpinsky:

"Dear K. Just when I happened to be in Geneva we received *gratifying* news from Russia. The text of the Russian Social-Democrats' reply to Vandervelde arrived too. We have therefore decided, instead of a separate manifesto, to issue a paper *Sotsial-Demokrat* (*The Social-Democrat*), the Central Organ.... By Monday we shall send you some slight corrections to the manifesto and a *different* signature (for after having got in touch with Russia we are coming out *more officially*)." (*Works*, Vol. 35, p. 119.)

Ilyich went on a lecture tour again at the end of October, first to Montreux, then to Zurich. Trotsky spoke at the lecture in Zurich, protesting against Ilyich calling Kautsky a "traitor." Ilyich deliberately put the case very strongly in order to make it quite clear what line people were taking. The fight with the defencists was in full swing.

The struggle was not an internal Party affair that concerned Russian matters alone. It was an international affair.

"The Second International is dead, vanquished by opportunism," Vladimir Ilyich maintained. Forces had to be rallied for a new International, the Third, purged of opportunism.

But what forces were there to back us?

The only M.P.'s who refused to vote for war credits besides the Russian Social-Democrats were the Serbian, of whom there were only two in the Serbian Parliament.

In Germany at the beginning of the war everyone had voted for war credits, but already on September 10 Karl Liebknecht, F. Mehring, Rosa Luxemburg and Clara Zetkin had drawn up a declaration protesting against the stand taken up by the majority of the German Social-Democrats. They got this declaration published in the Swiss newspapers only at the end of October, after having failed to get it published in the German papers. The most Left position of all the German newspapers was taken up at the very outset of the war by *Bremen Bürgerzeitung*, which declared on August 23 that the "proletarian international" was destroyed. In France the Socialist Party headed by Guesde and Vaillant had sunk to chauvinism. Among the rank and file of the Party, however, feeling against the war was pretty strong. Vandervelde's conduct was typical of the Belgian Party. In Britain the chauvinism of Hyndman and the whole British Socialist Party was rebuffed by MacDonald and Keir Hardie of the opportunist Independent Labour Party. There was a feeling against war in the neutral countries, but for the most part it bore a pacifist character. More revolutionary than the others was the Italian Socialist Party with its newspaper *Avanti*. It opposed chauvinism and exposed the selfish secret motives behind the appeals for war. It was backed by the vast majority of the advanced workers. On September 27 an Italo-Swiss Socialist Conference was held at Lugano. Our theses concerning the war were sent to this conference. The conference branded the war as an imperialist war and called upon the international proletariat to fight for peace.

On the whole, the voices against chauvinism, the voices of the internationalists still sounded very weak, isolated and uncertain, but Ilyich was sure that they would grow steadily stronger. His fighting spirit was high throughout the autumn.

That autumn is associated in my mind with the colourful picture of the Berne woods. It was a lovely autumn that year. In Berne we lived in Distelweg, a clean, quiet little street adjoining the Berne woods, which stretched for several miles. Inessa lived across the road, the Zinovievs a five-minute walk from us, and the Shklovskys a ten-minute walk. We used to roam for hours along the woodland paths, which were bestrewn with yellow leaves. Mostly the three of us went on these walks together—Vladimir Ilyich, Inessa and myself. Vladimir Ilyich spoke about his plans of struggle along international lines. Inessa was very enthusiastic about it all. She had begun to take a direct part in the rising struggle—she carried on correspondence, translated various of our documents into French and English, collected material, talked with people, etc. Sometimes we would sit for hours on a sunny wooded hillside, Ilyich jotting down notes for his articles and speeches, and polishing his formulations, I studying Italian with the aid of a Toussaint textbook, and Inessa sewing a skirt and basking in the autumn sunshine—she had not quite recovered yet from the effects of her imprisonment. In the evening we would all gather in Grigory's (Zinoviev's) tiny room—the three of them, Grigory, Lilina and their little boy Styopa, lived in a single room—and after playing about with little Styopa before he went to bed, Ilyich would make a number of concrete proposals.

The main points of the line of struggle were concisely formulated by Ilyich in his letter of October 17 to Shlyapnikov.

... Kautsky "is now *the most harmful of them all*. No words can describe how dangerous and mean are his sophisms which cover up the rascality of the opportunists (in the *Neue Zeit* (*New Era*) with smooth and slick phrases. The opportunists are an open evil. The German centre with Kautsky at its head, a hidden evil embellished for diplomatic purposes and dulling the eyes, the intelligence, and the consciousness of the workers, is more dangerous than anything else. Our task at present is a determined and open struggle against international opportunism and those who shield it (Kautsky). This is what we are going to do in the Central Organ which we shall soon issue (probably two pages). One must exert every effort to uphold the just hatred of the class-conscious workers for the hideous conduct of the Germans; one must draw from this hatred political conclusions *against* opportunism and *against* every concession to opportunism. This is an international task. It devolves upon us; there is nobody else. One cannot shirk it. The slogan of 'simply' re-establishing the International is incorrect (because the danger of a spineless conciliatory resolution along the line of Kautsky and Vandervelde is very, very great!). The slogan of "peace" is incorrect, as the slogan must be: converting the national war into civil war. (This conversion may take a long time, it may and will demand a number of preliminary conditions, but the work must all be conducted *along the line of such* a change, in this spirit and in this direction.) Not the sabotaging of the war, not undertaking sporadic individual acts in this direction, but the conducting of mass propaganda (and not only among 'civilians') that leads to the conversion of the war into civil war. In Russia, chauvinism hides behind phrases about *la belle France* and unfortunate Belgium (how about the Ukraine and others?), or behind the 'popular' hatred for the Germans (and 'Kaiserism'). It is therefore our absolute duty to struggle against those sophisms. In order that the struggle may proceed along a definite and clear line, one must have a slogan that summarizes it. This slogan is: For us *Russians*, from the point of view of the interests of the labouring masses and the working class of *Russia*, there cannot be the slightest doubt, absolutely no doubt whatever, that the *lesser* evil would be, here and now, the *defeat* of tsarism in the present war. For tsarism is a hundred times worse than Kaiserism. Not the sabotage of the war, but a struggle against chauvinism, all propaganda and agitation directed towards international rallying (drawing together, expressing solidarity, reaching agreements *selon les circonstances*) of the proletariat for the purpose of civil war. It would also be erroneous both to appeal for *individual* acts of firing at officers, etc., and to allow arguments like the one which says: We do not want to help Kaiserism. The former is a deviation towards anarchism, the latter towards opportunism. As to ourselves, we must prepare a mass (at least a collective) action in the army, not of one nation alone, and conduct *all* the work of propaganda and agitation in this direction. To direct the work (stubborn, systematic work that may require a long time) in the spirit of converting the national war into civil war—this is the whole issue. The moment for such a transformation is a different question; at present it is not clear as yet. We must allow this moment to ripen, we must systematically 'force it to ripen.'...

"The peace slogan is in my judgement incorrect at the present moment. This is a philistine's, a preacher's slogan. The proletarian slogan must be civil war.

"Objectively, from the fundamental change in the situation of Europe, there follows such a slogan for the epoch of mass war. The same slogan follows from the Basle resolution.

"We can neither 'promise' civil war nor 'decree it,' but it is our duty to work in *this direction*, if need be, for a very long time. You will find details in the article in the Central Organ." (*Works*, Vol. 35, pp. 120-22.)

Two and a half months after the outbreak of the war Ilyich had worked out a clear distinct line of struggle. It formed the dominant note of all his subsequent activity. The international scope of his activity gave a new tone to his whole work in connection with Russia, gave it fresh vigour and new colour. Without those long years of hard preliminary work devoted to the building up of the Party and the organization of the working class in Russia, Ilyich would not have been able to take the right line in regard to the problems raised by the imperialist war as quickly and firmly as he did. Had he not been in the thick of the international struggle, he would not have been able so firmly to lead the Russian proletariat to the victory of October.

Number 33 of *Sotsial-Demokrat* came out on November 1, 1914. Only five hundred copies of it were printed at first, but later it was found necessary to increase it by another thousand. Ilyich informed Karpinsky with joy on November 14 that the paper had been delivered at a point near the frontier and would soon be forwarded on.

With the aid of Naine and Graber a résumé of the manifesto was printed on November 13 in *La Sentinelle*, a Swiss newspaper published in French in the Neufchâtel working-class centre of Chaux-de-Fond. Ilyich was elated. We sent translations of the manifesto to French, English and German newspapers.

With the aim of developing propaganda among the French Vladimir Ilyich got in touch by letter with Karpinsky on the question of arranging a lecture by Inessa in French in Geneva. He wrote to Shlyapnikov about his addressing the Swedish congress. Shlyapnikov did address it, and his speech was a success. Thus little by little the Bolsheviks developed "international action."

Things were worse as far as contacts with Russia were concerned. Shlyapnikov sent some interesting material from St. Petersburg for No. 34 of the Central Organ, but along with this the paper had regretful occasion to publish a report about the arrest of the five Bolshevik Duma deputies. Connections with Russia weakened again.

While waging a passionate struggle against the betrayal of the workers' cause on the part of the Second International, Ilyich at the same time began an article on "Karl Marx" for Granat's Encyclopaedic Dictionary as soon as we arrived in Berne. This article, dealing with the teachings of Marx, opens with an outline of his philosophy under two headings: "Philosophic Materialism" and "Dialectics," followed by an exposition of Marx's economic theory, in which he describes Marx's approach to the question of socialism and the tactics of the class struggle of the proletariat.

Marx's teaching was not usually presented in this way. In connection with the chapters on philosophic materialism and dialectics, Ilyich began diligently to reread Hegel and other philosophers, and kept up this study even after he had finished the article. The object of his philosophic studies was to master the method of transforming philosophy into a concrete guide to action. His brief remarks on the dialectical approach to all phenomena made in 1921 during the trade-union controversy with Trotsky and Bukharin best testify to the great benefit which Ilyich derived in this respect from his philosophic studies begun upon his arrival in Berne; they were a continuation of his philosophic studies of 1908-1909, when he had combatted the Machists.

Struggle and studies, study and research with Ilyich were always strongly linked together, and closely bound up between themselves, although they may have appeared at first sight to run in parallels.

The beginning of 1915 saw the continuation of the strenuous work of consolidating the Bolshevik groups abroad. Definite understanding had been achieved, but the times were such that solidarity was needed more than ever before. Before the war the Centre of the Bolshevik groups, known as the Committee of Organizations Abroad, had been in Paris. Now it had to be transferred to a neutral country—to Switzerland, to Berne, where the office of the Central Organ was located. Agreement had to be reached on all points—appraisal of the war, the new tasks confronting the Party, and the methods of handling them; it was also necessary to define the work of the groups more definitely. The Baugy group, for instance (Krylenko, Bukharin, Rozmirovich), decided to publish abroad their own organ *Zvezda* (*Star*), and went about it with such precipitancy that they did not even arrange the matter with the Central Organ. We got to know about this plan from Inessa. Such a publication would hardly have been expedient in any case. There was no money with which to publish the Central Organ, and although there were no differences so far, they might easily arise. An unguarded phrase might be pounced on by opponents and exaggerated in every way. We had to keep in step together. It was such a time. A conference of groups abroad was called in Berne at the end of February. In addition to the Swiss groups there was the group from Paris represented by Grisha Belenky. He gave a full account of the defencist mood that prevailed among the Paris group on the outbreak of the war. The Londoners were unable to come, and were represented by proxy. The Baugy group came towards the end of the conference after long hesitation as to whether to come or not. Together with them came the "Japanese"—as we called the Kiev comrades Pyatakov and Bosch (sister of E. F. Rozmirovich), who had escaped from exile in Siberia by way of Japan and America. It was a time when we snatched desperately at every new person who was like-minded. We liked the "Japanese." Their arrival undoubtedly strengthened our forces abroad.

The conference adopted a clear resolution on the war, debated the United-States-of-Europe slogan (vehemently opposed by Inessa), outlined the character of the work of the groups abroad, decided not to publish a Baugy newspaper, and elected a new Committee of Organizations Abroad, consisting of the Berne comrades Shklovsky, Kasparov, Inessa Armand, Lilina and Krupskaya.

Kasparov lived in Berlin before the war (1913). Ilyich heard about him from our Baku comrades Yenukidze, Shaumyan and others. At that period the national question had claimed Ilyich's attention and he had been anxious to get into the closest possible touch with those who were interested in the question and had the right approach to it.

In the summer of 1913 Kasparov had written an article for *Prosveshchenie* on the national question. Ilyich had answered him: "I have received and read your article. The subject, in my opinion, has been chosen well and handled correctly, but it lacks literary finish. There is too much of—shall I say?—'agitation,' which is unsuitable in an article on a *theoretical* problem. I think you ought to re-write it, or let us try." (*Works*, 3rd Russ. ed., Vol. XXIX, p. 93.) The choice of a subject on the national question and its proper exposition meant a good deal, and Ilyich immediately got Kasparov wound up on the job of collecting material on the national question, and concretizing the things that interested him, confident that Kasparov would not overlook anything that was really essential and important. Planning a short visit to Berlin in January 1914, Ilyich wrote to Kasparov that it was necessary for them to meet, and suggested how it was to be done.

Moments of acute struggle and moments of uplift tend to bring people closer together. The workers' movement in St. Petersburg began developing swiftly in July 1914, and a letter was received about the rising revolutionary tide. Until then Ilyich had always addressed Kasparov in his letters "Dear Comrade," but on this occasion, knowing that Kasparov welcomed the revolutionary upsurge as enthusiastically as we did, he changed this mode of address. "Dear friend," Ilyich wrote him. "Will you please take the trouble of keeping us informed *throughout the revolutionary days in Russia*. We do not get any newspapers. Please...." (*Lenin Miscellany*, XIII, p. 241.) There follows a programme for maintaining contact.

When the war broke out Kasparov was obliged to leave Germany and move to Berne. He and Ilyich met like old friends. They saw each other in Berne every day, and soon Kasparov became one of the most intimate comrades of our group. That is how he came to be elected to the Committee of Organizations Abroad.

The rallying of our forces on an international scale

became the order of the day. How difficult that task was was shown by the London Conference of the Socialist parties of the Entente countries (Britain, Belgium, France and Russia), which was held on February 14, 1915. The conference was called by Vandervelde but organized by the British Independent Labour Party headed by Keir Hardie and MacDonald. Prior to the conference they had been opposed to the war and stood for international unity. The I.L.P. had first intended inviting delegates from Germany and Austria, but the French had declared they would not attend the conference if that were done. There were 11 delegates from Britain, 16 from France, three from Belgium, and three Socialist-Revolutionaries from Russia, and one delegate from the Menshevik Organizing Committee. We were to be represented there by Litvinov. It was obvious in advance what kind of conference it would be, and what could be expected of it, and it was therefore arranged that Litvinov would merely read the declaration of our Central Committee. Ilyich drew up a rough draft of the declaration for Litvinov. It put forward the demand that Vandervelde, Guesde and Sembat should resign immediately from the bourgeois cabinets of Belgium and France, and that all the Socialist parties should support the Russian workers in their fight against tsarism. The declaration stated that the Social-Democrats of Germany and Austria had committed a monstrous crime against socialism and the International by voting for war credits and concluding a "civil peace" with the Junkers, the clergy and the bourgeoisie, but that the Belgian and French Socialists had done no better. The workers of Russia extended a comradely hand to the Socialists who acted like Karl Liebknecht, like the Socialists of Serbia and Italy, like the British comrades of the I.L.P. and some of the members of the British Socialist Party, like our arrested comrades of the Russian Social-Democratic Labour Party.

"This is the road we call you to take, the road of socialism. Down with chauvinism, which is ruining the proletarian cause! Long live international socialism!" (*Works*, 3rd Russ. ed., Vol. XVIII, p. 123.) These were the concluding words of the declaration, which was signed by the Central Committee and by the representative of the Lettish Social-Democrats Bērziņš. The chairman did not give Litvinov a chance to read the declaration to the end. Litvinov therefore handed it over to the chairman and walked out declaring that the R.S.D.L.P. was not participating in the conference. After Litvinov's withdrawal, the conference adopted a resolution supporting the "war of liberation" until victory over Germany was achieved. Among those who voted for that resolution were Keir Hardie and MacDonald.

Meanwhile preparations were going forward for an international women's conference. The important thing was not only to have such a conference take place, but to avoid its assuming a pacifist character, and have it take up a definite revolutionary stand. A good deal of preliminary work was therefore involved, the brunt of which was borne by Inessa. Assisting the editors of the Central Organ in translating all kinds of documents, and having been directly engaged in the struggle against "defencism" from the very outset, she was admirably suited for the job. Besides, she knew foreign languages, and corresponded with Clara Zetkin, Balabanova, Kollontai and Englishwomen, thus helping to strengthen the early threads of international ties. Those threads were extremely weak and often broke, but Inessa kept mending them again and again. She corresponded with the French comrades through Staël, who lived in Paris. Contact with Balabanova was easiest of all. She worked in Italy and took part in the work of the *Avanti*. The revolutionary temper of the Italian Socialist Party was at its highest pitch at that time. Anti-defencist feeling was rising in Germany. On December 2 Liebknecht voted against war credits. Clara Zetkin convened the International Women's Conference. She was the secretary of the International Bureau of Socialist Women. Together with K. Liebknecht, Rosa Luxemburg and F. Mehring she

fought against the chauvinist majority in the German Social-Democratic Party. Inessa corresponded with her. As
for Kollontai, she had left the Mensheviks by that time.
She wrote to Vladimir Ilyich and me in January and
sent us a leaflet. "My dear respected comrade," Ilyich
wrote her in return. "Thank you very much for the leaflet
(the most I can do at present is to hand it over to the
local members of *Rabotnitsa* editorial board—they have
already sent a letter to Zetkin of apparently the
same content as yours)." (*Lenin Miscellany*, II, p. 221.)
Ilyich then goes on to clarify the position of the
Bolsheviks. "Apparently you do not entirely agree
with the civil war slogan, which you relegate, so to speak,
to a minor (I should even say to a conditional) place behind the slogan of peace. And you underline that 'what we
must put forward is a slogan that would *unite* us all.'

"Frankly, what I fear most of all at the present time
is just this kind of indiscriminate unity, which, in my opinion, is most dangerous and harmful to the proletariat."
(*Ibid.*) It was on the basis of Ilyich's position that Inessa corresponded with Kollontai about the conference. Kollontai was not able to attend it.

The international conference at Berne was held on
March 26-28. The largest and best organized delegation
was the German, headed by Clara Zetkin. The delegates
of the Russian Central Committee were Armand, Lilina,
Ravich, Krupskaya and Rozmirovich. The Polish "Rozłamowcy" were represented by Kamenska (Domskaya), who
kept together with the delegation of the Central Committee.
There were two more Russians representing the Organizing Committee. Balabanova represented Italy. Louise
Simanot, a Frenchwoman, was strongly influenced by Balabanova. The temper of the Dutch was sheerly pacifist.
Roland-Holst, who then belonged to the Left wing, could
not come; there was a delegate from the Troelstra Party,
which was out-and-out chauvinist. The English delegates
belonged to the opportunist I.L.P., and the Swiss dele-

gates were also pacifistically inclined. This tendency predominated. In comparison with the London Conference six weeks before, this one, of course, signified no little progress. The fact that women Socialists of the belligerent countries had gathered together at this conference was significant in itself.

Most of the German delegates belonged to the K. Liebknecht-Rosa Luxemburg group. This group had begun to dissociate itself from its chauvinists and fight its government. Rosa Luxemburg had been arrested. This held good only for home use. On the international rostrum, however, they thought they had to be as conciliatory as possible, since they represented a country that was winning battles at the fronts at the moment. If the conference, convened with such difficulty, broke up, they would be held responsible for it, and the chauvinists of all countries, the German social-patriots first and foremost would have exulted at its failure. Clara Zetkin, therefore, was inclined to make concessions to the pacifists, and this meant watering down the revolutionary essence of the resolution. Our delegation—the delegation of the Central Committee of the R.S.D.L.P.—supported the point of view of Ilyich as expressed in his letter to Kollontai. It was a matter not of any kind of unity, but of unity for revolutionary struggle against chauvinism, for the proletariat's uncompromising struggle against the ruling class. Chauvinism was not condemned in the resolution drawn up by a committee consisting of German, English and Dutch delegates. We submitted our own declaration. It was defended by Inessa, and supported by Kamenska, the representative of the Polish women. We were not supported by the conference. Everyone criticized our "splitting" policy. Events soon proved the correctness of our position, however. The tame pacifism of the English and the Dutch did not advance international action a single step. A greater role in hastening the end of the war was played by the revolutionary struggle and a clean break with the chauvinists.

Ilyich tackled the task of rallying the forces for the struggle on the internationl front with all the ardour of his nature. "No matter that we are so few," he said once. "We shall have millions with us." He drafted our resolution for the Berne Women's Conference, too, and followed all its proceedings. Obviously, it was very difficult for him to put up with the role of a sort of shadow-leader in the momentous events that were taking place around him and in which he longed with all his being to take a direct part.

One incident sticks in my memory. Inessa and I were visiting Abram Skovno in the hospital (he had undergone an operation), when Ilyich came along and urged Inessa to go and see Zetkin, and persuade her of the correctness of our position. She would have to see, she could not help seeing, he said, that sliding down into pacifism at such a time was impossible. All the issues at stake had to be emphasized very strongly. Ilyich cited argument after argument that was to be used to convince Zetkin. Inessa was not keen on going. She did not believe that anything would come of it. Ilyich insisted and pleaded warmly. Nothing came of Inessa's talk with Zetkin.

Another international conference was held in Berne on April 17—the Conference of Socialist Youth. A fairly large number of young men from various belligerent countries, who refused to go to the front and fight in the imperialist war, had gathered in Switzerland at the time, to which they had emigrated as a neutral country. These young men, it goes without saying, were revolutionary minded. It was no accident that the International Women's Conference was immediately followed by the Conference of Socialist Youth.

Inessa and Safarov spoke at the conference on behalf of the Central Committee of our Party.

In March my mother died. She had been a close comrade, who had helped in all our work. In Russia, during police raids, she would hide all illegal materials. She took parcels and messages to comrades in prison. She had lived with us in Siberia and abroad, done the house-keeping, entertained the comrades who came to see us, made special vests with illegal literature sewn up in them, written the "skeletons" for invisible-ink letters, etc. The comrades loved her. The last winter had been a very bad one for her. Her strength was at very low ebb. She had been homesick, but had had no one in Russia to take care of her there. She often had arguments with Vladimir Ilyich, but had always been solicitous about him, and Vladimir, too, had been considerate towards her. Once Mother sat looking glum. She was an inveterate smoker and had forgotten to buy cigarettes; it was Sunday, and no tobacco was to be obtained anywhere. Seeing this, Ilyich said: "What a thing to worry about—I'll get you some in a minute," and off he went to hunt up some cigarettes in the cafés. He found some and brought them home. Shortly before she died Mother said to me: "No, I won't go to Russia by myself. I'll wait until you two go." On another occasion she began to talk about religion. She considered herself religious, but had not gone to church for years, had never kept the fast, never prayed, and, in general, religion played no part in her life, but she did not like to talk about it. And now she had broken her rule, saying: "I believed in God in my youth, but after having lived and learned life, I saw what nonsense the whole thing was."

She had often expressed a desire to be cremated when she died. The little house in which we lived stood quite close to the Berne woods, and when the warm spring sun began to shine, she felt drawn to the woods. We went there together, and sat on a bench for about half an hour; she barely managed to walk back, and the next day her death agony started. We did as she had asked—cremated her body at the Berne Crematorium.

Vladimir Ilyich and I sat waiting in the cemetery, and in about two hours an attendant brought us a tin can with the ashes still warm in it, and showed us where to bury it.

Family life became more student-like than ever. Our

landlady, a devout old woman who worked as a presser, asked us to look for other lodgings as she wanted to let our room to religious-minded people. We moved to another room.

The trial of the five Duma deputies took place on February 10. All five Bolshevik deputies—Petrovsky, Muranov, Badayev, Samoilov and Shagov, together with L. B. Kamenev were sentenced to deportation.

In his article "What the Trial of the R.S.D.L.P. Group Has Proved," written on March 29, 1915, Vladimir Ilyich stated: "The facts show that in the very first months following the outbreak of the war, the class-conscious vanguard of the workers in Russia rallied *in deed* around the Central Committee and the Central Organ. However unpalatable this fact may be to certain 'groups,' it is incontrovertible. The words cited in the indictment: 'The guns should be turned not against our brothers, the wage slaves of other countries, but against the reactionary and bourgeois governments and parties of all countries'—these words, thanks to the trial, will spread and have already spread throughout Russia an appeal to proletarian internationalism, to proletarian revolution. The class slogan of the vanguard of the workers of Russia has now reached the broadest masses thanks to the trial.

"Widespread chauvinism among the bourgeoisie and part of the petty bourgeoisie, vacillations in the other part, and such an appeal of the working class—such is the actual objective picture of our political divisions. It is to this actual picture, and not to the good wishes of the intellectuals and founders of small groups that one must adjust one's 'prospects,' hopes and slogans.

"The *Pravda*-ist newspapers and work of the 'Muranov type'* have created unity among four-fifths of Russia's

---

* Muranov stated at the trial that he had organized the workers around the Party under the slogans of its Central Committee, and described the use of parliamentary methods for revolutionary purposes.—*Ed.*

class-conscious workers. About forty thousand workers bought *Pravda,* and many more read it. Even if war, prison, Siberia and penal servitude break five times more of them, ten times more—this stratum *can never be* destroyed. It is alive. It is imbued with the revolutionary spirit and anti-chauvinism. It *alone* stands among the masses of the people, in the very thick of them, as the spokesman of internationalism of the toiling, the exploited and the oppressed. It *alone* has stood its ground amid the general ruin. It alone leads the semi-proletarian strata *away from* the social-chauvinism of the Cadets, Trudoviks, Plekhanov and *Nasha Zarya* to socialism. Its existence, its ideas, its activities, its appeal to the 'brotherhood of wage slaves of other countries' have been revealed to the whole of Russia by the trial of the R.S.D.L.P. group.

"It is with this section that we must work. It is its unity that we must defend against the social-chauvinists. It is along this road alone that the working-class movement in Russia can develop towards social revolution and not towards national liberalism of the 'European' type." (*Works*, Vol. 21, pp. 153-54.)

Events soon proved that Lenin was right. He worked indefatigably to disseminate the ideas of internationalism, to expose social-chauvinism in all its varied forms.

After my mother's death I had a relapse of my old complaint and was ordered by the doctors to take the mountain air. Ilyich found through the advertisements a cheap boarding-house in a non-fashionable locality at the foot of the Rothorn in Sörenberg. We lived there in the Hotel Marienthal all through the summer.

Shortly before our departure the "Japanese" (Bosch and Pyatakov) arrived in Berne with a scheme for establishing abroad an illegal magazine in which all the most important questions could be comprehensively dealt with. The *Communist* was to be published under the auspices of the Central Organ, with P. and N. Kievsky (Bosch and Pyatakov) as associate editors. This arrangement was agreed upon. During the summer Ilyich wrote a comprehensive article for the *Communist* "The Collapse of the Second International," and in cooperation with Zinoviev he wrote, in preparation for the conference of internationalists, a pamphlet entitled *Socialism and War*.

We fixed up nicely in Sörenberg. All around there were woods and mountains, with even snow on the summit of Rothorn. The mail was delivered with Swiss punctuality. We found that even in such an out-of-the-way village as Sörenberg one could obtain any book one needed from the Berne or Zurich libraries free of charge. All you had to do was to send a post card to the library giving your address and the book you wanted. No questions were asked, no certificates or guarantees were demanded. Such a contrast to bureaucratic France! Two days later the book arrived in a cardboard wrapper with a tab tied to it with string, on one side of which was the address of the reader, on the other the address of the library that had sent it. This enabled Ilyich to work even in such an out-of-the-way place. Ilyich was lavish of praise for Swiss culture. He found he could work very well in Sörenberg. After a while Inessa came to stay with us. We would get up early, and before dinner, which was served throughout Switzerland at 12 o'clock, each of us would work in different nooks of the garden. Inessa often played the piano during those hours, and it was very pleasant to work to the sounds of music drifting down into the garden. In the afternoon we used to go for walks in the mountains sometimes for the rest of the day. Ilyich loved the mountains—he liked to climb the spurs of Rothorn towards the evening, when one got a beautiful view from the heights with the rose-tinted mist curling below, or to roam about the Schrattenfluh (a mountain about two kilometres from us) which we translated as "accursed steps." It was covered with a sort of corroded rock worn away by the spring streams, and it was impossible to climb to its broad flat summit. We seldom climbed the Rothorn, although it commanded a lovely view of the Alps. We went to bed at cockcrow, coming home with armfuls of alpine roses and berries; we were all passionate mushroomers—there were edible mushrooms galore, but lots of other fungus growth too, and we used to argue fiercely over the different kinds and names as if it were a resolution on some vital issue.

The struggle in Germany was beginning to rise. The *International*, a magazine founded by Rosa Luxemburg and Franz Mehring, appeared in April and was immediately suppressed. A pamphlet by Junius (Rosa Luxemburg) *The Crisis of German Social-Democracy* was published. An appeal of the German Left Social-Democrats written by Karl Liebknecht entitled "The Chief Enemy Is in Your Own Country" was issued, and at the beginning of June K. Liebknecht and Duncker drew up "An Open Letter to the Central Committee of the Social-Democratic Party and the Reichstag Faction" protesting against the attitude of the Social-Democratic majority towards the war. This "Open Letter" was signed by a thousand party functionaries.

In face of the growing influence of the Left Social-Democrats, the Central Committee of the German Social-Democratic Party decided on a countermove. On the one hand it issued a manifesto over the signatures of Kautsky, Haase and Bernstein against annexations and calling for party unity, and on the other it came out against the Left opposition in its own name and in the name of the Reichstag faction.

In Switzerland Robert Grimm called a preliminary conference for July 11 at Berne to discuss the preparations for the international conference of Left-wingers. The meeting was attended by seven persons—Grimm, Zinoviev, P. B. Axelrod, Warski, Valetsky, Balabanova and Morgari. As a matter of fact, apart from Zinoviev, there were no real Left-wingers at that preliminary conference, and one could gather from the drift of their talk that none of its participants was seriously interested in convening a conference of the Lefts.

Vladimir Ilyich was worried, and sent letters out in all directions—to Zinoviev, Radek, Bèrziņš, Kollontai and the Lausanne comrades—to make sure that places were secured for genuine Lefts at the forthcoming conference, and to ensure the greatest possible unity among them. By the middle of August the Bolsheviks had drawn up: 1) a manifesto; 2) draft resolutions; 3) a draft declaration, which were forwarded to comrades of the extreme Left for consideration. By October Lenin's and Zinoviev's pamphlet *Socialism and War* had been translated into German.

The conference was held in Zimmerwald on September 5-8. Delegates were there from eleven countries (thirty-eight delegates in all). What was known as the Zimmerwald Left group consisted of only nine people (Lenin, Zinoviev, Bèrziņš, Höglund, Nerman, Radek, Borchardt and Platten; after the conference Roland-Holst joined them). Other Russian delegates at the conference were Trotsky, Axelrod, Martov, Natanson, Chernov and a Bundist. Trotsky did not join the Left Zimmerwaldists.

Vladimir Ilyich left for the conference before it was due to open, and at a private meeting on the 4th made a report on the character of the war and the tactics to be applied by the international conference. The dispute centred around the question of the manifesto. The Lefts submitted their draft manifesto and resolution on the war and the tasks of the Social-Democrats. The majority rejected the draft of the Lefts and adopted a much vaguer and less militant manifesto. The Lefts signed the general manifesto. The following appraisal of the Zimmerwald Conference was given by Vladimir Ilyich in his article "The First Step": "Should our Central Committee have signed a manifesto that suffered from inconsistency and timidity? We think we should. Our disagreement, the disagreement not only of our Central Committee but of the whole Left, *international, revolutionary-Marxist* part of the conference is openly expressed in a special resolution, and in a special draft manifesto, and in a special declaration on the motives of voting for a compromise manifesto. We did not conceal one iota of our views, slogans and tactics. The German edition of our pamphlet *Socialism and War* was distributed at the conference. We have promulgated, are promulgating and shall promulgate our views to no less an extent than the manifesto will be promulgated. That this manifesto is a *step forward* towards a real struggle against opportunism, towards breaking and splitting with it, is a fact. It would be sectarianism to refuse to take this step *together* with the German, French, Swedish, Norwegian and Swiss minority, when we retain complete freedom and the full possibility to criticize inconsistency and achieve something greater." (*Works*, Vol. 21, pp. 353-54.)

At the Zimmerwald Conference the Lefts organized a bureau of their own and in general formed a distinct group.

Although Ilyich had written before the Zimmerwald Conference that the Kautskyites ought to have had our draft resolution presented to them: "The Dutch plus ourselves plus the Left Germans plus nought—that does not matter, it will not be Nought afterwards, but All," the rate of progress was nevertheless very slow indeed, and Ilyich could not reconcile himself to it. In fact, his article "The First Step" begins by emphasizing the slow rate of development of the revolutionary movement. "The development of the international socialist movement is making slow progress in the epoch of extremely acute crisis caused by the war." (*Ibid.*, p. 350.) It was therefore in a pretty irritable frame of mind that Ilyich returned from the Zimmerwald Conference.

The day after Ilyich's return we climbed the Rothorn. We climbed with "glorious zest," but when we got to the top Ilyich suddenly lay down on the ground in a rather uncomfortable position, and fell asleep almost right in the snow. Clouds gathered, then broke, and a wonderful view of the Alps opened before us, but Ilyich slept like the dead, without stirring. He slept for over an hour. Zimmerwald must have taken it out of him pretty badly.

It took several days rambling about the mountains and the general bracing atmosphere of Sörenberg to bring Ilyich round again. Kollontai was going to America, and Ilyich wrote urging her to do all she could in the way of rallying the American Left-wing internationalist elements. Early in October we returned to Berne. Ilyich went to Geneva to report back on the Zimmerwald Conference, and continued his correspondence with Kollontai about the Americans, etc.

The autumn was rather hot and close. Berne is chiefly an administrative and academic centre. It has many good libraries, and lots of scholars, but life there is soaked in a sort of petty-bourgeois dullness. Berne is very "democratic"— the wife of the Republic's highest official shakes her rugs out on the balcony every day, but the life of the women in Berne is wholly submerged in these rugs and the domestic comforts they stand for. We rented a room with electric lighting in the autumn, and moved our portmanteau and our books over. That same day the Shklovskys dropped in, and I began showing off the electric lights to them. When they had gone the landlady came bouncing in and demanded that we move out the very next day— she would not put up with anybody turning on the electricity in the daytime in her house. We decided that she was not all there, and took a room in a different place, a more humble place without electricity. This petty-bourgeois stamp lay upon everything in Switzerland. A Russian theatrical company, playing in German, once visited Berne. They showed L. Tolstoi's *The Living Corpse.* We went to see the play. The acting was fine. Ilyich, who heartily detested every kind of philistinism and conventionality, was greatly stirred by the play. He wanted to go and see it again afterwards. The Russians liked it very much. So did the Swiss. But to them the play appealed in quite a different way. They were terribly sorry for Protasov's wife, and took her troubles to heart. "What a good-for-nothing husband she went and married. Mind you, they were rich people of high standing, and could have lived so happily. Poor Liza!"

The autumn of 1915 found us busier than ever in the libraries and taking our usual walks, but nothing could shake off this feeling of being cooped up in a petty-bourgeois democratic cage. Out there the revolutionary struggle was mounting, life was seething, but it was all so far away.

Very little could be done in Berne by way of establishing direct contacts with the Lefts. I remember Inessa making a trip to French Switzerland to get in touch with the Swiss Lefts, Naine and Graber. Try as she might, she could not get to see them. They always had some excuse. Either Naine was out fishing, or Graber was busy with domestic affairs. "Father is busy today, it's our washing-day, and he's hanging out the washing," Graber's little daughter informed Inessa politely. Fishing and hanging out the washing are all very well in their way—Ilyich often stood guard over a pan of milk to see that it did not run over—but when the fishing-rod and the washing stood in the way of an important discussion about organizing the Lefts, then there was something wrong about it. Inessa got a passport in somebody else's name and went to Paris. On their return from Zimmerwald, Merrheim and Bourderon had set up in Paris a Committee for Restoring International Contacts. Inessa represented the Bolsheviks on it. She had to fight hard there for the Left line, which won the day in the long run. Inessa gave Ilyich a full account of her work in her letters.

"Dear Vladimir Ilyich," she wrote in a post card on January 25, 1916. "Thank you for your letter—it calmed me and cheered me up. As it happened I was upset that day over my failure with Merrheim. After reading what you say about Trotsky's refusal to contribute to the Dutch magazine, I am better able to account for Merrheim's refusal to take part in it—obviously there is a connection between the two. Your letter could not have been more to the point for another reason—in that it has now definitely strengthened the point of view I had formed as to the character of the work, but over which I had slightly wavered. On the whole, I am living well here, although I find it very tiring. Today, for instance, I waited for four hours to see somebody. But then I succeeded at last in getting a ticket to the national library, and a lot of information besides on how to use the catalogues and find what I wanted there. Well, I wish you the best. Sincerely yours."

Simultaneously with this letter Inessa sent a full account of her further activities, concealed in the covers of a book. This is what she wrote:

"Dear friends, I am writing just a few lines as I have very little time. Since last writing you, there have been two meetings of the Committee of Action. At one of them we discussed the appeal (about the 'minority,' of the French Party joining the German 'minority' and not the 'majority,' about the re-establishment of the International). Trotsky's draft was rejected and Merrheim's adopted instead, in which nothing is said about re-establishment, but merely that 'the International should be based on the class struggle, on the struggle against imperialism, on the struggle for peace. We support that kind of International.' Then it goes on to say that an International which would not be based on these foundations would be a deceit of the proletariat. I proposed several amendments—about the struggle against the social-chauvinists (I was told it would be inserted at the end), about the International fighting against imperialism (this was accepted), and finally I opposed that 'we support that kind of International,' and proposed the wording 'we shall reorganize the International on the basis, etc.' Merrheim and Bourderon let go at me for this 'reorganizing.' Merrheim said that we are Guesdists (old methods), that we think in the abstract, that we do not reckon with circumstances, that the Socialists in France will not hear of a split, and so on. I told him that an old-type Guesdist was not such a bad thing, that our present tactics were real and vital, as we could only rally the forces of the proletariat behind us by clearly and definitely opposing our point of view to that of the chauvinists; that the leaders' betrayal has evoked mistrust and disappointment; that many workers at the factories, on reading our pamphlet, said: 'This is very good, but there are no more Socialists'; that we must carry into the masses the good tidings that there *are* Socialists, that we can do it only by making a clean break with the chauvinists."

Inessa goes on to write about the work with the youth, the plan for publishing leaflets, about contacts with the mechanics, tailors, navvies and other sections of the syndicalists, etc. She did a great deal of work in our Paris group, and had met Sapozhkov, a member of the group, who had started by going to the front as a volunteer and who now shared the views of the Bolsheviks and had begun to conduct propaganda among the French soldiers.

Shklovsky organized a small chemical laboratory, and our people (Kasparov, Zinoviev) worked there for a livelihood. Zinoviev gazed with a pensive eye at the various tubes and retorts that had made their appearance in everyone's rooms.

The work that could be done in Berne was mostly theoretical. Many things had become clearer during the war. Characteristic in this respect was the question of a United States of Europe. The Declaration of the Central Committee, published in the Central Organ on November 1, 1914, said:

"The immediate political slogan of the Social-Democrats of Europe must be the formation of a republican United States of Europe, but in contrast to the bourgeoisie, which is ready to 'promise' anything in order to draw the proletariat into the general current of chauvinism, the Social-Democrats will explain that this slogan is utterly false and senseless without the revolutionary overthrow of the German, Austrian and Russian monarchies." (*Works*, Vol. 21, pp. 16-17.)

During the conference of the sections abroad held in March this slogan was hotly debated. The report of the conference stated: "... On the question of the slogan of a 'United States of Europe' the discussion took a one-sided political character, and it was decided to postpone the question until it had been dealt with on the *economic* side in the press." (*Ibid.*, p. 137.)

The question of imperialism, its economic essence, the exploitation of the weaker states by the powerful capitalist states, and the exploitation of the colonies, loomed large. The Central Organ, therefore, came to the conclusion that:

"From the standpoint of the economic conditions of imperialism, i.e., export of capital and the fact that the world has been divided up among the 'advanced' and 'civilized' colonial powers—a United States of Europe, under capitalism, is either impossible or reactionary.... A United States of Europe under capitalism is tantamount to an agreement to divide up the colonies." (*Ibid.*, pp. 309, 310.)

But perhaps it was possible to put forward another slogan, the slogan of a United States of the World? Here is what Ilyich wrote in this connection:

"A United States of the World (not of Europe alone) is the state form of the union and freedom of nations which we associate with socialism—until the complete victory of communism brings about the total disappearance of the state, including the democratic state. As a separate slogan, however, the slogan of a United States of the World would hardly be a correct one, first, because it merges with socialism; second, because it may be wrongly interpreted to mean that the victory of socialism in a single country is impossible, and it may also create misconceptions as to the relations of such a country to the others." (*Ibid.*, p. 311.)

This article is a good illustration of Ilyich's train of thought at the end of 1915. Clearly, it took the line of deeper study of the economic roots of the world war, i.e., of imperialism, on the one hand, and that of ascertaining the ways which the world struggle for socialism would follow, on the other.

It was on these problems that Vladimir Ilyich worked at the end of 1915 and in 1916, when he collected material for his pamphlet *Imperialism, the Highest Stage of Capitalism*, and read Marx and Engels over and over again in order to obtain a clearer idea of the epoch of socialist revolution, its ways and its development.

ZURICH

1916

In January 1916 Vladimir Ilyich started to write his pamphlet on imperialism for the Parus Publishing House. He attached tremendous importance to this question, believing that a real, profound appraisal of the present war was impossible unless the essence of imperialism, economically as well as politically, was made perfectly clear. He therefore undertook the job willingly. In the middle of February Ilyich had work to do in the libraries of Zurich, and we went there for a week or two, and then kept putting off our return day by day until, in the end, we stayed there for good, Zurich being a livelier place than Berne. There were a large number of revolutionary-minded young foreigners in Zurich, besides working-class elements; the Social-Democratic Party there was of a more Leftist tendency, and the petty-bourgeois spirit seemed to be less in evidence there.

We went to rent a room. At one place the landlady a Frau Prelog, looked more Viennese than Swiss. This was due to her having been employed for a long time as a cook in a Vienna hotel. We arranged to take a room at her house, but the next day she found out that her old lodger was coming back. He had been lying in the hospital with a broken head, and had now recovered. Frau Prelog asked us to find a room elsewhere, but offered us to come and have our meals with her at a fairly cheap price. We ate there for about two months. The food was plain but sufficient. Ilyich liked the simplicity of everything there—the fact that coffee was served in a cup with a broken handle, that we ate in the kitchen, that the talk was simple, talk not about the food, not about how many potatoes had to be used for this or that soup, but about matters that were of interest to the boarders. There were not many of them, though, and they kept changing. It was not long before we realized that we had landed in peculiar company, the "lower depths" of Zurich. One of the diners was a prostitute, who spoke without reserve about her profession, but who was much more concerned about the health of her mother and the kind of job her sister would find than about her own profession. A night nurse boarded there for several days, then other boarders began to turn up. Prelog's lodger did not have much to say for himself, but from what he did say it was clear that he was almost a criminal type. Our presence embarrassed no one, and, if the truth be told, the conversation of these people was more "human" and lively than that heard in the decorous dining rooms of a respectable hotel patronized by well-to-do clients.

I urged Ilyich to have his meals at home, as the crowd we dined with was likely to get us into a pretty mess one day. Certain aspects of Zurich's underworld, however, were not without interest.

Later, when reading John Reed's *Daughter of the Revolution*, I liked the way he described the prostitutes. He depicted them not from the angle of their profession or of love, but from the angle of their other interests. Usually writers give little attention to social conditions when describing the underworld.

Later, in Russia, when Ilyich and I went to see Gorky's *Lower Depths* at the Art Theatre—Ilyich was very keen on seeing the play—he was repelled by the theatricality of the production, the absence of those details of everyday life which gives the touch of authenticity and concreteness.

Afterwards, on meeting Frau Prelog in the street, Vladimir Ilyich always greeted her in a friendly manner. And we were always meeting her, as we had taken a room nearby in a side-street, in the home of a shoemaker by the name of Kammerer. The room was not exactly a bargain. It was a dingy old house, built, I think, way back in the sixteenth century, and had a smelly courtyard. For the same money we could have rented a much better room, but we liked our hosts. It was a working-class family with a revolutionary outlook, who condemned the imperialist war. The place could be truly called an "international." Our landlord and his family occupied two rooms, one room was occupied by the wife and children of a German baker who was in the army, one by an Italian, another by some Austrian actors who had a wonderful brindled cat, and the last room was occupied by us Russians. There was not a hint of any chauvinism, and once, when a whole women's international had gathered round the gas-stove, Frau Kammerer exclaimed with indignation: "The soldiers ought to turn their weapons against their governments!" After that Ilyich would not hear of moving to another place. Frau Kammerer taught me many useful things— how to cook satisfying meals cheaply and quickly. I learned other things too. One day the newspapers announced that Switzerland was having difficulty in importing meat, and the government therefore appealed to citizens to abstain from meat two days in the week. The butcher-shops still sold meat on "fast" days. I had bought meat for dinner, as usual, and, standing by the gas-stove, I asked Frau Kammerer what check there was as to whether the citizens were obeying the appeal, whether there were any inspectors going around the houses. "There's no need to check up," Frau Kammerer said, surprised at the question. "Once it has been published in the papers that there are difficulties, what working man, other than a bourgeois, maybe, will eat meat on meatless days?" Seeing my embarrassment, she added gently: "But that doesn't apply to foreigners." This intelligent proletarian approach won Vladimir Ilyich completely.

Going through my letters to Shlyapnikov for that period, I found one dated April 8, 1915. It is characteristic of the mood of that time. "Dear friend," I wrote, "I have received your letter of April 3, and was somewhat relieved. It had been painful to read your angry letters in which you had spoken about going to America and had been ready to blame everything and everybody. Correspondence is a beastly thing, it lets misunderstandings pile up one on top of the other.... In my missing letter I wrote in full detail why Grigory* could not be dragged either to Russia or to your parts. He took your reproach about his not having moved to Stockholm very much to heart. We can't afford to undermine the editorial board of our Central Organ and our foreign headquarters in general. The C.O., now more than ever, has succeeded in gaining ground during the war by dint of tremendous effort. Its editorial board has played no small part in the International. We can say that now outright, setting aside unnecessary modesty. The *Communist* would not have come out either had it not been for the editorial staff of the Central Organ. And the talk, the cares, and the worries it had cost! Still more so *Vorbote* (organ of the Zimmerwald Left). If we are going to deplete the editorial staff we shall have no one left to do the work. It isn't going to be so easy to

_____
* Grigory Zinoviev.—*Ed.*

get together a new editorial staff. There was Bukharin, with suggestions for sending him here and there; there was talk of his going to Cracow, then to Berne. Nothing could be done. Two people are not enough, and here you want to take one of them away. If you strip the foreign base there will be nothing to send across. Grigory sometimes gets fed up to the teeth with life abroad and then he doesn't know what to do with himself. And your reproaches only make things worse. Looking at it from the point of view of the usefulness of the work as a whole, Grigory should not be touched. There was a question of the whole editorial board moving over, but this brought up the question of money, of international influence, of police regime considerations. We put the question of money to the 'Japanese' point-blank, and they said they had none. In Stockholm life is much dearer. Here Grigory is working in a laboratory, we have libraries here, and that means a chance to earn at least something by writing. The problem of making a living will become more acute here, too, in the near future.

"As to Ilyich's supposed enthusiasm for emigrant affairs, the reproach is unfounded. He does not engage in them at all. International affairs claim more of his time and attention than ever, but that is unavoidable. True, his enthusiasm now is 'self-determination of nations.' In my opinion, if we want to make good 'use' of him now, we ought to insist on his writing a popular pamphlet on the subject. The question is by no means one of academic interest at the present time. There is great confusion on this question among international Social-Democracy, but that is no reason for putting it off. We had a dispute with Radek here last winter on the subject. Personally, that discussion was of great benefit to me." And I set forth on several pages the gist of this discussion and Ilyich's point of view.

Our life in Zurich was, as Ilyich described it in a letter home, "slow-poky" and somewhat detached from the local colony. We worked hard and regularly at the libraries. Every afternoon young Grisha Usievich—he was killed in 1919 during the Civil War—dropped in for half an hour on his way home from the emigrants' restaurant. Zemlyachka's nephew, who later went mad through starvation, used to visit us occasionally in the mornings. He went about in such ragged muddy clothes that he was refused admission to the Swiss libraries. He tried to catch Ilyich before he went to the library, saying that he had to discuss certain questions of principle with him. He got on Ilyich's nerves.

We started to leave the house earlier to take a stroll along the shore of the lake and have a chat before going to the library. Ilyich spoke about the book he was writing and the various thoughts that occupied his mind.

Those of the Zurich group we saw most often were Usievich and Kharitonov. Others I remember were Uncle Vanya (Avdeyev), a metal-worker, Turkin, a Ural worker, and Boitsov, who later worked in the Central Political Education Department. I also remember a Bulgarian worker, whose name I have forgotten. Most of the comrades of our Zurich group worked in factories, and were very busy; group meetings were comparatively rare. But then the members of our group had good connections with the workers of Zurich; they stood closer to the life of the local workers than was the case in other Swiss towns (with the exception of Chaux-de-Fonds, where our group was even closer to the mass of workers).

The Swiss movement in Zurich was headed by Fritz Platten. He was secretary of the Party, and joined the Zimmerwald Left group. He was the son of a worker, a simple ardent fellow, who had great influence over the masses. The editor of *Volksrecht*, Nobs, joined the Left Zimmerwaldians too. The young emigrant workers (of whom there were many in Zurich), headed by Willi Münzenberg, were very active and supported the Lefts. All this created intimate ties with the Swiss labour movement. Some comrades, who had never lived among the political emigrants abroad, are under the impression that Lenin had expected big things of the Swiss movement and believed that Switzerland was capable of becoming almost the centre of the future social revolution.

This is not so, of course. Switzerland never had a strong working class; it is mainly a country of health resorts, a small country living off the crumbs of the powerful capitalist countries. The workers of Switzerland, by and large, were not very revolutionary. Democracy and the successful solution of the national question were in themselves not enough to make Switzerland a centre of the social revolution.

It does not follow, of course, that no international propaganda was to be conducted in Switzerland and nothing was to be done to help revolutionize the Swiss labour movement and the Party, for it Switzerland were drawn into the war the situation might have undergone a swift change.

Ilyich read lectures to the Swiss workers and kept in close touch with Platten, Nobs and Münzenberg. Our Zurich group, with the cooperation of several Polish comrades (Broński was living in Zurich at the time), conceived the idea of joint meetings with the Swiss organization in Zurich. They got together in a small café called Zum Adler, not far from our house. Something like forty persons attended the first meeting. Ilyich spoke on current events, and stated his case in a sharp controversial manner. Although the people who had gathered were all internationalists, the Swiss were considerably taken aback by the sharp way in which the question was presented. I remember the speech of one of the representatives of the Swiss youth who said it was impossible to break through a stone wall with one's forehead. The fact remains that our meetings began to peter out, and the fourth one was attended only by us Russians and the Poles, who joked about it, then went home.

During the early months of life in Zurich Vladimir

Ilyich worked chiefly on his pamphlet on imperialism. He was deeply absorbed in this work, and made very many notes. He was particularly interested in the colonies, on which he had collected a mass of material; I remember his putting me to work, too, translating something about the African colonies from the English. He told me many interesting things. Afterwards, when rereading his *Imperialism*, I thought it much drier than his stories had been. He had studied the economics of Europe, America, etc., as the saying goes, to a T. Of course, he was interested not only in the economic system, but in the political forms that went with it and their influence on the masses. The pamphlet was finished by July. The Second Zimmerwald Conference (known as the Kienthal Conference) was held on April 24-30, 1916. Eight months had passed since the first conference, eight months of ever-spreading imperialist war, yet the face of the Kienthal Conference was not so strikingly different from that of the First Zimmerwald Conference. There had been a slight shift to the Left. The Left Zimmerwaldians had twelve instead of eight delegates, and the resolutions of the conference were a step forward. The conference strongly condemned the International Socialist Bureau, and adopted a resolution on peace, which stated: "It is impossible to establish lasting peace on the basis of capitalist society; the conditions necessary for its fulfilment will be created by *socialism*. By abolishing capitalist private property and, consequently, the exploitation of the masses of the people by the propertied classes, as well as national oppression, socialism will also do away with the causes of war. *Hence, the struggle for lasting peace can only be a struggle for the realization of socialism.*" (*Works*, 3rd Russ. ed., Vol. XIX, Appendix, p. 434.) For distributing this manifesto in the trenches three officers and thirty-two soldiers were shot in Germany in May. The German Government feared nothing so much as the revolutionization of the masses.

In its proposals to the Kienthal Conference, the Central Committee of the R.S.D.L.P. drew attention precisely to the necessity of revolutionizing the masses. They stated: "It is not enough that the Zimmerwald manifesto hints at revolution, saying that the workers must make sacrifices for their own cause and not for another's. The road the masses are to take must be clearly and definitely pointed out to them. The masses must know whither they are going and why. That revolutionary mass actions during the war, if successfully followed up, can lead only to the conversion of the imperialist war into a civil war for socialism, is an obvious fact, and to conceal this from the masses is harmful. On the contrary, this objective should be plainly pointed out, no matter how difficult its achievement may seem when we are only at the beginning of the road. It is not enough to say what the Zimmerwald manifesto says, namely, that 'the capitalists are lying when they speak about defending the motherland' in the present war, and that the workers in their revolutionary struggle should act regardless of their country's military situation; we must state clearly what is here only hinted at, namely, that not only the capitalists, but the social-chauvinists and the Kautskyites are lying when they hold the notion of defending the motherland as being applicable to the present imperialist war; that revolutionary action during the war is impossible without the menace of defeat to 'one's own' government, and that all and every defeat of the government in a reactionary war facilitates revolution, which alone is capable of securing a lasting and democratic peace. And lastly, it is necessary to tell the masses that unless they set up their own illegal organizations and press free from military censorship, i.e., an illegal press, no serious support for the nascent revolutionary struggle, its development, criticism of its various steps, rectification of its mistakes, and the systematic broadening and intensification of that struggle, is conceivable." (*Works*, Vol. 22, pp. 164-65.)

This proposal of the Central Committee affords a striking illustration of the attitude of the Bolsheviks and Ilyich to the masses—that of always telling the truth, the whole unvarnished truth to the masses without fear of it frightening them off. The Bolsheviks placed all their hopes in the masses; the masses, and only the masses, would achieve socialism.

I wrote to Shlyapnikov on June 1: "Grigory is very enthusiastic over Kienthal. I can only judge by reports, of course, but there seems to be far too much talk and no inner unity, of the kind that would serve as a pledge of the thing's solidity. Obviously the masses have not started 'shoving upwards' yet, as Badayev puts it, except perhaps, to some extent, the Germans."

A study of the economics of imperialism, an analysis of all the component parts of this "gear box," a sweeping review of the whole world-picture of imperialism—that last stage of capitalism—which was heading for ruin, enabled Ilyich to shed new light on a number of political issues and probe more deeply into the question of what forms the struggle for socialism would take in general and in Russia in particular. Ilyich was anxious to work out his ideas and give them time to fully mature, and so we decided to go to the mountains, all the more that my thyroid was giving me trouble again. The only cure for it was the mountains. We went for six weeks to the Tschudiwiese nursing home, high up in the mountain wilds quite close to the snowy summits, in the Canton of St. Gallen, not far from Zurich. It was a cheap place, costing 2¹/₂ francs a day per person. True, they kept us on a "dairy" diet there. In the morning we had coffee with milk and bread and butter and cheese, but no sugar; for dinner—milk soup, something made of curd-cheese, with milk for a third dish; at four o'clock we had coffee with milk again, and another milk meal in the evening. This milk cure had us howling at first, but after a while we reinforced it with raspberries and bilberries that grew all round in profusion. We had a clean room with electric light, but poorly furnished and without service. We did our own tidying up and cleaned our boots ourselves. This last duty was discharged by Ilyich, who, imitating the Swiss, took my mountain boots and his every morning and went with them to the shed where the boot cleaning was done, and there, exchanging banter with the other boot-blacks, he worked away with such zeal that once he knocked over a wicker-basket full of empty beer bottles amid general laughter. The crowd was a democratic one. A home that charged 2½ francs a day for board and lodging was not patronized by "respectable" folks. In some ways it reminded me of the French Bombon, except that the people were simpler, poorer, with the democratic spirit of the Swiss. In the evenings the proprietor's son played the accordion while the guests danced for all they were worth. The stamp of their feet could be heard till eleven o'clock. Tschudi-wiese was about eight kilometres from the station, and the only mode of communication was by donkey and narrow mountain trails. Everybody went on foot. Almost every morning a bell used to ring at six o'clock summoning people to give the walkers a send-off, which they did by singing some song about a cuckoo. Every couplet ended with the words: "Good-bye, cuckoo." Vladimir Ilyich liked his morning nap, and used to grumble and pull the blanket over his head. The crowd was anything but politically minded. Even the war was a subject that was never touched upon. Among the visitors was a soldier. His lungs being not very strong, his chiefs had sent him to take a milk cure at the government's expense. The military authorities in Switzerland take good care of the soldiers (Switzerland has a militia, not a regular army). He was quite a decent chap. Vladimir Ilyich walked round him like a cat round the cream bowl, and started a conversation with him several times about the predatory character of the war. The fellow did not argue, but obviously refused to rise to the bait. He was far more interested in his holiday at Tschudiwiese than in political questions.

We had no visitors at Tschudiwiese. There were no Russians living in the vicinity, and we lived a carefree existence, spending all day rambling about the mountains. Ilyich did no work at all there. During our walks in the mountains he spoke a lot about the questions that occupied his mind, about the role of democracy, and the positive and negative aspects of Swiss democracy, often expressing the same thought in different words. Clearly, these questions interested him deeply.

We spent the second part of July and the whole of August in the mountains. When we left everyone gave us the usual send-off by singing "Good-bye, cuckoo." As we were descending through the woods, Vladimir Ilyich suddenly caught sight of some edible mushrooms, and although it was raining, he began to pick them eagerly, as if they were so many Left Zimmerwaldians he were enlisting to our side. We were drenched to the skin, but picked a bagful of mushrooms. Naturally, we missed the train and had to wait two hours at the station for the next one.

Back in Zurich we rented our old room in Spiegelgasse.

During our stay at Tschudiwiese, Vladimir Ilyich had thought out his plan of work for the immediate future from every angle. The first thing, which was particularly important at the moment, was agreement on theoretical questions, the laying down of a clear theoretical line. There were differences with Rosa Luxemburg, Radek, the Dutch, Bukharin, Pyatakov, and to some extent with Kollontai. The sharpest differences were with Pyatakov (P. Kievsky), who had written an article in August entitled "The Proletariat and the Right of Nations to Self-Determination." After reading the manuscript, Ilyich sat down at once to write him a reply—a whole pamphlet entitled *A Caricature of Marxism and "Imperialist Economism."* The pamphlet was written in a very sharp tone, because by that time

Ilyich had arrived at a very clear and definite view of the relationship between economics and politics in the epoch of struggle for socialism. Underestimation of the political struggle in that epoch was characterized by him as imperialist economism. "Capitalism has won," wrote Ilyich, "*therefore* there is no need to think about political questions—argued the old 'Economists' in 1894-1901, who went to the extent of repudiating the political struggle in Russia. Imperialism has won—*therefore* there is no need to think about questions of political democracy, argue the modern 'imperialist Economists.'" (*Works*, Vol. 23, p. 17.)

The role of democracy in the struggle for socialism could not be ignored. "Socialism is impossible without democracy in two respects," Vladimir Ilyich wrote in the same pamphlet. "1. The proletariat cannot carry out a socialist revolution unless it has prepared for it by a struggle for democracy; 2. Victorious socialism cannot maintain its victory and bring humanity to the time when the state will wither away unless democracy is fully achieved." (*Ibid.*, pp. 62-63.)

These words of Lenin's were soon fully borne out by events in Russia. The February Revolution and the subsequent struggle for democracy prepared the way for the October Revolution. The constant broadening and strengthening of the Soviets, of the Soviet system, tends to reorganize democracy itself and to steadily give greater depth of meaning to this concept.

By 1915-1916 Vladimir Ilyich had gone deep into the question of democracy, which he examined in the light of socialist construction. As far back as October 1915 Ilyich had written a reply to an article by Radek (Parabellum) published in *Berner Tagewacht*: "According to Parabellum it works out that *for the sake of* the socialist revolution he spurns a consistently revolutionary programme in the field of democracy. That is wrong. The proletariat can win only through democracy, i.e., through putting into effect full democracy and linking up every step of its progress with democratic demands in their most emphatic wording. It is absurd to *offset* the socialist revolution and the revolutionary struggle against capitalism by *one* of the questions of democracy, in this case the national question. We must *combine* the revolutionary struggle against capitalism with a revolutionary programme and tactics in respect of *all* democratic demands, including a republic, a militia, election of government officials by the people, equal rights for women, self-determination of nations, etc. So long as capitalism exists all these demands are capable of realization only as an exception, and in incomplete, distorted form. Basing ourselves on democracy as already achieved, and showing up its deficiency under capitalism, we demand the overthrow of capitalism and expropriation of the bourgeoisie as an essential basis both for abolishing the poverty of the masses and for *fully* and *thoroughly* implementing *all* democratic transformations. Some of those transformations will be started before the overthrow of the bourgeoisie, others *in the course of* this overthrow, and still others after it. The social revolution is not a single battle but an epoch of a series of battles on all and every problem of economic and democratic transformations, whose completion will be effected only with the expropriation of the bourgeoisie. It is for the sake of this ultimate goal that we must formulate *every one* of our democratic demands in a consistently revolutionary manner. It is quite conceivable that the workers of a given country may overthrow the bourgeoisie *before* any single cardinal democratic transformation has been fully implemented. But it is quite inconceivable that the proletariat, as an historical class, will be able to defeat the bourgeoisie unless it has been prepared for it by being educated in a spirit of the most consistent and determined revolutionary democratism." (*Works*, Vol. 21, pp. 372-73.)

I quote these long passages because they so strikingly express the thoughts which had occupied Ilyich's mind at the end of 1915 and during 1916, thoughts which tinctured all his subsequent utterances. Most of his articles dealing with the questions of the role of democracy in the struggle for socialism were published later—the article against Parabellum in 1927, the pamphlet *Caricature of Marxism* in 1924. They are little known because they were published in symposiums with a small circulation. Yet these articles must be read if one is to understand the vehemence with which Vladimir Ilyich stated the case for the right of nations to self-determination. Considered in the light of Ilyich's general appraisal of democracy this vehemence is understandable. It should be borne in mind that the stand which one took on the question of self-determination was regarded by Ilyich as a touchstone of one's ability to correctly approach all democratic demands in general. All the disputes along this line with Rosa Luxemburg, Radek, the Dutch and Kievsky and a number of other comrades, were conducted from just this angle. In his pamphlet against Kievsky he wrote: "All nations will arrive at socialism—this is inevitable, but not all will do so in exactly the same way, each will contribute something of its own in one or another form of democracy, one or another variety of the dictatorship of the proletariat, one or another rate at which socialist transformations will be effected in the various aspects of social life. There is nothing more primitive from the viewpoint of theory or more ridiculous from that of practice than to paint, 'in the name of historical materialism,' *this* aspect of the future in a monotonous grey. The result will be nothing more than Suzdal daubing." (*Works*, Vol. 23, p. 58.)

The building up of socialism is not merely a matter of economic construction. Economics is only the foundation of socialist construction, its basis and premise; the crux of socialist construction lies in reconstructing the whole social fabric anew, rebuilding it on the basis of socialist revolutionary democratism.

This, if anything, is what most divided Lenin and Trotsky all the time. Trotsky failed to grasp the democratic spirit, the democratic principles of socialist construction, the process of reorganizing the entire mode of life of the masses. It was at that time, too—in 1916—that there already existed in embryo the differences which later arose between Ilyich and Bukharin. Bukharin's underestimation of the role of the state and the dictatorship of the proletariat was revealed in an article entitled "Nota Bene," written at the end of August in No. 6 of *Jugend-Internationale.* Ilyich wrote an article "Youth International" pointing out this mistake of Bukharin's. The dictatorship of the proletariat, ensuring the proletariat's leading role in the reconstruction of the whole social fabric—this is what interested Vladimir Ilyich most of all in the latter half of 1916.

Democratic demands were included in the minimum programme, and so in the first letter which Vladimir Ilyich wrote to Shlyapnikov after his return from Tschudiwiese, he criticized Bazarov for his article in *Letopisi (Annals)* advocating that the minimum programme should be done away with. Ilyich argued with Bukharin, who underestimated the role of the state, the role of the dictatorship of the proletariat, etc. He was angry with Kievsky for failing to understand the leading role of the proletariat. "Do not scorn theoretical agreement," he wrote to Shlyapnikov, "I assure you it is essential for our work during these difficult times." (*Works*, Vol. 35, p. 185.)

Vladimir Ilyich set to work rereading all that Marx and Engels had written on the state and making notes from their works. This equipped him with a deeper understanding of the nature of the coming revolution, and thoroughly prepared him for an understanding of the concrete tasks of that revolution.

On November 30 the Swiss Lefts held a conference on the subject of the attitude towards the war. A. Schmidt from Winterthur urged taking advantage of the democratic facilities in Switzerland for anti-militarist purposes. Ilyich wrote to Schmidt the next day suggesting that "a referendum be taken on the question, formulated as follows: for the expropriation of the big capitalist enterprises in industry and agriculture *as the only way* towards the complete abolition of militarism, or against expropriation.

"In this case," Ilyich wrote to Schmidt, "we shall, in our practical policy, say the same thing that we all admit in theory, namely, that the complete abolition of militarism is conceivable and practicable only in connection with the abolition of capitalism." (*Ibid.*, p. 206.) In a letter written in December 1916 and not published until fifteen years later, Lenin wrote on this question: "You think, perhaps, that I am so naive as to believe that such questions as that of the socialist revolution can be solved 'by persuasion'?

"No. I merely wish to give an *illustration*, and that only of one *particular point*, and that is: what *change* would have to take place in the whole of our Party's propaganda if we intended to take up a really serious stand on the question of *rejecting the defence of the motherland*! This is *only* an illustration to only a particular point—I do not claim any more." (*Lenin Miscellany*, XVII, p. 123.)

Questions of a dialectical approach to all events also occupied Ilyich's thoughts at that period. He fairly pounced on the following sentence in Engels' criticism of the draft of the Erfurt Programme: "... Ultimately such a policy can only lead one's own party astray. They put general, abstract political questions into the foreground, thus concealing the immediate concrete questions, the questions which at the first great events, the first political crisis, put themselves on the agenda." After copying out this passage Ilyich wrote in extra-large letters, putting the words in double parentheses: "((The abstract in the foreground, the concrete obscured!!)) *Nota bene*! Splendid! That hits it on the head! NB."

"Marxian dialectics demands a concrete analysis of every particular historical situation," Vladimir Ilyich wrote in his review of the pamphlet by Junius (*Works*, Vol. 22,

p. 303.) He strove at that period to take things in all their bearings and interrelations. It was from this standpoint that he approached both the question of democracy and that of the right of nations to self-determination.

In the autumn of 1916 and the beginning of 1917 Ilyich was completely absorbed in theoretical work. He tried to use every minute of the time the library was open, going there punctually at 9 a.m., sitting there till 12, coming home at ten past twelve to the minute (the library was closed from 12 to 1), going back again after lunch and staying there until 6 p.m. It was not very convenient for him to work at home. Our room, although it had plenty of light, over-looked the yard, from which came a terrible stink—a sausage factory adjoined our yard: We opened the window only late at night. On Thursday afternoons when the library was closed, we climbed the Zurichberg. Coming home from the library Ilyich would buy two bars of nut chocolate in blue wrappers at 15 centimes, and after lunch we took the chocolate and some books and went off to the mountain. We had our favourite spot there in the heart of the woods, where there were no people about, and Ilyich would lie in the grass deep in his reading.

At that period we had cut down our living expenses to a bare minimum. Ilyich searched hard for something to do to earn some money. He wrote to Granat, to Gorky, and to relatives about it, and once he even proposed to Mark Yelizarov, his sister Anna's husband, a fantastic scheme for publishing a "Pedagogical Encyclopaedia" on which I was to work. I was doing a lot of work then, studying pedagogics and familiarizing myself with the practical side of the school system in Zurich. Ilyich waxed so enthusiastic about this fantastic plan of his that he wrote about care being taken that no one should steal his idea.

The prospect of earning something by writing was not very bright, and so I decided to look for a job in Zurich. There was an Emigrants' Benefit Funds Bureau in Zurich directed by Felix Kohn. I became secretary of the Bureau and helped Felix in his work.

True, the income from this job was more mythical than real, but it was needful work. Comrades had to be helped to find work, all kinds of undertakings had to be arranged, and medical relief given. Funds were very low at the time, and we had more schemes for giving benefit than actual opportunities for rendering it. One scheme, I remember, was for setting up a sanatorium that would pay its own way. The Swiss had such sanatoriums, where the patients worked at gardening or making wicker-chairs in the open air for several hours each day, which helped considerably to reduce the cost of their upkeep. The number of consumptives among the political emigrants was very large.

And so we lived in Zurich, a quiet jog-trot life, while the situation grew steadily more revolutionary. In addition to his work in the theoretical field, Ilyich considered it extremely important to work out a correct tactical line. He believed the time was ripe for a split on an international scale, that it was time to break with the Second International, with the International Socialist Bureau, to break for good and all with Kautsky & Co., to start building up a Third International out of the Zimmerwald Left group. In Russia it was necessary at once to break with Chkheidze and Skobelev and the O.C.-ists,* with those, who, like Trotsky, did not understand that any idea of conciliationism and unity was unthinkable at that moment. It was necessary to wage a revolutionary struggle for socialism and to expose in the most ruthless manner the opportunists, who, instead of suiting the action to the word, were in reality serving the bourgeoisie and betraying the cause of the proletariat. Never before had Vladimir Ilyich been in such an uncompromising mood as he was during the last months of 1916 and the early months

---

* Followers of the O.C. (Organizing Committee) elected by the August bloc.—*Ed.*

Lenin in mountains of Zakopane, Poland, summer 1914

Lenin and a group of Russian exiles in Stockholm, April 13, 1917, on Vazagatan Street, several blocks from the Central Railway Station, where they were to entrain for Petrograd. On Lenin's left is Lingdkhagen, lord mayor of Swedish capital; wearing derby, Ture Nerman, editor of *politeken*, leading Swedish newspaper. Krupskaya can be distinguished in rear, and Inessa Armand to her front, right

of 1917. He was positively certain that the revolution was impending.

On January 22, 1917, Vladimir Ilyich addressed a youth meeting in Zurich, at which he spoke about the Revolution of 1905. There was quite a number of revolutionary-minded young people in Zurich at the time from other countries—Germany, Italy, etc., who refused to fight in the imperialist war, and Vladimir Ilyich wanted to bring home to them as fully as possible the experience of the workers' revolutionary struggle and the significance of the Moscow uprising; he considered the Revolution of 1905 a prelude to the coming European revolution. "Without a doubt," he said, "this coming revolution can only be a proletarian revolution, and in an even more profound sense of the word: a proletarian, socialist revolution in its content. This coming revolution will show to an even greater degree, on the one hand, that only grim battles, only civil wars, can free humanity from the yoke of capital; on the other hand, that only class-conscious proletarians can and will give leadership to the vast majority of the exploited." (*Works*, Vol. 23, p. 245.) Ilyich never for a moment doubted that such were the prospects. But, as to how soon that coming revolution would take place—that, of course, Ilyich could not know. "We of the older generation may not live to see the decisive battles of this coming revolution" (*Ibid.*, p. 246), he wound up rather wistfully. And yet Ilyich thought of nothing else, worked for nothing else but this revolution.

LAST MONTHS IN EMIGRATION.
THE FEBRUARY REVOLUTION

Departure for Russia

One day, after lunch, when Ilyich was about to go to the library and I had finished clearing away the dishes, Broński came in, saying: "Haven't you heard the news?

There's a revolution in Russia!" And he told us about the latest reports published in the special editions of the newspapers. After Broński had gone, we went down to the lake, on the shore of which all the newspapers were posted up as soon as they came out.

We read the reports several times. A revolution had really taken place in Russia. Ilyich's mind went to work at once. I hardly remember how the rest of the day and the night passed. Next day the second batch of official reports about the February Revolution found Ilyich writing to Kollontai in Stockholm: "*Never again* along the lines of the Second International! *Never again* with Kautsky! By all means a *more revolutionary* programme and tactics." And further on: "... *as before*, revolutionary propaganda, agitation and struggle with the aim of an *international* proletarian revolution and for the conquest of power by the 'Soviets of Workers' Deputies' (but not by the Cadet fakers)." (*Works*, Vol. 35, p. 239.)

Ilyich straightaway took a clear uncompromising line, although he had not yet grasped the scope of the revolution. He still gauged it by the scope of the 1905 Revolution, and said that the most important task of the moment was to combine legal work with illegal.

The next day, in reply to Kollontai's telegram asking for instructions, he wrote in a different vein, more concretely. He no longer spoke about the conquest of power by the Soviets of Workers' Deputies prospectively, but spoke about concrete preparations for seizing power and arming the workers, about the fight for bread, peace and freedom. "Spread out! Rouse new sections! Awaken fresh initiative, form new organizations in every stratum and *prove* to them that *peace* can come only with the armed Soviet of Workers' Deputies in power." (*Ibid.*, p. 241.) Together with Zinoviev, Ilyich set to work drawing up a resolution on the February Revolution.

The moment the news of the February Revolution was received, Ilyich was all eagerness to go back to Russia.

England and France would never have allowed any Bolsheviks to go through to Russia. That much was clear to Ilyich, who wrote to Kollontai: "We are afraid we shall not be able to leave this accursed Switzerland very soon." (*Ibid.*) With this in mind, he discussed with Kollontai in his letters of March 16 and 17 how best to organize contact with St. Petersburg.

As there were no legal ways of travelling, illegal ways would have to be used. But what ways? From the moment the news of the revolution was received, Ilyich had no sleep. His nights were spent building the most improbable plans. We could fly over by plane. But such an idea could only be thought of in a waking dream. Put into words, its unreality became at once obvious. The thing was to obtain the passport of some foreigner from a neutral country, best of all a Swede, who was less likely to arouse suspicion. A Swedish passport could be obtained through the Swedish comrades, but ignorance of the language was an obstacle to using it. Perhaps just a little Swedish would do? You might easily give yourself away, though. "Imagine yourself falling alseep and dreaming of Mensheviks, which will start you off swearing juicily in Russian! Where will your disguise be then?" I said with a laugh.

Nevertheless Ilyich wrote to Ganiecki enquiring whether there was any way of getting into the country through Germany.

On March 18, the anniversary of the Paris Commune, Ilyich went to Chaux-de-Fonds, a large Swiss labour centre. He went there gladly. Abramovich, a young comrade, worked at a factory there and took an active part in the Swiss labour movement. The thought of the Paris Commune, of utilizing its experience in the newly launched Russian revolutionary movement, and of avoiding its errors occupied Ilyich's mind a good deal those days, and so his lecture went off very well and he was pleased with it himself. His address impressed our comrades tremendously, but the Swiss thought it impracticable—even the

Swiss working-class centres had but a vague idea of what was going on in Russia.

The Russian emigrant groups of internationalists living in Switzerland met on March 19 to discuss ways of getting back to Russia. Martov proposed a plan for allowing emigrants to pass through Germany in exchange for German and Austrian prisoners of war interned in Russia. However, no one was inclined to accept this plan. Lenin was the only one who jumped at it. We would have to go about it carefully, he said. The best thing would be to have the negotiations started at the initiative of the Swiss Government. Grimm was authorized to enter into negotiations with the Swiss authorities. Nothing came of it, however. No replies were received to the telegrams sent to Russia. Ilyich fretted. "What torture it is for us all to sit here at such a time!" he wrote to Ganiecki in Stockholm. But he had already taken a grip upon himself.

Pravda started coming out in St. Petersburg on March 18, and on the 20th Ilyich started to send in his "Letters from Afar." They were five in number ("The First Stage of the First Revolution," "The New Government and the Proletariat," "Concerning a Proletarian Militia," "How To Achieve Peace," and "The Tasks Connected with the Building of Revolutionary Proletarian State System"). Only the first letter was published on the day Lenin arrived in St. Petersburg, three others were lying in the editors' office and the fifth had not even been sent to *Pravda*, as Lenin had started writing it just before leaving for Russia.

These letters strikingly reflect Ilyich's train of thoughts on the eve of his departure. I particularly remember what he then said about the militia. This question is dealt with in the third of the series—"Concerning a Proletarian Militia." It was not published until 1924, after the death of Ilyich. In it Ilyich expounds his ideas on the nature of the proletarian state. To obtain a really proper understanding of Lenin's book *The State and Revolution*, one must read these "Letters from Afar." The whole subject is treated in this article with extraordinary concreteness. Ilyich spoke about a new type of militia, consisting entirely of armed citizens, of adult citizens of *both* sexes. Besides its direct military duties, this militia was to effect prompt and proper appropriation and distribution of grain and other food surpluses, act as sanitary inspectors, see to it that every family had bread, every child a bottle of good milk, and that not a single grown-up in a rich family should dare to have any extra milk until the children had been provided for, that the palaces and rich homes should not stand empty, but be used as shelter for the homeless and destitute. "Who can carry out these measures except a people's militia, to which women should without fail belong equally with men?" Ilyich wrote.

"These measures *do not yet* constitute socialism. They pertain to the distribution of articles of consumption, and not to the reorganization of production.... How to classify them theoretically is not the point now. We would be committing a great mistake if we attempted to force the complex, urgent, rapidly developing practical tasks of the revolution into the Procrustean bed of narrowly conceived 'theory' instead of regarding theory primarily and mostly as a *guide to a c t i o n*." (*Works*, Vol. 23, p. 321.) The proletarian militia would *actually educate the masses* to take part *in all* state affairs. "Such a militia would draw the young people into political life and teach them not only by word of mouth, but also by action, by *work*." (*Ibid.*, p. 320.) "On the order of the day is the task of *organization*, but certainly not in the stereotyped sense of working only on stereotyped organizations, but in the sense of drawing unprecedentedly broad masses of the oppressed classes into an organization and of making this organization itself take over military, state and national-economic functions." (*Ibid.*, p. 322.)

Rereading this letter of Ilyich's today, after so many years, I can see him before me, as large as life: on the one hand, his extraordinary sober-mindedness, his clear appreciation of the necessity of an irreconcilable armed struggle and of the fact that no concessions or vacillation could be tolerated at that moment; on the other hand, his unremitting attention to the mass movement, to the organization of the broad masses in a new way, to their concrete needs, and to the immediate improvement of their conditions. Ilyich spoke about all these matters a great deal in the winter of 1916-1917, and especially in the period immediately preceding the February Revolution.

The negotiations dragged on. The Provisional Government obviously did not want to allow the internationalists entry into Russia, and the news from Russia pointed to certain vacillation among the comrades there. All this necessitated our speedy departure. Ilyich sent a telegram to Ganiecki, which the latter did not receive until March 25, saying: "Cannot understand delay. Mensheviks demand sanction of Soviet of Workers' Deputies. Send someone immediately Finland or Petrograd make possible arrangements with Chkheidze. Opinion Belenin desirable." (*Works*, 3rd Russ. ed., Vol. XXIX, p. 350.) By Belenin was meant the Bureau of the Central Committee. Kollontai arrived in Russia on March 18 and explained how matters stood with Ilyich's arrival. Letters were received from Ganiecki. The Bureau of the Central Committee issued instructions through him that "Ulyanov must come immediately." (*Lenin Miscellany*, XIII, p. 270.) Ganiecki re-telegraphed this message to Lenin. Vladimir Ilyich insisted that negotiations be opened through Fritz Platten, the Swiss Socialist-Internationalist. Platten came to a definite written understanding with the German Ambassador in Switzerland. The principal points of this agreement were: 1. That all emigrants were to be allowed to go regardless of their views on the war; 2. That no one could enter the railway car in which the emigrants were travelling without the permission of Platten. There was to be no inspection of passports or luggage; 3. That the passengers undertook to agitate in Russia for a corresponding number of Austro-German internees to be repatriated by way of exchange. Ilyich got busy making preparations for departure, and wrote to various comrades in Berne and Geneva, etc. The *Vperyod*-ists Ilyich was negotiating with refused to go. Karl and Kasparov, two close comrades who were dying in Davos, had to be left behind. Ilyich wrote them a farewell greeting. Or rather he added a postscript to my long letter. I wrote in detail about who was going, what preparations we were making and what our plans were. The few words that Ilyich added showed how well he understood the feelings of those who were staying behind.

"Dear Kasparov," he wrote, "I send you and Karl my heartiest greetings and wish you good cheer. You must have patience. I hope we shall meet soon in St. Petersburg. My best wishes to you both. Yours, Lenin." (*Lenin Miscellany*, XIII, p. 272.)

"I wish you good cheer. You must have patience...." Aye, that was just the thing. We never met again. Both Kasparov and Karl died soon after.

Ilyich wrote an article "The Tasks of the Russian Social-Democratic Labour Party in the Russian Revolution" for the Zurich paper *Volksrecht*, and a "Farewell Letter to the Swiss Workers" which ended with the words: "Long live the proletarian revolution *that is beginning* in Europe!" (*Works*, Vol. 23, p. 364.) He also wrote a letter "To Comrades Languishing in Captivity" in which he told them about the revolution that had started and the coming struggle. We had to write to them. While living in Berne we had started a fairly wide correspondence with Russian prisoners of war in German camps. We could not do much for them in the way of financial assistance, of course, but we did what we could, wrote letters to them and sent them literature. A number of close contacts were made. After our departure from Berne this work was continued by the Safarovs. We sent illegal literature to these prisoners of war, including Kollontai's pamphlet on the war, which was a great success, a number of leaflets, etc.

A few months before we left Zurich two prisoners of war turned up—one of them a Voronezh peasant named Mikhalyov, the other an Odessa worker. They had escaped from a German prisoner-of-war camp by swimming across Bodensee. They came to our Zurich group. Ilyich had long talks with them. Mikhalyov's stories about life among the prisoners of war were of great interest. He told us how the Ukrainian prisoners had first been sent to Galicia, how pro-Ukrainian agitation against Russia had been conducted among them, and how afterwards he and others had been transferred to Germany where they had been made to work for well-to-do farmers. "What wonderful management, not a crust of bread goes waste with them," Mikhalyov exclaimed. "When I get back to my home village I'll run the farm the same way as they do." He came of a family of Old Believers, and his grandfather and grandmother would not allow him to learn to read and write—literacy was supposed to be the mark of the devil. Nevertheless, during his captivity, he had learned to read and write. His grandparents sent him millet and pork fat, and the Germans looked on with astonishment as he cooked and ate millet porridge. Mikhalyov had counted on going to a people's university in Zurich, and was shocked to hear that there was none. He was interned. He got some work to do as a navvy and could not stop wondering at the downtrodden state of the Swiss working man. "Going to the office to draw my pay," he said, "I see the Swiss workers standing there and not daring to go into the office—they stood hugging the wall and peeping in through the window. What a downtrodden people! I went straight up, opened the door, walked in and got my money for my work!" Ilyich was greatly intrigued by this Voronezh peasant, who had only just learned to read and write and yet talked about the abject condition of the Swiss workers. Mikhalyov also described how a Russian priest once visited the prisoners' camp, but the soldiers began to shout and swear and refused to listen to him. One of the prisoners went up to him and kissed his hand, saying: "You'd better go away, Father, this is no place for you." Mikhalyov and his comrades asked us to take them with us to Russia, but we did not know how we would fare ourselves—we might all be arrested for all we knew. After our departure Mikhalyov crossed over to France, first living in Paris, then working at some tractor plant and later at some job in Eastern France, where there were a lot of Polish emigrants. In 1918 (or 1919—I do not remember which) Mikhalyov returned to Russia. Ilyich met him. Mikhalyov related how in Paris he and several other prisoners of war who had escaped from Germany were sent for by the Russian Embassy and asked to sign an appeal urging that the war be continued to a victorious end. And although important bemedalled officials spoke to them, the soldiers refused to sign it. "I got up and said the war should be stopped, and went away. The others slipped out on the quiet too," he said. He described the big anti-war campaign which the young people started in the little French town where he lived. Mikhalyov himself no longer resembled the Voronezh peasant we had first met. He wore a French cap, and khaki puttees, and his face was clean shaven. Ilyich fixed him up with some job in a factory, but all his thoughts were for his native village. The place had passed from hand to hand, from the Reds to the Whites and back again. The central part of the village had been burned down by the Whites, but his house was intact, and his grandparents were still alive. I learned all this from Mikhalyov himself, who came to see me at the Central Political Education Department. He told me that he was going home soon. "Why don't you go now?" I asked him. "I'm waiting for my beard to grow. If Grandma and Grandpa see me without it they'll die of grief!" This year I received a letter from Mikhalyov. He is working on the railway

343

in Central Asia, and writes that on Lenin Memorial Day he spoke at a workers' club about how he had met Ilyich in 1917 in Zurich and about our life abroad. Everyone had listened with interest, but had doubted the truth of the story, and so Mikhalyov asked me to confirm that he had really met Ilyich in Zurich.

Mikhalyov was a piece of real life. So also were the letters which our prisoners of war sent to our P.O.W. Relief Committee.

Ilyich could not leave for Russia without writing to them of what was uppermost in his mind at the moment.

When we received the letter from Berne telling us that Platten's negotiations had been successfully concluded, and that as soon as the protocol was signed we could start for Russia, Ilyich sprang to his feet: "Let us catch the first train." The train was due to leave in two hours. In those two hours we had to wind up our "household," settle with the landlady, return the books to the library, pack up and so on. "Go by yourself, I'll leave tomorrow," I said. But Ilyich insisted on us going together. In two hours everything was done—the books packed, letters destroyed, the necessary clothes and articles selected, and all affairs settled. We caught the first train to Berne.

All the comrades who were going to Russia gathered at the People's House in Berne. Among the passengers were the Zinovievs, the Usieviches, Inessa Armand, the Safarovs, Olga Ravich, Abramovich from Chaux-de-Fonds, Grebelskaya, Kharitonov, Linda Rosenblum, Boitsov, Mikha Tskhakaya, the Marienhoffs and Sokolnikov. Radek went under the guise of a Russian. Altogether thirty people were going, not counting curly-headed little Robert, the four-yeard-old son of a Bundist woman.

We were escorted by Fritz Platten.

The defencists raised a terrible hullabaloo about the Bolsheviks travelling through Germany. Naturally, the German Government gave permission for us to travel through Germany in the belief that revolution was a dis-

aster to a country, and that by allowing emigrant internationalists to return to their country they were helping to
spread the revolution in Russia. The Bolsheviks, for their
part, considered it their duty to develop revolutionary agitation in Russia, and made it their aim to bring about a
victorious proletarian revolution. They did not care what
the German bourgeois government thought about it. They
knew that the defencists would start a mud-slinging campaign against them, but that the masses in the long run
would follow their lead. At that time, on March 27, the
Bolsheviks were the only ones to take the risk of going
that way. A month later, over two hundred emigrants, including Martov and other Mensheviks, followed the same
route through Germany.

When boarding the train, no one examined either our
luggage or our passports. Ilyich withdrew completely into
himself, and his thoughts ran forward into Russia. The
talk during the journey was mostly of a trivial nature.
Robert's chirpy voice rang through the car. He took a
great liking to Sokolnikov, and would have no truck with
the women. The Germans went out of their way to show
that they had plenty of everything, and the cook served
up good square meals, to which our emigrant fraternity
was hardly accustomed. Looking out of the carriage window, we were struck by the total absence of grown-up men.
Only women, teenagers and children could be seen at
the wayside stations, on the fields, and in the streets of
the towns. This impression often came back to me during the early days of our arrival in Petrograd, where the
tramcars were packed with soldiers.

In Berlin our train was shunted to a siding. Just before
we came to Berlin, several German Social-Democrats had
got in in a special compartment. None of us spoke to
them except Robert, who looked into their compartment
and began interrogating them in French: "What does the
conductor do?" I don't know what the Germans told Robert, but I do know that they had no chance to put any

questions of their own to the Bolsheviks. On March 31 we arrived in Sweden. At Stockholm we were met by the Swedish Social-Democratic M.P.'s Lindhagen, Karlsson, Ström, T. Nerman and others. A red flag had been hung up in the waiting room and a meeting was held there. I have only a dim recollection of Stockholm, as all my thoughts were in Russia. The Provisional Government of Russia did not allow Fritz Platten and Radek into the country. It did not dare to stop the Bolsheviks, however. We crossed into Finland from Sweden in Finnish country sleighs. Everything was dear and familiar—the rickety old third-class carriages, the Russian soldiers. It made you feel good. It was not long before Robert woke up in the arms of an elderly soldier, and clasped him round the neck, chattering away to him in French and eating the sweet Easter cream-cheese with which the soldier was feeding him. We all huddled round the windows. The station platforms we passed were crowded with soldiers. Usievich leaned out and shouted: "Long live the world revolution!" The soldiers stared at him. A pale-faced lieutenant passed us several times, and when Ilyich and I went into the next car, which was empty, he sat down beside Ilyich and engaged him in conversation. The lieutenant was a defencist. They began a spirited argument. Ilyich, too, was very pale. Little by little the car filled with soldiers until it was packed tight. They stood up on the seats the better to be able to see and hear the man who was speaking in such understandable terms against the predatory war. Their faces grew tense as they listened with growing interest.

At Beloostrov we were met by Maria Ilyinichna, Shlyapnikov, Staël and other comrades. There were women workers there too. Staël kept urging me to say a few words of greeting to them, but words utterly failed me. The comrades got in with us. Ilyich asked whether we would be arrested on our arrival. The comrades smiled. Soon we arrived in Petrograd.

The masses of Petrograd—workers, soldiers and sailors —came to welcome their leader. Many of our close comrades were there, too, among them Chugurin, a student of the Longjumeau school, with a broad crimson sash across his shoulder and his face wet with tears. We were in the midst of a surging sea of people.

No one who has not lived through the revolution can have any idea of its solemn grandeur. Red banners, a guard of honour of Kronstadt sailors, searchlights from the Peter and Paul Fortress lighting up the way from the Finland Station to the Krzesińska Mansion,* armoured cars, files of working men and women guarding the road.

Chkheidze and Skobelev met us at the station in the capacity of official representatives of the Petrograd Soviet of Workers' and Soldiers' Deputies. Comrades conducted Ilyich to the royal waiting room where Chkheidze and Skobelev met us. When Ilyich stepped out on to the platform, a captain came up to him, stood at attention and reported. Taken by surprise, Ilyich returned the salute. A guard of honour was lined up on the platform, and Ilyich was led past it with all the rest of the emigrant fraternity following. Then we were seated in motor-cars, while Ilyich was placed on an armoured car, and all of us were driven to the Krzesińska Mansion. "Long live the socialist world revolution!" Ilyich shouted into the vast crowd swarming around us.

Ilyich already felt the beginning of that revolution in every fibre of his being.

We were taken to the Krzesińska Mansion, which then housed the Central Committee and Petrograd Committee of

---

* The Krzesińska Mansion (Krzesińska had been a favourite of Tsar Nicholas II) was seized by the revolutionary soldiers at the time of the February Revolution and served as the premises of the Petrograd Bolshevik Committee.—*Ed.*

the Party. The comrades arranged a tea party upstairs and wanted to organize speeches of welcome, but Ilyich switched the talk over to a subject that interested him now most of all—the tactics that had to be pursued. Crowds of workers and soldiers stood outside the Krzesińska Mansion, and Ilyich was obliged to address them from the balcony. The impressions of this meeting, and the tremendous revolutionary enthusiasm threw everything else into the shade.

We then went home to Lenin's sister, Anna Ilyinichna and her husband Mark Yelizarov. Maria Ilyinichna was living with them too. They lived in Shirokaya Street, on Petrograd Side. We were given a separate room. Little Gora, Anna Ilyinichna's foster son, had hung a slogan over our beds in honour of our arrival, reading: "Workers of All Countries, Unite!" Ilyich and I hardly spoke a word that night—no words could express what we felt that day; things were clear enough without words.

We were living at a time when every moment was precious. Ilyich had scarcely got up when comrades called for him to go to a meeting of Bolshevik members of the All-Russian Conference of Soviets of Workers' and Soldiers' Deputies. It was on an upper floor of the Taurida Palace. Lenin expounded his views as to what had to be done in a number of theses. In these theses he weighed the situation, and clearly set forth the aims that had to be striven for and the ways that had to be followed to attain them. The comrades were somewhat taken aback for the moment. Many of them thought that Ilyich was presenting the case in much too blunt a manner, and that it was too early yet to speak of a socialist revolution.

Downstairs a meeting of the Mensheviks was in progress. A comrade came from there insisting that Ilyich should make a similar report at a joint meeting of Menshevik and Bolshevik delegates. The Bolshevik meeting decided that Ilyich was to repeat his report at a general meeting of all the Social-Democrats. Ilyich did so. The meeting took place downstairs in the large hall of the palace. The first thing that struck me, I remember, was Goldenberg (Meshkovsky) sitting in the presiding committee. During the Revolution of 1905 he had been a staunch Bolshevik, one of our closest comrades in the struggle. Now he sided with Plekhanov and had become a defencist. Lenin spoke for about two hours. Goldenberg took the floor against him. He spoke very sharply, saying that Lenin had raised the banner of civil war in the midst of the revolutionary democrats. We could see now how far apart we had drifted. I also remember Kollontai's speech, in which she warmly defended Lenin's theses.

In his newspaper *Yedinstvo*,* Plekhanov called Lenin's theses "ravings."

Three days later, on April 7, Lenin's theses were printed in *Pravda*. This was followed the next day by an article in *Pravda* by Kamenev "Our Disagreements," in which he dissociated himself from these theses. Kamenev's article stated that they were the expression of Lenin's private views, which neither *Pravda* nor the Bureau of the Central Committee shared. It was not these theses of Lenin's that the Bolshevik delegates had accepted, but those of the Central Committee Bureau, Kamenev alleged. *Pravda* stood on its former positions, he declared.

A struggle started within the Bolshevik organization. It did not last long. A week later a general city conference of the Bolsheviks of Petrograd took place, at which Ilyich's point of view was upheld. The conference lasted eight days (from April 14 to 22), during which time a number of important events took place which showed that Lenin had been right.

---

* *Yedinstvo* (*Unity*)—a daily paper, published in Petrograd between March and November 1917 under Plekhanov's editorship. It united the extreme Right group of the Menshevik defencists and gave unqualified support to the bourgeois Provisional Government; waged a fierce struggle against the Bolshevik Party.—*Ed.*

On April 7, the day Lenin's theses were first published, the Executive Committee of the Petrograd Soviet voted in favour of the "Liberty Loan."*

The bourgeois and defencist newspapers started a furious hounding campaign against Lenin and the Bolsheviks. Kamenev's opinion meant nothing—everyone knew that Lenin's point of view would win the backing of the Bolshevik organization. The campaign against Lenin was the most effective way of popularizing his theses. Lenin had called the war an imperialist war of plunder, and everyone saw that he stood for peace in real earnest. This stirred the sailors and soldiers, stirred all those for whom the war was a life-and-death issue. On April 10 Ilyich addressed the soldiers of the Izmailovsky Regiment; on the 15th *Soldatskaya Pravda* (*Soldiers' Truth*) began to appear, and on the 16th the soldiers and sailors of Petrograd held a demonstration of protest against the campaign against Lenin and the Bolsheviks. On April 18 (May 1, New Style) a great May Day demonstration was held throughout Russia such as had never been seen before.

On the same day Milyukov, the Minister of Foreign Affairs, issued a statement in the name of the Provisional Government to the effect that it would continue the war to a victorious end and would fulfil all its obligations to the Allies. What did the Bolsheviks do? They showed up in the press what those obligations were. The Provisional Government, they pointed out, had pledged itself to fulfil the obligations incurred by the government of Nicholas II and the whole tsarist clique. They showed that those obligations had been incurred on behalf of the bourgeoisie.

When this became clear to the masses, they came out on the streets. On April 21 they demonstrated on Nevsky Prospekt. A counter-demonstration was held there by supporters of the Provisional Government.

---

* "*Liberty Loan*" was issued by the bourgeois Provisional Government in the spring of 1917 to meet military expenditures.—*Ed.*

These events united the Bolshevik ranks. The Petrograd organization of the Bolsheviks passed resolutions in the spirit of Lenin's views.

On April 21 and 22 the Central Committee passed resolutions clearly admitting the necessity of exposing the Provisional Government; it condemned the conciliatory tactics of the Petrograd Soviet, called for a re-election of workers' and soldiers' deputies, urged the strengthening of the Soviets, and the conduct of a wide explanatory campaign, while at the same time pointing out that attempts to immediately overthrow the Provisional Government were premature.

By the time the All-Russian Conference opened on April 24, three weeks after Lenin made public his theses, unity among the Bolsheviks had already been achieved.

After our arrival in Petrograd I saw little of Ilyich. He was working at the Central Committee and in *Pravda*, and addressing meetings. I went to work at the Secretariat of the Central Committee in the Krzesińska Mansion, but it was nothing like the secretarial job I had done abroad or that of 1905-1907, when I had done rather important work on my own under Ilyich's direction. Stasova was the secretary, and she had a staff of assistants to do the clerical work. My job involved talking to the Party workers who visited us, but I knew little about local activities at that time. Central Committee members came often, especially Sverdlov. I was a bit out of touch, though, and the absence of any definite duties was irksome. But then I drank in the life around me. The streets in those days presented a curious spectacle: everywhere people stood about in knots, arguing heatedly and discussing the latest events. I used to mingle with the crowd and listen. These street meetings were so interesting, that it once took me three hours to walk from Shirokaya Street to the Krzesińska Mansion. The house in which we lived overlooked a courtyard, and even here, if you opened the window at night, you could hear a heated dispute. A soldier would be sitting there, and he always had an audience—usually some of the cooks, or housemaids from next door, or some young people. An hour after midnight you could catch snatches of talk—"Bolsheviks, Mensheviks...." At three in the morning "Milyukov, Bolsheviks...." At five—still the same street-corner-meeting talk, politics, etc. Petrograd's white nights are always associated in my mind now with those all-night political disputes.

At the Secretariat of the Central Committee I had occasion to meet lots of people. Besides the Central Committee, the Krzesińska Mansion housed the military organization and *Soldatskaya Pravda* offices. Sometimes I attended the meetings of the Central Committee, where I got to know the people more closely, and followed the work of the Petrograd Committee. The youngsters and working-class youth interested me greatly too. The movement had taken hold of them. They represented different trends of opinion —Bolsheviks, Mensheviks, Socialist-Revolutionaries and Anarchists. There were up to fifty thousand young people in the organization, but at the beginning the movement was left pretty much to itself. I did some work among them. A direct contrast to this working-class youth were the senior pupils of the high schools. They often came in a crowd to the Krzesińska Mansion and shouted abuse at the Bolsheviks. They were obviously being thoroughly indoctrinated.

Shortly after our arrival—I do not remember the exact date—I attended a teachers' congress. There was a big crowd there. The teachers were completely under the influence of the Socialist-Revolutionaries. Prominent defencists spoke at the congress. On the day I went there, Alexinsky had addressed it in the morning before my arrival. There were altogether fifteen to twenty Social-Democrats there, including Bolsheviks and Menshevik-Internationalists. They gathered in a small separate room where they compared notes as to the kind of school to be aimed at. Many of those present at that meeting afterwards worked in the district councils. The mass of the teachers were drunk with the fumes of chauvinism.

On April 18 (May 1, New Style) Ilyich took part in the May Day demonstration. He spoke in the Okhta District and the Field of Mars. I did not hear him, as I was ill in bed that day. When Ilyich came home I was struck by his excited face. We usually attended May Day meetings when we lived abroad, but it was one thing to go to a May Day meeting sanctioned by the police, and quite another to follow a May Day procession of the revolutionary people, a people who had overthrown tsarism.

On April 21 I was to meet Ilyich at Danskoi's. The address given to me was No. 3 Staro-Nevsky and I walked all the way down Nevsky Prospekt. A big workers' demonstration was marching from the Nevskaya Zastava. Working people crowding the pavements greeted it as it passed. "Come along!" one young woman worker shouted to another standing on the pavement. "We're going to march all night!" Another crowd wearing hats and bowlers was coming from the other direction; it was greeted by hats and bowlers on the pavements. In the Nevskaya Zastava area workers predominated, but round about Morskaya Street and Politseisky Most the bowlers outnumbered them. Among this crowd the story passed from mouth to mouth about how Lenin had bribed the workers with German gold, and now they were all for him. "We must beat Lenin!" screamed a stylishly dressed young woman. "All those scoundrels ought to be killed!" shouted a man in a bowler. Class against class! The working class was for Lenin.

The All-Russian Party Conference, known as the April Conference, was held from April 24th to 29th. A hundred and fifty-one delegates attended. The conference elected a new Central Committee, and very important issues were discussed at it, namely, the political situation, the war, the inauguration of a Third International, the national question, the agrarian question and the Party programme.

I particularly remember Lenin's speech on the political situation. It brought out most strikingly Ilyich's attitude towards the masses, and showed how closely he followed their lives and interests. "There is no doubt that, as a class, the proletariat and semi-proletariat are not interested in the war. They are influenced by tradition and deception. They still lack political experience. Therefore, our task is that of patiently explaining. Our principles remain intact, we do not make the slightest compromise; yet we cannot approach those masses as we approach the social-chauvinists. Those elements of our population have never been Socialists, they have not the slightest conception of socialism, they are just awakening to political life. But their class-consciousness is growing and broadening with extraordinary rapidity. One must know how to approach them with explanations, and this is now the most difficult task, particularly for a party that but yesterday was underground." (*Works*, Vol. 24, pp. 205-06.)

"Many of us, myself included," said Ilyich in his speech, "have had occasion to address the people, particularly the soldiers, and it seems to me that even when everything is explained to them from the point of view of class interests, there is still one thing in our position that they cannot fully grasp, namely, in what way we intend to finish the war, in what way we think it possible to bring the war to an end. The masses are in a maze of misapprehension, there is an absolute lack of understanding as to our position, that is why we must be particularly clear in this case. (*Ibid.*, p. 202.)

"In approaching the masses, we must offer concrete answers to all questions." (*Ibid.*, p. 207.)

We must be able, said Ilyich, to carry on the work of explanation not only among the proletariat, but also among wide sections of the petty bourgeoisie.

Speaking of control, Vladimir Ilyich said: "To control, one must have power. If the broad masses of the petty-bourgeois bloc do not understand this, we must have the patience to explain it to them, but under no circumstances must we tell them an untruth." (*Ibid.*, p. 201.) Ilyich never stooped to demagogy, and this the soldiers and peasants who spoke to him always felt. Confidence, however, is not won off-hand. Even in those stirring times Ilyich kept a level head. "So far we are in the minority; the masses do not trust us yet. We can wait; they will side with us when the government reveals its true nature." (*Ibid.*, p. 202.) Ilyich had many talks with soldiers and peasants, and had already seen no few evidences of trust, yet he entertained no illusions. "The proletarian party would be guilty of the most grievous error if it shaped its policy on the basis of subjective desires where organization is required. We cannot assert that the majority is with us: in this case our motto should be caution, caution, caution. To base our proletarian policy on over-confidence means to condemn it to failure." (*Ibid.*, pp. 206-07.)

In concluding his speech on the political situation, Ilyich said: "The Russian Revolution has created the Soviets. No bourgeois country in the world has or can have such state institutions. No socialist revolution can function with any other state power. The Soviets of Workers' and Soldiers' Deputies must seize power not for the purpose of building an ordinary bourgeois republic, nor for the purpose of direct transition to socialism. The latter could not be accomplished. What, then, is the purpose? They must seize power in order to take the first concrete steps towards this transition, steps that can and should be made. In this case fear is the greatest enemy. The masses should be convinced that these steps must be taken immediately, that otherwise the power of the Soviets of Workers' and Soldiers' Deputies would be devoid of meaning, and would offer nothing to the people." (*Ibid.*, p. 211.)

Ilyich went on to speak about the immediate tasks confronting the Soviets. "Private ownership of land must be abolished. This is our first task, because the majority of the people are for it. To accomplish this we need the Soviets.

This measure cannot be carried out by means of the old government bureaucracy." (*Works,* Vol. 24, pp. 211-12.) He wound up his speech with an example showing what the struggle for power locally means. "I shall conclude by referring to the speech that made the strongest impression on me. I heard a coal-miner deliver a remarkable speech. Without using a single bookish word, he told how they had made the revolution. Those miners were not concerned with the question as to whether or not they should have a president. They seized the mine, and the important question to them was how to keep the cables intact so that production might not be interrupted. Then came the question of bread, of which there was a scarcity. And the miners again agreed on the method of obtaining it. Now this is a real programme of the revolution, not derived from books. This is a real seizure of power locally." (*Ibid.,* p. 212.)

Zinaida Krzhizhanovskaya once recalled my having told her about this miner's speech, and said: "What the miners need now is their own engineers. Vladimir Ilyich thinks it would be fine if Gleb* went down there."

We met lots of people we knew at the conference. I remember, among others, meeting Prisyagin, a former student of the Longjumeau school, and how his eyes shone as he listened to Ilyich's speech. Prisyagin is no longer among the living. He was shot by the Whites in Siberia in 1918.

Early in May 1917 Ilyich drafted amendments to the Party programme. The imperialist war and the revolution had brought about tremendous changes in social life, and this necessitated new evaluations and a new approach. The old programme was terribly outdated.

The outline of the new minimum-programme was imbued with a striving to improve, to raise the standard of living of the masses, and give greater scope to their activity.

---

* Krzhizhanovsky.—*Ed.*

I was becoming tired of my job at the Secretariat, and wanted to get into real work among the masses. I also wanted to see more of Ilyich, about whom I was getting very anxious. He was being hounded more and more. Going down the street in the Petrograd District you could hear the women saying to each other: "What's to be done with this Lenin fellow who's come from Germany? He ought to be drowned in a well, if you ask me." There was no doubt as to the source from which all those rumours about bribery and treachery came, but they did not make pleasant hearing nevertheless. It was one thing to hear the bourgeoisie talk like that, but quite another to hear it from the masses. I wrote an article for *Soldatskaya Pravda* about Lenin under the title "A Page from the History of the Party." Vladimir Ilyich looked through the manuscript and made some corrections, and the article was published in No. 21 of *Soldatskaya Pravda* for May 13, 1917.

Vladimir Ilyich used to come home tired, and I did not have the heart to question him about affairs. But both of us felt a need to talk things over the way we were used to doing—during a walk. We sometimes managed to go for a walk along the quieter streets of the Petrograd District. I remember once our taking such a walk together with Shaumyan and Yenukidze, and Shaumyan gave Ilyich some red badges, which his sons had asked him to give Lenin. Ilyich smiled.

We had known Stepan Shaumyan for a long time. He was tremendously popular with the Baku proletariat. He joined the Bolsheviks immediately after the Second Congress, and attended the Stockholm and London congresses. At the Stockholm Congress he was a member of the Mandate Commission. This congress was numerically much bigger than either the Second or the Third congresses. At those congresses we had known what every delegate stood for, but here there were many delegates whom we hardly knew. A sharp struggle was fought in the Mandate Commission over every delegate. I remember the tough time

Shaumyan had on this commission. I was not present at the London Congress. Afterwards, during our second period of emigration, we carried on a lively correspondence with the Baku comrades. I remember them enquiring of me the reasons for the split with the *Vperyod*-ists, and me having to give them a full account of what it was all about.

In 1913 Ilyich carried on a lively correspondence with Shaumyan on the national question. A very interesting letter was that of May 1914 in which Ilyich propounded the idea that the Marxists of all or most of the nationalities of Russia should submit to the State Duma the draft of a bill on the equal rights of nations and the defence of the rights of the national minorities. This draft, according to Lenin's idea, was to contain a complete interpretation of what we understand by equality of rights, including the question of language, the school and culture in general, in all its aspects. "It seems to me," wrote Ilyich, "that in this way we could popularly explain the folly of cultural-national autonomy and *quash* the adherents of that folly once and for all." (*Works*, Vol. 35, p. 106.) Ilyich even outlined such a draft.

In 1917, therefore, Ilyich was glad to see Stepan and discuss with him at first hand all the questions that then confronted the Bolsheviks in all their urgency.

I remember Ilyich's speech at the First All-Russian Congress of Soviets of Workers' and Soldiers' Deputies, which took place at the military school on Vasilyevsky Island. We walked down long corridors. The classrooms had been turned into dormitories for the delegates. The hall was crowded, and the Bolsheviks sat at the back in a small group. Lenin's speech was applauded only by the Bolsheviks, but there was no doubt about the strong impression it had made. Kerensky was said to have lain in a faint for three hours after that speech. I do not vouch for the truth of that story, though.

In June elections to the district councils were held. I went to Vasilyevsky Island to see how the election campaign was going. The streets were flooded with working people, most of them employees of the Tube Factory. There were also a lot of women workers from the Laferme Factory. This factory voted for the Socialist-Revolutionaries. Disputes raged all round; people were not discussing candidates or personalities, but the activities of the different parties and what they stood for. I was reminded of the municipal elections in Paris when we were there: we had been struck by the absence of political issues and by the extent to which the personal element predominated everywhere. Here the picture was just the reverse. Another thing that struck one was the extent to which the masses had politically matured since 1905-1907. It was obvious that all read the newspapers of the different political trends. One group was discussing the question whether Bonapartism was possible in this country or not. A squat figure, suspiciously spy-like in its snooping activity, looked oddly out of place among this crowd of workers, who had become so class-conscious during the last few years.

Revolutionary feeling among the masses was mounting.

The Bolsheviks had decided to hold a demonstration on June 10. The Congress of Soviets banned it by a ruling that no demonstrations were to be held in the course of three days. Thereupon Ilyich insisted that the demonstration arranged by the Petrograd Party Committee should be called off. He held that since we recognized the power of the Soviets we were bound to submit to the rulings of the Congress if we did not wish to play into the hands of our opponents. Yielding to the temper of the masses, however, the Congress of Soviets itself called a demonstration for June 18 (Old Style). It was scarcely prepared, however, for what happened. Nearly four hundred thousand workers and soldiers took part in the demonstration. Ninety per cent of the banners and posters bore the slogans of the Bolshevik Central Committee: "All Power to the Soviets!" "Down with the Ten Capitalist Ministers!" Only three posters supported the Provisional Government (one was the Bund's, the other the Plekhanov group's, and the third the Cossack Regiment's). Ilyich referred to the 18th of June as one of the days of the turning point. "The demonstration of June 18th," (July 1st, New Style) he wrote, "became a demonstration of the strength and the policies of the revolutionary proletariat which is giving direction to the revolution, and is showing the way out of the blind alley. Therein lies the colossal historical significance of the Sunday demonstration, and therein does it differ in principle from the demonstration which took place on the day of the funeral of the victims of the revolution, or from that held on the First of May. Then it was a universal *tribute* to the first victory of the revolution and its heroes, a glance backward, cast by the people over the first lap of the road to freedom and passed by them most quickly and most successfully. The First of May was a *holiday* of good wishes and hopes bound up with the history of the labour movement of the world, with its ideal of peace and socialism.

"Neither of the demonstrations aimed at pointing out the *direction* of the further advance of the revolution. Neither could point out that direction. Neither the first nor the second demonstration had placed before the masses, and in the name of the masses, any concrete and definite questions of the hour, questions as to whither and how the revolution must proceed.

"In this sense the 18th of June was the first political demonstration of *action*; it was an exposition of issues not in a book or in a newspaper, but in the street; not through leaders, but through the masses. It showed how the various classes act, wish to act, and should act, to further the revolution. The bourgeoisie had hidden itself." (*Works*, Vol. 25, pp. 91-92.)

The elections to the district councils were over. I was elected to the Vyborg District Council. Only Bolshevik candidates were returned here, and a few Menshevik-Internationalists. The latter refused to work on the council. Those who worked on it were all Bolsheviks—L. M. Mikhailov, Kuchmenko, Chugurin, another comrade and I. Our council was housed at first in the same building as the Party local, the secretary of which was Zhenya Yegorova. Lācis worked there too. Our council and the Party organization worked in close contact. This work in the Vyborg District taught me a great deal. It was an excellent school of Party and Soviet work. To me, who had lived abroad for so many years and had never had the pluck to address even a small meeting or write a single line for *Pravda*, such a school was very necessary.

The Vyborg District had a strong and active Bolshevik membership, who enjoyed the confidence of the masses of workers. Shortly after assuming office I took over the business of the Vyborg District branch of the Committee for Relief of Soldiers' Wives from my old friend and school chum Nina Gerd (Struve's wife), with whom we had taught together at the Sunday School, and, who, in the early years of the working-class movement, had been a Social-Democrat. Now we held opposing points of view on political matters. In handing over to me, she said: "The soldiers' wives don't trust us. No matter what we do they are never satisfied. They believe only in the Bolsheviks. Well then, take things into your own hands, perhaps you'll make a better job of it." We were not afraid to tackle the job, believing, that with the active cooperation of the workers, we would succeed in getting things going with a swing.

The mass of the workers displayed an amazing activity in the cultural as well as the political fields. Very soon we set up an Education Council on which all the factories and mills of the Vyborg District were represented. Of the various factory representatives I remember Purishev, Kayurov, Yurkin and Gordienko. We met every week and discussed practical measures. When the question of general literacy came up, the workers at the factories very quickly drew up a registry of all the illiterates. The employers were asked to provide premises for reading and writing classes, and when one of them refused to comply, the women workers kicked up a terrific row in the course of which it came to light that one of the rooms at the factory was occupied by a special squad of soldiers picked from the most chauvinistic battalions. In the end the employer was obliged to rent outside premises for the school. Class attendance and the teachers' work were supervised by the workers. A machine-gun regiment was quartered not far from the District Council. It was considered highly reliable at first, but this "reliability" quickly melted away. The moment the regiment was quartered in the Vyborg District agitation was started among the soldiers. The first to agitate in favour of the Bolsheviks were the women vendors of sunflower seeds, kvass, etc. Many of them were women workers whom I had known in the nineties and even during the Revolution of 1905. They were well-dressed, active at meetings, and politically alert. One of them told me: "My husband's at the front. We got on well together, but I don't know how things will be when he gets back. I'm for the Bolsheviks now, I'm going with them, but I don't know about him there at the front—whether he realizes that we've got to go with the Bolsheviks. I often lie thinking at night—what if he hasn't grasped it yet? I don't know whether I'll see him again, though. He may be killed, and I'm spitting blood, you know—I am going to the hospital." I shall never forget the thin face of that woman worker with the hectic flush in her cheeks, and her worrying about her and her husband possibly having to part because of differing views. But it was the working men and not the women who then took the lead in educational activities. They went deep into every detail. Gordienko, for instance, gave a good deal of his time to kindergarten work. Kuklin closely followed the work of the young people.

I, too, closely tackled the work among the youth. The Light and Knowledge League had worked out a programme of its own. Its members consisted of Bolshe-viks, Mensheviks, Anarchists and non-Party people. The programme was naive and primitive to a degree, but the dispute it gave rise to was very interesting. One of the clauses, for example, said that all members must learn to sew. One lad—a Bolshevik—remarked: "Why should we all learn to sew? I can understand if it's a girl having to learn it, because otherwise she won't be able to sew a button on her husband's trousers when the time comes, but why should we all learn!" This remark raised a storm of indig-nation. The boys as well as the girls protested, and jumped up from their seats. "Who said the wife must sew but-tons on trousers? What do you mean? So you stand for the old domestic slavery of women? A wife is her husband's comrade, not his servant!" The unfortunate mover of the women-only-learning-to-sew resolution was obliged to climb down. I remember a conversation with Murashov, another young man, who was a warm supporter of the Bol-sheviks. "Why don't you join the Bolshevik organization?" I asked him. "Well, you see," he said, "there were several of us young people in the organization. But why did we join? Do you think it was because we understood that the Bolsheviks were right? No, the reason was that the Bol-sheviks were distributing revolvers to their people. That's no good at all. You've got to have an intelligent reason for joining. So I returned my Party card until I got the thing straight in my own mind." I must say, though, that only revolutionary-minded young people belonged to the Light and Knowledge League; they would not have toler-ated anyone in their midst who upheld Right views. They were all active members, who spoke at meetings at their factories. Their trouble was that they were much too credulous. This credulity had to be combatted.

I had a lot of work to do among the women too. I had got over my former shyness and spoke wherever I had to.

I threw myself into the job with enthusiasm. I wanted to draw all the masses into social work, make possible that "people's militia" of which Vladimir Ilyich had spoken.

I saw still less of Ilyich when I started work in the Vyborg District. Those were crucial days and the struggle was mounting high. June 18 was not only a day when four hundred thousand workers and soldiers demonstrated under Bolshevik slogans, it was a day when the Provisional Government, after three months of vacillation, gave way at last to pressure from the Allies and launched an offensive at the front. The Bolsheviks had already started to agitate in the press and at meetings. The Provisional Government felt that the ground was slipping from under its feet. June 28 saw the beginning of the rout of the Russian army at the front; this greatly disturbed the soldiers.

At the end of June Ilyich went to the country for a few days' rest with Maria Ilyinichna. They stayed with the Bonch-Bruyeviches in the village of Neivola, near station Mustamäki (not far from Petrograd). Meanwhile the following events took place in Petrograd. The machine-gun regiment quartered in the Vyborg District decided to start an armed uprising. Two days before this, our Education Committee had arranged to meet the regimental Education Committee on Monday to discuss certain questions of cultural work. Naturally, no one came from the regiment. The whole machine-gun regiment had turned out. I went to the Krzesińska Mansion. On my way there I caught up with the machine-gunners. They were marching down Sampsonievsky Prospekt in orderly ranks. One incident impressed itself on my mind. An old workman stepped off the kerb and went towards the soldiers, bowing low to them and saying in a loud voice: "That's it, boys, stand up for us working folks." Among those present at the headquarters of the Central Committee were Stalin and Lashevich. The machine-gunners halted under the balcony of the Krzesińska Mansion, saluted, then marched on. Two more regiments marched up to the C.C. headquarters, followed by a workers' demonstration. That evening a comrade was sent to Mustamäki for Ilyich. The Central Committee had given the slogan to keep the demonstration a peaceful one, but the machine-gun regiment was already throwing up barricades. I remember Lashevich, who was in charge of Party work in this regiment, lying on the sofa in the office of the Vyborg District Council and staring up at the ceiling for a long time before going out to the machine-gunners to dissuade them from taking revolutionary action. It was hard on him, but such was the decision of the Central Committee. The factory workers had walked out. Sailors had arrived from Kronstadt. A huge demonstration of armed workers and soldiers was marching to the Taurida Palace. Ilyich spoke from the balcony of the Krzesińska Mansion. The Central Committee issued an appeal to stop the demonstration. The Provisional Government called out the military cadets and Cossacks. Fire was opened on the demonstrators in Sadovaya Street.

UNDERGROUND AGAIN

Arrangements were made for Ilyich to spend that night at the Sulimovs', in the Petrograd District. The safest place for Ilyich to hide in was the Vyborg District. It was decided that he would live with Kayurov, a worker. I called for Ilyich at the Sulimovs', and we went together to the Vyborg District. The Moskovsky Regiment was passing down a boulevard. Kayurov was sitting in the boulevard, waiting for us. When he saw us he got up and walked ahead. Ilyich followed him, and I turned off to one side. The military cadets wrecked the editorial office of *Pravda*. A meeting of the Petrograd Committee was held during the day in the caretaker's lodge of the Renault Plant, at which Ilyich was present. The question of a general strike was discussed. A decision was made not to call it. From there Ilyich went to the apartment of Fofanova, in Lesnoi

Prospekt, where he had an appointment with several members of the Central Committee. That day the workers' movement was suppressed. Alexinsky, *Vperyod*-ist and former deputy of the Petrograd workers in the Second Duma, who had once been our close associate, and Pankratov, member of the S.-R. Party and an old Schlüsselburger,* spread a slanderous rumour to the effect that Lenin, according to information in their possession, was a German spy. They aimed at paralyzing Lenin's influence. On July 6 the Provisional Government issued an order for the arrest of Lenin, Zinoviev and Kamenev. The Krzesińska Mansion was occupied by government troops. Ilyich moved from Kayurov's place to Alliluyev's, where Zinoviev was in hiding. Kayurov's son was an Anarchist, and the young people messed about with bombs; his house, therefore, was not quite a suitable place for hiding in.

On the 7th Maria Ilyinichna and I went to see Ilyich at the Alliluyevs' place. It happened to be a moment of vacillation with Ilyich. He argued the necessity of making his appearance in court. Maria Ilyinichna warmly protested against it. "Grigory and I have decided to appear—go and tell Kamenev," Ilyich said to me. Kamenev was staying at another flat not far away. I got up hastily. "Let's say good-bye," Ilyich checked me. "We may not see each other again." We embraced. I went to Kamenev and gave him Ilyich's message. In the evening Stalin and others persuaded Ilyich not to appear in court, and by so doing, saved his life. That evening our place in Shirokaya Street was raided. Only our room was searched. The raid was conducted by a colonel and another military man in a greatcoat with a white lining. They took some notes and documents of mine off the table. They asked me if I knew where Lenin was, and I gathered from that question that

---

* *Schlüsselburg*—a fortress for political prisoners in tsarist Russia.—*Ed.*

Lenin speaking in Taurida Palace, Petrograd, April 1917

Lenin disguised in wig and cap, and clean-shaven, August 1917 when, under the name of K. P. Ivanov, he hid in Finland to escape persecution by Provisional Government

he had not given himself up. In the morning I went to Smilga, who lived in the same street. Stalin and Molotov were there. There I learned that Ilyich and Zinoviev had decided to go into hiding.

Two days later, on the 9th, a gang of cadets came charging in and ransacked the whole flat. They took Mark Yelizarov, Anna Ilyinichna's husband, for Lenin. They questioned me closely about it. The Yelizarovs had a servant living with them, a country girl named Annushka. She was from some remote village and had no idea what was going on in the world. She was very keen on learning to read and write, and would snatch up her ABC book whenever she had a moment to spare, but learning did not come easy to her. "I'm a village dunce," she would cry ruefully. I tried to help her learn to read, and to explain what parties there were, what the war was all about, etc. She had no idea who Lenin was. I was not at home on the 8th, but the Yelizarovs afterwards told me what happened. A motor-car drove up to the house and a hostile demonstration was made. All of a sudden Annushka came running in, yelling: "Olenins or somebody have arrived!"

During the search the cadets questioned her, and pointing to Mark, asked what his name was. She did not know. They decided that she did not want to tell them. Then they searched the kitchen, and looked under her bed. This got Annushka's goat. "Why don't you look in the stove, maybe somebody's hiding in there!" she remarked. The three of us—Mark Yelizarov, Annushka and I, were taken to the General Staff Headquarters. There we were seated at a distance from one another, and each was guarded by a soldier with a rifle. After a while a bunch of infuriated officers burst into the room, ready to throw themselves at us. But a colonel came in—the same colonel who had been in charge of the first raid—and he looked at us and said: "These are not the people we want." Had Ilyich been there, they would have torn him to pieces. We were dismissed. Mark Yelizarov insisted on our being given a motor-car to go home in. The colonel promised and went away. Of course, no one gave us any car. We took a cab. The bridges were raised, and we did not get home until morning. We knocked at the door for a long time and were beginning to fear something had happened. At last the door was opened.

The Yelizarovs' place was searched a third time. I was at the District Council at the time. I came home to find the entrance to the building occupied by soldiers and the street full of people. I stood there awhile, then went back to the District Council. I could do nothing to help just the same. It was late by the time I got back to the council office, and there was no one there except the caretaker. Presently Slutsky came—this comrade had recently arrived from America with Volodarsky, Melnichansky and others. He was afterwards killed on the Southern Front. He had just escaped arrest and urged me not to go home, but to send someone down in the morning to find out what had happened. We went out to look for a place to sleep in, but we did not have any addresses of comrades. We wandered about the district for a long time until we got to Fofanova's, who put us up for the night. In the morning we learned that none of our people had been arrested and that this time the searchers had not been so rough as before.

Ilyich and Zinoviev were in hiding at Razliv, not far from Sestroretsk, in the house of Yemelyanov, an old underground Party worker employed at the Sestroretsk factory. Ilyich retained a warm feeling towards Yemelyanov and his family till the very end.

I spent all my time in the Vyborg District. The difference between the temper of the man in the street and that of the workers during the July days was very striking. The former could be heard muttering angrily in the trams and on every street corner, but as soon as one crossed the wooden bridge leading to the Vyborg District, one seemed to step into another world. I was up to my ears in work. Through Zof and others connected with Yemelyanov, I received Ilyich's notes giving various instructions. The reaction was rampant. On July 9 a joint meeting of the All-Russian Central Executive Committee and the Executive Committee of the Soviet of Workers' and Peasants' Deputies declared the Provisional Government to be "the government of salvation of the revolution." On the same day the "salvation" began. That day Kamenev was arrested; on July 12 an order was issued introducing the death penalty at the front; on July 15 *Pravda* and *Okopnaya Pravda* were suppressed, and an order was issued banning meetings at the front; arrests were made among the Bolsheviks in Helsingfors, and the Bolshevik paper there, *Volna* (*Wave*), was suppressed. On July 18 the Finnish Diet was dismissed, and General Kornilov appointed Commander-in-Chief; on July 22 Trotsky and Lunacharsky were arrested.

Shortly after the July days Kerensky hit on a scheme that was calculated to improve discipline among the troops; he decided to make an example of the machine-gun regiment which had started the demonstration in the July days by having it marched out, disarmed, into a square and there publicly degraded. I saw the disarmed regiment going out to the square. The soldiers were leading the horses by the bridles, and there was such smouldering hatred in their eyes, such resentment in their slow deliberate tread, that it was clear that no more stupid method could have been devised. As a matter of fact, the machine-gun regiment sided wholeheartedly with the Bolsheviks in October, and guarded Ilyich at Smolny.

The Bolshevik Party went over to a state of semi-legality, but it grew in strength and numbers. By the time of the opening of the Sixth Party Congress on July 26 it numbered 177,000 members—twice as much as at the All-Russian April Conference three months previously. The growth of Bolshevik influence, especially among the troops, was obvious. The Sixth Congress welded the forces of the Bolsheviks still closer. The appeal issued in the name of the Sixth Party Congress spoke about the counter-revolutionary position taken by the Provisional Government, and about the impending world revolution and the battle of classes. "Our Party," the appeal stated, "is entering this battle with its banner unfurled. It has firmly held this banner in its grasp. It has not lowered it before the oppressors and slanderers, before traitors to the revolution and flunkeys of capital. It will hold the banner aloft in the struggle for socialism, for the brotherhood of nations, for it knows that a new movement is rising and that the death hour of the old world is approaching." (*Works*, 3rd Russ. ed., Vol. XXI, p. 484.)

On August 25 Kornilov began his advance on Petrograd. The workers, those of the Vyborg District first and foremost, rushed to the defence of Petrograd. Our agitators were sent out to the units of Kornilov's so-called "Savage Division."* Kornilov's troops quickly became demoralized, and the advance petered out. Corps Commander General Krymov shot himself. I recall the figure of one of our Vyborg workers, a young man, who worked on the organization of literacy classes. He had been one of the first to go to the front. I remember him returning from the front and rushing straight off to the District Council with his rifle still on his shoulder. The literacy school was short of chalk. In came this young man, his face still wearing the flush of battle, put his rifle in a corner, and began talking excitedly about chalk and blackboards. In the Vyborg District I had an opportunity of daily observing how closely the workers linked the revolutionary struggle with the struggle for mastering knowledge and culture.

With the approach of autumn, it was no longer possible for Ilyich to live in the shanty at Razliv, where he was in

---

* *Savage Division*—the name of a division formed of highlanders from the Northern Caucasus during the First World War. General Kornilov tried to throw it against revolutionary Petrograd. Under the influence of revolutionary propaganda the Savage Division refused to march against Petrograd.—*Ed.*

hiding. He decided to cross over into Finland, where he wanted to write his book *The State and Revolution*, for which he had collected a mass of notes, and which he had thought out in every detail. In Finland it was also more convenient to follow the newspapers.

N. A. Yemelyanov procured for him a passport in the name of a fictitious Sestroretsk worker, and Ilyich was given a wig to put on and made up to look like a workman. Dmitry Leshchenko, an old Party comrade of 1905-1907 days and former secretary of our Bolshevik newspapers at whose place Vladimir Ilyich had often slept in those days (Leshchenko was now my associate in educational work in the Vyborg District), went to Razliv to photograph Ilyich for the passport. Jalava, a Finnish comrade who worked as an engine-driver on the Finnish Railway (he was well known to Shotman and Rahja), undertook to get Ilyich across under the guise of a fireman. And that is what he did. Jalava also served as a medium for communication with Ilyich, and I often went to see him to get letters from Ilyich—he lived in the Vyborg District, too. When Ilyich was settled in Helsingfors, he sent me a letter in invisible ink inviting me to join him; he gave his address and even sketched a plan by which I could find his place without having to ask anybody. The trouble was I had burnt the edges of the plan while heating the letter up over a lamp. The Yemelyanovs got a passport for me, too— that of an old Sestroretsk woman worker. I put a shawl on my head and went to the Yemelyanovs in Razliv, and they saw me across the frontier (no special permit beyond a passport was required for local inhabitants in crossing the border). An officer just glanced at my passport. I had to walk five versts through a wood to Ollila, a small station, where I was to catch a soldiers' train. Everything went off splendidly. The burnt edges of the plan gave me some trouble, though. I wandered about the streets for a long time before I found the one I wanted. Ilyich was ever so glad to see me. Obviously, he had been feeling desperately lonely, living here underground at a time when it was so important for him to be in the centre of preparations for the struggle. I told him all the news, and stayed in Helsingfors for two days. When I left Ilyich insisted on seeing me off, at least as far as the last turning before the railway station. We arranged that I would come again.

I visited Ilyich again about a fortnight later. I was a bit late and decided to go to Ollila by myself, without dropping in on the Yemelyanovs. It had begun to grow dark in the woods—it was late autumn—and the moon rose. My feet sank into the sand. I was afraid that I had lost my way, and I hurried along. When I reached Ollila I found the train had not arrived yet. I had to wait half an hour for it. The carriage was packed with soldiers and sailors, and I had to stand all the way. The soldiers spoke openly of an uprising. They only talked politics. The carriage was like a meeting room, tingling with excitement. No outsiders came in. One civilian did come in at first, but after hearing a soldier telling how they had thrown officers into the river at Vyborg, he slipped out at the next stop. No one took any notice of me. When I told Ilyich about this talk among the soldiers, his face became thoughtful, and no matter what he talked about afterwards it remained thoughtful all the time. Obviously, he was saying one thing and thinking of another —thinking of the uprising and how best to organize it.

On September 13-14 Vladimir Ilyich wrote his letter *Marxism and Insurrection* to the Central Committee, and at the end of September he moved to Vyborg from Helsingfors in order to be nearer to Petrograd. From Vyborg he wrote to Smilga in Helsingfors (Smilga, at the time, was the chairman of the Regional Committee of the Army, Navy and Workers of Finland) to the effect that *all attention* should be given to *military* preparation of the Finnish army and navy for the forthcoming overthrow of Kerensky. His mind was wholly occupied at the time with the problem of remodelling the entire machinery of government, reorganizing the masses along new lines, weaving anew the whole social fabric, as he expressed it. He wrote about this in his article "Can the Bolsheviks Retain State Power?", he wrote about this in his appeal to the peasants and soldiers, in a letter to the Petrograd City Conference to be read at a closed meeting, in which he now proposed concrete measures for seizing power; he wrote about this to the members of the Central Committee, the Moscow Committee and the Petrograd Committee of the Party, and the Bolshevik members of the Petrograd and Moscow Soviets.

ON THE EVE OF THE UPRISING

On October 7 Ilyich moved to Petrograd from Vyborg. It was decided to keep his whereabouts a strict secret, and not even the members of the Central Committee were to know his address. He was put up at Marguerite Fofanova's, in a big building on the corner of Lesnoi Prospekt, Vyborg District, tenanted almost exclusively by workers. It was a very convenient place, the family, including the servant, still being out in the country, where they had gone for the summer. Fofanova herself was an ardent Bolshevik, who ran all Ilyich's errands for him. Three days later, on October 10, Ilyich attended a meeting of the Central Committee at Sukhanova's apartment, where a resolution was adopted calling for an armed uprising. Ten members of the C.C. voted in favour of the resolution. They were Lenin, Sverdlov, Stalin, Dzerzhinsky, Trotsky, Uritsky, Kollontai, Bubnov, Sokolnikov, and Lomov. Zinoviev and Kamenev voted against it.

On October 15 a meeting of the Petrograd organization took place at Smolny (this in itself was significant). Delegates from the various districts were present, including eight from the Vyborg District. I remember Dzerzhinsky speaking in favour of an armed uprising, while Chudnovsky opposed it. The latter had been wounded at the front and his arm was in a sling. Deeply agitated, he argued that we would suffer inevitable defeat, that we should take our time about it. "Dying for the revolution is the easiest thing, but we shall only harm the cause of the revolution by letting ourselves be shot down," he said. Chudnovsky, in fact, did die for the revolution, losing his life during the Civil War. He was no phrasemonger, but his view was absolutely wrong. I do not remember the other speeches. When it was put to the vote the resolution in favour of an immediate uprising was carried by an overwhelming majority. The Vyborg delegates voted for it in a body.

Next day, the 16th, an enlarged meeting of the Central Committee was held at the offices of the Lesnoi Prospekt Sub-District Council, which was attended also by members of the Executive of the Petrograd Committee, the military organization, the Petrograd Trade-Union Council of factory committees, the Petrograd Okrug Committee and representatives of the railwaymen. Two lines were discussed at this meeting—that of the majority, who stood for an immediate uprising, and that of the minority, who were against it. Lenin's resolution was carried by an overwhelming majority of 19 votes, with 2 against and 4 abstentions. The question was decided. At a closed meeting of the Central Committee a Military Revolutionary Centre was elected.

Very few people were allowed to see Ilyich. The only ones who visited him were I, Maria Ilyinichna, and occasionally Rahja. I recall the following incident. Ilyich had sent Fofanova out on some errand; it was arranged in such cases that he was not to open the door to anyone or answer the bell. I was to knock at the door by a pre-arranged signal. Fofanova had a cousin, who attended some sort of military school. When I came that evening, I found the lad standing on the landing, his face a study. Seeing me, he said: "Someone's got into Marguerite's flat, you know." "What d'you mean?" I said. "Well, I came and rang the bell, and a man's voice answered me. Then I rang again and again, but no one answered any more." I told him a tale about Marguerite having gone to a meeting that day, and that it must have been his imagination playing him tricks. I did not calm down myself until I had seen him get on a tram and ride off. I went back and knocked in the pre-arranged manner, and when Ilyich opened the door I began to scold him. "The boy might have raised an alarm," I said. "I thought it was something urgent," Ilyich pleaded in excuse. I was running his errands, too, all the time. On October 24 he wrote a letter to the Central Committee urging the necessity of seizing power that very day. He sent Marguerite with this letter, but, without waiting for her to come back, he put on his wig and went off to Smolny. Not a minute was to be lost.

The Vyborg District was preparing for the uprising. Fifty women workers sat all night in the council office, where a woman doctor gave them instructions in first aid. In the rooms of the District Committee they were busy arming the workers; group after group came up and received weapons. But there was no one to be put down in the Vyborg District; only a colonel and several cadets who had come to have some tea at a workers' club were arrested. In the night Zhenya Yegorova and I went down to Smolny in a lorry to find out how things were going.

On October 25 (November 7), 1917, the Provisional Government was overthrown. State power passed to the Military Revolutionary Committee—a body of the Petrograd Soviet—which stood at the head of the Petrograd proletariat and garrison. On the same day the Second All-Russian Congress of Soviets of Workers' and Soldiers' Deputies formed a workers' and peasants' government. A Council of People's Commissars was set up and Lenin appointed its chairman.

Lenin, Simplest, most human, and yet most far-seeing and immovible

John Reed

John Reed's comment on Lenin, in an album drawn up by delegates at the Second Congress of the Communist International, July 1920

PART III

Lenin in Petrograd, January 1918

PREFACE TO PART III

I hesitated long before deciding to write this third post-October part of my reminiscences. Until our arrival in Russia in 1917 I had worked side by side with Ilyich. My work had been a direct aid to his activities, I had watched him day by day in his talks with people, and known every little detail of the things that had interested him. In the post-October period it was different. Under the new Soviet conditions of work the character of my secretarial activities underwent a change. Its scope was considerably narrowed. Ilyich persuaded me to take up work on the educational front. This work engrossed me completely. Still more gripping, of course, in all its colourful complexity, was the tumultuous life that surged all round me. True, the very intensity of this life somehow drew us still closer together. When disengaged Ilyich used to call me out from the People's Commissariat of Education to go for a walk together through the Kremlin, or to drive out of town to the woods, or simply to have a chat. But he was very busy all the time. I had got into the habit of not asking Ilyich any questions whenever we met, and he would never tell me about his recent experiences beyond a few casual remarks until some time had passed. Usually he would start off on a train of thought which those experiences had suggested. Even now, years afterwards, when rereading Ilyich's articles, I catch the very tones in which he had uttered this or that phrase in conversation before it had come to be written down in his article. But things like this baffle description. As a result reminiscences are bound to be very fragmentary and episodic. I had decided, therefore, to write no reminiscences at all covering the Soviet period. But then I thought that, given against the general background of events, such reminiscences, however fragmentary, might be of some interest. The background itself should merely be the setting, but not a history of events. I am not sure that I will be able to do it. However, since comrades are interested in every little detail that concerns Vladimir Ilyich, I shall try. The accompanying chapters are my first attempt at reminiscences of that type.

N. Krupskaya

December 12, 1933

THE OCTOBER DAYS

The seizure of power in October had been carefully thought out and prepared by the Party of the proletariat—the Bolshevik Party. The uprising during the July days had started spontaneously, but the Party, keeping a sober mind, had considered it premature. The truth had to be faced, and that truth was that the masses were still unprepared for an uprising. The Central Committee therefore decided to postpone it. It was no easy thing to restrain the insurgents whose fighting blood was up. But the Bolsheviks did their duty, painful though it was, for they appreciated the vital importance of choosing the right moment for the insurrection.

A couple of months later the situation had changed, and Ilyich, who was compelled to hide in Finland, wrote a letter to the Central Committee and to the Petrograd and Moscow committees between the 12th and 14th September, in which he said: "Having obtained a majority in the Soviets of Workers' and Soldiers' Deputies in both capitals, the Bolsheviks can and must take power into their hands." He then proceeds to show why the power had to be seized precisely at that of all times. The surrender of Petrograd* would lessen the chances of success. There was talk of a separate peace between the British and German imperial-

---

* Kerensky's Provisional Government was secretly planning to surrender Petrograd to the Germans in order to crush the revolution.—*Ed.*

ists. "To offer peace to the nations precisely now is to win," wrote Ilyich.

In his letter to the Central Committee he deals at length with the question of how to determine the moment for the insurrection and how to prepare it. "To be successful, insurrection must rely not upon conspiracy and not upon a party, but upon the advanced class. That is the· first point. Insurrection must rely upon a *revolutionary upsurge of the people*. That is the second point. Insurrection must rely upon such a *crucial moment* in the history of the growing revolution when the activity of the advanced ranks of the people is at its height, and when the *vacillations* in the ranks of the enemy and *in the ranks of the weak, half-hearted and irresolute friends of the revolution* are strongest. That is the third point."

At the end of his letter Ilyich indicated what had to be done in order to treat the insurrection in a Marxist way, i.e., as an art. "And in order to treat insurrection in a Marxist way, i.e., as an art, we must at the same time, without losing a single moment, organize a *headquarter staff* of the insurgent detachments, distribute our forces, move the reliable regiments to the most important points, surround the Alexandrinsky Theatre,* occupy the Peter and Paul Fortress, arrest the general staff and the government, and move against the cadets and the Savage Division such detachments as will rather die than allow the enemy to approach the centres of the city; we must mobilize the armed workers and call them to fight the last desperate fight, occupy the telegraph and the telephone exchange at once, place *our* headquarter staff of the insurrection at the central telephone exchange and connect it by telephone with all the factories, all the regiments, all the points of armed fighting, etc.

---

* *The Alexandrinsky Theatre* in Petrograd where the Democratic Conference convened by the bourgeois Provisional Government was in session. The government's aim was to broaden the social basis of its supporters.—*Ed.*

"Of course, this is all by way of example, only to *illustrate* the fact that at the present moment it is impossible to remain loyal to Marxism, to remain loyal to the revolution, *without treating insurrection as an art.*" (*Works*, Vol. 26, pp. 4, 8-9.)

Living in Finland, removed from the actual scene, Ilyich was terribly worried lest the opportune moment for the insurrection should be missed. On October 7 he wrote to the Petrograd City Conference, as well as to the Central Committee, the Moscow Committee, the Petrograd Committee and the Bolshevik members of the Petrograd and Moscow Soviets. On the 8th he wrote a letter to the Bolshevik delegates to the Congress of Soviets of the Northern Region, and worried about whether his letter would reach them. On the 9th he came to Petrograd himself and put up illegally in the Vyborg District, whence he directed preparations for the insurrection.

That last month Ilyich thought of nothing else, lived for nothing else but the insurrection. His mood and his deep conviction communicated themselves to his comrades.

His last letter from Finland to the Bolshevik delegates to the Congress of Soviets of the Northern Region is a document of the utmost importance. Here it is*:

"... Armed insurrection is a *special* form of political struggle, one subject to special laws which must be attentively pondered over. Karl Marx expressed this truth with remarkable saliency when he wrote that armed '*insurrection is an art quite as much as war.*'

"Of the principal rules of this art, Marx noted the following:

"1) Never *play* with insurrection, but when beginning it firmly realize that you must *go to the end.*

"2) Concentrate a *great superiority of forces* at the decisive point, at the decisive moment, otherwise the

_____

* Quoted from Lenin's letter "Advice of an Onlooker."—*Ed.*

enemy, who has the advantage of better preparation and organization, will destroy the insurgents.

"3) Once the insurrection has begun, you must act with the greatest *determination*, and by all means, without fail, take the *offensive*. 'The defensive is the death of every armed rising.'

"4) You must try to take the enemy by surprise and seize the moment when his forces are scattered.

"5) You must strive for *daily* successes, even if small (one might say hourly, if it is the case of one town), and at all costs retain the *'moral ascendancy.'*

"Marx summed up the lessons of all revolutions in respect to armed insurrection in the words of 'Danton, the greatest master of revolutionary policy yet known: *de l'audace, de l'audace, encore de l'audace.'*

"Applied to Russia and to October 1917, this means: a simultaneous offensive on Petrograd, as sudden and as rapid as possible, which must without fail be carried out from within and from without, from the working-class quarters and from Finland, from Revel and from Kronstadt, an offensive of the *whole* fleet, the concentration of a *gigantic superiority* of forces over the 15,000 or 20,000 (perhaps more) of our 'bourgeois guard' (the officers' schools), our 'Vendean troops' (part of the Cossacks), etc.

"Our *three* main forces—the navy, the workers and the army units—must be so combined as to occupy without fail and to hold *at the cost of any sacrifice*: a) the telephone exchange; b) the telegraph office; c) the railway stations; d) above all, the bridges.

"The *most determined* elements (our "shock forces" and *young workers*, as well as the best of the sailors) must be formed into small detachments to occupy all the more important points and to *take part* everywhere in all important operations, for example:

"To encircle and cut off Petrograd; to seize it by combined attack of the navy, the workers, and the troops—a task which requires *art and triple audacity.*

"To form detachments composed of the best workers, armed with rifles and bombs, for the purpose of attacking and surrounding the enemy's 'centres' (the military cadets' schools, the telegraph office, the telephone exchange, etc.). Their watchword must be: *'Rather perish to a man than let the enemy pass!'*

"Let us hope that if action is decided on, the leaders will successfully apply the great precepts of Danton and Marx.

"The success of both the Russian and the world revolution depends on two or three days of fighting." (*Works*, Vol. 26, pp. 151-53.)

This letter was written on the 21st, and the 22nd already found Ilyich in Petrograd. The next day there was a meeting of the Central Committee, at which a resolution was carried on his motion calling for an armed uprising. Zinoviev and Kamenev voted against it and demanded that a special plenary meeting of the Central Committee should be called. Kamenev demonstratively announced his resignation from the Central Committee. Lenin demanded that the severest measures of Party penalty should be imposed upon them.

Intensive preparations for the uprising were going forward and breaking down all opportunist resistance. On October 26 the Executive Committee of the Petrograd Soviet passed a resolution to set up a Military Revolutionary Committee. On October 29 an enlarged meeting of the Central Committee was held together with representatives of the Party organizations. The same day, at a meeting of the Central Committee, a Military Revolutionary Centre was set up to direct the uprising, consisting of Stalin, Sverdlov, Dzerzhinsky and others.

On the 30th the proposed organization of a Military Revolutionary Committee was endorsed by the Petrograd Soviet as a whole and not only its Executive Committee. Five days after this a meeting of the regimental committees acknowledged the Petrograd Military Revolutionary Committee as the leading organ of the military units in Petrograd, and passed a resolution not to obey the orders of the Staff unless they were endorsed by the Military Revolutionary Committee.

Already on November 5 the Military Revolutionary Committee had appointed commissars to the military units. The next day, November 6, the Provisional Government decided to prosecute the members of the M.R.C., and arrest the commissars appointed to the military units. The military cadets were called out to the Winter Palace. But it was too late. The military units stood for the Bolsheviks. The workers stood for the transfer of power to the Soviets. The M.R.C. was working under the direct guidance of the Central Committee, most of whose members, including Stalin, Sverdlov, Molotov, Dzerzhinsky and Bubnov, were members of the M.R.C. The uprising had begun.

On November 6 Ilyich was still in hiding at the flat of our Party member Marguerite Fofanova in the Vyborg District (House No. 92/1, Flat No. 42 on the corner of Bolshoi Sampsonievsky and Serdobolskaya streets). He knew that the uprising was about to take place, and fretted because he was not in the thick of it at such a crucial moment. He sent two messages through Marguerite saying that the uprising could not be delayed a moment more. That evening, at last, Eino Rahja, a Finnish comrade, came to see him. Eino, who was in close touch with the factories and the Party organization and served as a medium through whom Ilyich maintained contact with the organization, told Ilyich that the guards patrolling the city had been doubled, that the Provisional Government had given orders to raise the bridges across the Neva in order to cut off communication between the working-class quarters, and that the bridges were being guarded by detachments of soldiers. Obviously, the uprising was starting. Ilyich had intended asking Eino to send for Stalin, but had gathered from what Eino had told him that that was almost impossible. Stalin was probably at the M.R.C. in Smolny, the tramcars were probably not running, and it would take him a long time to get there. Ilyich decided to go to Smolny himself at once. He hurried away, leaving Marguerite a note, saying: "I am going where you did not want me to go. Good-bye. Ilyich."

That night the Vyborg District was arming in preparation for the uprising. One group of workers after another came to the District Committee to receive weapons and instructions. That night I went to see Ilyich at Fofanova's flat, only to learn that he had gone to Smolny. Zhenya Yegorova (Secretary of the Vyborg District Party Committee) and I tacked on to a lorry that our people were sending to Smolny. I was anxious to know whether Ilyich had reached Smolny in safety or not. I do not remember now whether I actually saw Ilyich in Smolny or only learned that he was there. At any rate, I know I did not talk to him, because he was completely absorbed in the business of directing the uprising, and when he did a thing he never did it by halves.

Smolny was brilliantly lit up, a scene of intense activity. Red Guards, representatives from the factories, and soldiers came from all over to receive instructions. Typewriters rattled away, telephones rang, our girls sat sorting out piles of telegrams, and on the second floor the M.R.C. was in continuous session. Armoured cars stood throbbing on the square outside, a field gun stood ready for action, and stacks of firewood had been built up in case barricades were needed. Guns and machine-guns stood at the entrance, sentries at the doors.

By 10 a.m. on October 25 (November 7, New Style), a manifesto "To the Citizens of Russia" issued by the M.R.C. of the Petrograd Soviet came off the press. It said:

"The Provisional Government has been overthrown. The power of state has passed into the hands of the organ of the Petrograd Soviet of Workers' and Soldiers' Deputies, the Military Revolutionary Committee, which stands at the head of the Petrograd proletariat and garrison.

"The cause for which the people have fought—the immediate proposal of a democratic peace, the abolition of landlord ownership of the land, workers' control over production and the creation of a Soviet Government—is assured.

"Long live the revolution of the workers, soldiers and peasants!" (*Works*, Vol. 26, p. 207.)

Although it was obvious that the revolution was victorious, the M.R.C. continued its activities as intensively as ever, occupying the government offices one after another, organizing guard duty, etc.

At 2.30 p.m. a meeting of the Petrograd Soviet of Workers' and Soldiers' Deputies was held. The Soviet hailed with acclamation the report that the Provisional Government no longer existed, that some of its ministers had been arrested and the rest were awaiting their turn, that the Pre-parliament* had been dismissed, and the railway stations, the general post and telegraph offices and the State Bank occupied. The Winter Palace was being stormed. It had not been captured yet, but its fate was sealed, and the soldiers were displaying wonderful heroism. The uprising had been a bloodless one.

Lenin's appearance at the meeting of the Soviet was greeted with a tumultuous ovation. It was characteristic of Ilyich that he made no big speeches in connection with the victory. He spoke instead about the tasks confronting the Soviet power, which had to be tackled in real earnest. He said that a new period in the history of Russia had been ushered in. The Soviet Government would carry on

---

* *Pre-parliament*—Provisional Council of the Republic, a consultative body under the Provisional Government elected at the Democratic Conference. The idea of setting up this body was to lead the country away from the Soviet revolution to the path of bourgeois constitutional development. The Pre-parliament was opened on October 20. The Bolshevik Party boycotted it.—*Ed.*

without the bourgeoisie. A decree would be issued abolishing private ownership of the land. A real workers' control would be established over industry. The struggle for socialism would be launched. The old machinery of state would be broken up and scrapped, and a new authority, the authority of the Soviet organizations, would be set up. We had the force of a mass organization which would carry all before it. The task of the day was to conclude peace. To do that Capital had to be defeated. The international proletariat, among whom signs of revolutionary unrest were beginning to appear, would help us to secure peace.

This speech struck home with the members of the Petrograd Soviet of Soldiers' and Workers' Deputies. Yes, a new period in our history was beginning. The strength of the mass organizations was invincible. The masses had risen, and the power of the bourgeoisie had fallen. We shall take the land from the landowners, and give the law to the factory owners, and, most important of all, we shall secure peace. The world revolution will come to our assistance. Ilyich was right. His speech was greeted with a storm of applause.

The Second Congress of the Soviets was to be opened that evening. It was to proclaim the power of the Soviets and give official recognition to the victory of the revolution.

Agitation was carried on among the delegates when they began to arrive. The government of the workers was to lean upon the peasantry, rally it behind them. The party that was supposed to express the views of the peasantry were the Socialist-Revolutionaries. The rich peasantry, the kulaks had their ideologists in the person of the Right Socialist-Revolutionaries. The ideologists of the peasant masses, the Left Socialist-Revolutionaries were typical representatives of the petty bourgeoisie, which wavered between the bourgeoisie and the proletariat. The leaders of the Petrograd Committee of the Socialist-Revolutionaries were Natanson, Spiridonova and Kamkov. Ilyich had met Natanson during his first emigration. At that time—in 1904—Natanson had stood fairly close to the Marxists, except that he had believed the Social-Democrats to be underestimating the role of the peasantry. Spiridonova was a popular figure at that time. During the first revolution, in 1906, she, then a girl of seventeen, had assassinated Luzhenovsky, the suppressor of the peasant movement in the Tambov Gubernia. After being brutally tortured, she was condemned to penal servitude in Siberia, where she remained until the February Revolution. The Left Socialist-Revolutionaries of Petrograd were strongly influenced by the Bolshevik temper of the masses. They were more favourably inclined towards the Bolsheviks than any of the others. They saw that the Bolsheviks were out in all earnest to confiscate all the lands of the landowners and hand them over to the peasants. The Left Socialist-Revolutionaries believed in introducing a system of equalized land-tenure; the Bolsheviks realized that a complete reconstruction of agriculture on socialist lines was necessary. However, Ilyich considered that the most important thing at the moment was to confiscate the landowners' lands. As to what turn further reconstruction would take, experience itself would show. And he gave his thoughts to the drafting of a decree on the land.

The reminiscences of M. V. Fofanova contain a very interesting item. "I remember," she writes, "Vladimir Ilyich asking me to get him all the back numbers of *Izvestia*, the organ of the All-Russian Soviet of Peasants' Deputies, which I did, of course. I do not remember exactly how many numbers there were, but they made a solid batch of material for study. Vladimir Ilyich spent two days over it, working even at night. In the morning he says to me: 'Well, I think I've studied these S.-R.'s inside out. All that remains is for me to read the mandate of their peasant electors.' Two hours later he called me in and said cheerfully, slapping one of the newspapers (I saw it to be the August 19 issue of the *Peasant Izvestia*): 'Here's a ready-made agreement with the Left S.-R.'s. It's no joke—this mandate has been signed by 242 local deputies. We shall use it as the basis for our law concerning the land and see if the Left S.-R.'s dare to reject it.' He showed me the paper with blue pencil markings all over it and added: 'The thing is to find a means by which we could afterwards reshape their socialization idea after our own pattern.' "

Marguerite was an agronomist by profession and she came up against these problems in her work. It was, therefore, a subject on which Ilyich willingly spoke to her.

Would the Left Socialist-Revolutionaries quit the congress or not?

The Second All-Russian Congress of Soviets opened at 10.45 p.m. on October 25 (November 7, New Style). That evening the congress was to be constituted, was to elect a presidium and define its powers. Of the 670 delegates only 300 were Bolsheviks; 193 were Socialist-Revolutionaries and 68 Mensheviks. The Right Socialist-Revolutionaries, Mensheviks and Bundists foamed at the mouth and thundered denunciations at the Bolsheviks. They read out a declaration of protest against the "military plot and seizure of power engineered by the Bolsheviks behind the backs of the other parties and factions represented on the Soviet" and walked out. Some of the Menshevik-Internationalists quitted too. The Left Socialist-Revolutionaries, who formed the overwhelming majority of the S.-R. delegates (169 out of 193), remained. Altogether fifty delegates quitted the congress. Vladimir Ilyich was not present at the opening night.

While the Second Congress of Soviets was being opened the Winter Palace was being stormed. Kerensky had escaped the day before, disguised as a sailor, and was rushed off to Pskov in a motor-car. The Military Revolutionary Committee of Pskov did not arrest him, although it had had direct orders signed by Dybenko and Krylenko to do so, and Kerensky left for Moscow to organize a crusade against Petrograd, where the soldiers and workers had taken the power into their own hands. The other ministers, headed by Kishkin, entrenched themselves in the Winter Palace under the protection of the military cadets and the women's shock battalion, which had been drawn up there for the purpose. The Mensheviks, Right S.-R.'s and Bundists were frantic with rage over the siege of the Winter Palace and went into hysterics at the congress. Erlich declared that some of the town-councillors had decided to go unarmed to the Palace Square and risk being shot down because the palace was being shelled. The Executive Committee of the Soviet of Peasants' Deputies, and the Menshevik and S.-R. groups decided to join them. After the Mensheviks and Socialist-Revolutionaries had walked out an interval was called. When the proceedings were resumed at 3.10 a.m. the congress was informed that the Winter Palace had been taken, the ministers arrested, the officers and cadets disarmed, and the Third Bicycle Battalion, which Kerensky had sent against Petrograd, had gone over to the revolutionary people.

When there was no doubt left that victory had been won and that the Left Socialist-Revolutionaries would not quit the congress, Vladimir Ilyich, who had hardly slept the previous night and had taken an active part all the time in directing the uprising, left Smolny and went to sleep at the Bonch-Bruyeviches', who lived in Peski, not far from Smolny. He was given a room to himself, but he could not fall asleep for a long time. He got up quietly so as not to wake anybody and began to write the Decree on Land, which he had already thought out in every detail.

Addressing the congress on the evening of October 26 (November 8, New Style) in support of the Decree on Land, Ilyich said:

"Voices are being raised here that the decree itself and the mandate were drawn up by the Socialist-Revolutionaries. What of it? Does it matter who drew them up? As a democratic government, we cannot ignore the decision of the rank and file of the people, even though we may disagree with it. In the fire of experience, applying the decree in practice, and carrying it out locally, the peasants will themselves realize where the truth lies.... Life is the best teacher and it will show who is right. Let the peasants solve this problem from one end and we shall solve it from the other. Life will oblige us to draw together in the general stream of revolutionary creative work, in the elaboration of new state forms.... The peasants have learnt something during the eight months of our revolution; they want to settle all land questions themselves. We are therefore opposed to all amendments to this draft law. We want no details in it, for we are writing a decree, not a programme of action." (*Works*, Vol. 26, pp. 228-29.)

We have all of Ilyich in those words—an Ilyich free from petty conceit (it does not matter who said it, so long as it says the right thing), taking into consideration the opinion of the rank and file, appreciating the power of revolutionary creative work, clearly understanding that the masses are best convinced by practice and experience, and that the hard facts of life would show them that the Bolsheviks' point of view had been correct. The Decree on Land submitted by Lenin was adopted. Sixteen years have passed since then. Landlord ownership has been abolished, and step by step, in a struggle against the old proprietary habits and views, new forms of farming have been created —collective farming, which now embraces the bulk of peasant households. The old small-farm methods and small-owner mentality are becoming a thing of the past. A strong and powerful basis for socialist farming has been created.

The decrees on Peace and Land were passed at the evening session on October 26 (November 8). On these points agreement was reached with the S.-R.'s. On the question of forming a government, however, the position was worse. The Left S.-R.'s had not quitted the congress because they had realized that such an action would have cost them their influence among the peasant masses, but the withdrawal on October 25 of the Right S.-R.'s and the Mensheviks, and their outcries against the adventurism of the Bolsheviks, the seizure of power, etc., etc., had deeply affected them. After the Right S.-R.'s and the others had left the congress, Kamkov, one of the leaders of the Left S.-R.'s, declared that they stood for a united democratic government, and that the Left S.-R.'s would do everything they could to have such a government set up. The Left S.-R.'s said they wanted to act as mediators between the Bolsheviks and the parties who had left the congress. The Bolsheviks did not refuse to negotiate, but Ilyich understood perfectly well that nothing would come of such talks. The Bolsheviks had not seized the power and made the revolution in order to hitch a swan, a pike and a crab to the Soviet cart, to form a government that would be incapable of pulling together and getting things done. Cooperation with the Left S.-R.'s, in Ilyich's opinion, was possible.

A talk on this question with representatives of the Left S.-R.'s was held a couple of hours before the congress opened on October 26. I remember the surroundings in which that conference was held. It was a room in Smolny with small settees upholstered in dark red. On one settee sat Spiridonova, and next to her stood Ilyich, arguing with her in a sort of gentle earnest manner. No agreement was reached with the Left S.-R.'s. They did not want to join the government. Ilyich proposed the appointment of Bolsheviks alone to the posts of socialist ministers.

The congress session of October 26 (November 8) opened at 9 p.m. I was present. I remember the speech Ilyich made in submitting his draft Decree on Land. He spoke calmly. The audience listened with rapt attention. During the reading of the Decree I was struck by the expression of one of the delegates who sat a little way off.

He was an elderly looking peasant, and under the stress of powerful emotion his face had assumed a wax-like appearance and his eyes shone with a peculiar light.

The death sentence, introduced by Kerensky at the front, was repealed, decrees on Peace, on Land and on Workers' Control were passed, and a Bolshevik Council of People's Commissars was formed as follows: Vladimir Ulyanov (Lenin)—Chairman of the Council; A. I. Rykov—People's Commissar for Internal Affairs; V. P. Milyutin—Agriculture; A. G. Shlyapnikov—Labour; V. A. Ovseyenko (Antonov), N. V. Krylenko and P. Y. Dybenko—Committee of Military and Naval Affairs; V. P. Nogin—Trade and Industry; A. V. Lunacharsky—Education; I. I. Skvortsov (Stepanov)—Finance; L. D. Bronstein (Trotsky)—Foreign Affairs; G. I. Oppokov (Lomov)—Justice; I. A. Teodorovich—Food Supply; N. P. Avilov (Glebov)—Post and Telegraph; and J. V. Djugashvili (Stalin)—Chairman of the People's Commissariat for the Affairs of Nationalities. The post of Commissar of Ways of Communication was left open.

Eino Rahja relates that when the list of first People's Commissars was being discussed at a meeting of the Bolshevik group, he had been sitting in a corner listening. One of the nominees had protested that he had no experience in that kind of work. Vladimir Ilyich had burst out laughing and said: "Do you think any of us has had such experience?" None had any experience, of course. But Vladimir Ilyich envisaged the People's Commissar as a new type of minister, an organizer and manager of one or another branch of state activity, who was linked closely with the masses.

Vladimir Ilyich's mind was hard at work all the time on the problem of new forms of administration. He was thinking of how to organize a machinery of government that would be free from the taint of bureaucratism, that would lean on the masses, organize their cooperation and assistance, and show itself capable of training a new type of administrative worker on this job. In the resolution of the Second Congress of Soviets concerning the formation of a workers' and peasants' government, this is expressed in the following words:

"The management of the different branches of state activity is entrusted to commissions whose make-up should ensure the implementation of the programme proclaimed by the congress in close unity with the mass organizations of the workers, sailors, soldiers, peasants and employees. The government power is vested in a collegium of chairmen of the said commissions, i.e., the Council of People's Commissars." (*Works*, Vol. 26, p. 230.)

I recall the talks I had with Ilyich on this subject during the few weeks he lived at Fofanova's. I was working at the time with tremendous enthusiasm in the Vyborg District, keenly observing the revolutionary activities of the masses and the radical changes that were taking place in the whole pattern of life. On meeting Vladimir Ilyich I would tell him about life in the district. I remember telling him about an interesting sitting of a People's Court which I had attended. Such courts had been held in some places during the Revolution of 1905—in Sormovo for one thing. Chugurin, a worker, whom I had met as a student of the Longjumeau Party school near Paris and with whom I was now working at the Vyborg District Council, was a native of Sormovo. It was his suggestion to start organizing such courts in the Vyborg District. The first court sat at the People's House. The place was packed with people standing shoulder to shoulder on the floor, benches and window sills. I do not remember now exactly what cases came before the court. They were not really offences in the strict sense of the word, but incidents of everyday life. Two suspicious characters were tried for attempting to arrest Chugurin. A tall swarthy watchman was "tried" for beating his young son, exploiting him and keeping him away from school. Many working men and women from among the public made warm speeches. The "defendant" kept wiping the sweat from his brow, and then, with the tears streaming down his face, promised not to ill-treat his son any more. Strictly speaking, it was not a court, but a public control of citizens' behaviour; we were witnessing proletarian ethics in the making. Vladimir Ilyich was greatly interested in this "court" and questioned me about it in detail.

Mostly I told him about the new forms of educational work. I was in charge of the Department of Education at the District Council. The children's school did not function in the summer, and most of the time I was busy with political education. In this respect my five years' experience at the Sunday Evening School in the Nevskaya Zastava District in the nineties came in very useful to me. These were different times, of course, and we could go ahead with the job unhampered.

Delegates from some forty factories got together every week and we discussed ways and means of carrying out one or another measure. Whatever we decided was immediately carried out. For example, we decided to do away with illiteracy, and the factory delegates, each at his own place of employment, organized the registration of illiterates, secured school premises and raised the necessary funds by bearing down upon the factory managements. A representative of the workers was attached to each such school and he saw to it that the school was supplied with all that it needed in the way of blackboards, chalk, ABC books, etc. Special representatives were appointed to see that right teaching methods were used and to find out what the workers had to say about it. We briefed these representatives and had them report back to us. We got together delegates of the soldiers' wives and discussed conditions in the children's homes, organized their inspection over the children's homes, gave them instructions, and carried out extensive explanatory work among them. We got together the librarians of the district, and together with them and the workers discussed the forms of work of the public libraries. A powerful impulse was given to the initiative of the workers, and the Department of Education rallied around itself considerable forces. Ilyich said at the time that this was just the style of work that our government offices and future ministers would have to adopt, a style of work modelled after these committees of working men and women, who were in the thick of things and were familar with the conditions of life and work of the masses and with everything that agitated their minds at the moment. Vladimir Ilyich was all the more keen to draw me out on these subjects in that he believed I understood how to enlist the masses on the job of running the government. He had some strong things to say afterwards about the "rotten" bureaucratism that had wormed its way in everywhere. Eventually, when the question came up of raising the responsibility of the People's Commissars and the Commissariats' department managers, who often shuffled it off on to the boards and commissions, the question of one-man management arose. Ilyich unexpectedly got me appointed a member of the commission under the Council of People's Commissars which was set up to investigate this question. He said we must be careful that one-man management should in no way override the initiative and independent activity of the commissions, or weaken the ties with the masses; one-man management had to be combined with an ability to work with the masses. Ilyich tried to make use of everyone's experience for building up a state of a new type. The Soviet Government, at the head of which Ilyich now stood, was faced with the task of setting up a type of state machinery such as the world had never yet seen, a machinery that relied on the support of the broad masses; the task was to remodel the whole social fabric and all human relations along new socialist lines.

But first of all the Soviet power had to be defended against the enemy's attempts to overthrow it by force and disrupt it from within. Our ranks had to be strengthened.

November 9-15 were days of struggle for the very existence of the Soviet power.

As a result of a thorough study of the experience of the Paris Commune, the world's first proletarian state, Ilyich noted what a ruinous effect the lenity which the working masses and the workers' government had shown towards their avowed enemies had had upon the fate of the Paris Commune. In speaking of the fight against the enemies, therefore, Ilyich was always inclined to put the case strongly for fear of the masses and himself showing too great lenity.

At the beginning of the October Revolution there had been far too much forbearance of this kind. Kerensky and a number of ministers had been allowed to escape, the cadets who had defended the Winter Palace had been set free on parole, and General Krasnov, who commanded Kerensky's advancing troops, had been left under domiciliary arrest. One day, while sitting in one of the waiting rooms at Smolny on a heap of army coats, I heard a conversation between Krylenko and General Krasnov, who had been brought to Petrograd under arrest. They had come in together, sat down at a small table standing all by itself in the middle of the large room, and dropped into a calm easy conversation. I remember being surprised at the peaceful nature of their talk. Speaking at a meeting of the Central Executive Committee on November 17, Ilyich had said: "Krasnov was treated leniently. He was merely put under domiciliary arrest. We are against civil war. But if, nevertheless, it continues, what are we to do?" (*Works*, Vol. 26, p. 252.)

Released by the Pskov comrades, Kerensky had engineered an attack on Petrograd; set free on parole, the cadets had revolted on November 11, and Krasnov, escaping from under domiciliary arrest, had organized a hundred-thousand-strong White army in the Don with the aid of the German Government.

The people were tired of the imperialist carnage and wanted a bloodless revolution, but the enemies compelled them to fight. Engrossed completely in the problems of socialist reconstruction of the entire social system, Ilyich was compelled to turn his attention to the defence of the cause of the revolution.

On November 9 Kerensky succeeded in capturing Gatchina. In an article "Lenin During the Days of the Uprising" (*Krasnaya Gazeta*, November 6, 1927) Podvoisky gives a vivid description of the tremendous work Lenin did during the days of Petrograd's defence. He describes how Lenin came to the Area Staff Headquarters and demanded a report on the situation. Antonov-Ovseyenko began to explain the general plan of operations, pointing out on the map the disposition of our forces and the probable disposition and strength of the enemy's forces. "Lenin examined the map closely. With the keenness of a profound and attentive strategist and general, he demanded explanations—why this point was not being guarded, why that point was undefended, why such a step was being contemplated instead of another, why Kronstadt, Vyborg, Helsingfors had not been called on for support, and so on. After comparing notes, it became clear that we had really made quite a number of blunders and not acted with the prompt urgency which the menacing situation in Petrograd called for in the matter of organizing the means and forces for its defence."

On the evening of the 9th Ilyich spoke with Helsingfors on the private line and arranged for two destroyers and the battleship *Respublika* to be sent to guard the approaches to Petrograd.

Vladimir Ilyich went to the Putilov Works with Antonov-Ovseyenko to check up whether the armoured train, which was so badly needed, was being built quickly enough. He talked with the workers there. Staff Headquarters was transferred to Smolny, and Lenin took a close interest in all its work, and helped it to mobilize the activity of the masses. Podvoisky writes that he began to appreciate Lenin's work after a delegate conference of workers' organizations, district Soviets, factory committees, trade unions and military units, which Lenin had called. "I saw here wherein Lenin's power lay," he writes. "During an emergency, he kept the concentration of our forces and means at its highest pitch of intensity. We squandered our energies, mustered and used our forces without plan, as a result of which our efforts lost much of their impact, and blunted the edge of the masses' activity, initiative and determination. The masses had not felt that iron will and iron plan which keeps all parts together as in a finely adjusted machine. Lenin kept driving home the idea that it was essential to make the utmost concentrated efforts for defence. Elaborating on this idea he unfolded to the conference an intelligible plan in which, as in an integral machine, everyone found a place for himself, for his factory or his unit. Right there, at the conference, every man was able to envisage concretely the plan of further work, and to feel his work to be linked with that of the whole collective body of the republic. As a result, he felt the responsibility which, from that moment, the dictatorship of the proletariat was imposing upon him. To attract the masses and bring it home to them that no leaders would do their job for them, but that they themselves would have to get down to work with their own hands if they wanted to arrange their lives on new lines and defend their state—this is what Lenin constantly strove to achieve, this is where he showed himself to be a true leader of the people, a leader who was able to make the masses face up to vital and essential issues and take the step towards their solution themselves, not by unconsciously following a leader, but by being profoundly conscious themselves of what they were doing."

In this Podvoisky was absolutely right. Ilyich was able to alert the masses, was able always to set concrete aims before them.

The workers of Petrograd rose in defence of their city. Old and young went off to the front to meet the troops of Kerensky. The Cossacks and the units that had been called up from the provinces were none too keen on fighting, and the Petrograd workers carried on agitation among them, argued with them. The Cossacks and soldiers whom Kerensky had mobilized simply quitted the front, taking guns and rifles with them. Kerensky's front was disintegrating. Nevertheless, many Petrograd workers lost their lives in defending the city. Among them was Vera Slutskaya, who had been an active Party worker in the Vasileostrovsky District. She went out to the front in a lorry and had her head blown off by a shell. Quite a number of our Vyborg District comrades were killed too. The whole district turned out to attend the funeral.

On November 11, when Kerensky was marching on Petrograd in full force, the military cadets, who had been released from the Winter Palace on parole, decided to help Kerensky and engineered a revolt. I was still living in Petrograd District at the time with Ilyich's relatives— this was before I moved to Smolny. Early in the morning fighting started near the Pavlovskoye Military School not far from where we lived. On hearing of the revolt of the cadets, the Red Guards and workers from the factories in the Vyborg District came to suppress it. Guns were used in the fighting, and our house shook. The people around us were scared to death. Early in the morning of that day, when I was leaving the house to go to the District Council, a housemaid from next door had come running towards me crying horrified: "You ought to see what they're doing! I just saw them bayonet a cadet just like a fly on a pin!" On the way I had met a fresh force of the Vyborg Red Guards coming up with another cannon. The revolt of the cadets was quickly suppressed.

The same day Ilyich addressed a conference of regimental representatives of the Petrograd garrison. In the course of his speech he said: "Kerensky's attempt was as pitiful an adventure as Kornilov's.* It is a difficult moment, though. Energetic measures are needed to improve the food supply and put an end to the hardships of war. We cannot wait, and we cannot tolerate a revolt of Kerensky's for a single day. If the Kornilovites organize a new offensive they will get the same answer as the cadet revolt received today. The cadets have themselves to blame. We have taken the power almost without any bloodshed. If there were any casualties they were on our side alone.... The government created by the will of the workers', soldiers' and peasants' deputies, will not tolerate any insults on the part of the Kornilovites." (*Works*, Vol. 26, p. 236.)

On November 14 Kerensky's revolt was suppressed. Gatchina was recaptured. Kerensky escaped. In Petrograd victory was complete. But in the country at large civil war was breaking out. On November 8 General Kaledin had proclaimed martial law in the Don Region and began to organize the Cossacks against the Soviet power. On November 9 the Cossack ataman Dutov had captured Orenburg. In Moscow things were dragging. The Whites had seized the Kremlin there. The fight was fiercer than in Petrograd.

The Right Socialist-Revolutionaries, the Mensheviks and other factions, who had quitted the Second Congress of Soviets on November 8, organized a Committee for the Salvation of the Motherland and the Revolution, around which they thought to rally all the opponents of the Soviet power. The committee had on it nine representatives of the Central Town Council, the whole presidium of the Pre-

---

* "Kornilov's attempt" refers to the counter-revolutionary plot organized in August 1917 by General Kornilov with the object of suppressing the revolution, smashing the Bolshevik Party and the Soviets and establishing a military dictatorship. To effect this coup Kornilov sent a cavalry corps against Petrograd. The Bolsheviks, with the support of the Soviets, organized the workers and soldiers for the fight and frustrated Kornilov's plot.—*Ed.*

parliament, three representatives from each of the executive committees of the All-Russian Soviet of Workers' and Soldiers' Deputies, the Soviet of Peasants' Deputies, and of the S.-R. and Menshevik factions, representatives of the Unity-Mensheviks, the Centroflot* and two representatives of Plekhanov's Unity group. They were out to save the country and the revolution from the Bolshevik "adventurers" who had seized the power behind their backs. But they could not do much. The slogans "For Peace," "For Land" were so popular among the masses that the latter rallied unhesitatingly around the Bolsheviks with tremendous enthusiasm. The Committee of Public Security, which had been formed in Moscow, joined the Petrograd Committee for the Salvation of the Motherland and the Revolution. It had been formed on the initiative of the Moscow Town Council, at the head of which stood the Right Socialist-Revolutionary Rudnev. The Moscow Committee of Public Security openly sided with the counter-revolution.

Troops had to be sent to Moscow to give a helping hand, but this could not be done on account of the stand which the All-Russian Executive Committee of Railway Employees had taken. The Railwaymen's Executive backed the dissentient factions that had quitted the congress, and the workers had no influence there. The Railwaymen's Executive declared that it took a "neutral stand" in the civil war that had started, and would not allow the troops of either side to pass. Actually, this "neutrality" hit the Bolsheviks and prevented them from sending troops to the assistance of Moscow. The sabotage of the Railwaymen's Executive was broken by the railway workers, who undertook to transport the troops themselves. On

---

* *Centroflot*—Russian abbreviation for Central Executive Committee of the All-Russian Navy. Consisted almost entirely of Socialist-Revolutionaries and Mensheviks. Supported the Provisional Government.—*Ed.*

November 16 the Military Revolutionary Committee in Petrograd sent a force to Moscow. The resistance of the Whites, however, was overcome in Moscow before those troops arrived.

At the most difficult moment, when the revolt of the military cadets had only just been suppressed in Petrograd, when Kerensky was still advancing, and fighting in Moscow was still in progress, a number of members of the Party Central Committee began to vacillate. They believed that concessions ought to be made, that the situation was desperate. These vacillations were most strikingly revealed in the negotiations with the Railwaymen's Executive. On November 9, the latter passed a resolution calling for the formation of a government of all the Socialist parties, from the Bolsheviks to the Popular Socialists,* and offering to act as mediators. At first only the Left wing of the Railwaymen's Executive entered into negotiations with the Central Committee, who authorized L. B. Kamenev and G. Y. Sokolnikov to represent it. The Mensheviks and the Right S.-R.'s took no part in the talks at first, but when they saw, as they thought, that the Bolsheviks had been driven into a corner as a result of Kerensky's attack and the state of affairs in Moscow, and learned that vacillations had started within the Central Committee, they became brazen to a degree. They came to the meeting of the Railwaymen's Executive on November 12-13 and demanded the repudiation of the power of the Soviets, the exclusion from participation in the government of those guilty of the October uprising, the removal, first and foremost, of Lenin, and the setting up of a new government headed by Chernov or Avksentyev. The Bolshevik delegation led by Kamenev did not withdraw from the meeting, thereby permitting discussion of the pro-

---

* *Popular Socialists*—a petty-bourgeois party defending the interests of the kulak elements in the countryside. It was represented on the Provisional Government.—*Ed.*

posals submitted by the Mensheviks and the Right S.-R.'s. The next day, on November 14, a meeting of the Central Committee was called, at which Lenin demanded that the talks with the Railwaymen's Executive, who had gone over to the side of the Kaledins and Kornilovs, should be broken off immediately. A resolution to that effect was adopted by the Central Committee. On the 17th, Nogin, Rykov, V. Milyutin and Teodorovich announced their resignation from the Council of People's Commissars on the grounds that they considered it necessary to form a socialist government of all the Socialist parties. They were joined by a number of other Commissars. Kamenev, Rykov, Zinoviev, Nogin and Milyutin announced their resignation from the Central Committee. All of them had stood for the formation of an all-party coalition government right after the victory of the October Revolution. The Central Committee demanded that they should submit to Party discipline. Ilyich was indignant and fought hard on this point. Zinoviev published a statement announcing his return to the Central Committee.

The further victories of the Bolsheviks and the Petrograd and Moscow organizations' sharp disapproval of these comrades' conduct (their resignation from the Central Committee and their official posts) enabled the Party to liquidate this incident fairly quickly. It took one's thoughts back to the past—to the Second Congress of the Party fourteen years earlier, in 1903. The Party then had only just begun to form, and Martov's refusal to join the editorial board of *Iskra* had provoked a serious crisis in the Party, which had caused Ilyich great distress. The present resignation of a number of comrades from the Central Committee and from their posts of Commissars merely created temporary difficulties. The uplift of the revolutionary movement had helped to quickly liquidate this incident, and Ilyich, who always spoke about what was on his mind at the moment during our walks together, never once mentioned this incident. His mind was set entirely on the problem of how to begin building up the socialist system of life, how to put into effect the resolutions passed at the Second Congress of Soviets.

On November 17, Ilyich spoke at the meeting of the All-Russian Central Executive Committee and the meeting of the Petrograd Soviet of Workers' and Soldiers' Deputies held jointly with army delegates from the front. His speeches breathed absolute confidence in victory, confidence in the correctness of the line which the Bolsheviks had taken, confidence in the support of the masses.

"The criminal inertia of the Kerensky Government brought the country and the revolution to the brink of disaster; truly, delay spells death, and in issuing laws that meet the hopes and wishes of the broad masses of the people, the new government is setting landmarks upon the path of development of new forms of life. The local Soviets, in keeping with local conditions, may modify, extend or supplement the basic principles which the government establishes. The basic factor of the new public life is the live creative effort of the masses. Let the workers set up a workers' control of their factories, let them supply the countryside with manufactures, barter them for grain. Every single commodity, every pound of bread should be accounted for, for socialism, above all, means accounting. *Socialism cannot be built up by decrees from above. Official bureaucratic automatism is alien to its spirit; living constructive socialism is the creation of the masses of the people themselves.*" (My italics.—*N.K.*) (*Works*, Vol. 26, pp. 254-55.)

Wonderful words!

"The power belongs to our Party, which has the support and trust of the broad masses of the people. Some of our comrades may have taken a stand that has nothing in common with Bolshevism. But the working masses of Moscow will not follow the lead of Rykov and Nogin," said Ilyich. (*Ibid.*, p. 256.)

He concluded his speech with the following words:

"The Central Executive Committee charges the Council of People's Commissars to nominate candidates for the posts of People's Commissars for Internal Affairs and Trade and Industry for the next meeting, and offers Kolegayev the post of People's Commissar of Agriculture." (*Ibid.*, p. 259.) Kolegayev was a Left Socialist-Revolutionary. He did not accept the proffered post. The party of Left Socialist-Revolutionaries still shirked responsibility.

The Mensheviks, Right S.-R.'s and others agitated for sabotage. The old government officials refused to work under the Bolsheviks, and did not come to their offices. Addressing the Petrograd Soviet on November 17, Lenin said: "They say we are isolated. The bourgeoisie has created an atmosphere of lies and slander around us, but I have not seen a soldier yet who has not hailed the passing of power into the hands of the Soviets with enthusiasm. I have not seen a peasant who was against the Soviets." (*Works*, Vol. 26, p. 262.)

And this gave Lenin confidence in victory.

On November 21, 1917, Yakov Sverdlov was elected Chairman of the All-Russian Central Executive Committee in place of L.B. Kamenev. He was nominated by Ilyich. The choice was an exceedingly happy one. Sverdlov was a man of great firmness. In the struggle for the Soviet power, in the struggle against the counter-revolution, he was indispensable. Moreover, there was a tremendous job to be done in organizing a state of a new type, and this job called for an organizer of exceptional ability. Sverdlov was just that kind of organizer.

Two years later, on March 18, 1919, after having accomplished a tremendous organizing job for the good of the country at a time of its greatest need, Sverdlov died. Lenin's speech at the special meeting of the All-Russian Central Executive Committee held in connection with his death, has gone down in history as a splendid memorial to that devoted champion of the working-class cause. "In the course of our revolution and its victories," said Lenin,

At the unveiling of a monument to Marx and Engels, Moscow,
November 7, 1918

Lenin with presidium of First Congress of the Communist International, the Kremlin, March 1919. Left to right: G. Klinger, G. Eberlein, Lenin, F. Platten

"Comrade Sverdlov has succeeded, more fully and wholly than anyone else, in expressing the most important and essential features of the proletarian revolution...." The most "profound and constant feature of this revolution and the condition for its victory," Ilyich continued, "has always been the organization of the proletarian masses, the organization of the working people. It is this organization of the millions of the working people that constitutes the finest conditions for the revolution, the deepest source of its victories.... It was this feature of the revolution that advanced to the fore such a man as Y. M. Sverdlov, who was an organizer *par excellence.*" Ilyich described Sverdlov as "a most clear-cut type of professional revolutionary," wholeheartedly devoted to the cause of the revolution, steeled by long years of underground illegal activity, a man who never lost touch with the masses, never left Russia, a revolutionary who "succeeded in becoming not only a leader beloved of the workers, not only a leader who was best and most widely familiar with the practical work, but also an organizer of the advanced proletarians.... It is to the remarkable organizing ability of this man that we owe whatever we have so far taken such pride in. He has secured for us the full opportunity for really organized, rational teamwork, worthy of the organized proletarian masses and fitting the needs of the proletarian revolution—organized teamwork without which we could not have achieved a single success, without which we could not have overcome a single one of those innumerable difficulties, a single one of those hardships which we have had to face till now and are compelled to face at the present moment." Ilyich characterized Sverdlov as an organizer who had won for himself an "unassailable reputation," an organizer of "the whole Soviet power in Russia" and "the most experienced" organizer of "the work of the Party, which created these Soviets and practically implemented the Soviet power." (*Works*, Vol. 29, pp. 70-74.)

The October Revolution altered the conditions of the revolutionary struggle. These new conditions of struggle demanded of a man greater determination, greater pertinacity, greater "stamina," to use a favourite word of Vladimir Ilyich, greater organizing scope. "The essence of socialism in the making is organization," Ilyich often said. It was no accident that the course of events brought to the fore men who were not afraid to shoulder responsibility, men whose abilities had been cramped by the conditions of the old underground; constant arrests and deportations had brought their organizing efforts to naught, while the need for secrecy had kept them in the background. One such man was Stalin, an outstanding organizer of the Party and of the victory of October. It was not for nothing that when candidates for People's Commissars were being nominated at the Second Congress of Soviets Ilyich proposed that Stalin should be appointed Chairman of the Commissariat for the Affairs of Nationalities. Ilyich had striven for years to bring about the liberation of the non-Russian nationalities and give them an opportunity for all-round development; during the last few years he had fought harder than ever for the right of nations to self-determination. I remember how closely he took to heart every little thing that had any bearing on this question, and how furious he got one day when I told him that there was some hesitation at the People's Commissariat of Education on the question as to whether historical monuments of value to the Poles should be restored to them or not. Ilyich hated great-power chauvinism with all his soul, and there was nothing he desired more passionately than that the Republic of the Soviets should offset the imperialist policy of oppressing the weaker nationalities by its own policy of complete liberation for those nationalities, a policy of comradely solicitude for their welfare. He knew Stalin's views on the national question very well, as they had often discussed the subject in Cracow. He was confident that Stalin would consider himself in honour bound to carry out in deed and not in word all that had been so carefully thought out and discussed on this subject during previous years. The nationalities had to be given the right to self-determination. The task was complicated by the fact that this right had to be enforced under conditions of acute class struggle. The work of putting into effect the nations' right to self-determination had to be combined with the struggle for the dictatorship of the proletariat and the implementation of the power of the Soviets. This question was closely linked with the question of the international struggle of the proletariat and the questions of the civil war. A broad mind, profound conviction and practical organizing ability were required of the person in charge of affairs on the national front. That is why Ilyich proposed Stalin for the job.

The problem of learning how to work the new way, learning new habits of mind, the problem of making leading, capable and tenacious builders of the socialist system out of yesterday's revolutionary opposition, loomed large before all Party workers.

* * *

Ilyich and I moved into Smolny. We were given a room there formerly occupied by a *dame de class*. It was partitioned off to make room for a bed. Admission to it was through the wash-room. A lift took you upstairs where Ilyich had his private office. Facing this was a small outer office used as a waiting room. Delegation after delegation came to see him. Most of them were from the front. Often, when going up to him, I would find him in the outer office. The room would be crowded with soldiers, all standing up and listening to Ilyich, who was talking to them by the window. Ilyich worked in the bustling atmosphere of Smolny, which was always crowded with people. Everyone came there, as if drawn by a magnet. Smolny was guarded by soldiers of the machine-gun regiment, the same regiment that had been quartered in the Vyborg District in the summer of 1917 and was completely under the influence of the workers there. It had been the first to come out in July 3, 1917, eager to join the fray. Kerensky had decided to make an example of the rebels. They were disarmed and marched out on to the square where they were publicly degraded. After that the machine-gunners hated the Provisional Government worse than ever. In October they fought for the Soviet power and afterwards took over guard duty at Smolny. One machine-gunner by the name of Zheltishev, an Ufa peasant, was told off to look after Ilyich. He was greatly attached to Ilyich and took care of him, attending to his wants and bringing him his meals from the canteen, which was then housed in Smolny. Zheltishev was naive to a degree. He was for ever wondering at things. Even the spirit-lamp set him wondering. I came into the room once and found him sitting on his haunches pouring spirits on the burning lamp that stood before him on the floor. Even the taps and the crockery set him wondering. The machine-gunners who were guarding Smolny once came upon a pile of caskets used by the young ladies of the former Smolny Institute. Curious to know what was in them, they prized them open with their bayonets. They found them to contain diaries, all kinds of knick-knacks and ribbons. The men gave them away to the children of the neighbourhood. Zheltishev brought me a trinket—a round little mirror with carving on it and the word "Niagara" in English letters. I still have it. Ilyich sometimes exchanged a word with Zheltishev, and the latter was prepared to do anything in the world for him. Zheltishev was supposed to attend on Trotsky, too, who lived opposite us with his family in the rooms formerly occupied by the head mistress of the Institute. But he did not like Trotsky. "He was much too bossy," he once wrote to me.

He is now living in a collective farm in the Bashkir Republic. He has a large family, is ailing, goes in for beekeeping, and writes to me occasionally, recollecting things about Ilyich.

I was at work all day, first in the Vyborg District Council, then in the Commissariat of Education. Ilyich was left pretty much to shift for himself. Zheltishev brought him his meals and bread—the usual rations. Maria Ilyinichna sometimes brought him some food from home, but he had no one to take regular care of his meals, as I was hardly ever at home. A young fellow named Korotkov recently told me of an incident connected with Lenin. He was a boy of twelve at the time, living with his mother, who was an office cleaner at Smolny. Once she heard someone walking about in the canteen. She looked in, and there was Ilyich standing at a table eating a piece of black bread and herring to which he had helped himself. He was somewhat taken aback at the sight of the office cleaner, and said with a smile: "I felt very hungry, you know." Korotkova knew Vladimir Ilyich. Once, during the days immediately following the revolution, Ilyich was coming down the stairs, which she was washing. She stood leaning on the banister, resting. Ilyich stopped and talked to her. She did not know who he was at the time. He said to her: "Well, Comrade, don't you find things better now under the Soviet power than under the old government?" And she answered: "Oh, I don't care, so long as I get paid for my work." Afterwards, when she got to know it had been Lenin, she could not get over it. She told that story of how she had answered Lenin as long as she lived. She is now an old-age pensioner, and her son, who had then been employed in the Forwarding Department of Smolny, has taken his degree as artist at the State Art and Crafts Workshops.*

And then, at last, Shotman's mother, a Finn, took matters in hand. She was very fond of her son and proud

---

* A higher institution of applied art, which existed in Moscow from 1918 to 1926.—*Ed.*

of the fact that he had been a delegate to the Second Party Congress and helped Ilyich to hide himself during the July days. Soon she had everything in the house ship-shape, the way Ilyich liked it, and put Zheltishev, and the cleaners, and the waitresses in the canteen through their paces. I could rest assured now, when going away, that Ilyich would be properly looked after and given his meals.

Late in the afternoon, when I came home from work, Ilyich (if he was disengaged) and I would go for a stroll round Smolny and have a chat. Few people knew Ilyich by sight in those days, and he used to go about unattended. True, the machine-gunners, seeing him go out, used to worry about it, and they saw to it that the Smolny area was kept clear of hostile elements. Once they ran in a dozen or so housewives who had collected on the corner and were railing loudly at Lenin. Malkov, the commandant of Smolny, sent for me the next morning and said: "We ran some women in yesterday—they were kicking up a row. What am I to do with them? Will you have a look at them?" For one thing it turned out that most of the women had slipped away, and the rest were such an ignorant lot far removed from politics that I laughingly advised Malkov to let them go. One of the women, on being released, came back and asked me in a whisper, pointing to Malkov: "Is that Lenin?" I dismissed her with a smile.

We lived in Smolny up to March 1918, when we moved to Moscow.

FROM THE OCTOBER REVOLUTION TO THE PEACE OF BREST

In his article of November 5, 1921, entitled "The Importance of Gold Now and After the Complete Victory of Socialism," Ilyich wrote:

"At such dizzy speed, *in a few weeks*, from October 25, 1917, to the Brest Peace, we built up the Soviet state, extricated ourselves from the imperialist war in a revolutionary manner and completed the bourgeois-democratic revolution so that *even* the great receding movement (the Brest Peace) left us sufficient room in which to take advantage of the "respite" and to march forward victoriously against Kolchak, Denikin, Yudenich, Pilsudski and Wrangel." (*Works*, Vol. 33, pp. 91-92.)

The few weeks which Lenin referred to for the most part cover the period of our stay at Smolny in Petrograd up to the middle of March, when we left for Moscow. Ilyich was the centre of all that activity, he organized it. That work was more than strenuous, it was work at high pressure that absorbed all of one's energies and strained one's nerves to breaking point. Tremendous difficulties had to be overcome and a desperate fight had to be waged, often a fight against one's closest colleagues. No wonder that, coming into his room behind the partition of our Smolny apartment late in the night, Ilyich could not fall asleep; he would get up again to ring someone up on the telephone and issue some urgent orders, and when he did fall asleep at last he would talk business in his sleep. Work at Smolny went on day and night. In the early days it was the centre of all activities—Party meetings and sittings of the Council of People's Commissars were held there, the different Commissariats carried on their work there, telegrams and orders were issued from there, and people flocked there from all over. And to think that the Council of People's Commissars at the beginning had an office staff of four wholly inexperienced people, who worked without a moment's respite, and did everything that had to be done in the course of business. Their functions were so vague and universal that it never entered anyone's mind to define and limit them. They were swamped with work, and Ilyich was often obliged to do ordinary office jobs, such as putting phone calls through, etc., etc. Use was made, of course, of the Party's clerical staff and the offices of the All-Russian Central Executive Committee and other bodies, but even that required a good deal of organizational work. It was all extremely primitive. The old machinery of state had to be broken up link by link. The bureaucratic apparatus resisted, and the personnel of the old ministerial and government offices went out of their way to sabotage the work and so prevent the Soviet power from setting up a new machinery of state. I remember how we "took power" at the Ministry of Education. Lunacharsky and we, a small group of Party people, went to the building of the Ministry which was situated at Chernyshov Bridge. The saboteurs had pickets outside the Ministry who warned all members of the staff and visitors that there was a walk-out there. Someone even tried to argue with us on the subject. Apart from the messengers and office cleaners there were no employees at the Ministry. We walked through empty rooms with desks from which the papers had not been cleared away. Then we went into a private office and there held the first meeting of the Board of the People's Commissariat of Education. The various functions were assigned among us. We decided that Lunacharsky was to make a speech to the junior office force, which he did. His warm speech was listened to with a kind of puzzled attention by the numerous audience, who had never before had the powers that be talk to them on such matters.

The state of affairs at the People's Commissariat of Education was not so bad, comparatively speaking. The bourgeoisie did not attach any great importance to it for one thing, and for another we had no great difficulty in getting the hang of things. Most of us were familiar with the organization of education. The Menzhinskys, for example, had worked for years in St. Petersburg as elementary school teachers. I had a lot of school experience, too, and all of us were propagandists and agitators. During our work at the district councils preceding the October Revolution we had acquired considerable organizing experience and contacts. My job was extra-school education

(Politprosvet),* a line in which I had the necessary experience and where the most important thing was to have the support of the Party and the working-class mass. This work could be started at once on entirely new lines with the backing of the mass. We were worse off in regard to financing, administration, accounting and planning, but quick progress was made under pressure from below, where the craving for knowledge was tremendous. Things here got under way.

Less favourable was the situation in such essential fields as food supply, finance and the banks. These strong points were strenuously defended by the bourgeoisie. Sabotage here was conducted with a vengeance. On the other hand, we had least experience and practical knowledge in these affairs. That is just what our enemies counted on—"they will not be able to do it." We were not very good at pushing things on either. Our young people—and not only the young, but those who came to the job in later years—often imagine that everything was simple—we took the Winter Palace, we defeated the cadets, we beat off Kerensky's offensive—and that was all. But when it comes to knowing how we set up the machinery of state and organized the work of the Commissariats, less interest is shown, although our first steps in the field of administration and the story of how we learned to fight for the cause of the proletariat in the everyday work of government are matters of considerable interest. The story of how we "took power" on the financial front, for example, is told with epic force by N. P Gorbunov in his memoirs describing how the office staff of the Council of People's Commissars was created during the October days. "In spite of the government's decrees and its demands that funds should be made available," writes Gorbunov, "the State Bank brazenly sabotaged. The People's Commissar of Finance

---

* *Politprosvet*—Department of Political Education under the People's Commissariat of Education in charge of extra-school work among adults.—*Ed.*

Menzhinsky* could do nothing to make the bank place at the government's disposal the funds that were necessary for the revolution. Not even the arrest of Shipov, the Director of the State Bank, helped. Shipov was brought to Smolny and kept there for a time under arrest. He slept in the same room with Menzhinsky and me. In the daytime this room was used as an office (of the Commissariat of Finance, I believe). I was obliged, as a mark of special courtesy and greatly to my annoyance, to let him have my bed while I slept on chairs." Pyatakov was appointed Director of the State Bank. He could do nothing at first, either. Gorbunov relates how Vladimir Ilyich handed him a decree signed by his own hand in which the State Bank was ordered to waive all rules and formalities and hand over to the Secretary of the Council of People's Commissars the sum of ten million rubles to be disposed of by the government. Osinsky was appointed government Commissar at the State Bank. When handing them—Gorbunov and Osinsky—the decree, Ilyich said: "Don't come back without money." The money was received. In face of the support given by the junior staff and messengers, and the threat of having the Red Guard called in, the teller was compelled to pay out the required sum. The operation was made under the cocked guns of the Bank's military guard. "We had difficulty with the bags for taking the money away in," writes Gorbunov. "We had not brought anything with us. At last one of the messengers lent us a couple of old sacks. We stuffed them full to the top with money, swung them on our shoulders and hauled them out to the motor-car. We rode back to Smolny, beaming. At Smolny we shouldered the bags again and lugged them into the private office of Vladimir Ilyich. Ilyich was not there. While waiting for him to come, I sat down on the sacks with a revolver in my hand, 'mounting guard.'

---

* Now Chairman of the Joint State Political Administration—OGPU.—*N. K.*

I handed the money over to Vladimir Ilyich with great solemnity. He received it as a matter of course, but actually he was very pleased. A wardrobe was requisitioned in the next room to house the first Soviet treasury. Chairs were put round it in a semicircle and a sentry put on guard there. The Council of People's Commissars issued a special decree fixing the manner in which this money was to be kept and used. Thus originated our first Soviet budget."

V. Bonch-Bruyevich describes the subsequent nationalization of the banks. This operation was directed by Stalin; Bonch-Bruyevich consulted him, made all the preparations, wrote out orders, and organized the transportation, twenty-eight detachments of riflemen, and so on. Twenty-eight banks had to be occupied, and twenty-eight bank directors arrested. "I told Malkov, the commandant of Smolny," Bonch-Bruyevich writes in his memoirs, "to have a good room prepared, completely isolated from the public, with twenty-eight beds in it, tables and chairs, and to make arrangements to have twenty-eight men put on the supply list, and first of all to have tea and breakfast ready for them at eight the next morning." The twenty-eight banks were occupied without any trouble. It took place on December 27, 1917. "Soon afterwards the Commissar of Finance put new men in charge of the banks. Many of the directors who had been arrested expressed a desire to continue work under the Soviet Government, and these were immediately released. Commissars were set up at the banks, and the work continued in so far as this was necessary for concentrating all currency and operations at the State Bank."

That is how we took power.

Our people were terribly nervous. Most of them were quite new to the business and lacked confidence in themselves. Often you would hear a comrade say: "I can't work like this any longer," but he went on working nevertheless, and picked things up quickly in the process of work.

New fields of state activity, new forms of work were being created.

On November 12 a decree was published establishing an 8-hour working day.

Workers' control having been mentioned in the appeal of the Second Congress of the Soviets, the workers started to put it into practice at once on a wide scale. As a matter of fact, the period preceding October had already prepared them for it. The employers had begun to reckon with the workers, and the workers had learnt to get what they wanted. All this had been sporadic, however. A committee met at Smolny under the chairmanship of Vladimir Ilyich, among the members of which were M. Tomsky, A. Shlyapnikov, V. Schmidt, Glebov-Avilov, Lozovsky and Tsiperovich. Some of the comrades stood for state control in place of the spontaneous workers' control, which very often took the form of seizure of the factories, mines and mills; others believed control should be introduced not at all the factories, but only at the big metal-works, on the railways, etc. Ilyich, however, did not think this activity should be narrowed and the workers' initiative restricted. Although a good deal might be done the wrong way, it was only in the struggle that the workers would learn real control. This point of view followed from his basic view of socialism: "Socialism cannot be built up by decrees from above ... living constructive socialism is the creation of the masses of the people themselves." (*Works*, Vol. 26, p. 255.) The committee came round to Ilyich's point of view. A decree was drafted, submitted to the All-Russian Central Executive Committee, and published on November 29. The mass of the workers was very active. Wide initiative came from below. Soon after the seizure of power the Factory Committees Council suggested the idea of setting up a Supreme Council of the National Economy, a fighting body of the proletarian dictatorship to direct all industry. The S.C.N.E. was to incorporate representatives of the workers and peasants. It was to be an organ of a new type. The decree instituting the S.C.N.E. was published on December 18, 1917.

The land questions were making slow progress. Teodorovich, the first Commissar of Agriculture, resigned in connection with the affair of the Railwaymen's Executive and went to Siberia. Schlichter had been nominated for the post, but he was living in Moscow and had not been told that his presence was required immediately in Petrograd, where Vladimir Ilyich, meanwhile, was besieged by peasants asking what was to be done with the land. On November 18 Vladimir Ilyich wrote "Reply to Peasants' Questions" and "To the Population." (*Works*, Vol. 26, pp. 263-67.) In his "Reply" he confirms the decree abolishing landlord ownership and calls upon the rural committees to take over the landowners' land themselves. In his "To the Population" he calls upon the population to "be watchful and guard like the apple of the eye your land, grain, factories, equipment, products, transport—all that henceforth will be wholly your property, public property." The same aim was pursued here as in the decree on workers' control, namely, to stir the masses to activity and build up their consciousness in the struggle. When Schlichter arrived Ilyich instructed him to proceed without delay to organize the reception of local peasant delegates and to give them concrete directions in connection with the land confiscation law. The next thing to do, said Ilyich, was to take over the ministerial machinery, to break down the sabotage and urgently draw up regulations concerning the land.

A special congress of Soviets of Peasants' Deputies opened on November 23. Vladimir Ilyich spoke twice at this congress, to which he attached great importance. Of the 330 delegates 195 were Left Socialist-Revolutionaries, who formed the decisive group; there was a struggle at the congress with the Right Socialist-Revolutionaries (of whom there were 65 delegates). After Lenin's second speech a resolution was carried, approving the work of the

Council of People's Commissars and the terms of the agreement with the Left Socialist-Revolutionaries. The Left S.-R.'s consented to participate in the government, and after some delay, they sent their representatives to the People's Commissariats. Kolegayev, a Left S.-R., became People's Commissar of Agriculture, but some time passed before he started work.

I saw very little of Ilyich during our stay in Petrograd. He was busy all the time interviewing soldiers', workers' and peasants' delegates, holding numerous conferences and working hard on the decrees that became the basis of the newly organized Soviet state. Sometimes, in the evening, or late at night, we would go for a little walk together around Smolny; more than ever before Ilyich felt a need to unburden his mind. He had little time to spare however. I got to know how things were going not so much from him as from outside. There were always lots of Party people to be met with in the corridors of Smolny. Comrades whom we had met abroad, during the events of 1905, or in Vyborg District work, discussed their affairs with me through old habit, and so I was kept in close touch with all that was doing. I had also many visitors at the Extra-School Department of the Commissariat of Education in which I was working. We had no Army Political Departments or trade—union culture departments in those days, and everyone used to come to the Commissariat of Education. Incidentally, I got to know many interesting details about the temper of the masses. I particularly remember the story of a comrade who had come from the front to get advice on how to organize educational work among the troops there. He spoke about the deep hatred which the mass of the soldiers bore towards the *gymnasium* schools and all the old culture of the master class. Soldiers were put up for the night in a high-school building, and they tore up and stamped on all the books, maps and copy-books which they could find in the desks and book-cases, and smashed up all the school supplies and appliances. "The

damned masters taught their children here." I was reminded of the nineties, when a worker attending the Sunday
School, after giving a detailed account proving the Earth
to be a globe, wound up with a mocking sceptical smile:
"Only you can't believe that, the masters made it up."
Ilyich and I often spoke about this distrust towards
the old science and learning on the part of the masses.
Later on, at the Third Congress of the Soviets, Ilyich
said:

"Previously the human mind and all its genius created
solely for the purpose of providing some with all the
blessings of technics and culture while denying to others
the bare necessities—education and development. Now all
the marvels of technics, all the conquests of culture will
belong to all the people, and from now on the human mind
and genius will never be used as a means of oppression, a
means of exploitation. We know that—and is not that great
historical task worth working for, worth giving all our
energies to? The working people will perform that titanic
historic job, for within them dwell the great slumbering
forces of revolution, regeneration and renewal." (*Works*,
Vol. 26, p. 436-37.) These words of Ilyich's showed the
backward masses that the old hateful science was becoming a thing of the past, and that the new science would
work only for the benefit of the masses. The masses had
to master it.

The Extra-School Department worked in close contact
with the workers, first and foremost those of the Vyborg
District. I remember how we cooperated with them in
drafting "The ABC of a Citizen"—a course of training
which every worker had to master if he wished to take
part in social work and in the activities of the Soviets and
the various organizations that would grow up around
them more and more as time went on. The workers for
their part kept us informed of what was going on in the
district. Production was being cut down, young workers
were being laid off at the factories, and food shortages

were becoming acute. On December 10 the Council of People's Commissars, on Lenin's motion, set up a special committee to elaborate the basic questions of the government's economic policy and organize a conference of food supply workers to discuss practical measures for combatting acts of pillage and improving the conditions of the workers. Two days after this the Council of People's Commissars adopted a number of resolutions drafted by Ilyich under which factories handling naval orders were to be switched over to productive work more needful to the people. It was no good simply closing down war production, as this would only create unemployment.

Ilyich pressed for the speedy organization of work at the Commissariat of Food Supply, which was to replace the Ministry of Provisions. The resistance of the old staff here was very strong. Besides, new ways had to be sought for drawing the mass of the workers into this activity, forms had to be discovered for organizing this cooperation.

In this wise the Soviet machinery of state was built up soon after the October Revolution; the old ministerial machinery of administration was scrapped, and Soviet organs of government were built up in its stead by hands that were as yet inexperienced and unskilful. There was still a lot left to do, but judging from what had been done in this respect by the beginning of 1918, tremendous progress had been made.

The Vyborg District arranged a New Year's Eve rally as a send-off for the Red Guards of the district who were leaving for the front. Many of these comrades had taken part in the fighting against the troops of Kerensky during their march on Petrograd. They were now going to the front to carry on propaganda for the Soviet Government, to rouse the activity of the soldiers, put a revolutionary spirit into the whole struggle. The New Year's Eve rally was organized in the spacious premises of the Mikhailovskoye Military Cadet School. The comrades who were going to the front were keen to see Ilyich, as was everyone else in the Vyborg District, and I suggested that he go there to celebrate the first Soviet New Year together with the workers. The idea appealed to Ilyich. We started out. We had a job getting out of the square. What with the janitors having been done away with and there being no one to clear the snow away, it required great skill on the part of the chauffeur to steer a passage through the piled up snow. We arrived at 11.30 p.m. The big "white" hall of the Mikhailovskoye School resembled a manège. Greeted warmly by the workers, Ilyich stepped up on the platform. Stimulated by the enthusiastic reception, he made a speech, which, although simple and unadorned, touched upon everything that had been uppermost in his mind of late. He spoke about what the workers had to do in order to organize their life anew through the medium of the Soviets. He spoke about how the comrades who were going to the front had to carry on their work there among the soldiers. When Ilyich finished he was given an ovation. Four workers grasped the legs of the chair on which he was sitting and raised it aloft amid loud cheers. I underwent the same treatment. After that a concert was given in the hall, then Ilyich had some tea in the staff room and chatted with the people there, and then we contrived to slip away unnoticed. Ilyich preserved a very pleasant memory of that evening. In 1920 he made me go with him to the workers' districts—that was already in Moscow— where he was eager to meet the workers again on New Year's Eve. We visited three districts that time.

At Christmas (Jan. 6-11, New Style) Ilyich and I and Maria Ilyinichna went to some place in Finland. Kosyura, who was working then in Smolny, fixed us up at some Finnish rest home, where Bērziņš happened to be taking his holiday. That spotless Finnish cleanliness with its white curtains everywhere reminded Ilyich of the days of his secret residence in Helsingfors in 1907 and again in 1917 on the eve of the October Revolution, when he had been writing his book *The State and Revolution* there. As a holiday, it wasn't much of a success. Ilyich sometimes even dropped his voice when speaking, the way we used to do when we were in hiding, and although we went for walks every day, there was no real zest in them. Ilyich's mind was occupied and he spent most of his time writing. The things he wrote during those four days, however, were not made use of, as he considered them unfinished. The articles that he then wrote, namely, "Those Scared by the Collapse of the Old and Those Fighting for the New," "How To Organize Competition," and "Draft Decree on Consumers' Communes," were not published until five years after his death, but they best show what problems his mind was wrestling with at the time. The questions that engrossed him most of all were how best to organize the everyday economic life, how best to arrange the workers' lives and improve the hard conditions they were living under at the time; how to organize consumers' communes, the supply of milk for the children, the removal of the workers to better apartments, and the organization of proper accounting and control which this involved; how to organize things in such a way as to draw the masses themselves into this work, to stir their initiative. Ilyich thought of ways for advancing the most gifted organizers from the midst of the workers. He wrote about emulation, and the organizing role it was destined to play.

We could not be long "holidaying," though. After four days of it we had to be getting back to Petrograd. I have a memory of a winter road, a ride through Finnish pine woods, a glorious morning, and Ilyich's thoughtful face. He was thinking about the coming struggle. The question of the Constituent Assembly, which was due to meet on January 18, had to be decided within the next few days. By the beginning of 1918 the question of the Constituent Assembly was quite clear. When the Second Party Congress in 1903 had adopted the Party programme, the socialist revolution had seemed a thing of the distant future. The immediate aim of the working-class struggle had been the overthrow of the autocracy. The Constituent Assembly had then been a militant slogan for which the Bolsheviks had fought ever since the congress with much greater persistency and determination than the Mensheviks. At that time no one yet clearly envisaged any concrete form of democratic organization of government other than that of a bourgeois-democratic republic. During the Revolution of 1905 the Soviets of Workers' Deputies which had originated spontaneously in the process of struggle, represented in embryo a new form of state power closely related to the masses. During the years of reaction Ilyich had deeply pondered that new type of organization and compared it with the forms of state organization that had been set up in the days of the Paris Commune. In addition to the Provisional Government, the February Revolution of 1917 had created an all-Russian organization of workers' and soldiers' deputies. At first the Soviets had followed the lead of the bourgeoisie, who, through their henchmen—the Mensheviks and the Right Socialist-Revolutionaries—had tried to convert the Soviets into instruments for obscuring the mass consciousness. Beginning from April, with Lenin's arrival in Russia, the Bolsheviks launched a wide campaign among the masses with the aim of raising the class consciousness of the workers and the poorest strata of the peasantry, and helped in every way to develop the class struggle.

The slogan "All Power to the Soviets," which the workers and peasants had inscribed upon their banners, virtually predetermined the direction which the struggle in the Constituent Assembly would take. One side would stand for the power of the Soviets, the other for the power of the bourgeoisie in the form of this or that type of bourgeois republic. The Second Congress of the Soviets had decided the question of the type of power beforehand, and the Constituent Assembly was called upon merely to form it and fill in the details. That is how the Bolsheviks saw it. The bourgeoisie, on the other hand, considered that the Constituent Assembly would be able to reverse the wheel of history, and by setting up a government of the bourgeois-republican type, liquidate the Soviets or, at least, reduce their role to naught. On the eve of the October Revolution new elections to the Soviets were held in which the Bolsheviks, carrying out the decisions of the Party, received a majority.

The Party understood long before the October Revolution that the Constituent Assembly would not take place in a classless society. As far back as 1905, in his pamphlet *Two Tactics of Social-Democracy in the Democratic Revolution* dealing with the resolution of the Menshevik "conference," which took place during the Bolsheviks' Third Congress of the Party in the summer of 1905, Vladimir Ilyich said that the Mensheviks, in their resolutions, called the slogan of the "Constituent Assembly" "a decisive victory," whereas "...the slogan of a popular constituent assembly *has been accepted* by the monarchist bourgeoisie (see the programme of the Osvobozhdeniye League) and accepted for the very purpose of conjuring away the revolution, of preventing the complete victory of the revolution, and of enabling the big bourgeoisie to strike a huckster's bargain with tsarism." (*Works*, Vol. 9, p. 29.)

And in 1917—twelve years later—the Bolsheviks took the power in October without waiting for any Constituent Assembly.

However, the Provisional Government had cultivated certain illusions around the idea of the Constituent Assembly. To shatter those illusions it was necessary for the Constituent Assembly to be convoked and an effort made to convert it to the service of the revolution, and if that proved impossible, to show the masses how harmful it was, to dispel all the illusions about it, and wrest this instrument of agitation against the new power from the hands of the enemy. There was no sense in postponing the convocation of the Constituent Assembly, and already on

November 10 the Council of People's Commissars announced its decision for the Constituent Assembly to be convoked at the appointed time. On November 21 the All-Russian Central Executive Committee adopted a corresponding resolution. Did the Bolsheviks have a majority in the Constituent Assembly? They had the proletariat, the vast majority of the proletariat behind them, while the Mensheviks at that time had lost almost all influence among the workers. At the decisive points—in Petrograd and Moscow—the proletariat was not only Bolshevik-minded, but was a class-conscious revolutionary force steeled in fifteen years of struggle. In addition, it had succeeded in ranging the peasantry behind it. The slogans demanding peace and land, adopted at the Second Congress of the Soviets, had won for the Bolsheviks half the votes of the army and navy. The Socialist-Revolutionaries collected the vast majority of the peasants' votes. The Socialist-Revolutionaries split up into Rights and Lefts. The Left S.-R.'s were in the majority and had the backing of the poor peasants and most of the middle peasants. After the Second Congress of the Soviets the Central Committee of the Socialist-Revolutionaries expelled the Left members of the party who had taken part in that congress. The Special Congress of the Soviets of Peasants' Deputies held on December 8—Lenin spoke there—recognized the Soviet power. The day after Ilyich made his speech the congress went to Smolny in a body and joined the All-Russian Central Executive Committee of the Soviets of Workers' and Soldiers' Deputies which was in session there. The Special Congress of the Soviets of Peasants' Deputies ruled that representatives of the Left Socialist-Revolutionaries were to join the government. The same day Ilyich wrote an article in *Pravda* "Alliance Between the Workers and the Toiling and Exploited Peasants." (*Works*, Vol. 26, pp. 298-300.)

The Special Congress of Soviets of Peasants' Deputies showed that the influence of the October Revolution and of the letters from soldiers at the front, who were siding more and more with the Bolsheviks, was making itself felt in the countryside, where the poor and middle peasants were lining up with the Soviet power. The peasants had not yet learned the difference between the Left and Right Socialist-Revolutionaries. They had voted for the S.-R.'s in general, but actually the majority clearly stood for the Left Socialist-Revolutionaries. Vladimir Ilyich submitted to the All-Russian Central Executive Committee the idea of introducing the right of recall in regard to previously elected deputies. That right, he said, was virtually the right of the constituency to control what its deputy was saying and doing. It still existed, by virtue of former revolutionary traditions, in the U.S.A. and in certain Swiss cantons. The right of recall was sanctioned by the All-Russian Central Executive Committee, and a corresponding decree was issued on December 6, 1917. The Provisional Government, as far back as August, had set up a committee for elections to the Constituent Assembly consisting of Constitutional Democrats (Cadets) and Right Socialist-Revolutionaries. This committee had gone out of its way to side-track the work of preparing for the elections and refused to submit its progress report to the Council of People's Commissars. On December 6, the day the decree instituting the right of recall was passed, Uritsky was appointed Commissar to direct the activities of this committee. The latter refused to work under his direction and was arrested, but on December 10, on Lenin's order, the committee members were released. On December 6 the All-Russian Central Executive Committee resolved that the Constituent Assembly would be opened upon the arrival of its four hundred delegates in Petrograd. On December 11 the right Socialist-Revolutionaries and Constitutional Democrats attempted to organize a demonstration, but apart from a comparatively insignificant number of intellectuals no workers or soldiers took any part in it. On December 13 the electoral committee was dismissed.

The Bolsheviks launched a wide campaign explaining the issues involved. On December 14 Lenin addressed a meeting of the A.R.C.E.C. on the question of the Constituent Assembly. He said: "We are told to convoke the Constituent Assembly as planned. No fear! It was planned against the people. We made the revolution in order to be guaranteed that the Constituent Assembly would not be used against the people.... Let the people know that the Constituent Assembly will not be convened the way Kerensky wanted it. We have introduced the right of recall, and the Constituent Assembly will not be what the bourgeoisie have planned it to be. With the assembly only a few days off, the bourgeoisie are organizing civil war, increasing sabotage, and jeopardizing the truce. We shall not let ourselves be deceived by formal slogans. They want to sit in the Constituent Assembly and organize civil wars at the same time." (At that time, in the south, near Rostov-on-Don, sanguinary fighting, organized by General Kaledin, was in progress.—N.K.) "...We shall tell the truth to the people. We shall tell the people that its interests are above those of a democratic institution. We should not go back to the old prejudices under which the interests of the people are subservient to formal democratism. The Cadets shout: 'All power to the Constituent Assembly,' but actually they mean 'All power to Kaledin.' We must tell that to the people, and the people will approve of us." (*Works*, Vol. 26, pp. 316, 317-18.)

On the next day, December 15, Ilyich spoke at the Second All-Russian Congress of Peasants' Deputies at which Spiridonova presided. The congress was a very stormy one. The Right S.-R.'s walked out.

It became increasingly clear that a sharp struggle would break out over the Constituent Assembly, vacillations and Right-wing moods began to make themselves felt among the Bolshevik group of the Constituent Assembly. A meeting of the Party Central Committee devoted to this question was held on December 24. It was decided to have a C.C. report made at the group of the Constituent Assembly and theses drafted on the question of the Constituent Assembly. Lenin was entrusted with both tasks. He drew up the theses and the next day made a report in Smolny at a meeting of the Bolshevik group of the Constituent Assembly. The theses were unanimously adopted and published the next day in *Pravda*. They set before the Constituent Assembly a clear demand: recognition of the Soviet Government and of the revolutionary policy that it was pursuing on the questions of peace, the land, workers' inspection and the struggle with the counter-revolution.

The opening of the Constituent Assembly was fixed for January 18, 1918.

The preparations for the Constituent Assembly, which the Party, under Ilyich's leadership, had been making with such care and thoroughness, were an important phase in the consolidation of the Soviet power; it was a struggle against formal bourgeois democracy for genuine democracy enabling the working masses to develop immense revolutionary activities in all fields of socialist construction.

The work done in connection with the convocation of the Constituent Assembly showed how, step by step, it had struck deep-root among the masses and gained their support, how it had organized the masses for the struggle, and helped the Soviet and Party cadres to form close links with the masses.

A great deal still remained to be done in the way of organizing preparations for and conducting the Constituent Assembly.

The Right Socialist-Revolutionaries were pressing for a fight against the Bolsheviks. The extreme Right-wingers set up a military organization, which made an abortive attempt on Lenin's life on January 1. This organization made active preparations for an armed revolt, which was planned for January 18, the opening day of the Constituent

Assembly. Although the Central Committee of the S.-R. Party did not officially support this military organization, it was aware of its activities and shut its eyes to them. This military organization associated itself with the Constituent Assembly Defence League, whose object was to coordinate the activities of all the anti-Bolshevik organizations. The Defence League consisted of extreme Right Socialist-Revolutionaries, Menshevik Defencists, Popular Socialists, and certain Constitutional Democrats. Although it developed a great activity, the Defence League did not succeed in winning over to its side either the workers or the garrison of Petrograd.

The demonstration of January 18 was a one-sided limited affair, but rumours were rife in town that an armed revolt was being prepared. The Bolsheviks got ready to face it. The Constituent Assembly was to meet at the Taurida Palace. A military staff was set up. Among its members were Sverdlov, Podvoisky, Proshyan, Uritsky and Bonch-Bruyevich. The city and the Smolny area were marked off into sectors, and the workers volunteered to guard them. The crew of the cruiser *Aurora* and two companies off the battleship *Respublika* were called out to guard the Palace and patrol the streets in the vicinity. The armed revolt which the Constituent Assembly Defence League had been planning did not come off. Its hybrid demonstration, held under the slogan of "All Power to the Constituent Assembly," came up against our workers' demonstration marching under the slogan of "Long Live the Soviet Power" at the corner of Nevsky and Liteiny prospekts. There was an armed clash, which was quickly liquidated. Bonch-Bruyevich was as busy as can be, phoning, giving orders, and surrounding Ilyich's trip to the Palace with the greatest secrecy. He rode with Ilyich in the car himself, I, Maria Ilyinichna, and Vera Bonch-Bruyevich being the other occupants. We drove up to the Taurida Palace by way of a side-street. The gates were locked, but on the horn giving the pre-arranged signal, they were opened to let us through and then locked again. The guard conducted us into a special apartment set aside for Ilyich. It was somewhere on the right side of the main entrance, and the way to the meeting hall ran through a glassed-in passage. The main entrance had a queue of delegates and crowds of spectators standing round it, and of course it was more convenient for Ilyich to use a different entrance. But all this mysterious theatricality rather irritated him. We sat drinking tea, talking to the different comrades who came in. I remember Kollontai and Dybenko among others. We sat there rather long, as a meeting of the Bolshevik group was in progress, and it was a pretty stormy one. Varvara Yakovleva, a Muscovite, was in the chair. The Muscovites stood firm on the question of the Constituent Assembly, and some of them even went a bit too far—they were for breaking up the Constituent Assembly at once, overlooking the fact that things had to be done in such a way that the masses would clearly realize why the Constituent Assembly had to be dismissed.

The Constituent Assembly was to be opened by Yakov Sverdlov.

The sitting opened at 4 p.m. On his way to the hall Ilyich reminded himself that he had left his revolver in his overcoat pocket. He went back for it, but the revolver wasn't there, although no strangers had entered the apartment. Obviously one of the guards had removed it. Ilyich rebuked Dybenko for the lack of discipline among the guards. Dybenko was very upset. When Ilyich came back from the meeting hall Dybenko handed him his revolver, which the guard had returned.

Sverdlov was a bit late, and the Constituent Assembly decided to have its session opened by its eldest member Shvetsov, a Socialist-Revolutionary. The latter had got up on the platform and started maundering, when Sverdlov came hurrying in. He went up to the speaker's desk, took the bell away from Shvetsov, pushed him aside, and announced in his deep loud voice that the Central

Executive Committee of the Soviets of Workers', Soldiers' and Peasants' Deputies had authorized him to open the meeting of the Constituent Assembly. Then, on behalf of the C.E.C. he read out the text of the Declaration of the Rights of the Toiling and Exploited Peoples written by Lenin and edited by him in cooperation with Stalin and Bukharin, the text of which had been published in *Pravda* the day before. The Declaration had been adopted by the All-Russian Central Executive Committee together with a ruling that "any attempt on the part of any person or institution whatsoever to assume one or another function of state power will be regarded as a counter-revolutionary act. Any such attempt will be suppressed by the Soviet Government by every means at its disposal, including the use of armed force." (*Works*, Vol. 26, p. 389.)

The Declaration announced that "Russia is hereby declared a Republic of Soviets of Workers,' Soldiers' and Peasants' Deputies. All power centrally and locally belongs to the Soviets. ... The Soviet Russian Republic shall be constituted on the basis of a free union of free nations as a federation of Soviet National Republics." It approved the laws passed by the Second Congress of Soviets. The decisions adopted by the Council of People's Commissars were to have been endorsed by the Constituent Assembly. "While supporting the Soviet Government and the decrees of the Council of People's Commissars, the Constituent Assembly considers its tasks completed with the establishment of the fundamental bases for a socialist remodelling of society." (*Ibid.*, pp. 385, 387.)

The Right wing of the Constituent Assembly had quite different ideas concerning the activities of the Assembly, which, they believed, would do nothing less than take all the power into its hands. The Right Socialist-Revolutionaries were in the majority. They nominated Chernov Chairman of the Assembly, while the Bolsheviks and the Left Socialist-Revolutionaries nominated Spiridonova. Chernov received 244 votes, Spiridonova—151.

The Bolsheviks voted for Spiridonova because the issue at stake was whether the Constituent Assembly would vote for the Soviet power or not. The Left Socialist-Revolutionaries at the time sided with the Bolsheviks, and the nomination of Spiridonova was calculated to bring home to the peasantry the fact that the working class aimed at a close alliance with the peasantry, that the Bolsheviks stood for such an alliance. The propaganda value of Spiridonova's nomination was therefore an important factor.

After the election of the chairman (Chernov), the proceedings were opened. Chernov, on behalf of the Right Socialist-Revolutionaries, spoke on the land question. His words were greeted with a shout from the Left benches: "Long live the Soviets, who have given the peasants the land!" Bukharin, who took the floor after Chernov, submitted a motion for the Declaration of the All-Russian Central Executive Committee to be considered first. The first thing that had to be decided was who the Assembly stood for— "Kaledin, the cadets, the factory owners, the merchants, the directors of the discount banks, or the grey army coats, the workers, soldiers and sailors?" Tsereteli spoke on behalf of the Mensheviks. He attacked the Bolsheviks, trotted out the bogy of civil war, and suggested that all the power be taken over by the Constituent Assembly.

Many years have passed since then. We have seen how the Social-Democrats of Germany and other capitalist countries, using the same old methods of soft-soaping, the scare of civil war, and all kinds of promises, have betrayed the working class and paved the way to power for the fascists, those brutal thugs and bestial champions of the perishing class of landowners and capitalists, who stand in mortal fear of the Communists and preach civil peace by word while helping the landowners and capitalists by deed to arrogantly exploit the working people and plunge them into another world war more devastating than the first.

The Bolsheviks, however, saw clearly where conciliation with the Right S.-R.'s and the Mensheviks led to. Addressing himself to the Right S.-R.'s and Mensheviks, Skvortsov said: "It is all over between us. We shall see the October Revolution against the bourgeoisie through to the end. You and we are on different sides of the barricades."

Vladimir Ilyich did not speak. He sat on the platform steps, smiling ironically, joking and jotting down notes. He obviously felt out of it all. Among his papers is the beginning of an article in which he describes his impressions of that meeting of the Constituent Assembly: "A tiresome, painful, dreary day in the elegant rooms of the Taurida Palace, whose very appearance differs from that of Smolny as elegant but lifeless bourgeois parliamentarism differs from the proletarian, simple Soviet apparatus, which, though in many ways still disorderly and unfinished, is alive and vital." "After the real live Soviet work among the workers and peasants who are engaged in the *real job* of felling the forest and grubbing up by the roots landlord and capitalist exploitation, I suddenly found myself transported to a 'strange world' among visitors from the other world, from the camp of the bourgeoisie and its voluntary and involuntary, conscious and unconscious followers, hangers-on, servants and defenders. From a world of struggle of the working masses and their Soviet organization against exploitation to a world of sweetish phrases, smooth empty declamations, promises and promises based as before on conciliation with the capitalists." (*Works*, Vol. 26, pp. 393, 392.)

Only 146 deputies voted in favour of discussing the Declaration of the All-Russian Central Executive Committee, with 247 against. The Bolsheviks and Left Socialist-Revolutionaries demanded an adjournment. The Bolshevik group of the Assembly met to discuss their further course of action. It was decided not to return to the meeting hall. Raskolnikov and Lobov were sent there to announce that the Bolsheviks were quitting the Assembly, and to state the reasons why. The group also decided not to dismiss the Assembly, but give it a chance to see the session through. It lasted until 4.40 a.m. on January 6, after which it broke up. The next day the All-Russian Central Executive Committee decreed that the Constituent Assembly was to be dissolved. No more meetings of the Assembly were held.

The dissolution of the Constituent Assembly was received by the masses with passive indifference. Its prestige stood very low and its dismissal caused no stir whatever. A stumbling block to further work had been removed from the path. A check had been put to all conciliatory moods.

*　*　*

While this stumbling block to progress had been removed, the more formidable task of extricating the country from the hole of imperialist war in which it was floundering still remained to be tackled.

On November 8, the Second Congress of Soviets adopted the Decree on Peace. The early days of the Soviet power's existence had passed in military struggle—with the advancing troops of Kerensky and the rebel cadets—and in a fight with conciliatory vacillations within the Central Committee of the Party. On November 20 General Dukhonin, the Supreme Commander-in-Chief, was ordered to suspend hostilities and begin negotiations for an armistice with the Central Powers. On November 22, when a telephone conversation with General Dukhonin made it clear that he was sabotaging the order of the Council of People's Commissars, he was dismissed and Krylenko was appointed Supreme Commander-in-Chief in his stead. Later in the day Vladimir Ilyich drew up a radio message to all regimental, divisional, corps, army and other committees, to all soldiers of the revolutionary army and sailors of the revolutionary fleet, calling upon them

Red Square, May Day, 1919. In group with Lenin are Vladimir Zagorsky (in cap, at right), Secretary of Moscow Party Committee, killed by a terrorist a few months later; Krupskaya, and in profile next to her, Anna Rozovskaya, member of Moscow Committee; left, holding newspaper, Maxim Litvinov

Lenin and commanders reviewing troops of citizen trainees, Red Square, Moscow, May 25, 1919

to take matters into their own hands. His chief hope was the soldier mass, not the generals.

"Soldiers!" ran the message. "The cause of peace is in your hands! Do not allow the counter-revolutionary generals to frustrate the great cause of peace, surround them by a guard in order to avert acts of summary justice unworthy of a revolutionary army and to prevent these generals from evading the trial that awaits them. Maintain the strictest revolutionary and military order.

"Let the regiments at the front immediately elect plenipotentiaries to start formal negotiations for an armistice with the enemy.

"The Council of People's Commissars empowers you to do so.

"Keep us informed in every possible way of every step in the negotiations. The Council of People's Commissars is alone empowered to sign the final treaty of armistice.

"Soldiers, the cause of peace is in your hands! Vigilance, restraint and energy, and the cause of peace will triumph!

"In the name of the Government of the Russian Republic,

> V. Ulyanov (Lenin),
> Chairman of the Council of
> People's Commissars
> N. Krylenko,
> People's Commissar of War and
> Supreme Commander." (Works,
> Vol. 26, p. 280.)

On November 21, the Soviet Government submitted the Decree on Peace to the representatives of the Entente in Russia for their consideration.

On November 23, Ilyich spoke at the All-Russian Central Executive Committee. He said that our chances were very favourable. He spoke about revolutionary fraternization. "We have a chance to get in touch with Paris by radio telegraph, and when the peace treaty will have been drawn up we shall be able to tell the French people that it is ready to be signed within two hours and that it depends on them whether an armistice will be concluded. We shall see what Clemenceau then has to say." (*Ibid.*, p. 282.) On November 23, the press began publication of the secret treaties with other countries. They clearly revealed how brazenly the governments had been lying to the masses and fooling them.

On November 23 the Soviet Government requested the neutral countries to officially notify the enemy governments of its readiness to start peace negotiations.

On November 27 a reply was received from the German Commander-in-Chief consenting to start negotiations for an armistice.

Speaking at a meeting of the A.R.C.E.C. on November 23, Ilyich said:

"Peace cannot be concluded only from above. Peace must be secured from below. We do not believe the German General Staff an iota, but we do believe the German people. Without the active participation of the soldiers peace concluded by the commanders-in-chief is unstable." (*Ibid.*, p. 284.)

In Germany the situation was none too good. There was an acute food shortage, and the people were tired of the war. Germany believed that an armistice with Russia would leave her hands free to deal with France, and with Paris under her heel, she would then be able to tackle Russia.

Upon receiving the reply of the German command, the Council of People's Commissars immediately got in touch with the Allies (France, Britain, Italy and the U.S.A.), asking whether they agreed to start negotiations for an armistice with the enemy powers on December 1.

The Allies did not answer, and over the head of the Soviet Government wrote to General Dukhonin, who had been dismissed, protesting against the conclusion of a separate peace.

On December 1 our delegation, headed by Ioffe, left for the front. The other members were Karakhan, Kamenev, Sokolnikov, Bitsenko, Mstislavsky, and one representative each from the workers, peasants, sailors and soldiers.

The next day the Council of People's Commissars issued an appeal to the German workers.

Peace negotiations were started on December 3. The Soviet delegation announced its declaration in which the aims of the negotiations were proclaimed to be "the achievement of universal peace without annexations or indemnities in which the right to national self-determination would be guaranteed." It also proposed that an offer be made to all the other belligerents to take part in the negotiations. On December 5 an agreement was signed suspending military operations for one week. On the 7th the People's Commissariat of Foreign Affairs wrote once more to the representatives of the Allies to "define their attitude towards peace negotiations." No reply was received.

On the 11th our delegation, augmented by Pokrovsky and Weltman (Pavlovich), left for Brest again.

Peace negotiations were resumed on December 13, and the armistice prolonged until January 14. The negotiations fell through.

On December 25 the Germans announced on behalf of the Central Powers that they agreed to peace without annexations or indemnities on condition that the peace treaty was signed by all the belligerents. They knew that the latter would not agree, and their declaration was merely designed to shift all the responsibility for the continuation of the war on to the Entente.

Until the end of December the nature of the negotiations was agitational rather than anything else. The advantage gained from them was a temporary armistice and the development of a wide agitation for peace among the German troops and ours.

From the beginning of 1918 the negotiations assumed a different character. Early in January Ludendorf and

Hindenburg, who stood for a militarist policy of annexation, sent an ultimatum to Wilhelm II threatening to resign unless their demand for the prosecution of a vigorous annexationist policy at Brest-Litovsk and the taking over of negotiations by the military command was complied with. The conduct of negotiations passed into the hands of General Hoffman.

On January 7 our delegation, now headed by Trotsky, left for Brest again. Peace negotiations were resumed on January 9. This time the German delegation began to issue ultimatums. By January 20 the German attitude was clear. The only alternative to continued war was an annexationist peace, that is, peace on the conditions that we ceded to them *all* the territory that they occupied and paid them indemnity (under the guise of defraying the cost of maintenance of prisoners of war) to the amount of about three thousand million rubles payable over a number of years.

In the middle of January 1918 a general strike broke out in Vienna, provoked by the acute food shortage, the desire for peace and the indignation of the workers at the annexationst policy of the Central Powers at Brest-Litovsk. The strike affected almost the whole country and led to the setting up of a Soviet of Workers' Deputies. A few days later a strike broke out in Berlin, which, according to official reports, involved half a million workers. Strikes occurred in other cities as well. Soviets of Workers' Deputies were formed. The strikers demanded the proclamation of a republic and the conclusion of peace. However, no revolution was yet in sight. All the power was in the hands of Wilhelm II, Hindenburg, Ludendorf, in the hands of the bourgeoisie.

Ilyich pinned his hopes in a coming world revolution. On January 14 at the send-off given to the first socialist troop trains leaving for the front, he said: "The peoples are already awakening, they already hear the ardent call of our revolution, and soon we shall no longer be alone.

442

Our army will be joined by the proletarian forces of other countries." (*Works*, Vol. 26, p. 381.)

But that was still a thing of the future. It was characteristic of Ilyich that he never deceived himself, no matter how sad the realities were; he was never drunk with success, and always had a sober outlook. He did not always find it easy, though. Ilyich was anything but coldly rational, a sort of calculating chess-player. He felt things very intensely, but he had a strong will, he had lived through a good deal and thought things out for himself, and was able to face the truth without flinching. In this particular case he put the matter bluntly: an annexationist peace is a dreadful thing, but are we in a position to fight? Ilyich was constantly talking with soldiers' delegations that came from the front; he carefully studied the situation at the front and the state of our army, and attended a delegate conference of the First Army Congress on Demobilization. Writing of that congress in his memoirs, Podvoisky says: "The congress was due to take place on December 25, 1917, but it was opened on December 30. . . . During the five intervening days conferences were held with the most prominent delegates. Though they were of a preliminary nature, those conferences were of decisive importance. One of them was attended by Lenin, Chairman of the Council of People's Commissars, who, after listening to the detailed reports of the delegates from the most important armies, put to them three questions: 1. Was there any reason to believe that the Germans would attack us? 2. Would the army be able, in the event of a German offensive, to remove the munitions, materiel and artillery from the front-line area to the rear? 3. Would the army, in its present condition, be able to hold the German advance?

"The majority of the conference answered the first question in the affirmative, and the second and third in the negative, owing to the spirit of demobilization that prevailed among the soldiers, their increasing defection, and the exhausted state of the horses as a result of short fodder supplies." About three hundred delegates were present at that conference. It fully convinced Ilyich of the impossibility of continuing the fight with the Germans at that particular moment. Without yielding to pessimism—indeed, he was conducting an intensive campaign at the time for organizing the Red Army for the country's defence—he framed the question clearly: at the moment we cannot fight. "Go to the front," Ilyich advised the comrades who thought that war was possible. "Hear what the soldiers have to say about it."

Kravchenko recently told me about a talk she had had with Ilyich at that period. She had been working at Motovilikha, in the Urals. Petrograd was one thing, Perm and the Urals another. There was no immediate threat of an enemy advance there, and the homeward-bound soldiers had not come that far yet. The fighting spirit in the Urals stood high. The workers were organizing military detachments and preparing guns. Kravchenko was sent to see Ilyich and tell him that the Urals would back the country. On arriving in Petrograd Kravchenko called on Spunde, a Urals comrade, who was working at the State Bank. He lived on the premises. The simple iron cot on which he slept stood lonesomely and incongruously in one of the large conference halls. This little detail gives a picture of those days and is reminiscent of the conditions under which the arrested director of the State Bank Shipov was kept in custody. Spunde directed Kravchenko to Smolny, where Ilyich was. There, in the corridors, she met Goloshchokin, who had come from the Urals on the same mission. He was also going to see Ilyich. While they stood there talking, Ilyich came out of his office. Seeing Goloshchokin, he went up to them and started asking how things were going in the Urals. They told him what the feeling was among the Urals workers and what they had come here for. "We'll have a talk in the evening," Ilyich said. All of a sudden he looked ill. "Meanwhile go and take a walk, hear what the soldiers say in the streets," he added. "And we heard such an earful," Kravchenko related, "that our heads were splitting by that evening. The impressions of it were so strong that they overshadowed all else." Kravchenko does not even remember whether they had that talk with Ilyich or not.

Goloshchokin, too, recollects that meeting. Ilyich had asked him to interview the soldiers' delegations. Goloshchokin heard out their reports, ascertained the prevailing temper, then went and reported to Ilyich about it. Ilyich came out to the delegates, answered their questions, and told them what the state of affairs was; he kindled them with the fire of his enthusiasm. On this job Goloshchokin had it forcibly brought home to him that Ilyich was right. At the Seventh Congress he no longer needed convincing, he had no more vacillations.

At the Seventh Congress of the Party, held at the beginning of March, 1918, Ilyich said that during the first weeks and months following the October Revolution—in October, November and December—we had passed from triumph to triumph on the internal front of struggle against the counter-revolution, against the enemies of the Soviet power. The reason for this was that world imperialism had trouble enough of its own to be bothered with us. Our revolution had taken place at a time when cataclysmic disasters in the shape of the extermination of millions of people had overwhelmed the vast majority of the imperialist countries, when, after three years of fighting, the belligerent countries were at a deadlock, and the question arose objectively as to whether the nations, reduced to such a state, could go on fighting. It was a moment when neither of the two gigantic predacious groups could immediately throw themselves at one another or unite against us. Ilyich, at the Seventh Congress, described the first period of the Brest negotiations in the following words: "A tame domestic animal lay beside a tiger and tried to persuade him that peace should be without annexations and indemnities." In the latter half of January the Brest negotiations had assumed a different character: the preying wolf of German imperialism had seized us by the throat, and we had to answer immediately, either by agreeing to an annexationist peace or by continuing the war, knowing beforehand that we would be beaten in it. Lenin's point of view, in the long run, prevailed, but the inner-Party struggle, which had lasted two months, told on him very painfully. Ilyich had been pressing for the conclusion of peace. He had been backed wholeheartedly by Sverdlov and Stalin, supported without vacillation by Smilga and Sokolnikov. But the overwhelming majority of the Central Committee members and their following, the men with whom the October Revolution had been made, had been against Lenin. They had challenged his point of view, and drawn the local committees into the struggle. The Petrograd Committee and the Moscow Regional Committee had been against him too. The "Left" Communist* faction had begun to issue their own daily paper in Petrograd (*Communist*) in which they had talked themselves into such ridiculous statements as that it were better to let the Soviet power perish than to conclude a shameful peace, and argued about a revolutionary fight without regard for the actual balance of forces. They held that concluding peace with the German imperialist government was tantamount to surrendering all our revolutionary positions and betraying the cause of the international proletariat. Among the "Left" Communists were quite a number of intimate comrades with whom Ilyich had been working hand in hand for years and whom he

---

* "*Left Communists*"—a faction within the Party, formed in 1918, which opposed the conclusion of the peace of Brest and drove the Party towards war with Germany, which, as matters then stood, might have proved disastrous to the Soviet power. As a result of Lenin's struggle with the "Left Communists" the majority of them at the end of 1918 acknowledged their mistakes and ceased their factional activities.—*Ed.*

had been accustomed to look to for support during critical moments of the struggle. Now a void had been formed round him. The things he was accused of! Trotsky had a good deal to say. A lover of fine words, who liked to strike an attitude, he thought not so much of how to get the Soviet Republic out of the war and give it a respite to recuperate and rally the masses, as to cut a figure ("We conclude no degrading peace, we fight no war"). Ilyich called this a lordly, grand-seignior pose, and the slogan an adventurist gamble which gave the country over to pillage and anarchy, a country where the proletariat had taken over the helm of power and great construction was being started.

The majority of votes on the Central Committee had been against Lenin at first. On January 24 the majority (nine members) voted for Trotsky's motion—we conclude no peace and demobilize the army—with seven voting against. On February 3, on the question whether peace should be concluded now or not, five voted for and nine against; on February 17 five voted for an immediate offer of peace to Germany and six against; on February 18, on the question of whether we should offer the Germans to resume peace negotiations, six voted for and seven against.

Not until the Germans, on February 23, had presented their terms and demanded a reply within forty-eight hours, while their troops began to advance and take town after town, did the situation change. Lenin declared that if this policy of revolutionary phrasemongery continued he would resign from the Central Committee and the government. Voting on the question of whether to accept the German terms or not gave the following result: seven in favour and four against, with four abstentions including Trotsky, who shrank from taking upon himself responsibility on such a momentous issue at such an important time. The leading five who voted for concluding peace even on the Germans' terms (Lenin, Sverdlov, Stalin, Sokolnikov and Smilga) were joined by Zinoviev and Stasova. The opponents of peace were allowed freedom of agitation.

447

The advance of the Germans, however, had had an instantaneous sobering effect. By the time the Seventh Congress of the Party took place Lenin's standpoint had won over the vast majority. On March 8 the congress adopted a resolution in favour of endorsing the peace treaty signed at Brest-Litovsk by thirty votes against twelve, with four abstentions. On March 16 the Fourth Congress of Soviets, held in Moscow, ratified the Brest treaty by 704 votes against 285 with 115 abstentions.

Of this period of struggle for the peace of Brest two moments stand out in my memory. An extended meeting of the Party Central Committee was held on January 21, 1918. Winding up the debates, Ilyich felt the hostile glances of his comrades upon him. He had set forth his view with apparently little hope of being able to convince those present. I can almost hear the unutterably weary and bitter tone in which he said to me, when his speech was over: "Ah, well, let's go!" No one would have been more pleased than Ilyich if our army had been able to fight back, or if a revolution had broken out in Germany, which would have put an end to the war. He would have been glad to know that he had been wrong. But the more optimistic his comrades were, the more wary and guarded did Ilyich become. I remember another moment. During the very difficult time between the middle of January and the end of February Ilyich and I often went for walks together along the Neva around Smolny. Ilyich was worried, and at such moments he felt a need to unburden his mind to someone who stood close to him. I do not remember now exactly what he said, but it was in the same vein as his speech at the Seventh Congress of the Party. Even today I cannot read that speech without emotion. I hear Ilyich's voice and all his intonations in the words: "It will be a good thing if the German proletariat will be able to come out. But have you measured, have you discovered such an instrument that will determine that the German revolution will break out on such and such a day? No, that you do not know, and neither do we. You are staking everything on this card. If the revolution breaks out, everything is saved. Of course! But if it does not turn out as we desire, supposing it does not achieve victory tomorrow—what then? Then the masses will say to you: you acted like gamblers—you staked everything on a fortunate turn of events that did not take place, you proved unfit for the situation that actually arose in place of an international revolution, which will inevitably come, but which has not ripened yet." (*Works*, Vol. 27, pp. 79-80.)

Reading this, memory takes me back to the Neva, to our stroll there along the embankment in the dusk. The western sky over the river is flooded with the crimson glow of Petrograd's winter sunset. That sunset reminds me of my first meeting with Ilyich at the pancake party at Klasson's in 1894. Going back from the Okhta District along the Neva my comrades told me about Ilyich's brother. And here we were, Ilyich and I, walking down the Neva again, while he kept repeating over and over again the reasons why the standpoint of "no peace, no war" was fundamentally wrong. On our way back, Ilyich suddenly stops, and his tired face lights up as he lets fall: "You never know!"—meaning, a revolution may have started in Germany for all we know. In Smolny he reads the latest telegrams reporting that the Germans are advancing. His face becomes clouded and drawn, and he goes into his office to ring up. The revolution in Germany did not start until November 9, 1918. On November 13, 1918, the All-Russian Central Executive Committee annulled the treaty of Brest-Litovsk.

ILYICH MOVES TO MOSCOW, HIS FIRST MONTHS OF WORK IN MOSCOW

The German advance and the capture of Pskov by them showed what danger the government was exposing itself to by remaining in Petrograd. In Finland civil war had broken out. It was decided to evacuate to Moscow. This was essential from the organizing point of view as well. The work had to be done in the centre of the country's economic and political life.

On March 12 the Soviet Government moved to Moscow, the centre of Soviet Russia, which was at a safer distance from the frontiers and closer to a number of provinces with which closer contact had to be made.

On March 11, the day of the evacuation, Ilyich wrote an article entitled "The Main Task of Our Day," which was published in *Izvestia* on March 12. This article was programmatic, and at the same time strikingly characteristic of Ilyich's mood at the time.

The article begins with a quotation from Nekrasov's poem *Who Can Be Happy and Free in Russia*:

> *Thou art so pitiful,*
> *Poor, and so sorrowful,*
> *Yet of great treasure full,*
> *Mighty, all-powerful,*
> *Russia, my Mother!*

Briefly, in a few pithy sentences, Ilyich deals with the significance of the great proletarian revolution, then mentions the humiliating character of the Brest peace. Further, he writes of the struggle for a mighty and abundant Russia:

"Russia will become so if she casts aside all dejection and all phrasemongering, if she clenches her teeth, musters all her forces, strains every nerve, tightens every muscle, and if she understands that salvation lies *only* along that road of the international socialist revolution upon which we have set foot. It is by marching forward along that road, undismayed by defeats, it is by laying stone by stone the firm foundation of a socialist society, and by working with might and main for the building of discipline and self-discipline and for consolidating everywhere organization, order, efficiency, the harmonious cooperation of all the forces of the people, and over-all accountancy and control of the production and distribution of products—that is the way to build up military might and socialist might." (*Works*, Vol. 27, p. 135.)

"Since October 25, 1917, we are defencists," wrote Ilyich. "We are for 'defence of the motherland'; but that patriotic war towards which we are moving is a war for a socialist motherland, for socialism as a motherland, for the Soviet Republic, as a *detachment* of the world army of socialism." (*Ibid.*, pp. 136-37.)

Now, eighteen years after this article was written, when we have advanced far along the path of socialist construction and achieved decisive victories of socialism in our country, when we are "marching through life with a song," when we can already say with full right that our socialist homeland has achieved abundance and might, when millions, with an energy and initiative unprecedented in history, are winning the goal that was so brilliantly expressed by Lenin in his article "The Main Task of Our Day"— that article looks so matter of fact and natural. But one has to recollect those days in order to appreciate the full impact of that article.

Ilyich was full of energy, prepared cap-à-pie for the struggle.

At first we (Ilyich, Maria Ilyinichna and I) were put up at the National Hotel in Moscow (then called the First House of Soviets), where we had two rooms with a bath on the first floor. It was spring, and Moscow's generous sun was shining brightly. Okhotny Ryad—an open marketplace—began just outside the hotel. This was a colourful spot of old Moscow with its market stalls and shops whose owners had once knifed the students. Lots of people came to see Ilyich, many of them military men.

On March 18 the English landed a party of 400-500 marines in Murmansk ostensibly for the purpose of guarding the military stores set up there by the Entente under the tsarist government. The idea behind this landing party was clear.

At the National we were fed on English tinned meat with which the English fed their soldiers at the front. Once, during the meal, Ilyich remarked: "I wonder what we're going to feed our own soldiers with at the fronts?" Life at the National, nevertheless, was like a bivouac. Ilyich was eager to settle down in permanent quarters where he could get down to work.

It was decided to house the government offices and the principal members of the government in the Kremlin. We were to live there too.

I remember Sverdlov and Bonch-Bruyevich conducting us to the Kremlin for the first time to see our future apartment. We were allotted one in the building of the Court of Chancery. An old stone staircase, the steps of which had been worn down by the feet of generations of visitors, led to the second floor where the public prosecutor of the High Court used to have his apartment. It was planned to give us the kitchen with three rooms adjoining it which had a separate entrance, the rest of the apartment being assigned to house the offices of the Council of People's Commissars. The largest room was set aside as a conference hall (the meetings of the Council of People's Commissars of the U.S.S.R. are still being held there). Adjoining this was Ilyich's private office, which stood closer to the main entrance used by visitors. It was all very convenient. The building was in a filthy state, though; the stoves were broken and the ceilings cracked. Our future apartment was the dirtiest place of all—the caretakers had been living there. The place needed doing up.

We were given temporary lodgings—two clean rooms— in the so-called Cavalier Chambers of the Kremlin.

Ilyich liked to stroll about the Kremlin, which commanded a sweeping view of the city. He liked best of all to walk along the pavement facing the Grand Palace, where there was plenty to fill the eye. He was also fond of taking walks along the wall below, where there was lots of greenery and few people.

In one of the temporary rooms which we occupied there was an old publication lying on a table containing pictures of the Kremlin with historical notes concerning its buildings and towers. Ilyich liked to thumb through that album. The Kremlin of those days (1918) bore little resemblance to the Kremlin of today. Everything in it breathed of a bygone splendour. Next to the Chancery building was the pink-painted Chudov Monastery with its small latticed windows; by the steep bank stood the statue of Alexander II; below, nestling against the wall, stood some ancient church. Opposite the Chancery, workers were at work in the Kremlin building. There were no new squares or buildings then. The Kremlin was guarded by Red Army men.

The old army was demoralized and had been disbanded. A new army, a strong revolutionary army imbued with the spirit of enthusiasm and the will to victory, had to be built up.

At the beginning the Red Army bore little resemblance to a conventional army. It was burning with enthusiasm, but in outward appearance it was primitive. The men had no uniforms, and each one wore the clothes he had come in. There were no definite regulations or system of rules. The enemies of the Soviet power sneered at the Red Army men, and did not believe that the Bolsheviks were capable of creating a strong, well-knit army. The man in the street was scared of the Red Army soldiers, who looked like brigands to him. Adoratsky had a woman translator working for him in 1919, and when he asked her to come to the Kremlin to get some work, she did not dare to for fear of the Red Army men who were guarding the Kremlin.

Foreigners particularly were struck by the absence of the customary discipline and conduct on the part of the guards.

Ilyich told me of a visit which Mirbach paid him. The sentry outside Ilyich's office usually sat at a little table, reading a book. In those days no one saw anything peculiar in it. When peace with Germany was concluded and the German Ambassador, Count Mirbach, arrived in Russia, he paid the customary visit to the representative of the government in the Kremlin—the Chairman of the Council of People's Commissars Lenin. The sentry outside Ilyich's room was sitting and reading, and when Mirbach approached the door he did not even look up. Mirbach glanced at him in surprise. Afterwards, on coming out, Mirbach stopped next to the seated sentry, took the book he was reading, and asked his interpreter to translate the title for him. The book was a translation of Bebel's *Die Frau und der Sozialismus*. Mirbach returned it to the sentry without saying a word.

The Red Army men were studying hard. They realized that knowledge was needful for victory.

In passing down the corridor to his office with his hurried step, carrying an armful of newspapers, books and papers, Ilyich always had a friendly greeting for the guards. He was aware of their enthusiasm, of their readiness to die for the Soviets.

At the Seventh Party Congress (March 6-8, 1918) it had been decided to conclude peace with the Germans, albeit it was an onerous and humiliating peace. That decision had been the outcome of a bitter struggle. The speaker on the question of ratifying the peace treaty with Germany, which was examined together with the political report of the Central Committee, was Lenin, with Bukharin on behalf of the group of "Left Communists" as co-reporter. The fight was a sharp one. The congress was attended by 46 delegates with decisive votes representing 300,000 Party members. The Party in those days was not what it is now—it lacked the unity which has since been achieved. Thirty of the 46 delegates voted for the ratification of the Brest-Litovsk peace and 12 against, with 4 abstentions. In other words, about a third of the delegates were against the line of the Central Committee, against Lenin's line. Among them were many prominent Bolsheviks. On February 23 six of them announced their resignation from high posts in the administration and the Party, and reserved full freedom of agitation both within and outside the Party. On February 24 the Moscow Regional Bureau passed a resolution of no confidence in the Central Committee, refused to submit to those of its rulings which "would be connected with the implementation of the terms of the peace treaty with Austro-Germany," and in the explanatory note to its resolution declared that "a Party split in the near future is scarcely avoidable." The Moscow Regional Bureau early in 1918 acted as the organizational centre of the "Left Communists" on an all-Russian scale.

One can understand the vehemence with which Lenin opposed the "Left Communists" and their revolutionary phrasemongering. On February 21, 1918, he wrote in *Pravda*:

"We must fight against revolutionary phrasemongering, fight at all cost, so that it may not be said of us afterwards in words of bitter truth: 'revolutionary phrasemongering about a revolutionary war killed the revolution.'" (*Works*, Vol. 27, p. 10.)

Ilyich knew that the masses would back him and not the "Left Communists." The Fourth Extraordinary All-Russian Congress of Soviets was to ratify the peace treaty. The "Left Communists" were even prepared to put up with the loss of the Soviet power. In their declaration of February 24 they said: "In the interests of the international revolution we consider it expedient to consent to the possible loss of the Soviet power, which has now become purely formal." That phrase shocked Ilyich profoundly. Addressing a meeting of the Moscow Soviet of Workers', Peasants' and Red Army Deputies on March 12, he said with more than his usual vehemence and passion:

"The Russian revolution *has given that which so sharp-ly distinguishes it from the revolution in Western Europe.* (My italics.—*N.K.*) It has given a revolutionary mass, prepared for independent action by 1905; it has given Soviets of Workers', Soldiers' and Peasants' Deputies—bodies immeasurably more democratic than all previous ones—which have made it possible to educate and raise the downtrodden masses of the workers, soldiers and peasants, and make them follow our lead." (*Ibid.*, pp. 138-39.)

In the same speech Ilyich gave his appraisal of the Provisional Government and the conciliators. Referring to the February Revolution, he said:

"If the power had then passed to the Soviets, if the conciliators, instead of helping Kerensky to drive the army into the cannons' mouth, had then come forward with a proposal for a democratic peace, the army would not have been in such a ruinous state. They should have told it: stand by calmly. It should have held in one hand the torn secret treaty with the imperialists and an offer of democratic peace to all nations, and in the other hand a rifle and gun, and the front should have been fully preserved. That is when the army and the revolution could have been saved." (*Ibid.*, p. 139.)

Now, when our Red Army, equipped according to the latest word of science, stands by calmly, strong and organized, these words of Lenin's sound so near and familiar to every conscious citizen of our great country! But then, at the Fourth Extraordinary All-Russian Congress of Soviets, which took place on March 14-16, Ilyich, addressing the representatives of the Soviets with the same deep earnestness and sincerity with which he always addressed the masses, casually let fall a phrase that characterizes him as a revolutionary and fighter:

"They say we are surrendering the Ukraine, which Chernov, Kerensky and Tsereteli are out to ruin; we are told: traitors, you have betrayed the Ukraine! I say: comrades, I have seen a thing or two in the history of the revolution, more than enough to be daunted by the hostile glances and shouts of people who let themselves be carried away by their feelings and are unable to reason." (*Ibid.*, p. 158.)

Hostile glances and shouts could not deter Ilyich, not even those of his most intimate comrades. But he was only human, and these clashes with people with whom he had been so closely associated distressed him greatly; he did not sleep at nights, and his nerves were in a bad state. On this occasion, however, a split was avoided. The Fourth All-Russian Congress of Soviets ratified the peace treaty by 724 votes against 276, with 118 abstentions. This congress was attended not only by the Bolsheviks, of course. The Mensheviks, Communist-Anarchists and Right and Left Socialist-Revolutionaries voted against the signing of the peace treaty. Their representatives opposed the acceptance of the German peace terms at the meeting of the All-Russian Central Executive Committee on February 23. With 724 votes cast against 276, this meant a sweeping victory for Lenin's line.

The question of the peace treaty with the Germans having been settled, Ilyich regarded this as a respite which had to be made use of for developing the activities of the Soviet Government within the country to the utmost. He started to write his pamphlet *The Immediate Tasks of the Soviet Government.* Sverdlov was a frequent visitor of ours in the Cavalier Chambers. Seeing Ilyich at work, he persuaded him, after much argument, to use a stenographer, and sent him one of the best on the staff. Nothing came of it, though. The presence of the stenographer embarrassed Ilyich, and try as the former would to persuade Ilyich not to take any notice of him, the work made no headway. Ilyich's method of working was to write a couple of pages first, then spend a long time thinking how better to express himself. He could not do this in the presence of a stranger. Not until 1923, when he was seriously ill and could not do his own writing, did he start to dictate his articles, extremely difficult though he found it. He dictated them to Fotieva, Glyaser, Manucharyants and Vo-lodicheva. These women had been working a long time in his secretariat and he was not so shy of them. Even so, one could often hear his embarrassed laugh through the door of his room.

Between the end of March and April 1918 Ilyich worked hard at his article *The Immediate Tasks of the Soviet Government*. It was published in *Izvestia* on April 28 and served as a guide to action for the Bolsheviks for years to come. Nowhere, I believe, did Ilyich deal with the main difficulties of socialist construction in our country in such a simple, vivid and striking manner as he did in that pamphlet. At the time of the October Revolution our country was a land of small-scale peasant farming. The peasant millions were steeped in the psychology of the petty proprietor, where each thought only of himself, of his own household and patch of land, and did not care for anyone else. "Each for himself, and God will take care of the rest," the peasant argued. Ilyich had written about that petty-proprietor mentality and its harmfulness dozens of times, but now that with the dismissal of the Constituent Assembly the question of power had been definitely settled and the peace of Brest made possible a certain respite, the problem of re-educating the masses and cultivating in them a new psychology, a collectivist psychology, loomed large.

The great proletarian revolution, while overthrowing the landowners and the capitalists, had at the same time opened the floodgates of petty-bourgeois instincts. The landowners' property was being seized and shared out, and increasingly used for purposes of profiteering. These petty-bourgeois passions had to be brought under control, the masses had to be re-educated, a new socialist structure had to be created, and the administration organized. During March and April 1918 all these problems absorbed Ilyich completely.

How to organize a nation-wide accounting and control, how to raise the productivity of labour, how to teach people to work, to draw the masses into public activities, make them socially alert citizens, how to reorganize work and work discipline on new lines—this is what Ilyich wrote of in *The Immediate Tasks of the Soviet Government*. He also wrote about *socialist emulation* in this pamphlet.

Rereading it today tells one such a lot. Today everyone understands what a tremendous role socialist emulation has played in the business of socialist construction, but at that time the question was somehow passed over (partly, no doubt, on account of the civil war which commenced soon after). Socialist emulation was first widely applied on a mass scale during the years of struggle for the First Five-Year Plan, beginning approximately with 1928—ten years after Ilyich had written about it.

This pamphlet contains a special chapter entitled "Raising the Productivity of Labour." Ilyich, as always, dealt with the question in all its aspects and bearing on a number of other fundamental issues.

"The raising of the productivity of labour first of all requires that the material basis of large-scale industry shall be assured, *viz.*, the development of the production of fuel, iron, the engineering and chemical industries.... Another condition for raising the productivity of labour is, firstly, the raising of the educational and cultural level of the masses of the population. This is now taking place extremely rapidly, and only those who are blinded by bourgeois routine are unable to see it; they are unable to understand what an urge towards light and initiative is now developing among the 'lower ranks' of the people thanks to the Soviet form of organization. Secondly, a condition for economic revival is the raising of the discipline of the toilers, their skill, their dexterity, increasing the intensity of labour and improving its organization." (*Works*, Vol. 27, p. 228.)

Lenin dealt with the question of raising the productivity of labour from the angle of socialist emulation problems. He pointed out in this pamphlet that the task of raising labour efficiency was a long-range problem:

"...While it is possible to capture the central power in a few days, while it is possible to suppress the military resistance (and sabotage) of the exploiters even in different parts of a great country in a few weeks, the capital solution of the problem of raising the productivity of labour requires, at any rate (particularly after a most terrible and devastating war), several years. The protracted nature of the work is certainly dictated by objective circumstances." (*Ibid.*)

Today, at the beginning of 1936, when we are witnessing the Stakhanov movement, when the new technics created under the First and Second Five-Year plans have given rise to a movement from below aimed at increasing labour efficiency, when we have achieved a tremendous upsurge in labour productivity, Ilyich's pamphlet *The Immediate Tasks of the Soviet Government* appears to us in a new light and strikes home with a fuller and clearer impact.

Vladimir Ilyich spoke a good deal with workers and peasants, and could not help noticing at every step an inaptitude for work, coupled with an attitude, fostered by centuries of task labour, which regarded work as a curse, as something that had to be reduced to a minimum. The revolution had done away with the bullying, swearing and driving class of foremen and bosses, and the worker was glad to be rid of them, glad to be able to sit down and have a smoke when he was tired without anyone driving him. At the beginning the factory organizations readily released the workers to attend all kinds of meetings. I remember a woman worker coming to me once at the Commissariat of Education to receive some certificate or other. During our conversation I asked her what shift she was working in. I thought she was working in the night shift, otherwise she would not have been able to come to the Commissariat in the daytime. "None of us are working today. We had a meeting yesterday evening, everyone was behindhand with her domestic work at home, so we voted to knock off today. We're the bosses now, you know." When you tell this to comrades now, eighteen years later, they hardly believe it and do not think it was typical. For early 1918, however, this was a typical case. The bosses and exploiters with their bullying foremen and driving overseers had been got rid of, but that the factory had now become public property, that that property had to be taken care of, and the productivity of labour raised, was something that had not yet been brought home to people. That is why Lenin was so emphatic about this aspect of the problem; he could face the truth when need be. The workers had to be educated to an intelligent work attitude, and all labour had to be organized on efficient lines.

Ilyich particularly showed up the Left Socialist-Revolutionaries in this pamphlet. Those representatives of the petty bourgeoisie had failed to grasp the importance of practical efficient work, which they looked upon as narrow practicalness, and "gradualness" while they dreamt of a "revolutionary war," and so on.

The class on which Ilyich relied and in whose gift of leadership he implicitly believed, despite the fact that that class still had to develop and work hard at its self-improvement, was the proletariat. "The only class that can lead the toiling and exploited masses is the class that unswervingly follows its path without losing courage and without giving way to despair even at the most difficult, arduous and dangerous stages. Hysterical spurts are of no use to us. What we need is the steady march of the iron battalions of the proletariat."

With these words the pamphlet *The Immediate Tasks of the Soviet Government* ended.

It appeared as an article in *Izvestia* on April 28, and on April 29 Ilyich addressed a meeting of the All-Russian Central Executive Committee.

To enable the workers' *active* of Moscow to hear Ilyich's report on the immediate tasks of the Soviet Government, the meeting was held at the Polytechnical Museum. Ilyich was greeted with a tumultuous ovation and listened to with rapt attention. Obviously, the question was one of keen interest to everybody. Ilyich spoke there with extraordinary fervour. Even today one cannot read that speech without emotion. Ilyich spoke about the distinguishing features of our revolution, the causes of its triumph, the difficulties of socialist construction in a petty-bourgeois country; he characterized our bourgeoisie and its weaknesses, urged that we should learn organization of production from the Western and American bourgeoisie, from the trust organizers; he scathingly criticized the Left Socialist-Revolutionaries, the representatives of the petty-bourgeois elements, criticized our "Left Communists" who had succumbed to that influence, although he still called them our friends of yesterday, today and tomorrow; he spoke about the role of the proletariat, about the influence of the petty-bourgeois element, the significance of socialist organization. and the necessity of our proletariat organizing on new lines—only then would it be capable of rallying the masses behind it.

"Until the advanced workers learn to organize the millions," said Ilyich, "they are not Socialists or creators of a socialist society, and they will not acquire the necessary knowledge of organization. The way of organization is a long way, and the tasks of socialist construction demand long hard work and corresponding knowledge in which we are lacking." (*Works*, Vol. 27, p. 268.)

In his speech at the Central Executive Committee on April 29 Ilyich also said that the proletariat, who had learnt discipline in big industry, would appreciate the significance of the May Day slogan which the Central Committee of the Party had put forward: "We have overcome Capital, and we shall overcome our own lack of organization." He spoke about the importance of the railways:

"...Without the railways we shall not only have no socialism, but we shall all die of starvation like dogs while the grain lies right next to us," for "that is the crux of the matter, a manifestation of the most striking connection between the town and the country, between industry and agriculture, on which socialism is founded. To combine this for regular activity in the interests of the whole population, the railways are needed." (*Ibid.*, p. 277.)

How understandable, how familiar that speech sounds today, eighteen years after!

At that time, to be sure, not everyone had grasped its significance, but it had stirred people's minds, kindled the flame of enthusiasm among the masses.

On March 29 after the Fourth Congress of Soviets, the "Left Communists" at the head of the Moscow Regional Bureau of the Communist Party decided after all to publish their own weekly journal *Communist* to propound their views. The first issue, which appeared on April 20, contained the editorial "Theses on the Present Situation." Ilyich's speech at the Central Executive Committee on April 29 was largely a reply to these views. He dealt with them more fully in his articles "'Left-Wing' Childishness and the Petty-Bourgeois Mentality," published in *Pravda* on May 9 and 11, 1918. An interesting feature of these articles was the passage concerning socialization, in which Ilyich wrote:

"We will pass to the misfortunes of our 'Left' Communists in the sphere of home policy. It is difficult to read phrases such as the following in the theses on the *present* situation without smiling.

"...'The systematic use of the surviving means of production is conceivable only if a most determined policy of socialization is pursued'... 'not capitulation to the bourgeoisie and its servile petty-bourgeois intelligentsia, but the utter rout of the bourgeoisie and the complete break-down of sabotage.'

"Dear 'Left Communists,' how determined they are... but what little judgement they display! What do they mean by pursuing 'a most determined policy of socialization'?

"One may or may not be determined on the question of nationalization or confiscation. But the whole point is that even the greatest possible 'determination' is not enough to pass *from* nationalization and confiscation *to* socialization. The misfortune of our 'Lefts' is that by their naive, childish combination of words: 'most determined policy of socialization' they reveal their utter failure to understand the crux of the question, the crux of the 'present' situation. The misfortune of our 'Lefts' is that they have missed the essence of the 'present situation,' *viz.*, the transition from confiscation (the carrying out of which requires above all a determined policy) to socialization (the carrying out of which requires a *different* quality in the revolutionary).

"Yesterday, the main task of the moment was, as determinedly as possible, to nationalize, confiscate, beat down and crush the bourgeoisie and break down sabotage. Today, only a blind man could fail to see that we have nationalized, confiscated, beaten down and broken more than we have been able to *keep count of*. And the difference between socialization and simple confiscation lies precisely in the fact that confiscation can be carried out by means of 'determination' alone, without the ability to count up and distribute property, *whereas socialization cannot be brought about without this ability*." (*Ibid.*, pp. 300-01.)

Today, when the long path of collective-farm organization is behind us and we have witnessed the "dizzy-with-success" phenomenon, we are better able to appreciate these utterances of Lenin's.

Analyzing the material of the "Left Communists" published in the journal *Communist*, Lenin gave the following critical appraisal of the "Left Communists":

"Every page of the *Communist* shows that our 'Lefts' have no conception of iron proletarian discipline and how it is achieved; that they are thoroughly imbued with the mentality of the declassed petty-bourgeois intellectual." (*Works*, Vol. 27, p. 296.)

Only four issues of the *Communist* were published, the June issue being the last.

The opposition of the Left Socialist-Revolutionaries to Lenin's policy was far more vigorous.

On May 2-3, 1918, the Left Socialist-Revolutionaries headed by Spiridonova and Karelin demanded that the People's Commissariat of Agriculture should be fully controlled by them. Their demand was made in the form of an ultimatum. Lenin consulted the Bolsheviks then working in the Commissariat of Agriculture (V. N. Meshcheryakov, S. Sereda and others). The Bolshevik group was emphatically against it. The Central Committee of the Party rejected this demand of the Left Socialist-Revolutionaries. The influence of the Left Socialist-Revolutionaries in the Commissariat of Agriculture was curtailed.

On May 22 Ilyich wrote to the workers of Petrograd:

"Comrades, the other day your delegate, a Party comrade, a worker in the Putilov Works, called on me. This comrade drew a detailed and extremely harrowing picture of the famine in Petrograd. We all know that the food situation is just as acute in a number of the industrial gubernias, that famine is knocking just as cruelly at the door of the workers and the poor generally.

"And side by side with this we observe an orgy of profiteering in grain and other food products. The famine is not due to the fact that there is no grain in Russia, but to the fact that the bourgeoisie and the rich generally are putting up a last decisive fight against the rule of the toilers, against the state of the workers, against the Soviet power, on this most important and acute of issues, the issue of bread. The bourgeoisie and the rich generally, including the rural rich, the kulaks, are sabotaging the grain

465

monopoly; they are disrupting the distribution of grain undertaken by the state for the purpose and in the interests of supplying bread to the whole of the population, and in the first place to the workers, the toilers, the needy. The bourgeoisie are disrupting the fixed prices, they are profiteering in grain, they are making a hundred, two hundred and more rubles profit on every pood of grain; they are disrupting the grain monopoly and the proper distribution of grain by resorting to bribery and corruption and by deliberately supporting everything tending to destroy the power of the workers, which is endeavouring to put into effect the prime, basic and root principle of socialism: 'He who does not work, neither shall he eat.'" (*Ibid.*, p. 355.)

Profiteering was rife in Moscow at the time. I recollect an amusing incident. Ilyich and I went for a ride to Vorobyovy Hills. Few people knew Ilyich by sight at the time, and when he walked about the streets he attracted no attention. I saw a well-fed looking peasant sitting with an empty sack, rolling himself a cigarette. I went up to him and started a conversation, asked him how he was living, how he was off for grain. "We're not bad off at all these days," he said. "We've got lots of grain and do a good trade. People in Moscow are hungry, they're afraid there won't be any bread at all soon. Bread fetches a good price these days, it's a very profitable business. You've got to be careful the way you go about it, though. I've got some regular families I deliver bread to, and get paid cash down without any bother...."

Ilyich came up and listened to our talk. "I've got one family living at Boloto..." the peasant was saying. "Boloto?" I queried. "Where's that?" The peasant stared at me. "Where do you come from that you don't even know Boloto?" As I afterwards found out, Boloto was the name of a market-place* (Government House now stands there)

---

* *Boloto* in Russian also means a swamp.—*Ed.*

where vegetables and apples were sold. "I'm a Petrograder," I said. "I'm new to Moscow."

"Oh, a Petrograder," the peasant said. The word started him off on a new train of thought, and after a pause he added: "That Lenin's a nuisance. I don't understand the man. Muddle-headed, if you ask me. His wife wanted a sewing machine, so he goes and gives orders for all the sewing machines to be taken away in all the villages. My niece had hers taken away too. The whole Kremlin is cluttered up with sewing machines, they say." I avoided looking at Ilyich for fear that I would burst out laughing.

That well-to-do farmer and petty proprietor could not imagine Lenin not helping himself to something or other when he had the chance. This suburban farmer had heard that Lenin had spoken something about machines, and he could not understand why Lenin should be bothering his head about machines.

Daft though this conversation was, it showed what a difficult path confronted the Party and the Soviet Government in the struggle for socialism, the struggle against the rich, the kulaks, against the psychology of the petty proprietor, against inefficiency, ignorance and the economic backwardness of our country.

At the end of May Ilyich wrote a letter to the workers of Petrograd. Not all of Ilyich's articles and speeches are written in the same vein. It all depended on whom they were intended for. His letter of May 22 was written for people in whom he placed his hopes and in whose constructive genius he implicitly believed—the Petrograd workers. He wrote to them:

"Petrograd is not Russia. The Petrograd workers are only a small part of the workers of Russia. But they are one of the best, the advanced, most class-conscious, most revolutionary, most steadfast detachments of the working class and of all the working people of Russia, and one of the least liable to succumb to empty phrases, to spineless despair and to the intimidation of the bourgeoisie.

And it has frequently happened at critical moments in the life of nations that even small advanced detachments of advanced classes have carried the rest after them, have fired the masses with revolutionary enthusiasm and have accomplished tremendous historic feats." (*Works*, Vol. 27, pp. 358-59.)

Vladimir Ilyich wrote to the Petrograd workers about the immense organizing job that confronted them. He attached the greatest importance to organizing work.

"Heroism displayed in prolonged and persevering organizational work on a national scale is immensely more difficult than, but at the same time immensely superior to, heroism displayed in an uprising," wrote Ilyich. "But the strength of working-class parties, the strength of the working class always lay in that it looks danger boldly, squarely and openly in the face, that it does not fear to admit danger and soberly weighs the forces in its 'own' camp and in 'the other' camp, the camp of the exploiters. The revolution is progressing, developing and growing. The tasks we face are also growing. The struggle is broadening and deepening." (*Ibid.*, p. 360.)

Ilyich's confidence in the victory of the revolution fired the enthusiasm of the masses.

His own hard work was an example of that heroic organizing job of which he had spoken.

Besides organizing the country's defence against its foreign and internal enemies, and assuming the leadership in the civil war, which had already started by that time, Vladimir Ilyich did a tremendous job in organizing socialist construction. He put through decrees on the nationalization of industry, wrote instructions for the workers of the nationalized enterprises, made reports at the trade-union congresses, the Supreme Council of National Economy and the First Congress of Councils of National Economy, addressed the Congress of Labour Commissars, delegate meetings of the factory Party units, and conferences of the factory committees, received delegations of the Petrograd, Yelets and other workers, spoke to the mobilized Communists leaving for the front, and at the same time, at the moments of gravest crisis—on May 25, just before the introduction of martial law in Moscow, he submitted to the Council of People's Commissars a draft decree concerning the inauguration of a Socialist Academy of Social Sciences; on June 5 he addressed a meeting of internationalist teachers, on June 10 he drew up an appeal in connection with the Czechoslovak counter-revolutionary insurrection, and later in the day submitted a proposal to the Council of People's Commissars for enlisting the services of the engineers; two days before the attempt upon his life he addressed the Education Congress where he spoke about the school being a tremendous factor in the building up of socialism.

Every week Ilyich spoke at district meetings, sometimes twice a day or more.

This directional work among the masses bore fruit. It was this, more than anything, that helped to achieve victory.

Rereading the history of the Civil War of 1918 today, when the whole picture had been pieced together and we now have a clear idea of the desperate struggle for existence that was waged by the old landlord and capitalist system, one realizes that the revolution had won because the masses were mustered for the struggle, because a tremendous job of work had been done among them, because the masses had had it brought home to them what the struggle was about, and because that struggle was something near to them which they could understand.

In the spring and summer of 1918 Ilyich lived in Moscow and worked at high pressure. Whenever he had a moment to spare he would go motoring outside Moscow with his sister Maria and me, always visiting new places, riding and thinking and filling his lungs with the fresh air. He would take notice of every little thing around him.

The middle peasants sympathized with the Soviet power, which stood for peace and was against the landlords, but they did not think it had come to stay, and were nothing loath on occasion to pass some humorous remark about it.

I remember once driving up to a bridge which had a look of very doubtful security about it. Vladimir Ilyich asked a peasant, who was standing by the bridge, whether the car could safely cross it. The peasant shook his head and said with a chuckle: "I'm not so sure. It's a Soviet bridge, if I may be pardoned for saying so." Ilyich often afterwards laughingly repeated the phrase that peasant had used.

On another occasion we were returning from a drive and were about to pass under a railway bridge when a herd of cows coming the other way blocked our path. Those cows coolly ignored all motor traffic and made way for no one on the road. We were obliged to stop. A peasant who walked past looked at Ilyich with a grin and said: "You had to give way to the cows all right."

The peasants did not sit on the fence long, though. In the middle of May the class struggle flared up and made them come off it.

The summer of 1918 was an extremely difficult one. Ilyich no longer wrote anything, and he did not sleep at nights. A photograph of him, taken shortly before he was shot at, shows him standing with a brooding air, looking as though he had just recovered from a serious illness.

It was a very difficult time.

The bourgeoisie, having lost all in the great proletarian revolution, was seeking aid from abroad. Now it took money from the Allies to organize revolts, now it called in the German troops, giving the population over to plunder and anarchy, plunging about from one orientation to another. The Germans helped the Finnish Whites and occupied the Ukraine, the Turks came to the aid of the Azerbaijan Mussavatists and the Georgian Mensheviks, the Germans occu-

At 9th Congress of Russian Communist Party, Sverdlovsky Hall in Kremlin, March-April 1920

In Kremlin study, with H. G. Wells, October 1920

pied the Crimea, the British occupied Murmansk, the Allies helped the Czechoslovaks and the Right Socialist-Revolutionaries to cut Siberia off from the central provinces. Grain shipments from the Ukraine and Siberia were stopped, and Moscow and Petrograd were starving. The ring of fighting fronts kept narrowing.

On May 21, Ilyich wrote in a telegram to the Petrograd workers:

"...The plight of the revolution is critical. Remember, *only you* can save the revolution, there is no one else....

"Time is short: after painful May will come still more painful June and July and perhaps part of August." (*Works*, Vol. 27, p. 354.)

The spell of counter-revolutionary uprisings roused and rallied the kulaks. They hoarded their grain. The struggle with famine merged with the struggle against the counter-revolution. Vladimir Ilyich pressed for the organization of the Poor Peasants' Committees,* and agitated strongly for the workers to join the Food Detachments,** as their revolutionary experience would come in useful in the coun-

---

* *Poor Peasants' Committees*, set up on June 11, 1918, during the bitter class struggle in the countryside, when the country was suffering acutely from a food shortage. Their functions were, among others, to distribute grain and other necessaries, and agricultural implements, to render assistance to the local food supply authorities in confiscating grain surpluses from the kulaks. These committees were the bases of the dictatorship of the proletariat in the rural districts, and it was largely through them that the Red Army cadres were enlisted from among the peasant population. After having served their purpose these committees were done away with in December 1918. —*Ed.*

** *Food Detachments* were set up in 1918 owing to the acute food shortage within the country. Detachments of workers and poor peasants were sent to the grain producing districts to buy surplus stocks of grain from the kulaks at fixed prices or to requisition them. The detachments played an important role in supplying the population with food, in politically educating the poor peasants, and combatting kulak sabotage of grain collection. They were abolished after the end of the civil war.—*Ed.*

tryside. The fight for bread at that moment—he told the workers—was a fight for socialism.

It was necessary, Ilyich wrote to the Petrograd workers, for "the advanced worker, *as the leader* of the poor, *as the leader* of the toiling masses of the countryside, *as the builder of the state of toilers* to 'go among the people.'" He said that the fight-hardened experienced workers were the vanguard of the revolution.

"That is the sort of vanguard of the revolution—in Petrograd and throughout the country—that must sound the call, must *rise in their mass*, must understand that the salvation of the country is in their hands, that from them is demanded a heroism no less than that which they displayed in January and October 1905 and in February and October 1917, that a great *'crusade'* must be organized against the grain profiteers, the kulaks, the parasites, the disorganizers and bribe-takers, a great *'crusade'* against the violators of strictest state order in the collection, transportation and distribution of bread for the people and bread for the machines.

"The country and the revolution can be saved only by the mass effort of the advanced workers. We need tens of thousands of advanced and steeled proletarians, class-conscious enough to explain matters to the millions of poor peasants all over the country and to assume the leadership of these millions...." (*Ibid.*, pp. 361, 359.)

The workers of Petrograd responded to the appeal of Ilyich. They organized a "crusade." The poor peasants began to rally closer around the Soviet power. On June 11 the All-Russian Central Executive Committee decreed the organization of the Poor Peasants' Committees. The poor peasants began to look upon Lenin, of whom they had heard so much from the workers and soldiers, as their leader. Ilyich took care of the poor, but the poor also took care of Ilyich. Lydia Fotieva, Ilyich's secretary, relates how a Red Army man of a poor peasant family came to the Kremlin and cut off half of his loaf for Lenin. "Let him eat it, these are hungry times," he said. He did not even ask to see Ilyich, but just asked to have him pointed out to him from a distance when he passed by.

Ilyich got very angry when any attempts were made to create favoured living conditions for him, pay him a big salary, and so forth. I remember how angry he was over a pail of *khalva*, which Malkov, then commandant of the Kremlin, once brought him.

On May 23 Ilyich whote a note to Bonch-Bruyevich:
"V.D. Bonch-Bruyevich,
Business-Manager,
Council of People's Commissars.

"In view of non-fulfilment by you of my insistent demand to notify me on what grounds my salary was raised from 500 to 800 rubles per month as from March 1,1918, and in view of the obvious illegality of such a rise, which you have made arbitrarily by arrangement with the Secretary of the Council N.P. Gorbunov in direct violation of the decree of the Council of People's Commissars dated November 23, 1917, I herewith severely reprimand you.

"Chairman of the Council of People's Commissars

V. Ulyanov (LENIN)"
(*Works,* Vol. 35, p. 272).

The Germans concluded the peace of Brest with Soviet Russia and ceased hostilities, but did not abandon their plans for seizing Russia. During the Brest negotiations the German Government had entered into an agreement with the Ukrainian Rada, promising it their assistance in the fight against the Bolsheviks. After occupying the Ukraine and overthrowing the Soviet power there, the Germans dismissed the Rada, too, and set up in its place the tsarist General Skoropadsky as hetman—ruler of the Ukraine. The Ukraine virtually became a German colony. Grain, cattle, sugar and raw materials were shipped from the Ukraine to Germany in vast quantities.

The German imperialists did their utmost to fan the flame of civil war. Cossack ataman Krasnov, who escaped to the Don, appealed to the Germans for assistance, and they helped him to raise and rally White Guard Cossack units.

The Germans helped the White Finns to suppress the revolution in Finland and take brutal reprisals against the Finnish revolutionaries.

But the Germans were not the only ones to take aggressive action. At the beginning of April the Japanese and the British landed in Vladivostok.

Already in April a number of anti-Soviet parties had united and formed a Revival League. It consisted of Socialist-Revolutionaries, Cadets, Popular Socialists, Mensheviks and the "Unity" group. The League concluded an agreement with the Entente for Entente troops to be sent to Russia against the Bolsheviks and for the Czech Corps to be used for engineering a coup in Russia and overthrowing the Soviet Government. At the time of Kerensky the Czech Corps had numbered 42,000 strong, and included many Russian reactionary generals and officers. The plan of the revolt was discussed with the French Military Mission by members of the Socialist-Revolutionary Central Committee and representatives of the Siberian Socialist-Revolutionaries. It was decided that the Czechoslovak troops, evacuated to the Far East, would occupy strong points on the Ural, Siberian and Ussuri railways.

At the end of May the Czechoslovaks occupied Chelyabinsk, Petropavlovsk, Taiga railway station, and Tomsk, and at the beginning of June—Omsk and Samara. At the end of May a White Guard plot sponsored by the League was discovered in Moscow; a revolt had been engineered in the Crimea, and the stage was set for a mutiny in the Baltic Fleet. On June 4 a bourgeois-nationalist government was formed in the Crimea. On June 19 there was a counter-revolutionary revolt in Irkutsk, on June 20—in Kozlov and Ekaterinburg, on June 29 a monarchist plot was discovered in Kostroma, and on June 30 a bourgeois government was proclaimed by the Siberian Regional Duma. The Socialist-Revolutionaries worked hand in hand with the bourgeoisie. On June 8, after the capture of Samara by the Czechoslovak Corps, a Constituent Assembly Committee was set up there. On June 19 the Right Socialist-Revolutionaries raised a revolt in Tambov, and the next day assassinated Volodarsky in Petrograd.

The Left Socialist-Revolutionaries, too, took to the ways of counter-revolution.

On June 24 they decided to assassinate the German Ambassador Mirbach and engineer an armed revolt against the Soviet power. On June 27 the British landed in Murmansk. On July 1 White Guard troop-trains formed under the direction of the French Mission were arrested in Moscow. On July 4 the All-Russian Congress of Soviets was opened, and on July 6 Mirbach was assassinated, and a revolt organized in Moscow and Yaroslavl.

Speaking at the Fifth Congress of Soviets on July 5, Ilyich had taken the Left Socialist-Revolutionaries to task for their woolliness, their panic-mongering and failure to grasp the situation, but he had not thought them capable of falling so low as counter-revolution.

On July 6 Left S.-R.'s Blyumkin and Andreyev presented themselves at the house of the German Embassy in Moscow and asked for a private audience with Count Mirbach. After throwing a bomb at him and killing him, they escaped to the Cheka* detachment under the command of Left S.-R. Popov, which was located in Trekhsvyatitelsky Street. Simultaneously the whole Central Committee of the Socialist-Revolutionary Party moved over there. Head of the Cheka Dzerzhinsky, who went there to arrest the murderers, was himself arrested. Popov's detachment sent patrols out into the nearby streets, who arrested the Chairman of the Moscow Soviet Smidovich, People's Commissar of Post and Telegraph Podbelsky, one of the heads of the Cheka Lācis and others, and seized the General Post Office. The Left S.-R. Central Committee promulgated through-

---

* *Cheka*—the All-Russian Extraordinary Commission.—*Ed.*

475

out Russia and the Czechoslovak front a report announcing the revolt in Moscow, and calling for war against Germany. In face of the hostilities started by the Left Socialist-Revolutionaries, the Council of People's Commissars took military action against Popov's detachment which numbered about two thousand infantrymen with eight guns and an armoured car. On July 8 Trekhsvyatitelsky Street was sealed off and shelled. The Socialist-Revolutionaries attempted to retaliate by opening fire on the Kremlin. Several shells landed in the courtyard. After a brief resistance Popov's detachment withdrew and escaped by way of the Vladimir Road, where they shortly afterwards dispersed. About three hundred prisoners were taken.

After the suppression of the Socialist-Revolutionaries in Trekhsvyatitelsky Street, Ilyich wanted to have a look at the house in which the rebels had set up their temporary headquarters. We drove down there together in an open car. As we were passing the Oktyabrsky Station, we heard a shout of "Stop!" from round a corner. Not seeing who it was shouting, our chauffeur Gil drove on without stopping, but Ilyich told him to pull up. Meanwhile, somebody had started shooting a revolver from around the corner, and a group of armed men came running up. They were our own people. "What's the idea, comrades, shooting from round the corner when you don't see whom you're shooting at!" Ilyich rebuked them. They were greatly put out. Ilyich asked the way to Trekhsvyatitelsky Street. We were allowed into the house without delay and conducted through the rooms. Ilyich had been curious as to why the Socialist-Revolutionaries had chosen that particular house for their headquarters and how they had organized its defence, but he soon lost interest in that question: the house's location and interior arrangements were not of the slightest interest from that point of view. What struck us there were the floors, which were thickly strewn with scraps of torn paper. Apparently, during the fight, the Socialist-Revolutionaries had torn up all their documents.

Although it was late in the afternoon, Ilyich wanted to go for a ride in Sokolniki Park. At a level crossing we ran into a Komsomol patrol. "Stop!" We stopped. "Documents!" Ilyich showed his document reading "V. Ulyanov, Chairman of the Council of People's Commissars." "Tell us another one!" the young men sneered. They arrested Ilyich and took him down to the nearest militia station. There he was immediately recognized, and the men in charge laughed heartily. Ilyich came back, and we drove on. We turned into Sokolniki Park, and as we were driving down one of the roads, we heard shooting again. It appeared that we had been passing a munition store. Our papers were examined and we were allowed to pass with a grumbled remark about our riding about God knows where at unearthly hours. Riding back we had to pass the same youth patrol post, but when the lads caught sight of our car from afar they instantly disappeared.

On July 8 the Fifth Congress of Soviets resolved to expel from the Soviets the Left Socialist-Revolutionaries, who had supported the revolt of July 6-7. On July 10 the congress adopted the Soviet Constitution and wound up its proceedings.

The situation was extremely difficult throughout July.

The commander of the troops fighting the Czechoslovaks was the Left Socialist-Revolutionary Muravyov. He had sided with the Soviet power after October, had fought the troops of Kerensky and Krasnov, who had been advancing on Petrograd, had fought against the Central Rada, and on the Rumanian front. But when the S.-R. revolt started on July 6-7, Muravyov went over to their side and wanted to turn his troops against Moscow. The units upon which he had been relying, however, refused to follow his lead; he had counted on the backing of the Simbirsk Soviet, but the Soviet withdrew its support; his arrest was ordered, but he put up a resistance and was killed. Simbirsk was shortly afterwards taken by the Czechoslovaks. The latter were advancing on Ekaterinburg, where Nicholas II was kept prisoner. On July 16 we had him and his family shot. The Czechoslovaks came too late to save him—they took Ekaterinburg on July 23.

In the north the British and French troops seized part of the Murmansk railway.

The Mensheviks of Baku called in British troops.

The White Volunteer Army took Tikhoretskaya, then Armavir.

The Germans demanded that a battalion of their troops should be allowed into Moscow to guard the Embassy.

Desperate though the situation was, Ilyich never lost heart. His mood is best revealed in his letter to Clara Zetkin, dated July 26.

"My dear Comrade Zetkin," he wrote. "Thank you heartily for your letter of June 27 which Comrade Gerta Gordon brought me. I will do everything I can to help Comrade Gordon.

"We are all delighted that you, Comrade Mehring and other 'Spartacist comrades' in Germany are 'with us heart and soul.' This makes us confident that the best elements of the West-European working-class, despite all difficulties, will come to our aid.

"We here are now experiencing what are perhaps the most difficult weeks of the whole revolution. The class struggle and the civil war have penetrated into the depths of the population: everywhere in the countryside there is a cleavage—the poor are for us, the kulaks are furiously against us. The Entente has bought the Czechoslovaks, the counter-revolutionary revolt is raging, and the whole bourgeoisie is making every effort to overthrow us. Nevertheless, we firmly believe that we shall avoid this 'customary' (as in 1794 and 1849) outcome of the revolution and defeat the bourgeoisie.

"My sincerest greetings, gratefully yours

Lenin"

(*Works,* Vol. 35, p. 282).

To this was added a postscript:

"The new state seal has just been brought to me. Here is an impress. It reads: Russian Socialist Federative Soviet Republic. Workers of all countries, unite!"

The counter-revolutionary revolt continued to rage unabated. The Czechoslovaks captured Kazan, the Anglo-French troops took Arkhangelsk, where a Socialist-Revolutionary Supreme Government of the Northern Region was formed. In Izhevsk the S.-R's launched a revolt; the Izhevsk Right S.-R. troops occupied Sarapul; the Soviet troops abandoned Chita; the Volunteer Army took Ekaterinodar, but the failure of the Moscow and Yaroslavl uprisings caused some vacillation in the ranks of the Socialist-Revolutionaries. The fighting between the Germans and the Allies, which started with renewed force, diverted their attention from Russia. On August 16 the Czechoslovaks were defeated on the River Belaya. The consolidation of all our armed forces began to take shape; a number of important organizational measures was taken, and decrees were issued enlisting the workers' organizations to the business of grain purveyance and providing for the organization of harvesting and stop-the-way detachments—the grain situation had somewhat improved and the closing down of the bourgeois newspapers had put a stop to public excitation. Agitation against intervention was increased among the foreign workers. On August 9 the Commissariat of Foreign Affairs made an offer of peace with the Allied powers to the Government of the United States.

Feeling that the ground was being cut away from under their feet, the Right Socialist-Revolutionaries decided to assassinate a number of Bolshevik leaders, Lenin among them.

On August 30 Petrograd reported to Ilyich that Uritsky, the head of the Petrograd Cheka, had been assassinated at 10 a.m.

That evening Ilyich, at the request of the Moscow Committee, was to address meetings in the Basmanny and Zamoskvoretsky districts.

479

Bukharin had been dining with us that day, and during the meal he had kept urging Ilyich not to go. Ilyich had dismissed his fears with a laugh, and, then, in order to have done with the subject, he said that he probably would not go. Maria Ilyinichna had been feeling unwell that day and kept indoors. Ilyich came in to see her dressed for going out, and she started asking him to take her with him. "On no account. You stay at home," he said, and went off to the meeting without taking any guard with him.

We were having a conference on education in the building of the Second Moscow State University. Two days before that Ilyich had spoken there. The conference was drawing to a close and I was making ready to go home. I had promised to give a lift to a school-teacher acquaintance of mine, who lived in the Zamoskvoretsky District. A Kremlin car was waiting for me outside, but the chauffeur was a stranger to me. He drove us to the Kremlin, but I told him to take our passenger home first; the chauffeur did not say anything, but on reaching the Kremlin he stopped the car and made my companion get out. I was surprised at the high-handed way he carried things and was going to give him a piece of my mind, when we drove up to our entrance in the C.E.C. courtyard, where Gil, our chauffeur, who always drove us in the car, met me outside. He began telling me that he had driven Ilyich to the Michelson Works and a woman there had shot at Ilyich and wounded him slightly. Obviously, he was trying to break the news to me gently. He looked very upset. "Tell me—is he alive or not?" I demanded. Gil said he was, and I ran inside. Our apartment was crowded; strange-looking overcoats hung on the hall-stand, and the doors were all wide open. Next to the hall-stand stood Sverdlov, looking grave and grim. Glancing at him, I decided that it was all over. "What are we going to do?" was all I could say. "It's all been arranged with Ilyich," he said. My worst fears are confirmed, I thought. I had to pass through a small room, but it seemed an eternity to me. I entered our bedroom. Ilyich's bed had been moved into the middle of the room, and he was lying on it with a bloodless face. Seeing me, he said in a low voice after a minute's pause. "You've come, you must be tired. Go and lie down." The words were irrelevant, but his eyes said something quite different: "This is the end." I went out of the room so as not to upset him, and stood in the doorway so that I could see him without being seen myself. When I was in the room I hadn't noticed who was there, but now I saw Lunacharsky in there—he had either just gone in or had been in there before. He was standing at Ilyich's bedside looking down at him with frightened piteous eyes. Ilyich said to him: "What's there to look at."

Our apartment was like a camp. Vera Bonch-Bruyevich and Vera Krestinskaya—both of them doctors—were fussing around the sick man. A dressing-station had been fixed up in the small room adjoining the bedroom, inhalation bags had been brought, medical assistants sent for, and all kinds of phials, and solutions, and cotton wool had appeared.

Our temporary domestic help, a Lettish woman, was so frightened that she locked herself up in her room. Someone got busy in the kitchen lighting the oil-stove, and Comrade Kizas rinsed blood-stained dressings and towels in the bath tub. The sight of her reminded me of the first nights of the October Revolution at Smolny, when she had sat up for nights without getting a wink of sleep, going through the telegrams that had come pouring in from all sides.

At last the surgeons arrived—Vladimir Rozanov, Mints and others. There was no doubt about it—Ilyich's condition was dangerous, his life hung by a thread. When Gil, together with some other comrades from the Michelson Works, had brought him to the Kremlin and wanted to carry him in, Ilyich would not let them. He had walked up to the second floor by himself. Blood flooded his lung. The doctors also feared a puncture of the gullet, and forbade him to drink anything. He suffered from thirst. Shortly after the doctors had gone, leaving a hospital nurse with him, he asked the nurse to go out and call me in. When I came in Ilyich was silent for a while, then said: "Fetch me a glass of tea, will you." "Didn't the doctors say you were not to drink anything," I answered. The trick had not worked. Ilyich shut his eyes, saying: "All right, you can go." Maria Ilyinichna was busy with the doctors. I stood by the door. I went to Ilyich's private office at the end of the corridor three times during the night—Sverdlov and other comrades sat up all night there on chairs.

The attempt on Vladimir Ilyich upset not only all the Party organizations, but the broad masses of the workers, peasants and Red Army men. What Lenin meant for the revolution was suddenly brought home to them with special force. The press bulletins concerning his condition were followed with anxiety.

On the evening of August 30 a statement was issued by the Party over Sverdlov's signature concerning the attempt on Lenin's life. It said: "The working class will respond to attempts against its leaders by rallying its forces and by a ruthless mass terror against all the enemies of the revolution."

The attempted assassination of Lenin made the working class close its ranks and work still harder.

The Party of the Socialist-Revolutionaries began to break up.

The day after the attempt on Lenin, a statement was published in the newspapers by their Moscow Bureau saying that the Socialist-Revolutionary Party was not privy to the crime. Already after the July revolt of the Left S.-R.'s its members had begun to withdraw from the party, especially workers. A section of the party calling itself *Narodnik*-Communists had split away. This section, headed by Kolegayev, Bitsenko, A. Ustinov and others, had been opposed to violent action against the peace of Brest, to acts of terrorism, or to active struggle against the Communist Party. The remaining membership had tended still more rightward and supported the kulak revolts, but their influence was on the wane. The attempt on Lenin intensified this process of disintegration in the Socialist-Revolutionary Party and undermined its influence among the masses still more.

The hopes of the enemies of the Soviet Government were dashed. Ilyich pulled through. The doctors' reports grew more optimistic day by day. They and everyone else who surrounded Ilyich cheered up. Ilyich cracked jokes with them. He was forbidden to move about, but on the quiet, when there was nobody in the room, he tried to sit up. He was eager to get back into harness. At last, on September 10, *Pravda* reported him to be out of danger, and added a note from him to the effect that he was convalescing and asked people to stop bothering the doctors with phone calls enquiring about his health. On September 16, Ilyich was permitted to attend the Council of People's Commissars. He was so excited and nervous that he could hardly stand on getting out of bed, but he was glad to be able to get back to work at last.

On September 16, Ilyich presided over a meeting of the Council of People's Commissars. Later in the day he wrote a message of greeting to the Conference of Proletkult Organizations. The Proletkult was a great influence in those days. A shortcoming of the Proletkult, in Ilyich's opinion, was that its work was insufficiently linked with the general political tasks of the struggle, that it did not do enough towards stimulating the consciousness of the mass, advancing workers to the fore, and preparing them for administration of the state through the medium of the Soviets. In his message of greeting to the conference he made it a point of mentioning the political tasks that confronted Proletkult. Another article written by him a couple of days later was "On the Character of Our Newspapers" in which he urged the newspapers to have a keener eye for what was taking place around them. "Closer to life. More attention to the way the mass of the workers and peasants are *in deeds* building something *new* in their everyday work. More verification of the fact to what extent this new is communistic." (*Works*, Vol. 28, p. 80.)

Vladimir Ilyich started work by coming straight to grips with the food problem. He took an active part in drafting the decree introducing the tax in kind for farmers. However, he quickly realized that this daily round of intensive administrative work was too much for him, and he consented to take a fortnight's holiday in the country. He was taken to Gorki, the former country house of Reinbot, ex-governor of Moscow. It was a fine house with verandas, a bathroom, and electric lighting, richly furnished, and standing in an excellent park. The ground floor was occupied by the guards—until the attempt on his life this matter of a bodyguard had been very haphazard. Ilyich was unused to it, and the guards themselves had but a faint idea of what they were supposed to do. They greeted Ilyich with a speech of welcome and a big bunch of flowers. Both the guards and Ilyich felt exquisitely embarrassed. The surroundings, too, were new and strange to us. We had been accustomed to living in humble dwellings, in inexpensive rooms or cheap boarding-houses abroad, and here, in these rich chambers, we did not know what to do with ourselves. We chose the smallest room to live in—Ilyich died in that room six years later. But even that small room had three large plate-glass windows and three cheval-glasses. It was some time before we got used to the house. The guards took time fitting themselves into it too. I remember the following incident. It was the end of September, and getting rather cold. The large room adjoining the one we had moved into had two fireplaces in it. We had got used to fireplaces in London, where in most of the houses it is the only form of heating. "Light the fire, will you," Ilyich said. The guard fetched some wood and began looking round for the chimney pipe, but there wasn't any. Well, thought the guards, maybe these foreign fireplaces don't have chimneys. They lit the fire. But that fireplace proved to be there merely for decoration, and was not made to be heated. A fire started in the garret, and had to be put out with water, as a result of which part of the ceiling plaster came down. Gorki afterwards became Ilyich's regular summer haunt. By that time the place had been properly "mastered" for the purpose of relaxation and work. Ilyich took a liking to the balconies and the big windows.

He was rather weak after his illness and it was quite a time before he felt strong enough to go outside the grounds. He was in high spirits, what with the sense of recovering health and the realization that a turning point had been reached in the whole situation. Things at the front were beginning to look up. The Red Army was winning. On September 3 the workers in Kazan rose against the Czechoslovaks and the Right Socialist-Revolutionaries, who had seized the power. On the 7th the Soviet troops took Kazan, on the 12th Volsk and Simbirsk, on the 17th Khvalynsk, on the 20th Chistopol, and on October 7 Samara. On September 9 the Soviet troops occupied Grozny and Uralsk. Obviously, things had taken a turn for the better. On the anniversary of the Soviet power Lenin rightfully remarked in his speech that the scattered detachments of the Red Guard had now been moulded into a strong Red Army.

We received regular reports at Gorki testifying that the revolution in Germany was gathering head.

On October 1 Ilyich wrote to Sverdlov in Moscow:

"Things have so 'accelerated' in Germany that we must not lag behind. And that is what we are doing.

"*Tomorrow* a joint meeting must be called of

    The Central Executive Committee

    The Moscow Soviet

    The district Soviets

    The trade unions, etc., etc.

"A number of reports should be made on *the beginning of the revolution in Germany.*

"(The victory of *our* tactics of struggle against German imperialism, and so forth.)

"Adopt a resolution

"The international revolution has approached *in a week* to within such a distance that it is to be reckoned with as an event of the *immediate future.*

"No alliances either with the Government of Wilhelm or the Government of Wilhelm+Ebert and other scoundrels.

"As for the German working-class masses, the German toiling millions, when they started with their spirit of protest (so far *only* spirit),

we are beginning to prepare for them a brotherly alliance, **grain**, military aid.

"We shall all give our lives to help the German workers in pushing forward with the revolution which has started in Germany.

"Deductions:

1) Ten times more effort in procuring grain (sweep up *all* stocks both for ourselves and *for the German* workers).

2) Ten times more *enrolment* in the army.

We must have an army of 3 millions *by the spring* to help the international workers' revolution.

"This resolution to be telegraphed over the whole world Wednesday night.

"Fix the meeting for 2 p.m. on Wednesday. We shall start at 4. Give me the floor for a 15-minute speech. I shall come down and go back again. Send the car for me tomorrow morning (and tell me on the phone that you *agree*).

"Greetings,

Lenin"
(*Works*, Vol. 35, pp. 301-02).

This consent was not given, despite Ilyich's earnest request. His health was a matter of great concern. The joint meeting was due to be held on Thursday, the 3rd, and on Wednesday, the 2nd, Ilyich wrote a letter to the meeting. The joint meeting heard the letter and adopted a resolution along the lines suggested by Lenin. This resolution was promulgated by telegraph to all countries and throughout Soviet Russia and published the next day in *Pravda*.

Ilyich knew that no car would be sent for him, yet he sat by the roadside that day, waiting for it. "You could never tell!"

Unrest was growing among the German workers. Lenin always attached tremendous importance to the theoretical struggle, to the clarity of theoretical positions. He knew that Kautsky, who had written a number of works popularizing the doctrine of Marx and had criticized the opportunist views of Bernstein, enjoyed considerable prestige in Germany, and was therefore all the more upset and shocked at the extracts from Kautsky's article against Bolshevism published in *Pravda* on September 20. He wrote immediately to Vorovsky, who was living in Switzerland at the time, where he acted as the official representative of Soviet Russia, to the effect that Zetkin, Mehring and the others ought to publish a statement on theoretical principles making it clear that on the questions of dictatorship Kautsky was presenting the case of vulgar Bernsteinism, not Marxism. Ilyich wrote that it was necessary to have his booklet *The State and Revolution*, in which he deals with Kautsky's reformist platform, translated into German as soon as possible, and asked that a copy of Kautsky's pamphlet *The Dictatorship of the Proletariat* should be sent to him as soon as it came out, and that all Kautsky's articles on Bolshevism should be sent to him.

During his rest at Gorki, Ilyich undertook the task of exposing Kautsky. The result was his pamphlet *The Proletarian Revolution and the Renegade Kautsky*. Its last lines were written on November 9, 1918. It ends with the words:

"That same night news was received from Germany announcing the beginning of a victorious revolution, first in Kiel and other northern towns and ports, where the power has passed into the hands of Soviets of Workers' and Soldiers' Deputies, then in Berlin, where, too, power has passed into the hands of a Soviet.

"The conclusion which still remained to be written to my pamphlet on Kautsky and on the proletarian revolution is now superfluous."

On October 18 Ilyich had returned to Moscow. On the 23 he wrote to our ambassador in Berlin:

"Convey immediately our most ardent greetings to Karl Liebknecht. The liberation of the imprisoned representatives of the revolutionary workers of Germany is a sign of the new epoch, the epoch of victorious socialism which is now being ushered in both for Germany and the whole world.

"On behalf of the Central Committee of the Russian Communist Party (Bolsheviks)

"Lenin Sverdlov Stalin."

On October 23 when Karl Liebknecht was released from prison, the workers held a demonstration outside the Russian Embassy.

On November 5, 1918, the German Government accused the Soviet representatives in Berlin of having taken part in the revolutionary movement in Germany, and demanded that the diplomatic and consular representatives of Soviet Russia headed by the Soviet Ambassador Ioffe should leave the country immediately. On November 9, Ioffe, who was on his way back to Russia with the embassy staff, was returned to revolutionary Berlin by the Berlin Soviet of Workers' and Soldiers' Deputies.

The first anniversary of the Soviet power was celebrated in a spirit of elation. Towards the end of October Ilyich took part in the drafting of an appeal to the Austrian workers in the name of the Central Executive Committee and the Council of People's Commissars, and on November 3 he addressed a demonstration held in honour of the Austro-Hungarian revolution. It was decided to hold the Sixth All-Russian Congress of Soviets during the anniversary days. The congress opened on November 6 with a speech by Ilyich "On the Anniversary of the Proletarian Revolution." Later in the day he made a speech at the ceremonial meeting of the All-Russian Central and Moscow Councils of Trade Unions, and at the evening ceremony of the Moscow Proletkult. On the 7th he spoke at the unveiling of the memorial plaque to the fighters of the October Revolution.

On the 7th Ilyich unveiled the Marx and Engels monument and spoke about the importance of their teachings, their foresight:

"We are living in happy times, when this prophecy of the great Socialists is beginning to be realized. We see the dawn of the international socialist revolution of the proletariat breaking in a number of countries. The unspeakable horrors of the imperialist butchery of nations are everywhere evoking a heroic rise of the oppressed masses, and are lending them tenfold strength in the struggle for emancipation.

"Let the memorials to Marx and Engels again and again remind the millions of workers and peasants that we are not alone in our struggle. Side by side with us the workers of more advanced countries are rising. Stern battles still await them and us. In common struggle the yoke of capital will be broken, and socialism will be finally won!" (*Works*, Vol. 28, pp. 146-47.)

On November 8, 9, 10 and 11 Ilyich was completely carried away by the news of the German revolution. He was continuously addressing meetings. His face beamed with joy, as it had beamed on May 1, 1917. The days of the first October anniversary were the happiest days in his life,

Never for a moment, however, did Ilyich forget what a difficult path still lay ahead of the Soviet power. On November 8 he addressed a conference of the peasant poor of the Moscow Region.

The delegates gathered at the Moscow Conference of the Poor Peasants' Committees looked pleased. One tall delegate, dressed in a blue caftan, stopped before the bust of a scientist as he was going upstairs, and remarked with a smile: "We could do with that in the village." The delegates spoke mostly about what they would take and how they would share it among themselves. Ilyich spoke to an audience of poor individual farmers for whom the questions of collectivization of agriculture, the collective cultivation of the land were not a pressing problem. Comparing the temper among the delegates of the Poor Peasants' Committees with that of the delegates to the Second Congress of Collective Farmers, one is amazed at the progress that has been made, the tremendous task that has been achieved.

Ilyich realized that this was going to be a long job. He clearly saw all the difficulties, but considered it a decisive issue. "The conquest of the land, as every other conquest by the working people, is only secure when it rests on the activity of the working people themselves, on their own organization, their determination and revolutionary steadfastness.

"Did the toiling peasantry have such an organization?

"Unfortunately, they did not, and therein lies the root cause of all the struggle's difficulty." (*Works*, Vol. 28, p. 153.)

Ilyich indicated the path of organization. It was to get the upper hand of the kulaks and to join forces with the working class.

"... If the kulak is left intact, if we do not get the better of those blood-suckers, we shall inevitably have the tsar and the capitalist back again.

"The experience of all the revolutions that have so far

occurred in Europe strikingly proves that the revolution inevitably suffers defeat unless the peasantry gets the upper hand of the kulaks.

"All European revolutions ended in naught precisely because the countryside failed to get the better of its enemies. The workers in the towns overthrew the tsars—yet after a while the old order of things was re-established." (*Ibid.*, p. 153.)

"In former revolutions the poor peasants had nowhere to turn for support in their difficult struggle against the kulaks.

"The organized proletariat—which is stronger and more experienced than the peasantry (it gained that experience in earlier struggles)—is now in power in Russia and is in possession of all the means of production, the mills, the factories, the railways, ships, etc.

"The poor peasants now possess a reliable and powerful ally in their struggle against the kulaks. The poor peasants know that the city is behind them, that the proletariat will help them, is in fact already helping them with every means in its power." (*Ibid.*, p. 154.)

"The kulaks awaited the Czechoslovaks impatiently. They would most willingly have enthroned a new tsar, in order to continue their exploitation with impunity, in order to continue to dominate the farm labourer and to continue to grow rich.

"And salvation was wholly due to the fact that the village united with the city, that the proletarian and semi-proletarian elements of the countryside (*i.e.*, those who do not employ the labour of others) started a campaign against the kulaks and the parasites together with the city workers." (*Ibid.*, p. 155.)

Ilyich goes on to outline the prospects of reorganizing the whole system of rural life.

"The solution lies only in social cultivation of the land.... Salvation from the disadvantages of small-scale farming lies in communes, cultivation by artels, or peasant associations. That is the way to raise and improve agriculture, to economize forces and to combat the kulaks, parasites and exploiters." (*Ibid.*, p. 156.)

November 16, 1918, saw the opening of the First All-Russian Congress of Women Workers, held under the auspices of the Committee of the C.C. of the Russian Communist Party (Bolsheviks) for Agitation and Propaganda Among the Women Workers. Inessa Armand, Samoilova, Kollontai, Staël, and A. D. Kalinina worked hard on the organization of this congress. It was attended by 1,147 delegates. It was a congress of women workers only, and no peasant women were present—we had not got to that yet. Neither was the question of the work among the national minorities raised at that congress. In his speech at the congress, however, Ilyich spoke of what was uppermost in his mind, namely, of the village and of how women could be emancipated only under socialism. "Only when we shall pass from small household economy to social economy and to social tilling of the soil," said Ilyich, "will women be fully free and emancipated. It is a difficult task. Committees of Poor Peasants are now being formed, and the time is at hand when the socialist revolution will be consolidated.

"It is only now that the poorer section of the population in the villages is organizing, and in these organizations of the poor peasants socialism is acquiring a firm foundation.

"It has often happened before that the cities became revolutionary and the countryside took action afterwards.

"The present revolution has the countryside to rely on, and therein is its significance and strength." (*Ibid.*, p. 161.)

In every speech he made, Ilyich spoke about the peasantry and the collectivization of the land. In conversation and during our walks he often touched on the subject of Karl Marx's letter to F. Engels in 1856, in which Marx wrote: "The whole thing in Germany will depend on the possibility of backing the proletarian revolution by some second edition of the Peasant War. Then the affair will be splendid...."*

Addressing the First All-Russian Congress of Land Departments on December 11, 1918, Lenin said:

"It is impossible to live in the old way, in the way we lived before the war. And the waste of human toil and effort associated with individual, small-scale peasant production can no longer be tolerated. The productivity of labour would be doubled or trebled, the economy of human labour in agriculture and human production would be doubled and trebled, if a transition were made from this disunited, small-scale production to social production. (*Works*, Vol. 28, p. 319.)

While living in Switzerland I had suffered from a serious form of goitre. An operation and mountain air had checked the disease to some extent, but its aftereffects had told on my heart and undermined my strength. After the attempt on Ilyich's life, the shock of it and the worry over his health caused a serious relapse in my own condition in the autumn. The doctors kept me in bed, gave me all kinds of medicines, and forbade me to work, but it didn't help. There were no nursing homes in those days. I was sent to a forest school at Sokolniki, where all talk about politics and work was taboo. I made friends there with the children, and Ilyich visited me almost every evening, in most cases with Maria Ilyinichna. I lay there during the end of December 1918 and January 1919. The children very soon came to regard me as a close friend and told me about everything that agitated their minds. Some showed me their drawings, others told be how they had gone skiing; a nine-year-old boy was grieved that there was no one to cook dinner for his mother; usually he had done it. He cooked a soup from potatoes, and "fried" potatoes in water; when his mother came home

---

* K. Marx, F. Engels, *Selected Correspondence*, Moscow, p. 111, —*Ed.*

from work she would find dinner ready, waiting for her. There was a little girl at the forest school who had been transferred there from an orphanage. She had picked up some typical habits there, such as worming herself into the good graces of the strict teacher, and telling lies. She had a mother, a prostitute, who lived at Smolensky Market. The mother and daughter were passionately fond of each other. Once the girl told me with tears in her eyes that her mother had come to see her in freezing cold weather with almost nothing on her feet; her lover had stolen her boots and sold them to buy drinks, and her mother had frozen her feet. The girl was always thinking about her mother; she did not eat her bread rations, and put them away for her mother; after dinner she would hunt about for crusts, and if any were left over, would collect them for her mother.

Many of the children told me about their lives. The school had little to do with real life. In the morning the pupils had their lessons, then they went out skiing, and in the evening they made fir-tree decorations.

Ilyich often joked with the children. They became very fond of him, and looked forward to his coming. At the beginning of 1919 (Old-Style Christmas) the school arranged a fir-tree party for the children. With us in Russia the Christmas tree was never associated with any religious rites; it was just an evening party to amuse the children. The children invited Ilyich to the party. He promised to come. He asked Bonch-Bruyevich to buy as many presents as he could for the children. On his way to me that evening with Maria Ilyinichna, his car was held up by bandits. The latter were taken aback when they learned who it was they had attacked. They made Ilyich, Maria Ilyinichna, the chauffeur Gil and Ilyich's bodyguard—whose hands had been engaged holding a jug of milk—get out of the car and drove away in it. At the forest school we were all waiting for Ilyich and Maria Ilyinichna and wondering why they were so late. When they reached the school at last they looked rather queer. Afterwards, in the passage, I asked Ilyich what the matter was. He hesitated for a moment for fear of upsetting me, then we went into my room and he told me all about it.

I was glad that he was safe and sound.

1919

The year 191? was a year of sharp civil war against Kolchak, Deniki₁₁ and Yudenich. The fight was conducted under extremely dificult conditions of famine and widespread economic ruin. Factories and mills were at a standstill, and the railways were completely disorganized. The Red Army was not properly organized yet and was poorly armed. In many places the Soviet power was not properly established yet, and had not identified itself with the population. Parties hostile to the Soviet power, all those elements who had lived in clover under the old regime—the servants of the landowners and capitalists, the kulaks, tradesmen, etc.—carried on a furious agitation against the Bolsheviks, and played on the ignorance and lack of information among the peasant mass to spread all kinds of cock-and-bull stories among them.

Lenin's name, however, already enjoyed great prestige everywhere. Lenin was against the landowners and the capitalists. Lenin stood for the land, for peace. Everyone knew that Lenin was the leader of the struggle for the power of the Soviets. The masses knew that in every out-of-the-way corner of the country. But Lenin took no direct part in the fighting, he was not at the fronts, and it was difficult for illiterate people in those days, people whose outlook was limited by the secluded life they led, to imagine how anyone could effect leadership at a distance. And so legends grew up around the name of Lenin. The fishermen of Lake Baikal in far-away Siberia, for instance, related about ten years ago, how at the height of a battle with the Whites, Ilyich had come flying up in an airplane

495

and helped them to overcome the enemy. In the North Caucasus people said that although they had not seen Lenin, they knew for certain that he had fought there in the ranks of the Red Army, only he had done so secretly, so that nobody knew, and had helped them to gain a victory.

Today the workers and collective farmers know that although Ilyich had not been at the fronts, he had been with the Red Army all the time heart and soul, he had always been thinking about it, caring for it. They know how hard he had been working to direct the policy into the right channels. He was Chairman of the Council of People's Commissars; his activities were varied, but whatever form they took, they were intimately bound up with the questions of the civil war, the questions of the struggle for the power of the Soviets. On March 13, 1919, Ilyich addressed a meeting in Petrograd at which he spoke about the successes and difficulties facing the Soviet power.

"For the first time in history an army is being built on closeness, on inseparable closeness, one might say, *inseparable unity between the Soviets and the army.* (My italics.—*N.K.*) The Soviets unite all the working people and the exploited—and the army is built up on the principle of socialist defence and class-consciousness." (*Works*, Vol. 29, p. 47.)

This unity of interests was expressed in a thousand little ways. The Soviet Government was the Red Army man's own familiar government.

Ilyich liked to sleep with the windows open. Every morning the singing of the Red Army men, who lived in the Kremlin, would burst into the room from outside. "We shall die to a man for the power of the Soviets," sang the young voices.

Ilyich knew perfectly well what was going on at the fronts. He was in direct touch with the fronts and headed the whole struggle, while at the same time he lent an attentive ear to what the masses were saying about the war. I was sometimes present during Ilyich's talks with

Making notes at a session of Third Congress, Communist International,
Moscow, June-July 1921

In Kremlin study with Parley P. Christensen, Presidential candidate of the Farmer-Labor Party in the U.S. elections of 1920, when he got nearly a million votes

different people, and I noticed how good he was at drawing them out on subjects that interested him. And he was interested in the whole situation, in everything that went on at the fronts.

I remember being present at a report made to Ilyich concerning the mistrust towards the old military specialists on the part of the Red Army men. At the beginning we had been obliged to take lessons from the old military specialists—that much, the Red Army men understood, but they regarded them nevertheless with suspicion and were intolerant of even their petty faults. This was understandable when one remembers what a gulf there had been between the commanding officers and the soldiers under the old regime. After the man who had made the report had gone, Ilyich spoke to me about the strength of the Red Army lying in the fact that its commanders stood so close to the mass of the soldiers. We were reminded of Vereshchagin's pictures portraying the war with Turkey in 1877-1878. They were fine paintings. He has one battle scene in which the commanding officers are shown standing on a mound, watching the battle from afar. Spruce officers in gloves watch the soldiers dying in battle through binoculars, themselves standing at a safe distance. I first saw this picture when I was ten. My father had taken me to the exhibition of Vereshchagin's paintings, and his pictures had burned themselves into my memory for a lifetime.

Ilyich once received a letter from Professor Dukelsky, in Voronezh, who demanded comradely treatment of specialists on the part of the Red Army men. Ilyich answered him with an article in *Pravda*, in which he said:

"Show a comradely attitude towards the exhausted soldiers, the tired-out workers, embittered by centuries of exploitation, and then the rapprochement between the workers of physical and mental work will advance in gigantic strides." (*Ibid.*, p. 207.)

I was once present during Lunacharsky's report to Ilyich after a visit of his to the front. Lunacharsky, of course, was no great specialist in military matters, but Ilyich kept asking him such questions, kept linking together a number of seemingly unrelated facts and steered the speaker skilfully into such channels, that it turned out to be a report of absorbing interest. Ilyich always knew what to ask this or that person and how to get the information he wanted from him. He talked with many workers going to or coming from the front. Ilyich had a good idea of the face of the Red Army, he knew that most of the Red Army men were peasants. He knew the peasantry well, knew how the toiling peasantry had been exploited by the landowners, how they hated the landowners, and what a tremendous motive force it was in the civil war. He did not idealize the individual farmer, though (and the peasants in those days were all individual farmers); he knew how strong and tenacious the petty-bourgeois mentality was among the peasantry, how difficult it was for the peasants to organize, how helpless, in fact, the peasant was in those days in the matter of organization.

The crux of socialist construction is organization, Ilyich never tired of repeating. He attached tremendous importance to questions of organization, and set his hopes on the working class, on its organizing experience, its close ties with the peasantry. Ilyich demanded that the entire experience of the old army and the old specialists should be mastered, he demanded that knowledge and science should be placed at the service of the working people of the Soviet Republic.

The policy of the Soviet Government was directed the right way.

In his interview with the first American labour delegation in September 1927, Stalin said:

"Is it not known that the outcome of the civil war was that the armies of occupation were driven from Russia and the counter-revolutionary generals were wiped out by the Red Army?

"It turned out that the *fate of a war is decided in the last analysis* not by technical equipment, with which Kolchak and Denikin were plentifully supplied by the enemies of the U.S.S.R., but *by a correct policy, by the sympathy and support of the vast masses of the population.* (My italics.—*N.K.*)

"Was it an accident that the Bolshevik Party proved victorious then? Of course not."*

The policy of the Soviet Government in 1919 was directed towards strengthening the ties with the masses.

"If we call ourselves a Party of Communists," said Ilyich, "we should realize that only now, when we have finished with external obstacles and scrapped the old institutions does the first task of a real proletarian revolution—that of organizing dozens and hundreds of millions of people—face us actually and fully for the first time." (*Works*, Vol. 29, p. 310.)

At the Second All-Russian Congress of Soviets in October 1917 Ilyich said that the crux of socialist construction was organization, and seventeen months later, in March 1919, at the time of the Eighth Congress of the Party, when the Soviet power was securely on its feet, the problems of organization loomed large. All the questions which Ilyich dealt with at the Eighth Congress were closely linked with the problems of organization. He spoke about office staffs, about bureaucracy and culture, about how the lack of culture stood in the way of socialist construction, prevented the broad masses from being drawn into socialist construction, hampered the fight against survivals of the past and interfered with the rooting up of bureaucracy; he spoke about the village, about strengthening the influence of the proletariat not only upon the rural workers and the poor, but upon the broadest sections of the peasantry, the middle peasants, who lived by their own labour without exploiting hired labour;

---

* J. V. Stalin. *Works*, Vol. 10, Moscow, 1954, p. 111.—*Ed.*

he said that they had to be made the mainstay of the Soviet power, that they had to be catered to in the matter of supply; he spoke about the cooperative movement, and said that communism should be built out of what capitalism had left us as a legacy, that communism could not be built up with the hands of the Communists alone, that the old specialists, science, the whole experience of bourgeois construction had to be made use of for our own purposes.

The important thing in all this work was for people to know not only what link had to be grasped in order to pull out the whole chain, but *how* that link had to be grasped, how the chain was to be pulled out.

Two days before the congress Yakov Sverdlov, the Chairman of the All-Russian Central Executive Committee, died. In his speech at Sverdlov's funeral, Ilyich spoke about his ability to link theory with practice, about his moral prestige and organizing talent, laying special stress on the value of his work as an *organizer of the broad proletarian masses*:

"... This professional revolutionary never for a moment lost touch with the masses. Although the conditions of tsarism necessitated his working chiefly underground, illegally, as did most of the revolutionaries at that time, Comrade Sverdlov managed even then, in his underground and illegal activity, to march shoulder to shoulder and hand in hand with the advanced workers, who already from the beginning of the twentieth century began to take the place of the previous generation of revolutionaries from amongst the intelligentsia.

"It was at that time that the advanced workers came into the job by the dozen and the hundred and cultivated in themselves that hard tempering in the revolutionary struggle combined with the closest contact with the masses without which the revolution of the proletariat in Russia could not have succeeded." (*Works*, Vol. 29, p. 72.)

At the Eighth Congress of the Party Sverdlov was to have made a report on the organizational work of the

Central Committee. This report was made instead by Lenin.

Speaking of Sverdlov, Ilyich said:

"'Possessing as he did a vast, an incredibly vast memory, he kept in it the greater part of his report, and *his personal acquaintance with the work of organization locally* (my italics—*N.K.*) would have enabled him to make this report. I am unable to replace him even in one-hundredth degree ... dozens of delegates were received by Comrade Sverdlov daily and more than half of them were probably not Soviet officials but Party workers." (*Ibid.*, p. 140.)

Ilyich spoke about Sverdlov having been an excellent judge of people with a remarkable flair for practical matters:

"It is to the remarkable organizing talent of this man that we owe what we have so far taken such legitimate pride in. It is to him we owe the possibility of efficient, expedient and really organized teamwork, the kind of work that would be worthy of the organized proletarian masses and meet the needs of the proletarian revolution—that organized teamwork without which we could not have scored a single success, without which we would not have overcome a single one of those innumerable difficulties, a single one of those painful trials through which we have already passed and are now obliged to pass.

"...We are profoundly convinced that the proletarian revolution in Russia and throughout the world will bring to the fore groups and groups of people, numerous layers of the proletarians and the toiling peasantry, who will provide that practical experience, that *collective*, if not individual, *organizing talent* (my italics—*N.K.*) without which the many-millioned armies of proletarians would not be able to achieve victory." (*Ibid.*, pp. 73, 75.)

In recent years, especially in 1935-1936, we are witnessing a remarkable and rapid growth in the *organizing talent of the masses*. The conferences of Stakhanovites, combine operators, tractor drivers, Soviet land workers, and workers of the Soviet republics afford us an example of this collective organizing genius which has been developed during the period of Soviet Government.

We are not mere units, we are thousands. . . .

None but a blind man could fail to grasp what a tremendous power the collective organizing genius of the proletarian masses represents.

* * *

The mentality of the petty proprietor was a special obstacle to the organization of administrative and army work during the early years of the Soviet Government's existence.

At the First All-Russian Congress on Extra-School Education in May 1919 Ilyich spoke at some length on the question of this petty-proprietor anarchic mentality, which hampered the proper organization of work.

"The broad masses of the petty-bourgeois working population, while striving towards knowledge and smashing up the old, could introduce nothing of organized or organizing value." (My italics—N.K.)

And further:

"We are still suffering in this respect from muzhik naïveté and muzhik helplessness, like that peasant, who, after robbing the master's library, ran home, fearing that someone would take it away from him, because the idea that there could be a correct distribution, that the public chest is not something hateful, but the common property of the workers and the toiling population—that consciousness was still lacking in him. The undeveloped peasant mass is not to blame for this, and from the point of view of the development of the revolution this is quite legitimate—it is an inevitable phase, and when the peasant took the library home and kept it there in secret, he could not act otherwise, because he did not understand that the libraries of Russia could be joined together, that there would be enough books to gratify the thirst of the literate and teach the illiterate. Now we must combat the survivals of disorganization, chaos and ridiculous departmental disputes ... not set up parallel organizations, but create a single planned organization. In this small job is reflected the basic task of our revolution. If it fails to solve this task, if it will not emerge upon the path of creating a really planned united organization in place of Russian muddle-headed chaos and absurdity, that revolution will then remain a bourgeois revolution, for the basic characteristic of a proletarian revolution heading for communism consists precisely in this." (*Works*, Vol. 29, pp. 308, 309-10.)

Ilyich here revealed the roots of anarchism, which denies all planned collective effort, all forms of state organization, on the principle of "I do as I please."

Ilyich and I often talked about anarchism. I remember our first conversation on that subject at Shushenskoye. On joining Ilyich in Siberian exile, I examined with interest his album containing photographs of political convicts. Between two photographs of Chernyshevsky, I saw one of Zola. I asked him why he kept a photograph of Zola in his album. He began telling me about Dreyfus, whom Zola had defended, then we began comparing notes about Zola's books, and I told him what a deep impression his novel *Germinal* had made upon me—I had first read it when I was deep in study of the first volume of Marx's *Capital*. *Germinal* describes the French labour movement and contains, among others, the figure of a Russian Anarchist Suvarine, who strokes a pet rabbit while at the same time repeating that everything should be "smashed and destroyed" (*tout rompre, tout dètruire*). Ilyich had spoken warmly about the differences between an organized socialist labour movement and anarchism. I dimly recollect another talk with Ilyich on the same subject of the Anarchists on the eve of his departure to attend the Tammerfors Conference in 1905. I have recently reread Ilyich's article "Socialism and Anarchism," relating to that period, in which he gives an excellent characterization of anarchism: "The philosophy of the Anarchists is bourgeois philosophy turned inside out. Their individualistic theories and their individualistic ideals are the very antithesis of socialism. Their views express, not the future of bourgeois society, which is irresistibly heading towards the socialization of labour, but the present and even the past of that society, the domination of blind chance over the scattered, isolated small producer. Their tactics, which amount to the negation of the political struggle, disunite the proletarians and in fact convert them into passive participants of one or another set of bourgeois politics; because it is impossible for the workers really to detach themselves from politics." (*Works*, Vol. 10, p. 55.)

This was what Ilyich and I had talked about in 1905.

In May 1919 the First All-Russian Congress on Extra-School Education was held. It was greeted by Ilyich. The congress was attended by eight hundred delegates, among whom there were many non-Party people. The general atmosphere was one of enthusiasm—many of the delegates were preparing to go to the front—but we, Bolsheviks, who had organized the congress, saw that on many questions the delegates lacked a clear understanding of Soviet democracy, of that which distinguished our Soviet democracy from bourgeois democracy, and we asked Ilyich to make another speech at the congress. He consented and delivered a long speech on May 19 on the subject of "The Deception of the People by the Slogans of Freedom and Equality." He spoke about how the people were deceived by these slogans in the capitalist states, said that the Soviet power—the dictatorship of the proletariat—would now lead the masses to socialism, and spoke about the difficulties that still confronted the Soviet Government.

"This new organization of the state is being born with the greatest difficulty because to overcome disorganizing, petty-bourgeois lack of discipline is the most difficult thing, is a million times more difficult than overcoming the landlord violator or the capitalist violator, but it is a million times more fruitful for the creation of a new organization free from exploitation. When proletarian organization solves this task, then socialism has won finally. The whole of the activity of both extra-school and school education must be devoted to this." (*Works,* Vol. 29, pp. 345-46.)

But if a struggle was needed against anarchist moods in the business of building up the Soviet power, all the more necessary was it in the Red Army. Anarchist moods there took the form of sheer insubordination. The experience of the civil war in the Ukraine best illustrates these difficulties in organizing the Red Army. Ilyich spoke about this on July 4, 1919, when he addressed a joint meeting of the All-Russian Central Executive Committee, the Moscow Soviet of Workers' and Peasants' Deputies, the Moscow Council of Trade Unions and delegates of Moscow's factory committees.

Ilyich spoke about the difficulties of the first year of civil war, when we were obliged to form our detachments hastily one after another.

"The extremely low level of proletarian political consciousness in the Ukraine," Ilyich said, "combined with weakness and poor organization, Petlura* disorganization, and the pressure of German imperialism, provided fruitful soil for enmity and guerrilla methods. In every detachment the peasants snatched up arms, elected their ataman or headman in order to set up a local authority. They ignored the central authorities completely, and every headman imagined himself to be a local ataman who could

* *Petlura*—head of a counter-revolutionary bourgeois-nationalist movement in the Ukraine during the period of foreign military intervention and civil war. This brief period of Petlura-ist rule was attended by mass shootings of the population and a wave of savage Jewish pogroms.—*Ed.*

settle all Ukrainian questions himself regardless of what was being undertaken in the centre." (*Ibid.,* pp. 424-25.)

Ilyich went on to say that this lack of organization, these guerrilla methods and chaos, were having a disastrous effect on the Ukraine. It was an experience that would leave its mark upon the country.

"This lesson of disorganization and chaos has been realized in the Ukraine," Ilyich said. "I will be a turning point for the whole Ukrainian revolution, and will affect the whole development of the Ukraine. It is a turning point which we, too, have passed, a change from guerrilla methods and the throwing about of revolutionary phrases—we can do anything!—to a realization of the necessity of long, hard, dogged organizational work. It was the path we entered upon many months after October and achieved considerable success in. We look to the future absolutely confident that we shall overcome all difficulties." (*Ibid.,* p. 426.)

Ilyich's hopes were fulfilled. Our Red Army became a model of socialist organization.

At that time, in 1919, most of the Red Army men were individual peasant farmers, who were not afraid of hard work, but in whom the mentality of the petty proprietor was still strong. Ilyich therefore considered it very important to have all the fronts strengthened by proletarian elements. He wrote a letter to the Petrograd workers about rendering aid to the Eastern Front, when the situation there became critical; he made a speech at a meeting of the All-Russian Central Council of Trade Unions, addressed the railway workers of the Moscow terminus, spoke about fighting Kolchak at a conference of Moscow factory committees and trade unions, wrote to the workers and peasants concerning the victory over Kolchak, spoke about the role of the Petrograd workers, delivered a speech to the mobilized workers of the Yaroslavl and Vladimir gubernias, who were going out to the Denikin front and to help defend Petrograd against Yudenich, wrote an appeal to the workers and Red Army men of Petrograd in connection with the Yudenich threat, and wrote a letter to the workers and peasants of the Ukraine about the victory over Denikin.

The organization of the Red Army was steadily improving.

In proportion as the Soviet power struck root and the civil war opened the eyes of the masses as to who was their real friend and their real enemy, the influence of the Left Socialist-Revolutionaries weakened. Feeling the ground slipping from under their feet, they banded with the Anarchists with whom they organized a bomb outrage in Leontyevsky Street on September 25, where the Moscow Committee of the Party was discussing questions of agitation and propaganda. Twelve were killed, including the Secretary of the Moscow Committee Zagorsky, and fifty-five were wounded. We first heard the news of the outrage from Inessa Armand, who came to see us. Her daughter had been at that meeting.

* * *

While pointing out the scattered isolated character of small peasant economy and the adverse effect it had upon the lives and outlook of the peasants, Ilyich from the very outset stressed the need for passing over to collective forms of husbandry. He said that large-scale collective associations had to be set up for the common cultivation of the land in the form of agricultural communes and artels. He considered that the urban and agricultural workers would be the initiators in this matter, and supported all and every initiative by the workers in this respect. We know that as early as in the spring of 1918 he supported the initiative of the Obukhov and Semyannikov workers who went out to Semipalatinsk in Siberia to organize agricultural artels. He supported all efforts on a more modest scale to organize the collective cultivation of the land.

Ilyich, of course, had no illusions. He constantly spoke about the conditions that had to be created before mass collectivization of agriculture could be made practicable. At the Thirteenth Congress of the Party he spoke about tractors, about mechanized land cultivation, and the necessity of rousing the peasants, without which collectivization would make no real headway, while at the same time he believed that every initiative in the setting up of collective farms should be supported.

In the spring of 1919 Ilyich posed the question of organizing a collective farm of a new type to the workers of Gorki, where he lived. However, most of the workers there were unprepared for it. Reinbot, the former owner of Gorki, had picked Lettish workers for his estate, whom he had tried to keep apart, isolated from the rest of the population. The workers of Gorki, like all the Lettish workers, hated the landowners, but they were ill fitted at the time for collective work, for organizing the estate along state-farm lines.

I remember, how, at a meeting at the manor, Ilyich earnestly tried to talk them over. But nothing came of his persuasive efforts. The Reinbot property was shared out, and Gorki turned into an ordinary state-run farm. Ilyich wanted the state farms to serve as a model of efficient large-scale farming to the peasants; the latter knew how to run a small farm, but they still had to learn how to run a large one.

The manager of Gorki at the time—Vever—did not grasp Ilyich's ideas in regard to the state farm. One day, when Ilyich was out walking, he met Vever and asked him how the state farm was helping the local peasants. Vever looked puzzled and answered: "We sell seedlings to the peasants." Ilyich asked him no more questions, and when he had gone, looked at me ruefully and said, "He doesn't understand the very question." He afterwards became rather exacting towards Vever, who did not understand that the state farm had to serve as a model of efficient large-scale farming for the peasants.

One day, early in 1919, I received a visit at the Extra-School Education Department from Balashov, an old pupil of mine at the Sunday Evening School. He had worked in Nevskaya Zastava, and later, during the period of reaction, had served two years in prison. He told me that he had studied agriculture, especially market-gardening, and now wanted to tackle the job. He united seven peasant households (relatives) and organized a social kitchen-garden, which they decided to work together without hired labour. They organized an agricultural artel and grew fine cabbages on it under contract with the Red Army. This undertaking though did not survive. The Committee of Poor Peasants took all the cabbages for themselves, and Balashov was jailed. He wrote to me from prison. At Ilyich's request Dzerzhinsky sent men down to investigate the affair. It turned out that former detectives had wormed their way into the committee. Balashov was released, but the undertaking was dropped.

Those market-gardening artels—they were fairly popular at the time—came up against stiff resistance due to underestimation of their significance. At Blagusha, for instance, there were market-gardening courses organized by A. S. Butkevich with an allotment garden attached to them. Our Education Department supported those courses. In February 1919, Butkevich's son, himself an agronomist and specialist on market-gardening, organized on this allotment a sort of cooperative society of trainees (most of them workers of the Gnome & Rom Factory and the Semyonov Mills) under whose rules the crop was shared proportionately to the number of work hours put in. Young Butkevich experimented with fertilizers, new varieties and new methods of planting. The crop of vegetables was higher than at any of the other common allotments in the neighbourhood, and forty-five working-class families were provided with vegetables all the year round.

The Extra-School Department supported this undertaking, but the Moscow Education Department, which had a big say in things those days, took the courses' allotment away on the grounds that "providing some 45 or 50 families with vegetables was a matter of trivial social significance compared with work organization in the school." It failed at the time to appreciate the propaganda value of collective forms of husbandry. The school farm for the sake of which the Moscow Education Department had appropriated this allotment was itself a failure.

It is difficult today to imagine the obstacles which such undertakings found themselves up against in 1919. Those obstacles—and there were many of them—are now forgotten, but the people who took part in those undertakings have hardly forgotten them. Vladimir Ilyich was particularly interested in such undertakings.

To bring the peasant masses to identify themselves with the organization of farms on collective lines required a long period of preparatory work among the bulk of the peasantry. Ilyich was being constantly made aware of this when he read letters from peasants. One such letter concerning the situation in the countryside (the letter is dated February-March 1919) has a marginal note by Ilyich: "A cry for the middle peasant."

The question of the attitude towards the middle peasant loomed large at the Eighth Congress of the Party (March 18-23, 1919). In his speech at the opening of the congress Ilyich formulated the issue with unmistakable clarity:

"Implacable war against the rural bourgeoisie and the kulaks brings to the forefront the task of organizing the proletariat and semi-proletariat of the countryside. But for a party that wishes to lay the solid foundations of a communist society the next step is to correctly solve the question of our attitude towards the middle peasants. This is a task of a higher order. We were not able to deal with it on a broad basis until the essential conditions of the Soviet Republic's existence were assured."

And further on:

"We have entered such a phase of socialist construction when it is necessary, on the basis of our experience in rural work, to draw up concretely and in detail the basic rules and directions by which we should be guided in order to *take a firm stand for alliance* in regard to our attitude towards the middle peasants." (*Works*, Vol. 29, pp. 124-125.)

At this congress Ilyich spoke about the necessity of a comradely approach to the middle peasant, about the impermissibility of using coercion, and about the necessity of assisting him, first and foremost in the matter of mechanizing farming processes, relieving and improving his economic position, and raising his standard of living and culture. Ilyich spoke a lot about raising the cultural level of the village, and about how we were constantly coming up against the stumbling block of insufficient culture among the masses. He spoke about the enforcement of Soviet laws being hampered by the low cultural level: "...Besides the law, there is a cultural level, which is subject to no laws."

Remarking on certain limitations in the electoral rights of the peasantry, he said:

"...As we point out, our Constitution was obliged to introduce this inequality because the cultural level was low and because with us organization was weak. But we do not make this an ideal; on the contrary, in the programme the Party undertakes to work systematically for the abolition of this inequality between the more organized proletariat and the peasantry, an inequality we shall have to abandon as soon as we succeed in raising the cultural level. We shall then be able to get along without these limitations." (*Ibid.*, p. 163.)

Now, when the countryside is collectivized, when the mechanization of agriculture has become a reality, when the village has reached a much higher level of education and culture, this directive of Ilyich's has become attainable. The new Constitution of the Soviet Union gives full and equal suffrage to both the workers and the peasants. Reading this Constitution makes one's heart beat faster; it is the fruit of long years of work, guided by the Party into the proper channels.

A week after the Eighth Party Congress, at a meeting of the All-Russian Central Executive Committee on March 30, 1919, during which he proposed M.I. Kalinin as a candidate for the post of Chairman of the All-Russian Central Executive Committee in place of the late Y. Sverdlov, Ilyich said that Kalinin had a record of twenty years' Party work, that this St. Petersburg worker, who was at the same time a peasant by origin from the Tver Gubernia, had preserved close ties with peasant economy and was constantly renewing and refreshing those ties, that he showed a comradely approach to the broad masses of the working people. The middle peasants would see in the person of the highest representative of the Soviet Republic one of their own people. The nomination of Kalinin would serve as a practical means of organizing a number of direct contacts between the highest representative of the Soviet power and the middle peasants, would tend to bring them closer together.

Ilyich's hopes, as we know, were completely fulfilled. Kalinin is extremely popular with the peasant masses, who love him.

Ilyich's daily work showed what careful attention had to be given to all questions that concerned the interests of the middle peasant.

The Skopin Uyezd Consultative Congress sent a delegation of three peasants to Ilyich on March 31, 1919, with instructions "to petition for the middle and lower-than-middle peasants to be relieved of the air tax," "to petition for the complete repeal of the milch cow mobilization, because there is only one milch cow left among our population per 8 to 10 persons, besides which we are suffering from violent epidemics of typhus, the Spanish flu and other such diseases, and milk is the only food product for the sick. As to other products, such as butter and fats, these are completely lacking and unobtainable anywhere." The instructions also said something about horses and contained details of the tax collection.

Ilyich looked through the "mandate," and without asking any questions as to what the "air tax" could mean, he immediately answered the peasants of the Skopin Uyezd to the point:

"The imposition of a special tax on the peasants with incomes below the average is *unlawful*," he wrote. "Steps have been taken to lighten the burden of taxation for the *middle* peasants. A decree will be issued in a day or two. On the other questions I shall immediately demand information from the People's Commissars. You will be duly informed.

"*V. Ulyanov*".

April 5, 1919

(*Lenin Miscellany*, XXIV, p. 44).

He made a note for his Secretary on the peasants' letter: "Remind me at C.P.C. to speak to **Sereda** and (*F r u m k i n*) *Svidersky*. To be drafted by arrangement between *P.C. of Agriculture* and *P.C. of Food Supply*."

Ilyich demanded attention to the needs of the population on the part of all the administrative bodies.

Lenin's solicitude for the children was strikingly manifested during the famine that prevailed in 1919. The food situation became critical in May. At the second meeting of the Economic Commission Ilyich raised the question of rendering relief in kind to the children of the workers.

Towards the end of May 1919 the situation got worse. There were lots of grain, thousands of tons of it, in the Ukraine, the Caucasus and in the East, but the civil war had cut off all communications, the central industrial districts were starving. The Commissariat of Education was swamped with complaints about there being nothing to feed the children with.

On May 14, 1919, the army of the North-Western Government launched an offensive against Petrograd. On May 15 General Rodzyanko had taken Gdov, the Estonian and Finnish White Guard troops started to advance, and fighting began at Koporskaya Bay. Ilyich was concerned about Petrograd. It was characteristic of him that at this very same time, on May 17, he put through a decree for children to be fed free of charge. This decree provided for the improvement of the food supply for children and the welfare of the working people, and ordered that such supplies should be issued free of charge to all children up to 14 irrespective of their parents' ration class. The decree applied to the large industrial centres of sixteen non-agricultural gubernias.

June 12 brought news of the treachery of the Krasnaya Gorka garrison. On the same day Ilyich signed an order of the Council of People's Commissars extending the decree of May 17 concerning free food supplies for children to a number of other localities. The age limit was raised to 16 years.

Red tape in the matter of rendering relief to the needy was particularly hateful to Ilyich. On January 6, 1919, he wired to the Cheka in Kursk:

"Immediately arrest Kogan, member of the Kursk Central Purchasing Board, for not having helped 120 starving workers of Moscow and sent them away empty-handed. Publish it in newspapers and leaflets so that all employees of purchasing agencies and food supply authorities should know that formal and bureaucratic attitude and failure to help the starving workers will be severely punished, if need be—shot. Chairman of Council of People's Commissars *LENIN.*" (*Ibid.*, p. 168.)

Ilyich took special care to have the People's Commissariats stand as close to the worker and peasant masses and the Red Army as possible.

I was working at the Commissariat of Education, and saw evidences of Ilyich's keen interest in this matter at every step. Our Extra-School Department was visited by a mass of people—men and women workers, peasants, soldiers from the front, teachers and Party workers. Our Department became a sort of rendezvous to which Party people came to enquire about Ilyich and tell about their own work, to which workers came for advice as to how best to organize propaganda and agitation work, to which Red Army soldiers and commanders came, as well as workers who were closely associated with the village.

I remember a young Red Army man complaining that the wrong books were being sent them, that the newspapers did not reach them and that they had no propagandists. He demanded that more propagandists should go out. He was not the only one who came, of course, but that young fellow was so desperately earnest about it that he sticks in my memory.

A young commander, newly arrived from the front, told us agitatedly how his company, billetted in a *real* school somewhere out west, had made short work of "master-class" culture. The real schools were privileged institutions. The Red Army men had smashed up all the appliances and torn the textbooks and exercise books to bits. "This is master-class property," they said. On the other hand, their thirst for knowledge was stronger than ever. There were no textbooks to be had. The old textbooks with their prayers for the Tsar and the Fatherland were destroyed by the Red Army men. They demanded textbooks that had a bearing on real life and on their own experiences.

At the Extra-School Education Congress which Ilyich addressed a resolution was passed calling on the delegates to go out to the front. Many of them went. Among them was Elkina, an experienced school-teacher. She went to the Southern Front. The Red Army men asked to be taught to read and write. Elkina started giving them lessons based on the analytic-synthetic method of the textbooks then in use: "Masha ate *kasha* (porridge)," "Masha made butter," etc. "What are you teaching us!" the Red Army men started protesting. "Who the dickens is Masha? We don't want to read that stuff!" And Elkina constructed her ABC lessons on different lines: "We are not slaves, no slaves are we."

It was a success. The Red Army men quickly learned to read and write. This was the very method of combining instruction with real life that Ilyich had been urging all the time. There was no paper to print new textbooks on. Elkina's textbook was printed on yellow wrapping paper, and in a note explaining her method Elkina described how to learn to write without using pen and ink. One has merely to recollect what paper the notice announcing the First Congress of the Third International was printed on to understand why Elkina wrote about this. It was not a case of failure to appreciate the role of the textbook. The Red Army men quickly learned to read and write by Elkina's ABC book.

"...There cannot be the slightest doubt of the existence of a tremendous thirst for knowledge and of tremendous progress in education—mostly attained by means of extra-school methods—of tremendous progress in educating the toiling masses. This progress cannot be confined within any school framework, but it is tremendous," Ilyich said at the Eighth Party Congress. (*Works*, Vol. 29, p. 161.)

Our political-education workers Sergievskaya, Ragozinsky and others visited the fronts. We received numerous letters from the fronts. Here is an extract from the letter of a front-line comrade, a Petrograd worker, who had co-operated with us in organizing political-educational work in the district. "I have just read the newspaper for the 7th reporting the opening of the Congress on Extra-School Education," he wrote. "Yes, Nadezhda Konstantinovna, when you travel the length and breadth of Soviet Russia you see what a lot our Department has to do and how needful this extra-school work is. I'm afraid I won't be able to follow all the congress proceedings. I am waiting for a train at station Inza to take me to station Nurlat. I have been appointed inspector-instructor, and I am going to inspect the 27th Division. It's a big job, and the main thing, a new one both in general and for me in particular. The recommendation which Vladimir Ilyich has given me obliges me to fulfil the trust in the best way I possibly can. Referring to that recommendation, one comrade said: 'I'd give my life for such a letter.' I'll write you when I've done the job. Give Vladimir Ilyich and all my acquaintances my sincere regards. Army in the Field. Political Department."

We had visitors from the front as well as letters. Ilyich asked for the more interesting visitors to be directed to him.

Our Department devoted no less attention to explanatory work among the peasantry.

The question of propaganda among the peasantry had long been receiving the attention of Ilyich. We know what trouble he had gone to in building up a popular literature and symposiums of collected articles, and having a popular newspaper published for the village (*Bednota*).

On December 12, 1918, the Council of People's Commissars had issued a decree "On the Mobilization of Literate People and the Organization of Propaganda of the Soviet System." This decree called for the organization of readings of decrees and the most important articles and pamphlets in working-class districts, and especially in the villages. These readings were to have been organized first and foremost by our Department. Ilyich was a hard task-master. These readings were held; they awoke a desire for knowledge. "We're not going to take sides or join any party," the peasants of the Arzamas Uyezd told our agitator who went down there. "When we've learnt to read we'll read everything for ourselves, and then no one will be able to take us in."

A section for work in the village was set up at the Eighth Congress of the Party, in the name of which Ilyich made his report. The section consisted of sixty-six delegates. Sereda, Lunacharsky, Mitrofanov, Milyutin, Ivanov, Pakhomov, Vareikis, Borisov and others were elected to the committee for drafting the theses.

All this goes to show what tremendous attention the Party and Ilyich devoted to this question.

I remember with what interest Ilyich used to listen to everything our Department succeeded in learning about the life of the peasants and what their attitude was to one or another question.

A peasant of the Moscow Gubernia, who was working at some building site, once called on us for some books. He told us about the profiteering practised before the revolution among the army contractors, who had made fortunes out of the business. We directed him to Lunacharsky. He came back and told us: "He was very nice. He made me sit down on the sofa, while he walked up and down, up and down, speaking ever so well. He gave me some books. Promised to give me some vizool gadgets as well (visual aids.—*N.K.*). I'm afraid to take 'em, though. He says they won't cost anything, but I'm afraid I'll be taxed for those vizool things afterwards." Nevertheless he took away a collection of all kinds of placards and school aids. He became a frequent visitor at our Department. We called him the Vizool Gadget man. It is characteristic that Ilyich gave more attention to another incident related by this builder. It was about the school-teacher who lived in their village. She did not receive any salary, yet she did not give up her work at the school, and in the evenings gave lessons to the adults, whom she taught to read and write. The Vizool Gadget man told us that he had bought her a pair of boots, as her old ones were completely worn out.

In 1919, many villages were still cut off from the rest of the world. There was no radio in those days. The illiterate population (in the Simbirsk Gubernia, where Ilyich was born, eighty per cent of the population in 1919 was still illiterate) did not read the newspapers—in fact, there weren't any newspapers owing to the shortage of paper; the central newspapers had a very restricted circulation for the same reason, and never reached the villages. Book deliveries had not been organized properly and the bookshops sent out unbelievable stuff. The village was all agog for news of what was going on in the world, but its only source of information were rumours.

Ilyich listened attentively to my stories about how the peasants called on us with naive questions, how monstrously ill-informed they were in regard to the practical measures of the Soviet Government, its structure, their own rights and obligations, what ignorance there was in the countryside, how naive their illiterate letters were, letters penned for them by the village "scholars" in a clerkly flourishing hand full of curlicues, and how those free-lance scribes made them pay through the nose for those letters.

I showed the letters to Ilyich. He used to read them with interest. He advised me to give more attention to the organization of enquiry desks at our reading rooms and village recreation halls. He had experience in consultation service in exile in the village of Shushenskoye, where the peasants from the neighbouring villages used to come to him every Sunday for advice. In December 1918 he drafted rules of management for the government offices, in which he urged the setting up of similar local enquiry offices by the various government departments. "These enquiry offices must not only give the required information, both oral and in writing, but draw up applications free of charge for the illiterate and those who are unable to do so clearly," Ilyich wrote in his "Draft Rules of Management for Soviet Institutions." (*Works*, Vol. 28, p. 327.)

"Rules concerning the days and hours of reception should be posted up in every Soviet institution both inside and outside in a manner accessible to all without passes. The reception room should be so arranged that everyone could have free and easy access to it without passes.

"A book should be kept in every Soviet institution containing a brief record of the applicant's name, the gist of his request and to whom the matter has been directed.

"On Sundays and holidays reception hours should be observed." (*Ibid.*)

These draft rules were not published until 1928—ten years later, but Ilyich's directives were known to the Extra-School Department, and it was on his insistence that we began to pay greater attention to the organization of enquiry services at the reading rooms. The village librarians gained prestige as a result of this work, and in 1919 they were a definite influence in the countryside. Enquiry-desk work was linked with propaganda of the Soviet power, propaganda of the decrees issued by the Soviet Government.

* * *

Enquiry service was only one of the things Ilyich thought about. On April 12, 1919, a decree was published over the signatures of Kalinin, Lenin and Stalin, providing for the reorganization of the State Control (Stalin was then People's Commissar of State Control). This decree said:

"The old bureaucracy has been destroyed, but the bureaucrats remain. They have brought with them into the Soviet institutions the spirit of conservatism and red tapery, inefficiency and loose discipline.

"The Soviet Government declares that it will not tolerate bureaucratism in whatever form, that it will banish it from Soviet offices by determined measures.

"The Soviet Government declares that only the participation of the broad masses of the workers and peasants in the administration of the country and extensive control over the organs of government will eliminate the faults in the machinery of state, will rid the Soviet institutions of the bureaucratic evil and decidedly advance the cause of socialist construction."

On May 4, 1919, a decree was issued instituting a Central Bureau of Applications under the People's Commissariat of State Control, followed on May 24 by a decree instituting local branches of the Central Bureau.

Ilyich urged an unremitting struggle against bureaucratism in Soviet offices.

Bureaucratism with us in Russia was held up to ridicule in the literature of the sixties, especially by the *Iskra* (Chernyshevsky-ist) poets.* These poets (Kurochkin, Zhulev and others) had a strong influence on our generation. They branded all the numerous manifestations of bureaucratism, red tape and corruption. Verses by the *Iskra* poets and all kinds of anecdotes concerning red tape were a sort of folklore of the intellectuals during the sixties. Anna Ilyinichna and I were often reminded of that literature in recent years; she had an excellent memory. That literature was very popular in the Ulyanov family. Satire had done its work at the time by enabling our generation to suck in with their mother's milk, so to speak, a healthy hatred of bureaucratism. It was Ilyich's cherished desire to wipe that blemish off the face of the Soviet land.

Ilyich himself was extraordinarily considerate towards people and the letters that he received. This is borne out by the documents published in *Lenin Miscellany*, XXIV.

Ilyich received a mass of complaints and he dealt with them himself.

On February 22, 1919, he sent the following telegram to the Yaroslavl Gubernia Executive Committee:

"Soviet employee Danilov complains that the Cheka has confiscated from him three poods of flour and other products purchased during eighteen months on his work earnings for a family of four. Check most carefully. Wire me results.

"Chairman, Council of People's Commissars

Lenin"

(*Lenin Miscellany*, XXIV, pp. 171-72).

---

* *Iskra*—a satirical magazine, close to the Revolutionary-Democrats' journal *Sovremennik*, which was under the ideological guidance of Chernyshevsky in the sixties of the 19th century. The first number of which appeared in 1859. Its founder was the poet V. Kurochkin. The nucleus of the magazine were poets D. Minayev, V. Bogdanov, N. Kurochkin, G. Zhulev, N. Loman and others. *Iskra* was in the lead of progressive literature, and was subjected to persecution for its trend, until it was closed down in 1873.—*Ed.*

Another telegram to the Gubernia Executive Committee of Cherepovets ran:

"Check complaint Yefrosinia Yefimova, soldier's wife of village Novoselo, Pokrovsk Volost, Belozersk Uyezd, concerning confiscation of grain for common barn, although her husband has been prisoner of war over four years and she has family of three without a farm help. Report to me results investigation and your measures.

"Chairman, Council of People's Commissars

Lenin"

(*Ibid.*, p. 173).

Such instances could be cited by the hundred. I refer to those kept in the Archives of the Lenin Institute, but how many more are there that have not survived! In June 1919, when I went away for a two months' trip on the Volga and the Kama on the agitation steamboat *Krasnaya Zvezda*, Ilyich wrote to me: "I read the letters addressed to you asking for assistance and try to do what I can about it." When a person's mind is engaged on some important problem, it is extremely difficult and exhausting for him to switch over twenty times a day to all kinds of petty affairs. The only time Ilyich could give his mind up completely to any problem was when he took walks or went out shooting. Comrades recollect how, in such cases, Ilyich would unexpectedly utter some word or phrase which showed what his mind was working on at the moment.

Recollecting how Ilyich used to deal with "trifles," some comrades say: "We did not look after him properly, he was swamped by trivial affairs; we should not have troubled him with all those piddling affairs." That may be so, but Ilyich considered that attention to trivial details was extremely important, and that only such attention could make the Soviet administrative apparatus really democratic, not in a formal way, but in a proletarian democratic way.

And, as he had previously done in the building up of the Party, when he had tried, by personal example, to teach

522

the comrades a correct approach to the problems of agitation, propaganda and organization, so did he now, as head of the Soviet state, endeavour to show how work should be carried on in the government offices, how bureaucratism in every shape and form should be banished from the machinery of the state, and that machinery brought closer to the masses. His telegram to the Novgorod Gubernia Executive Committee in June 1919 is characteristic of him:

"Apparently Bulatov has been arrested for complaining to me. I warn you that I shall have the chairmen of the gubernia executive committees, the Cheka and members of the executive committee arrested for this and see that they are shot. Why did you not answer my question immediately?

"Chairman, Council of People's Commissars

Lenin"

(*Lenin Miscellany*, XXIV, p. 179).

Ilyich tried to purge the machinery of the state of bureaucratism; he demanded a considerate attitude towards every person on the staff, demanded that those in charge should know their staffs, help them in their work and create the necessary facilities for efficient work. Ilyich constantly questioned me about the members of my own staff and got to know them; he advised me how to make better use of one or another worker. He constantly enquired what I was doing for them, how they were off for food, and how their children were faring. He studied the members of my staff, whom he had never set eyes on, and I was sometimes surprised to find that he knew them better than I did.

There are numerous records showing Ilyich's solicitude for the members of his own staff.

At a meeting of the C.P.C. on March 8 Ilyich wrote the following note to his secretary concerning Khryashchova, a member of the Board of the Central Statistical Department:

"If Khryashchova lives a long way and walks home, it's a shame. Explain to her tactfully when opportunity offers that she can leave earlier on the days when statistical questions do not come up, or not come at all." (*Ibid.*, p. 287.)

Ilyich showed particular concern for the living conditions of staff workers. It was a time when even high-ranking officials and their families did not have enough to eat. It transpired that A. D. Tsyurupa, Markov of the Commissariat of Transport, and others were starving.

On August 8, 1919, Ilyich wrote the following letter to the Organizing Bureau of the Central Committee:

"I have just received additional information from a *reliable* source that Board members are *starving* (for instance, Markov of the Commissariat of Transport). I insist most energetically that the C. C. should: 1) order the Central Executive Committee to issue a grant of 5,000 rubles by way of relief to all Board members (and those of equal position); 2) put them all permanently on *maximum* quotas for specialists.

"It is a shame, really—they are starving and their families are starving!!

"100 to 200 people should be better fed." (*Ibid.*, p. 317.)

* * *

At the end of April a turning point was reached on the Eastern Front. The Red Army began to score victories. Ufa and a number of other towns were recaptured from the Whites. The offensive against Ekaterinburg and Perm was developing successfully. At the end of June the agitation steamboat *Krasnaya Zvezda* was fitted out for a trip on the Volga as far as the Kama, then up the Kama as far as possible, then down the Volga to the last navigable place of safety. The task of the *Krasnaya Zvezda* was to follow in the wake of the Whites and agitate for the line adopted at the Eighth Party Congress, and consolidate the Soviet power everywhere. The Political Commissar on the *Krasnaya Zvezda* was V. Molotov. The boat was equipped with a cinema and a printing plant and had radio and a large stock of books. It was staffed by representatives of various

Commissariats (I represented the Commissariat of Education) and the trade unions.

Before sailing I had a long talk with Ilyich about what we had to do, how to assist the population, what questions had to be focussed on, and what things we had to study more carefully. Ilyich would have liked to go himself but he could not give up his work for a minute. On the eve of my departure we talked all through the night. Ilyich went to the station to see me off, and made me promise to write him regularly and talk with him on the private line. I went up the Volga and the Kama as far as Perm.

Molotov was in charge of all the work. He got us together before each stop, and we discussed what we were going to do, what we were going to lay special stress on. After each stop we reported back on what we had done and compared notes. That trip was extremely useful to me. I had lots of things to talk to Ilyich about after that trip, and he listened to me with tremendous interest, going into every little detail.

We held endless meetings during the trip, and addressed mass meetings at the Bondyuzhsky Works, in Votkinsk, Motovilikha, Kazan, Perm, Chistopol, Verkhniye Polyany, and so on. Our ship's newspaper reckoned that I had addressed 34 meetings. I am no orator, but the things I spoke to the men and women workers about, to the Red Army men and the peasants, were things that deeply agitated them and intimately concerned them. Wherever the Whites had been, the hatred of the population towards them was intense. I shall never forget the meeting at the Votkinsk Works, where the Whites had shot almost all the teenagers—those "accursed Bolshevik spawn" as they called them. The crowded mass meeting sobbed to a man when we started singing the revolutionary funeral march. There was hardly a family there that had not had a son or daughter killed. Never shall I forget the story of how partisan girls and school-teachers were flogged to death, never shall I forget the countless outrages and acts of violence which the peasants—mostly middle peasants—living around the Kama told us about.

The ignorance among the population was very great. Peasant women were still afraid to send their children to the nurseries. A furious agitation against the Soviet power was being conducted among the school-teachers. I saw an instance of that agitation at Chistopol. However, the close contact which the rural teachers had with the peasant and working-class masses induced many of them to side with the peasants and the workers. At the Izhevsk Works 95 out of 96 engineers had run away with Kolchak, but the wife of one of them, a school-teacher in Izhevsk and a former class-mate of mine at the high school, did not run away with her husband but remained with the Reds. "How could I leave the workers?" she said to me when we met.

The privileged intellectuals sided with Kolchak at the time, and went away with the Whites; our chief agitators were men and women workers, and Red Army men. They stood close to the masses. The Second Army had a rather peculiar agitator: he had been a priest before the October Revolution, but after October he became an agitator for the Bolsheviks. At a meeting of five thousand Red Army men in Perm he spoke of the Soviet power's intimate link with the masses. "The Bolsheviks," he said, "are today's apostles." When asked by a Red Army man in the audience: "What about baptism?" he answered: "That would take a couple of hours to explain, but briefly it's pure eyewash!" The speeches of the army commanders from among the workers were very convincing. I told Ilyich about this meeting and how one commander had said: "Soviet Russia is unconquerable on account of its squarity and sizability." We laughed, but afterwards, with the fall of the Hungarian Republic, Ilyich said that, strictly speaking, that commander had been right—we had room to manoeuvre in during the civil war.

Azin, a Red Army commander, came to see me on the boat at Yelabug. He was a Cossack, ruthless to the Whites and deserters, a man of reckless daring. He spoke to me chiefly about the care he was taking of the Red Army men. His men loved him. I received a letter this year from a Red Army man who had fought Kolchak under him. Every line of the letter breathes of warm love for Azin. Recently Pastukhov, a member of the Central Executive Committee, related how a detachment of the Red Army under the command of Azin had suddenly burst into Izhevsk, which was still occupied by the Whites, riding horses whose manes were plaited with red ribbons, and captured the jail in which prisoners under sentence of death were kept (including Pastukhov's seventy-year-old father and his youngest eleven-year-old brother; Pastukhov's two other brothers had been killed at the front). Azin afterwards fell into the hands of the Whites on the Lower Volga and was tortured to death.

The agitation of the *Krasnaya Zvezda* was very effective in Tataria, where the population gave their fullest support to the Soviet power.

Vladimir Ilyich asked me about everything in full detail; he was particularly interested in what I told him about the Red Army, the temper of the peasants, of the Chuvashes and the Tatars, and about the growing trust towards the Soviet power among the masses.

* * *

The latter half of 1919 was much more difficult than the first. This especially applied to September, October and the beginning of November. The civil war was spreading. Kolchak had been defeated, but the Whites were bent on capturing the centres of the Soviet power—Moscow and Petrograd. Denikin started to advance from the south, where he had seized a number of important points in the Ukraine, and Yudenich began to advance from the west, and already stood at the approaches to Petrograd. The victories of the Whites encouraged the enemies who had been lying in hiding. At the end of November a counter-revolutionary organization connected with Yudenich and subsidized by the Entente was discovered in Petrograd.

All the time that Denikin and Yudenich were winning Vladimir Ilyich received a lot of anonymous letters of a threatening character, some of them with caricatures. The intelligentsia was still vacillating, and only the more progressive sections of it headed by Timiryazev had gone over to the Soviets. The Anarchists, supported by the Socialist-Revolutionaries, had engineered a bomb explosion on the premises of the Moscow Committee of the Party in Leontyevsky Street on September 25, in which a number of our comrades were killed.

Famine and poverty were rife. The Red Army had to be strengthened, its fighting spirit sustained, and plans for conducting the struggle at the battle fronts had to be thought out. The Red Army, the population and working-class centres in the rear had to be supplied with grain, explanatory and agitation work had to be launched on a wide scale, and the whole administrative machinery had to be built up on new lines—not on the old bureaucratic lines, but along new Soviet lines; new cadres had to be selected and trained, one had to go into a mass of petty details.

Although Ilyich's confidence in victory never weakened for a moment, he worked from morning till night, and the tremendous burden of all those cares gave him no sleep. He would get up in the night and start ringing up on the telephone to check whether this or that order of his had been carried out, or to send another telegram somewhere. He spent most of his time in his office, receiving people, and hardly stayed at home during the day. I saw still less of him during those hectic months; we almost stopped going out for walks together, and I did not like going into his office on private matters for fear of interrupting his work.

The most acute problem was that of grain. The simple purchase of the required amount of grain under the ex-

In Gorki, where Lenin was convalescing, August-September 1922

In Kremlin study, October 4, 1922

isting conditions of small peasant holdings and wild speculation was simply unthinkable. Some kind of planning and system had to be introduced here, a number of laws enforced and suitable people mobilized for the purpose. It was not mere accident, therefore, that Alexander Tsyurupa was appointed People's Commissar of Food Supply on January 17, 1919. We had known him for a long time; I had been in exile with him in Ufa.

His father was a petty employee (secretary of the Town Council) in Aleshki, Tavrida Gubernia. Alexander was born in 1870, the same year as Ilyich. Theirs had been a large family of eight; his father died early, his mother made a living by sewing, and Alexander started giving lessons at an early age. He went to a primary school, then the town school and the secondary agricultural school. By profession he was an agronomist, and was familiar with rural economy and peasant life. He was first imprisoned for being a revolutionary in 1893, and was arrested again in 1895. Beginning from 1897 he worked as a statistician in Ufa. There he belonged to a group of Social-Democrats who did active work among the railway workers and the workers of the neighbouring factories. We had worked together there. He met Ilyich once or twice in Ufa when Ilyich came to see me, and afterwards we regularly corresponded. He wrote for *Iskra*. We knew him as a convinced ardent revolutionary. In 1901 he had organized a May Day strike in Kharkov, and in 1902 had worked in Tula in a group of which Sophia Smidovich, Veresayev and Lunacharsky's brother had been members. In 1902 he was arrested in Samara, and 1905 found him working again in Ufa.

Beginning from 1914 Tsyurupa began to take an active part again in revolutionary Bolshevik work. Ilyich, who was an excellent judge of people, thought very highly of him. He was an extremely modest man, neither orator nor writer, but a splendid organizer, a practical man who knew his business and was familiar with the village. At the same time he was a splendid revolutionary, who was not afraid of difficulties, and threw himself wholeheartedly into the job of whose significance he was fully aware. He worked under the direction of Ilyich, who appreciated him, took care of his health. Seeing him tired and overworked Ilyich, half in jest, half in earnest, reprimanded him for not taking proper care of "state property" (our domestic slang term for devoted Communists). Ilyich liked Alexander Tsyurupa as a comrade too.

The Soviet Government's food policy at the time consisted in the organization of a grain monopoly, that is, prohibition of all private trade in grain, compulsory deliveries of surplus grain to the state at fixed prices, the prohibition of hoarding, strict stock-taking of all surpluses of grain, the proper transportation of grain from places where there was a surplus to places where there was a shortage, and the laying in of stocks for consumption and sowing. Strictly speaking, this was a section of planned economy, socialist economy, but it had to be practised under conditions when the very foundations of that economy had not yet been reorganized, when peasant farming still remained uncollectivized.

On July 29-30, 1919, the Moscow Soviet and the Moscow Trade-Union Council called a conference of factory committees, representatives of trade-union head offices, delegates of the Moscow Central Workers' Cooperative Society, and the "Kooperatsia" Society Council to organize a united consumers' society in Moscow. The conference was attended also by Mensheviks and supporters of the independent cooperative movement. Vladimir Ilyich spoke at this conference on July 30; he wished the conference success in its work, but stressed that everything depended upon whether we would win the civil war and remodel the social system on new lines, as only this could give the cooperative movement the right direction.

He said that it was only twenty months since the October Socialist Revolution had taken place, and, naturally, that was too short a time in which to remodel the whole social system. Ilyich said that it was necessary to get the better not only of the old institutions, not only of the land-owners and the capitalists, but also of the old habits bred by capitalism and the conditions of small peasant econo-my, habits which had grown into the very bones of the pet-ty proprietor in the course of centuries.

Today, when collective farming has become the predom-inant form of agriculture in our country, everyone under-stands what Lenin had been driving at. He had talked about replacing individual farming by collective farming. He said that a last and decisive battle was being waged between capitalism and socialism, that only the victory of socialism could help once and for all do away with hunger, exploi-tation, and the profiting of one from the labour of another. He spoke about the Bolsheviks having started on the path of socialist grain collection for supplying the Red Army and the working-class population. These grain purchases during the first year amounted to only thirty million poods.

"The next year," said Ilyich, "we laid in over 107 million poods, despite the fact that we had been much worse off in a military respect and in respect of free access to the richer grain-producing territories, as we were cut off effectively from the Ukraine and the greater part of the south as well as Siberia. Nevertheless, as you see, our grain purchases have trebled. From the point of view of the work of our food supply organizations this is a great success, but from the point of view of providing the non-agricultural areas with grain this is very little, because when a careful check-up of food conditions among the non-agricultural population and, especially, the working-class population in the towns, was made, it was discovered that in the spring and summer of this year the worker in the towns received approximately only half his food from the People's Commissariat of Food Supply and was obliged to get the rest on the free market and from profiteers, paying in the first case only a tenth of all his expenses, and in the latter case nine-tenths. The profiteers, as may have been expected, are making the worker pay nine times more than the price the state charges for this bread. Considering these exact data showing our food situation, we must admit that we are still half in old capitalism, with one foot there, and have only half climbed out of this morass, this quagmire of profiteering and taken the *path of really socialist collections of grain*, when grain has ceased to be a commodity, an object of profiteering and an object and cause for squabbling, for fighting, and for the impoverishment of many."

Ilyich went on to say:

"A decisive and final struggle is now going on against capitalism and free trade, and for us it is now a battle royal between capitalism and socialism. If we win this fight there will be no return any more to capitalism and the old order, to all that has been." (My italics.—*N.K.*) (*Works,* Vol. 29, pp. 481-82, 487.)

In a number of speeches made in 1919 Ilyich explained to the working men and women, the peasants and Red Army men the meaning and significance of the Soviet Government's food policy and spoke about collective farming. Experience has confirmed the correctness of the policy that was then pursued.

Besides his concern for providing grain for the Red Army Ilyich was constantly thinking how to strengthen the ranks of the Red Army and raise its discipline. He believed that the best way of doing this was to reinforce the ranks of the Red Army, made up mostly of peasants, with workers. That is why he so warmly greeted the Petrograd workers who were going to the front, into the thick of the fight, and he greeted the Moscow workers for the same reason. He relied upon the workers, attached tremendous importance to their advancement to posts of authority in the capacity of commissars and army commanders. He called upon the Red Army men to be unremittingly vigilant. In a letter to the workers and peasants in connection with the victory over Kolchak, Ilyich warned:

"... The landlords and capitalists have not been destroyed and do not consider themselves vanquished; every intelligent worker and peasant sees, knows and realizes that they have only been beaten and have gone into hiding, are lying low, very often disguising themselves by a 'Soviet' 'protective' colouring. Many landlords have wormed their way into state farms, and capitalists into various 'chief administrations' and 'centres,' acting the part of Soviet officials; they are watching every step of the Soviet Government for it to make a mistake or show weakness, so as to overthrow it, to help the Czechoslovaks today and Denikin tomorrow.

"Everything must be done to track down these bandits, these landlords and capitalists who are lying low, and to ferret them out, *no matter what guise they take*, to expose them and punish them ruthlessly, for they are the worst foes of the working people, skilful, shrewd and experienced, who are patiently waiting for an opportune moment to set a conspiracy going; they are saboteurs, who stop at no crime to injure the Soviet power. We must be merciless towards these enemies of the working people, towards the landlords, capitalists, saboteurs and Whites.

"And in order to be able to catch them we must be skilful, careful and class-conscious, we must watch out most attentively for the least disorder, for the slightest deviation from the conscientious observance of the laws of the Soviet power. The landlords and capitalists are strong not only because of their knowledge and experience and the assistance they get from the richest countries in the world, but also because of the force of habit and the ignorance of the broad masses, who want to live in the 'good old way' and do not realize how essential it is that the laws of the Soviet power be strictly and conscientiously observed."
(*Works*, Vol. 29, pp. 514-15.)

This call for vigilance frightened many people. Many a story was told to Ilyich of how the Red Army men sometimes dealt with one or another capable commander only because he was "one of the gentry," or because some order of his was not to their liking, or on some other trivial excuse. All this was told to Ilyich with a sneer, as much as to say: "There are your fine Red Army men for you!"

Of course, there were many cases of men being blamed not for what they ought to be blamed, or blamed for something someone else had done; people were prevented from seeing things right by lack of knowledge, by the small-proprietor criterion of what was good and what was bad, by an anarchic approach to a number of questions. Ilyich kept hard at us educational workers, demanding that we should develop wider educational activities among the adult workers, peasants and Red Army men, that we should not handle this business in a formal official manner, but should broaden the horizon of our adult pupils, infuse the spirit of Party into all our teaching. He demanded that we should by every means in our power open the door to higher education to those for whom it had been previously closed.

It was in 1919 that a number of decrees were issued throwing open for all the door to the higher educational institutions. Workers' Faculties* were organized, numerous workers' courses were set up, and the first Soviet-Party School** was organized in 1919.

I would come to Ilyich—at the end of 1919 he looked very bad (there is a photo of him going to the courses, which shows how bad he looked—worn out and harassed) —and he would sit there silent. I knew that all I had to do to take him out of himself was to tell him something about the life of the Workers' Faculty students or the Soviet-Par-

---

* *Workers' Faculties* first came into being in 1919. Their aim was to attract the proletarian and peasant masses into the higher schools in order to raise cadres of the intelligentsia, cadres of specialists from among the workers and peasants. The task of these faculties was to prepare students for the universities.—*Ed.*

** *Soviet-Party Schools* set up for the training of Party and administrative cadres—propagandists, Party and administrative personnel, political-education workers and cooperative movement organizers. —*Ed.*

ty School. And there was plenty to tell him about. He was interested in hearing how people were becoming more socially alert, how they were increasingly becoming aware of the tasks that faced them. We discussed the subject a good deal.

A Party Week was organized in Petrograd between August 10 and 17; at the same time, in accordance with the ruling of the Eighth Party Congress, a re-registration of Party members was carried out, which lasted till the end of September. Between October 8 and 15 a Party Week was held in Moscow.

On October 11 Ilyich wrote his article "The Workers' State and Party Week" which gave a forceful expression of his views on the Party, on what the new government apparatus should be, and how important it was to staff it with as many workers and peasants as possible.

"Party Week in Moscow falls at a difficult time for the Soviet power," Ilyich wrote in that article. "Denikin's successes have given rise to a frenzied increase of plotting on the part of the landlords, capitalists and their friends, and increased efforts on the part of the bourgeoisie to sow panic and undermine the strength of the Soviet system by every means in their power. The vacillating, wavering, ignorant petty bourgeois, and with them the intelligentsia, the Socialist-Revolutionaries and Mensheviks, have, as is usually the case, become more wobbly than ever and were the first to allow themselves to be intimidated by the capitalists.

"But the fact that Party Week in Moscow falls at such a difficult time is, I think, rather an advantage to us, for it is much better for the cause. We do not need Party Week for show purposes. We do not need fictitious Party members even as a gift. Our Party, the party of the revolutionary working class, is the only government party in the world which is concerned not in increasing its membership but in improving its quality, and in purging itself of 'self-seekers.' We have more than once carried out re-registration of Party members in order to get rid of these 'self-seekers' and to leave in the Party only politically enlightened elements who are sincerely devoted to communism. We have taken advantage of the mobilizations for the front and of the subbotniks to purge the Party of those who are only 'out for' the benefits accruing to membership of a government party and do not want to bear the burden of self-sacrificing work for communism.

"And at this juncture, when intensified mobilization for the front is in progress, Party Week is a good thing because it offers no temptation to the self-seekers. We extend a broad invitation into the Party only to the rank-and-file workers and to the poor peasants, to the labouring peasants, *but not* to the peasant profiteers. We do not promise and do not give these rank-and-file members any advantages from joining the Party. On the contrary, just now harder and more dangerous work than usual falls to the lot of Party members.

"All the better. Only sincere supporters of communism, only persons who are conscientiously devoted to the workers' state, only honest working people, only genuine representatives of the masses that were oppressed under capitalism, will join the Party.

"And it is only such members that we need in the Party.

"We need new Party members not for advertisement purposes but for serious work. These are the people we invite into the Party. To the working people we throw its doors wide open." (*Works*, Vol. 30, pp. 45-46.)

Further Ilyich repeated what he had said at the funeral of Sverdlov—that there were many talented organizers and administrative workers among the working class and the peasantry. It was to these that he appealed to tackle socialist construction.

"If you are sincere supporters of communism, set about this work boldly, do not fear its novelty and the difficulty it entails, do not be put off by the old prejudice that only those who have received a formal training are capable of this work." (*Ibid.*, pp. 46-47.)

The article ended with the words: "The mass of the working people are with us. That is where our strength lies. That is the source of the invincibility of world communism."

Ilyich, in those difficult times, ceaselessly appealed to the workers and the Red Army men in speeches and articles. His words roused them. The workers of Yaroslavl, Vladimir and Ivanovo-Voznesensk went to the front en masse.

"The power of the workers' and peasants' *sympathy* for their vanguard," wrote Ilyich, "was *itself* sufficient *to work wonders*.

"It is indeed a miracle: the workers who have experienced the untold torments of hunger, cold and economic ruin have not only kept their spirit up, preserved all their devotion to the Soviet power, all their energy of self-sacrifice and heroism, but are taking upon themselves, despite their unpreparedness and inexperience, the burden of steering the ship of state! And this at a time when the storm has reached a furious pitch.

"The history of our proletarian revolution is full of such miracles. Such miracles will lead certainly and positively —whatever the separate painful ordeals may be—to the complete victory of the world Soviet Republic." (*Works*, Vol. 30, pp. 53-54.)

The young people, too, were eager to go to the front. We political-education workers were busy at the time with the first Soviet-Party School, at which we tried to give the young people not a "formal" training, of which Ilyich so sharply disapproved, but knowledge that would equip them to grasp and meet the events they were living through. We were awfully glad when Ilyich came to address the graduates of the first Soviet-Party School on October 24, 1919.

"Comrades," he began. "You know that what has brought us here together today is not only a desire to celebrate the graduation by most of you of the course at the Soviet school but also the fact that about half of all the graduates have decided to go to the front in order to give fresh, extraordinary and substantial aid to the troops who are fighting there."

After describing the difficult situation at the fronts without any attempt to gloss it over, Ilyich went on: "That is why, hard though this sacrifice is—the sending to the front of hundreds of graduates who are so badly needed for work in Russia—we have nevertheless consented to grant your wish." (*Ibid.*, pp. 57, 62.)

Ilyich then went on to describe the work that confronted the Soviet-Party School graduates:

"To those who are going to the front as representatives of the workers and peasants there can be no choice. Their slogan should be—death or victory. Each of you should be able to approach the most backward and undeveloped Red Army men in order to explain the situation to them in the plainest language from the standpoint of the working man, help them at a time of difficulty, remove all vacillations, teach them to combat the numerous manifestations of sabotage, inertia, deceit or treachery. You know that there are still many such manifestations in our ranks and among the commanders. This is where we need men who have gone through a course of training, who understand the political situation and are in a position to help the broad masses of the workers and peasants in their fight with treachery or sabotage. Besides personal bravery, the Soviet power looks to you to render the utmost assistance to the masses, to put a stop to all vacillations among them, and prove to them that the Soviet power has forces to which it resorts whenever it is in difficulties." (*Ibid.*, pp. 63-64.)

The Soviet-Party School graduates justified the confidence placed in them.

Ilyich's speech was also a programme for all our political-education workers.

It was not only at public meetings that Ilyich spoke about what was uppermost in his mind. He spoke about it at home, too, especially when close comrades visited us. At the end of 1919 a frequent visitor was Inessa Armand, with whom Ilyich liked to discuss the prospects of the movement. Inessa's daughter had been at the front, and had narrowly escaped being killed during the bomb outrage in Leontyevsky Street on September 25. I remember Inessa coming to us once with her youngest daughter, Varya, who was quite a young girl at the time and afterwards became a staunch member of the Party. Ilyich liked to indulge in day-dreaming in their presence; I remember how Varya's eyes used to sparkle. He liked to chat with our domestic help Olimpiada Zhuravlyova, mother of the woman writer Boretskaya. Zhuravlyova had previously worked in the Urals as an unskilled worker at an ironworks and afterwards as office cleaner at *Pravda*. Ilyich thought she had a strong proletarian instinct. Sitting in the kitchen (by force of old habit he liked to have his meals in the kitchen), Ilyich liked to talk with her about the future victories.

Ilyich was not mistaken—we celebrated the second anniversary of the Soviet power with victories.

When Denikin at the beginning of October threatened Orel, the Central Committee of the Party sent Stalin to the Southern Front as a member of the Revolutionary Military Council. Stalin proposed a new plan for an offensive, which was adopted by the Central Committee. Vladimir Ilyich fully supported it. Things at the Southern Front quickly took a turn for the better. On October 19 our troops dealt a crushing blow to generals Shkuro and Mamontov at Voronezh. On the 20th Orel was recaptured, and on October 21 the Pulkovo battles inaugurated the defeat of Yudenich, who had been advancing on Petrograd.

On the anniversary of the October Revolution Ilyich sent ardent greetings to the workers of Petrograd, wrote an article in *Pravda* "The Soviet Power and Women's Position" and an article for the peasants in *Bednota* "Two Years of Soviet Power."

On November 7, Ilyich addressed a joint meeting of the All-Russian Central Executive Committee, the Moscow Soviet, the All-Russian Central Council of Trade Unions, and factory-committee delegates on the subject of "Two Years of Soviet Power." Ilyich did not like speaking at ceremonial meetings, and his speech at this one was a purely business-like speech without any propaganda. It was none the less a stirring speech, which roused enthusiasm and a storm of applause.

Ilyich said that the most important achievement of the Soviet power during the past two years had been "the lesson at building up the workers' state ... the workers' participation in running the state." "...The most important job that we did was that of remodelling the old machinery of state, and hard though this work was, we see the results of the efforts of the working class in the course of two years and can say that in this field we have thousands of representatives of the workers who have been through the whole fire of struggle, ousting the representatives of the bourgeois state step by step. We see workers not only at the state apparatus, we see their representatives in the food supply business, a sphere that was dominated almost exclusively by representatives of the old bourgeois government, the old bourgeois state. The workers have created a food supply apparatus."

The percentage of workers on the government staffs rose from thirty to eighty in 1919.

The most important task of all that was being handled, Ilyich said, was that of making leaders of the proletariat. They were being made at the front, in all fields of administrative activity. Ilyich stressed the role of the subbotniks, the importance of enrolling workers into the Party. In Moscow alone as many as over fourteen thousand new members of the Party were enrolled during Party Week. Ilyich spoke about the reserves we had in the person of the worker and peasant youth, who had been reared under the conditions of active struggle. But the main thing to which attention had to be paid, Ilyich said, was the building up of proper relations with the peasant millions, the necessity of conducting a wide explanatory campaign among the peasantry. He spoke about how the civil war was opening the eyes of the peasantry to the true state of affairs. Ilyich spoke calmly. The general mood was one of elation.

Mayakovsky, who was then popular with the political-education workers, expressed this mood in his poem dedicated to the second anniversary of the October Revolution:

> *Let it be by a drop,*
> *by two,*
> *merge your spirits in world-wide fusion*
> *to boost*
> *by everything each can do*
> *the workers' exploit*
> *called*
> Revolution!
> *Congratulators*
> *don't knock at the door?*
> *shrivelling up*
> *with fear?*
> *What the hell do we need them for?*
> *What's ten?*
> *We'll come*
> *to our hundredth year.*

When we celebrated the twentieth anniversary of the October Revolution, and summed up the achievements on the front of socialist construction as recorded in the new Constitution of the Soviet Union, we all thought of Ilyich, of Ilyich's words and directives.

NAME INDEX

A

Abramovich—337, 344

Adler, Victor—172, 176, 279, 283

Adoratsky, V. V.—177, 453

Akimov, V.P.—64, 92

Alexander III—14

Alexandrov, M. S. (O!minsky)— 83, 103, 106, 108, 121

Alexandrova, E. M. (Stein, Jacques)—82-83, 93

Alexeyev, N. A.—56, 70, 75

Alexinsky, G A.—138, 148, 157, 158, 167, 171-173, 179, 184, 198, 208, 243, 250-252, 352, 366

Aliluyev, S. Y.—366

Andreyev, L.—122, 135, 182

Andreyev (Left S.-R.)—475

Andreyeva, M. F.—135, 173, 184

Aptekman, O. V.—48

Armand, Inessa (Blonina)—213, 219-220, 223, 225, 227, 235 241, 261, 266-269, 271, 274- 275, 281, 287, 292, 297, 300- 303, 312-314, 344, 492-507, 539

August—see Krasikov P. A.

Avdeyev (Uncle Vanya)—321

Avksentyev, N. D.—405

Avramov—161

Axelrod, P. B.—23, 54-56, 58, 65- 67, 84, 87, 94, 96, 156, 175, 308-309

Azin—527

B

Babushkin, I.V. (Bogdan)—16, 23, 48, 54, 61, 77, 80-81, 125

Badayev, A. Y.—241, 244-256, 273, 305, 325

Bagocki—236, 238, 263

Bakin—137

Balabanova, A.—300, 308

Balashov—266-268

Balmont, V. A.—135, 137

Baramzin, Y.V.—41, 43, 47

Baransky, N. N.—141

Bask—146

Baturin—192

Bauman, N. E. (Victor, Tree, Rook, Sorokin)—77, 78, 81, 96

Bazarov, V.A.—106, 135, 148, 166, 179, 183, 251, 331

Bebel, A.—226, 454

Beethoven—221, 269

Belenky, Abram—225

Belenky, Grigory—225, 297

Belostotsky (Vladimir)—218, 231